CHILDREN OF FATE

CHILDREN OF FATE

Childhood, Class, and the State in Chile, 1850–1930

Nara B. Milanich

Duke University Press   Durham and London

2009

© 2009 Duke University Press

All rights reserved

Printed in the United States of America on acid-free paper ∞

Designed by C. H. Westmoreland

Typeset in Warnock with Whitman display

by Keystone Typesetting, Inc.

Library of Congress Cataloging-in-Publication Data

appear on the last printed page of this book.

FOR MY PARENTS

FOR NICOLA, GIACOMO, AND LUCA

CONTENTS

ILLUSTRATIONS AND TABLES

Tables

ACKNOWLEDGMENTS

Like all books with past lives as dissertations, this one has gone through multiple reincarnations. Along the way, it has incurred many, many debts. As a Fulbright scholar in Chile in 1995, I first broached the themes and materials that would lead to this project. I received funding for my dissertation from the Social Science Research Council International Dissertation Research Fellowship, the Henry Hart Rice Research Fellowship, the Yale Program in Agrarian Studies, and the Whiting Fellowship in the Humanities. More recently, this project greatly benefited from support from the National Endowment for the Humanities. I also wish to acknowledge the generous maternity leave policy at Barnard College. It seems fitting that one of the first beneficiaries of the newly revamped college policy would write a book about children.

I hope that this book succeeds in communicating some of the richness of the historical materials I worked with and the great fun I had while doing so. At the Archivo Nacional in Santiago, I wish to thank Mario Monsalve, Ricardo Valenzuela, and Marco Reyes Collao for their assistance and for permitting access to uncatalogued materials in the basement of the archive. I also thank Dionisio Ortiz and Guillermo Torres for their cheery forbearance on chilly winter mornings in the reading room. These highly capable staff members consistently went beyond the call of professional duty. Mr. Monsalve also collaborated in the transfer of judicial documents from a closet in the First Criminal Court of San Felipe, where they lay in danger of imminent deterioration, to a safer home in the Archivo Nacional. The late Germán Rosales Pérez provided transportation, and Mauricio Silva Pizarro, Judge of the First Criminal Court of San Felipe, and Max Cancino, Secretary of the Court, also assisted in the matter. The staff of the Archivo del Siglo XX (Archivo Nacional de la Administración) was similarly helpful. I am grateful to Dr. Ricardo Cruz-Coke Madrid, director of the Museo Nacional de Medicina "Dr. Enrique Laval," housed in the Faculty of Medicine at the Universidad de Chile, for his personal interest in this project. Until her retirement, Mireya Olivares, the library's indefatigable *bibliotecaria*, was a true model of professional dedication as well as a pleasure to work with. In the Biblioteca Nacional, Liliana Montecinos ran a tight ship in the reading room. Hugo Castillo Palacios and Jimena Rosenkranz assisted with photographic reproduction, as did Marina Molina of the Museo Histórico Nacional's photographic archive. Ivonne Urriola Pérez and Soledad Zárate generously shared source materials. Finally, Priscilla Rocha Caamaño, a master's student in history at the Universidad de Santiago de Chile, provided extremely thoughtful research assistance.

When I ventured out of libraries and archives and into convents and welfare asylums in search of research materials, Madre Luz Galdames of the Congregación de las Hijas de San José, Protectoras a la Infancia, welcomed my interest in her congregation and generously facilitated access to documents relating to their early history. I also acknowledge the warmth of Madre Augusta Meza B. of the Congregación de las Hermanas de la Providencia, who in addition to allowing me to browse through the correspondence of Madre Bernarda Morin, the congregation's founder, cajoled me with cups of hot tea. Madre Augusta and I were both immersed in overlapping research projects: Mine was of course an academic study. Hers was the case for the beatification of Madre Bernarda, an effort that continues. At the Sociedad Protectora de la Infancia, President Alicia Amunátegui de Ross generously gave of her time to help me understand the Protectora and her family's role within it. I also acknowledge her husband, the late Jorge Ross Ossa, for his encouragement in this project. Whether or not they would agree with the conclusions of this study, I was impressed by the strength of their convictions and the depth of their dedication to their cause. I hope that my respect for them is evident here.

This study would have turned out very, very differently were it not for a fateful encounter with the 1999 Santiago phonebook. There I discovered that the Casa Nacional del Niño, the contemporary incarnation of the Casa de Huérfanos, Santiago's historic foundling home, was alive and well, located on the same site as its nineteenth-century predecessor in Providencia, a neighborhood that takes its name from the congregation that ran the asylum. I approached the Casa Nacional in a distinctly un-Chilean fashion, unidentified and unannounced, seeking research leads.

Director María Cristina Rojas took a chance on a stranger and graciously agreed to share with me the extraordinary cache of nineteenth-century documentation that had been stored for decades in a closet behind a playroom. The Casa Nacional's nutritionist and historian, Carlos Eduardo Sánchez Aravena, assisted in this project in many ways. He cheerfully clambered up the ladder to reach the dustiest tomes in the farthest reaches of the closet, allowed me to stay after hours, and was always interested to hear about my day's findings. Were it not for Carlos and his abiding commitment to the institution's past, the documents so generously shared with me might well have been disposed of long ago.

Working with these extraordinary materials was a privilege, not the least because of the circumstances in which I did so. The Casa Nacional is, after all, not an archive or a library: it is a children's asylum that at any given time houses some 100 infants and toddlers. I was provided with an office across the hall from a playroom and so found myself poring over the institution's nineteenth-century history with the hubbub of its present-day wards in the background. Leonardo, Mateo, and Aurora, among many other young people, certainly enriched that research experience.

Books have genealogies as sure as people do. I locate the origins of this project in a course I took at the Universidad de Santiago de Chile in 1995. The seminar, team-taught by Alfredo Jocelyn-Holt and Julio Pinto, was titled "Los de Arriba y Los de Abajo en Chile Decimonónico" (Rich and Poor in Nineteenth-Century Chile). It was there I first read Augusto Orrego Luco's essay "La cuestión social," from which the title of the book derives, and began to think about structures of hierarchy in Chile. While this project has undergone many incarnations since its life as a dissertation, the distinctive intellectual mark of each of my graduate advisors, Nancy Cott, Gil Joseph, and Stuart Schwartz, remains unmistakably palpable throughout. It is only in retrospect that I can say how truly formidable their influence has been. I thank them as well for support and encouragement that has endured long after graduate school. More recently, this project has benefited from new intellectual communities. I did not originally conceive of this book as a history of childhood. Thanks to the small but extraordinarily dynamic intellectual community that is the Society for the History of Children and Youth, including Paula Fass, Steve Mintz, and Bengt Sandin, it became one.

Books, I discovered, are as much about talking as writing. This one has benefited from conversations with and feedback from friends, colleagues, and *miembros del gremio*, including Azun Candina, Consuelo Figueroa, Igor Goicovic, Tobias Hecht, Liz Hutchison, Ivan Jablonka, Deborah Meacham, Joe Miller, Jolic Olcott, Catalina Policzer, Jorge Rojas, René Salinas, Shobana Shankar, Rebecca Wilkin, and Soledad Zárate. Amy Chazkel, Bryan McCann, Tori Langland, and Mark Overmyer-Velásquez continue to be wonderful and important *compañeros* long after graduate school. I thank as well my friends in Davis, Chuck Walker, Zoila Mendoza, Andrés Resendez, Tom Holloway, Krystyna von Hennenberg, Luis Guarnizo, and Marisol de la Cadena. I express gratitude to the Barnard History Department for the supportive environment they provide for junior faculty. My colleagues at Barnard and in the broader Columbia and New York Latin American History communities read parts of this book in supportive, thoughtful, and dynamic seminars. Individual chapters of this book greatly benefited from the feedback of Constanza Castro, John Coatsworth, Debbie Coen, Betsy Esch, Federico Finchelstein, Carlos Gálvez, Abosede George, Paul Gootenberg, Tom Klubock, Dorothy Ko, Ariel Mae Lambe, Claudio Lomnitz, José Moya, Julia del Palacio, Pablo Piccato, Caterina Pizzigoni, Thom Rath, Lisa Tiersten, Carl Wennerlind, and Carlos Zúñiga-Nieto. I am grateful to Linda Lewin and Steve Mintz for reading an earlier version and to Joe Miller for helping me think through issues of tutelary servitude. Amy Chazkel provided an extremely thoughtful reading of the final manuscript, as well as a welcome dose of camaraderie, even as she was finishing her own book. Nicola Cetorelli and my mom brought an economist's and anthropologist's sensibility, respectively, to their reading of the manuscript and were ever mindful of the big picture. Betsy Kuznesof and Heidi Tinsman deserve special thanks for working through this manuscript not once but twice. I am very grateful for their exceptionally constructive and generously rendered critiques. Thanks as well to Valerie Millholland, Miriam Angress, Leigh Barnwcll, and Ncal McTighe, at Duke University Press, as well as to Ariel Mae Lambe, Sonya Manes, and Lynn Walterick, for their expert guidance, patience, and good humor in shepherding this book to completion.

I have Luis Ortega, Diana Veneros, and their daughter Antonia to thank for many of my best memories of Chile. Santiago would have been a much hungrier city were it not for the many, many *cazuelas de ave* I enjoyed at their home, and a much lonelier one were it not for the many conversations about history and politics we shared beneath the backyard *parra*. At key moments, they also provided crucial institutional assistance that furthered this project.

This is a book about kinship and the material and symbolic benefits it confers. It is therefore only fitting to recognize my family's myriad and immeasurable contributions to its making. It is sometimes said that a historian's personal familiarity with the subjects of inquiry facilitates his or her scholarship. This may be true for some fields, but I am not convinced it is true for the history of children! Neither Luca nor Giacomo helped me finish this book any faster. Giacomo impatiently inquired when I would write a book *for* children instead of *about* them. On the other hand, thanks to them I developed tremendous empathy for the mothers, fathers, caretakers, and *comadres* I encountered in the historical record. And of course they provide daily opportunities to appreciate dimensions of childhood not explored in this book. Nicola Cetorelli's devoted support, unwavering encouragement, and superhuman forbearance over more than ten years have been truly instrumental to this book's journey. He will be possibly even more relieved at its completion than I am. Finally, I express profound gratitude for the steadfast and loving support of Jerry Milanich—personal assistant, babysitter extraordinaire, and dad—and Maxine Margolis—critic, trailblazing role model, and mom. In the spirit of nineteenth-century Chilean elites' genealogical veneration, I dedicate this book, with love, to all of them.

INTRODUCTION

State, Class Society, and Children in Chile

The Children, the Judge, and the Doñas

The initial report brought to the judge's attention in November 1894 concerned three neglected and abused children living in a poor neighborhood of Santiago. An official was dispatched to 66 Maipú Street, but, as he recounted in his report, the woman who opened the door was singularly uncooperative. At first she refused to present the children in question and then produced three healthy-looking ones. Eventually, the official was shown a girl whose "sickly condition made me suspect [the report of abuse] was true." After ordering the arrest of the woman and several other inhabitants, he searched the house and found two other children who had been hidden under a bed.

The official identified the youngsters as Delia, Ricardo, and José Manuel Puelma, siblings between the ages of approximately seven and ten. He described the children's "sad state" in detail: dressed in filthy rags, they exhibited "hunger in the true sense of the word." Delia had worms on her scalp, and José Manuel and Ricardo displayed "a thinness that provoked horror." Photographs taken at the judge's instruction show the children posed on a cobblestone street with a wooden chair as a prop, barefoot, swathed in rags, staring plaintively at the camera or rotated to expose their scars.

The judge paid for the children to be clothed and fed at his personal expense and the next day questioned them about their situation. They confirmed they were orphans living with relatives and described, in a statement that would later be excerpted in lurid detail in the newspapers, how they habitually ate garbage out of a canal. The threesome could not say how old they were and did not know the identity of their mother or

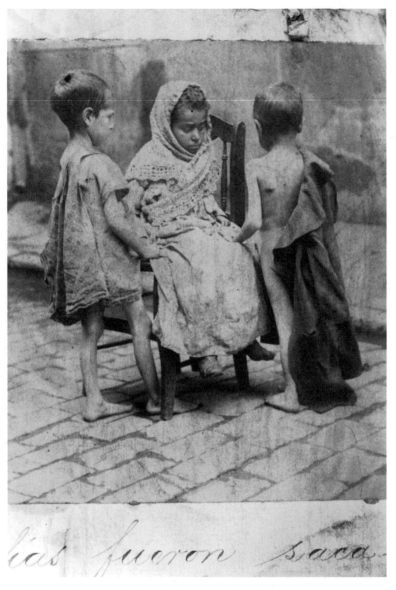

1. Children of fate: the Puelma children when they first arrived at the court in November 1894. *Source: Archivo Nacional Histórico de Chile.*

how long their parents had been dead. Subsequent testimony confirmed they were illegitimate, born of an adulterous and possibly incestuous union of a well-off father and a poorer woman to whom he was related. The "crime of Maipú Street" generated extensive press coverage at a moment of blossoming public preoccupation with poor children. Eventually, two caretakers were convicted of attempted homicide.

And what became of the children? Several days after they were taken into court custody, Doña Emiliana Subercaseaux appeared before the judge, requesting that they be delivered to her care. A prominent member of the Santiago elite and widow of Don Melchor Concha y Toro (of viticultural fame), Doña Emiliana had no personal connection to the case. But she wished to place the children in the asylum that she and an associate, Doña Josefina Gana de Johnson, had recently founded. The judge granted her request, and the logs of the Sociedad Protectora de la Infancia record the Puelma trio as the very first wards admitted to an institution that, in succeeding decades, would succor tens of thousands of poor children. After a stay of unspecified duration, the asylum placed Delia and José Manuel with a "trusted señora," for whom they probably worked as servants in exchange for material sustenance and moral tutelage. According to the logs, José Manuel and his brother Ricardo were eventually sent to workshops associated with Santiago's main orphanage, where they would receive instruction in artisanal trades. Thereafter all documentary traces of the Puelmas vanish, but a probable fate can be reconstructed from the experiences of countless other poor and parentless minors in this society. Delia would come of age as a domestic servant, the dependency of an impoverished childhood morphing seamlessly into the subordination of adult servitude. After a few years in the workshops, her brothers would emerge with few prospects for becoming independent artisans, landing casual employment in an urban household or perhaps a rural estate. They too would join an unskilled and dependent underclass.[1]

My research on children and family in nineteenth-century Chile led me in 2000 to the offices of Doña Alicia Amunátegui de Ross. The member of a prominent family, Doña Alicia was the president of the Sociedad Protectora de la Infancia, the asylum inaugurated by the Puelmas, which had celebrated its centenary several years before. She had presided over la Protectora, as it was known, for more than twenty-five years and displayed a passionate commitment to its mission. When she talked about the organization, which provided services to more than 5,000 needy children and employed a staff of hundreds, she used the first-person singular. Doña Alicia's bond with the Protectora was not just a product of the years she had devoted to its good works, however. Her relationship was more intimate and profound: It was familial. For as she explained to me, Doña Josefina, the Protectora's second founder, was her great-grandmother. And Doña Emiliana, who had solicited the Puelmas from the court, was the great-grandmother of her husband. For over a century, four generations of women from the same tightly knit elite clan had led the Protectora. Prompted by my questions about the asylum's history, Doña Alicia and her husband, Don Jorge Ross, provided a careful exegesis of their respective genealogies. The couple's knowledge of their family histories was striking: they could spontaneously name most of the twelve children of a great-grandmother. This genealogical veneration, shared by earlier generations of Chilean elites, is particularly conspicu-ous given that asylums like the Protectora have historically received children like the Puelmas—poor, abandoned, illegitimate, or orphaned minors with little if any knowledge of their natal identity.

Doña Alicia, Don Jorge, their great-grandmothers, and the Puelma children embody the significance of family for Chileans of all social levels. In the present but especially in the past, membership in a family had broad cultural meanings and important social and legal consequences, implying access to resources both material and symbolic. For elites, kin networks were a fundamental basis of economic and political power; for plebeians, they were a source of support and a buffer against a precarious existence. Familial belonging also harbored status associations. Elites' conceit of class was rooted in genealogy, but for the poor, the capacity to sustain social reproduction across generations could never be taken for granted, and many individuals were cut off from natal kin ties.

This book examines the linkage of two categories of social relations usually considered separately, those of class and those of family. The articulation of social hierarchy and family is a theme running through the social, cultural, and political history of Latin America. From the colonial period to the present day, patterns of marriage, child rearing, kinship, sexuality, and household structure have diverged widely between social groups. This book argues that familial patterns emerge in, are sustained

2. Doña Emiliana Subercaseaux, her husband Don Melchor Concha y Toro, and two eldest sons, Carlos and Daniel, ca. 1865. *Courtesy of the Museo Histórico Nacional.*

by, and help reproduce the profound social hierarchies that have characterized Latin American societies historically. Such dynamics are clear
enough in a colonial society of castes in which, to give a well-known
example from eighteenth-century Spanish America, imperial authorities
managed racial mixing through marriage regulation. But they were also
operative in the context of a liberal, constitutional republic of formal,
legal equality. Drawing on evidence from Chile in the latter half of the
nineteenth century and first decades of the twentieth, I argue that the
republican reconfiguration of rights and entitlements, dependencies and
differences, was rooted in cultural ideologies, social practices, and legal
structures surrounding family. Although the connection between class
and family has been deeply embedded in Latin American cultures and
histories, scholars have not systematically probed this relationship.

My analysis focuses on a particular dimension of family, namely, the
status of children, practices of child rearing, and filiation. *Filiation* refers
to "relations of descent from parents to children," but this definition is
deceptively simple.[2] Neither a natural nor a priori category, filiation was
defined socially and legally, its definition varied across classes, and its
meanings changed over time. Filiation demarcated proximity to some
but also difference and distance from others, for in delineating who was
kin, law and social practice simultaneously defined who was an *ajeno* or
an *extraño*, an outsider or stranger. The logic by which some people
came to be defined as kin and others as outsiders illuminates gender and
generational relationships within the family but also relationships of
hierarchy and class beyond it.

The distinction between kin and ajeno was most immediately consequential for children, because it determined who would rear them and in
what capacity. While all children began their lives dependent on others,
all forms of dependency were not equal. Children like the Puelmas, with
no natal kin, were forced to rely on charitable largesse. Even as the tutelage of benefactors safeguarded early survival, it tended to ensure lifelong subordination. The distinction between individuals reared within
kin networks and those reared beyond them also had a legal dimension.
Kin dependency conferred legal rights (and obligations) on those considered sons and daughters, but the dependency of those reliant on charitable largesse was entirely extralegal. Child-rearing practices thus implicated different modes of dependency, different textures of social and

legal relations. They referenced alternatively inclusion and exclusion. As such, children provide a privileged vantage point for exploring the making of subordination and the operation of postcolonial social hierarchies in general.

As the distinction between rights versus largesse suggests, the state, and in particular the law, is central to this story. The codification of civil law in the nineteenth century transformed law and legal culture surrounding filiation, enhancing the power of men over women and fathers over children. In shaping hierarchies of gender and generation, family law also reinscribed those of class. Yet the state did not just "regulate" kinship; it employed kinship as a central category of legibility and legal personhood, reading the identity of individuals through their family relations. This reliance on kinship was profoundly paradoxical, for the state's bureaucratic protocols simultaneously undermined the legal and social ties of certain children to their kin origins. For example, the Civil Code, civil registry, and child welfare asylums systematically expunged the familial identities of children who were illegitimate. State policy, in other words, deployed kinship but generated "kinlessness," helping create an underclass of individuals bereft of the entitlements of family, dependent on the charity of others, and marginalized from public bureaucracies that defined legal identity with reference to kinship.

While the Puelma children's passage through the courts and publicly subsidized welfare asylums reflects the protagonism of the state, public institutions were hardly the only contexts relevant to their lives. Most of the Puelmas' early years were actually spent in private households. Indeed, in managing their plight, the court and the asylums repeatedly recurred to private patrons, such as the "trusted señora" who took in Delia and José Manuel. From the last decades of the nineteenth century, in Chile as in other modernizing societies, poor children were branded a matter of urgent public concern. But shifting the focus from the grandiose rhetoric of children's welfare to the reality of their lives reveals the persistence of private, informal, and extralegal forms of social provision. Indeed, the nineteenth-century liberal legal regime reflected conflicting impulses between greater and lesser state control over families and the domestic sphere.

In recent years, state formation has occupied a privileged place in analyses of Latin American society and culture. This book contributes to that literature by showing how the Chilean state both absorbed and shaped a key category of social and cultural practice: kinship. It shows how the liberal state's engagement with kinship and childhood oscillated between asserting new powers of intervention and conspicuously abdicating others. But this analysis also partially displaces the abiding focus on state formation. Probing social practices and power relations beyond the state, I suggest that far from seeking to commandeer the private, liberal state formation perpetuated this realm of social practice. Children thus elucidate the dynamics, but also the limits, of liberal state power in relation to a reconfigured private sphere.

State and Class Society in Nineteenth-Century Chile

Chile was one of more than a dozen independent nations to emerge from the collapse of the Spanish Empire. But as contemporaries and historians alike have long observed, its republican trajectory, which began with the declaration of independence in 1810, diverged in significant ways from that of its neighbors. The political anarchy of the independence period gave way to a centralized and relatively stable state. As in other Latin American polities, political debate was framed by the conflict between liberals, who advocated a secular, constitutional republic and (at least in theory) a society of equals, and conservatives, who as defenders of Catholicism and the colonial legacy of order and hierarchy espoused a more authoritarian political vision and a less democratic social one. Yet despite their intensity, in Chile these ideological debates rarely led to open violence. The country would experience relative political stability and economic expansion for much of the rest of the century. Compared to the weak states, acute and persistent political violence, and caudillismo that characterized much of nineteenth-century Latin America, the Chilean nation-state was by most measures a uniquely coherent and consolidated entity.

The demise of imperial rule marked the end of a colonial society in which individuals had been legally classified by color and caste, as free and enslaved, noble and plebeian. And it heralded the rise of a constitutional republic grounded in a formal commitment to equality before the law; it is in this sense that we can talk about a "liberal" state even in the context of enduring conservative power. The nascent republic abolished noble titles and coats of arms (1817), civil discrimination against Indians (1819), and slavery (1823), making it the first Hispanic American republic to declare emancipation. Even the frankly authoritarian Constitution of 1833 pledged to "ensure to all inhabitants of the republic . . . equality before the law. In Chile there are no privileged classes."[3] The new republic was free of the all-pervasive legacy of racial slavery of Brazil—the scope and economic significance of slavery in Chile had been limited—as well as the enduring ethnic distinctions of the Andes. Racial categories were eliminated from bureaucratic practice by the 1850s, and discourses on race tended to emphasize and extol the homogeneity of a mestizo populace born of conquering Spaniards and vigorous "Araucanian" Indians.[4] Racialized and racist ideas deeply inflected social and political discourse, but racial difference was not the tortured crucible of national identity that it would become elsewhere in the hemisphere.

Yet against this backdrop of formal, legal equality and a rhetoric of ethnic homogeneity, social distinctions of class were entrenched, persistent, and profound. Rather than eliminating the relations of dependency that organized society, as we will see, liberalism in some ways strengthened them. Whether critics or defenders, most contemporary observers concurred that society was divided into two distinct groups, the rich and the poor. They usually regarded the poor as an undifferentiated mass, labeled *los de abajo, el pueblo, el bajo pueblo,* or, in more paternalistic moments, *nuestro pueblo.* This mestizo underclass was overwhelmingly rural and landless. Most rural dwellers were dependent on *haciendas,* the great landed estates that controlled perhaps 75 percent of agricultural lands. Bound to the estates by customary arrangements steeped in paternalism, *inquilinos,* or tenant farmers, exchanged their labor and that of family members for access to land and perquisites. Their relative stability contrasted with the itinerant *gañanes,* peons who worked, according to the census definition, "for a daily wage without fixed residence or employment." Fueled by the growing commercialization of the agrarian economy, by 1865 this great, unskilled "errant mass," as it was frequently styled, accounted for a third of workers. By the 1880s, urbanization was accelerating, and migration between countryside, cities, and mines, as well as circulation among occupational categories, increasingly blurred the distinction between rural and urban poor.[5]

Plebeians, in turn, were starkly distinguished from their social superiors, *la gente decente* or *los de arriba*. Thanks to the increased profitability of traditional economic activities like agriculture and mining and new opportunities in banking and commerce, the late-nineteenth-century Chilean upper classes were considerably wealthier than their colonial predecessors. They also maintained a grip on the state that was seriously contested only in the early twentieth century. Landownership was particularly central to elite power, according status, political control, and a sense of identity.[6] The Chilean upper classes readily absorbed immigrants and others made wealthy through new economic opportunities, but their limited numbers and tendency toward economic and commercial diversification made them a remarkably cohesive group.[7] Multi-stranded webs of kinship and marriage further enhanced elite unity.

Indeed, the story of the Chilean elite is inevitably a story of families. It is not by chance that the nineteenth-century upper classes are referred to not only as the "aristocracy," the "bourgeoisie," and the "oligarchy" but also as "influential families," "the most important families," and the "great families."[8] It is impossible to account for the Chilean elite's enduring political and economic power without reference to kinship. Kinship helped shape how elites weathered the transition to independence as well as patterns of property ownership and business leadership among twentieth-century "landlords and capitalists." The nineteenth century may well have marked the apex of kin-based elite power in Chile and in Latin America. The classic example is that of the Errázuriz family, which between the 1830s and the 1920s boasted two presidents, two archbishops, and fifty-nine parliamentarians (with as many as six serving simultaneously). As the historian and statesman Benjamín Vicuña Mackenna noted, Santiago in the 1860s "was not a city of men but of relatives." The intimacy of a political class composed of "relatives" may help explain how Chile, in spite of sometimes acute ideological conflict between liberals and conservatives, largely avoided the internecine political violence that plagued neighboring republics. Meanwhile, kinship has historically proven crucial not only to elites' economic and political power but to their identity as a class. To this day, "aristocratic sentiment" among the Chilean upper classes is profoundly rooted in notions of *estirpe*, or lineage.[9]

The standard characterization of nineteenth-century Chile as a society of rich and poor inevitably misses some of its nuances. It obscures the

3. The power of lineage: the Errázuriz family on the Hacienda El Huique (Colchagua), ca. 1895. Pictured is President Federico Errázuriz, his wife, two children, and unidentified relatives and friends. *Courtesy of the Museo Histórico Nacional.*

slow rise of a small but growing middle class. More pointedly for our purposes, it obscures how hierarchy and dependency pervaded all levels of this social order and the significance of status distinctions *within* the popular classes. Manifestly subordinate to his hacendado, an inquilino might nevertheless serve as *patrón*, or master, to a young, landless peon residing in his household. Artisans were masters to their apprentices. Modest wives and widows benefited from the presence of young *criados*, child wards they reared as household servants.

Within this graded social landscape, family helped define dependency and demarcate difference. In contemporary parlance, a respectable individual was said to be of *familia decente*—as opposed to "the great majority, which is composed of the poor and of people of unknown family [*de familia desconocida*]."[10] This characterization referenced not only the aristocratic genealogies of elites but also the way family structure harbored meaning at all social levels. Take the expressions *padre de familia* and *hijo de familia*. Legally, a padre de familia was a man who exercised paternal authority (*patria potestad*) over his minor children, and an hijo/a de familia was a minor subject to paternal authority. In social parlance, however, the terms accrued additional layers of meaning. A padre de familia was a morally upright authority figure who oversaw a legally constituted household that enjoyed at least a degree of material independence (hence not, for example, an itinerant peon). The term *madre de familia* had no existence in civil law, but it was used in social discourse to refer to a respectable wife and mother who presided over her own household (thus, not an unmarried woman or a domestic servant, even if she had children). An hijo (or hija) de familia, in turn, referenced a minor son or daughter inserted within the household's structures of affect and authority, as opposed to a young person reared in a non-natal household as a servant, or a minor forced to leave home to work at a young age.[11] Thus, the phrase "de familia"—a seemingly redundant qualifier of roles that were by definition familial (padre, madre, hijo)—was in fact not redundant at all. It obliquely referenced the fact that not all fathers, mothers, or children lived in what were normatively recognized to be "families," that is, in patriarchal households. And it alluded to the fact that even in patriarchal households, women and children could be inserted in very different roles (as servile dependents, rather than as wives or hijos). "Family" thus marked a distinct, and distinctly privileged, set of gendered and generational dependencies to which not all progenitors, nor all offspring, belonged.

Discourses of class in nineteenth-century Chile were (and, in historiographic appraisals, are) so hegemonic and categorical that it is easy to forget that "rich" and "poor" were in fact social and historical categories. By showing how status was acquired in the first place, children illuminate the social production of hierarchy and the fact that its logic was neither predetermined nor unchanging. They also reveal hidden vulnerabilities of the Chilean social order, how differences officially deemed innate and immutable were in practice reflexively treated as acquired and precarious.[12] These dynamics are particularly visible at the margins. Examining the life histories of elites' extramarital children, who could be accepted or rejected by their progenitors, explains how and why some offspring became kin and others did not. The experiences of parentless children reared in others' households, sometimes as sons and daughters and sometimes as servile subordinates, are similarly instructive. In a social order formally based on fixed and stable status categories, illegitimates and child servants straddled an uneasy divide between proximity and distance, kin and stranger, intimate peer and lowly subordinate. Such scenarios further reveal the striking power of male household heads to determine the boundaries of the family—and concomitantly, the class status of the individuals included within, or excluded from, its embrace. By showing how social dependencies could prove ambiguous and status categories contingent, children expose embedded social logics at odds with hegemonic articulations of class.

Ultimately, then, this book is a history of children and family. But it is also a history of social inequality and class. It is abundantly clear that in modern Latin America, profound social inequalities have coexisted alongside the promise of formal equality. How have these inequalities been produced and reproduced? This book finds one answer to this question in the generative relationship of status to family. It is a relationship that holds lessons about the nature of inequality in modern Latin America. Hierarchical social modes imply that an individual's position in life is predetermined by birth, by family background, or by other ascriptive characteristics (of race, gender, etc.). Yet hierarchy does not for this reason imply stasis. I show how the production and reproduction of status required continuous, active, and often creative maintenance, particularly when law eschewed overt discrimination and external markers such as color proved unreliable in social practice and unpalatable in republican principle. Class hierarchy, in short, is not a thing; it is a process, one whose dynamism becomes apparent when we attend not only to the consequences of social status but to the ways it is acquired in the first place.

This depiction of class as contingent, experiential, and actively constructed echoes recent analytic approaches to race and ethnicity as well as gender. In the past two decades, rich and revealing threads of scholarship have probed the historical construction of race and gender in general and their intersections with experience, identity, and ideology in particular. This scholarship reflects a broad turn to subjectivities that traditional Marxist frameworks considered secondary to the true motor of historical change, class. In privileging the category of class hierarchy, this book does not seek to reassert the primacy of class. Rather, it seeks to approach its analysis with some of the same critical sensibilities that scholars now routinely apply to those other social categories.

Filiation as "an Unsolvable Problem": Men, Women, and Children in Nineteenth-Century Chile

A brief overview of family and filiation in nineteenth-century Chile sets the stage for this analysis. Explorations of plebeian families usually begin by considering labor and household structure on the hacienda, where contemporaries and historians alike have identified two contrasting familial patterns.[13] The first was that of the stable, sedentary inquilinos, who married, had children, and remained rooted for generations on a single hacienda. As one contemporary critic observed, the system of service tenancy may have been feudal, but at least "that home, that field, those animals, those children are guarantees that the inquilino gives to society." More disturbing were the unmarried, propertyless male peons who migrated perpetually, the "nomadic mass, without family, without a home of their own" whom authorities inevitably associated with social disorder.[14] The enhanced profitability of agriculture, a consequence of new international grain markets and the penetration of railroads, would only exacerbate the distinction. As landowners turned superfluous workers off their property to appropriate land previously dedicated to subsistence cultivation, more people were severed from inquilino household economies and their "guarantee" of order and stability.

Women were among the most likely to migrate. Considered dispensable to agricultural production, they found their livelihoods further undermined by the decline of traditional textile production in the face of foreign imports. Women left for provincial towns and urban areas, where a burgeoning market for domestic help generated a protoproletarian legion of servants, laundresses, cooks, and seamstresses. In 1875, these occupations collectively accounted for almost 85 percent of female employment.[15] Such migrants were unlikely to marry, in part because of imbalances in sex ratios: men outnumbered women on haciendas and in mining centers while the reverse was true in provincial towns and cities. In the provincial towns of the central valley, in the suburban settlements ringing Santiago, and, slightly later, in the urban slums of the city proper, female-headed households multiplied.[16]

The social organization of gender profoundly shapes the social condition of children. Yet neither historians of women and gender nor historians of family and childhood have explored this relationship systematically. Particularly conspicuous in the Chilean case, it is a subtext of this study. In a context of gendered migration and settlement patterns, illegitimacy was ubiquitous. According to official statistics, almost certainly significant underestimates, more than 20 percent of children in the 1850s, 30 percent in the 1890s, and between 30 and 40 percent in the 1910s and 1920s were born out of wedlock. In provincial San Felipe, over 50 percent of testators in the 1850s made bequests to illegitimate children or grandchildren or were illegitimate themselves; there is no reason to suppose this community was particularly prone to illegitimacy.[17] By way of comparison, around 1870 France's illegitimacy rate was 7.4 percent; Italy, 6.5 percent; Spain, 5.5 percent; and England 5.4 percent.[18]

"Illegitimacy" is a vague category that masks very different social and sexual arrangements, ranging from serial monogamy, to long-term, "marriage-like" consensual unions, to rape. It is thus less a sociological descriptor than an expression of an elite moral vision that censured all sexuality beyond the bounds of formal marriage. Given the range of unions associated with "illegitimate" birth, its significance for children themselves was never predetermined. Nevertheless, birth status had potentially profound consequences. A historically ubiquitous phenomenon, illegitimacy in Latin America has been explored primarily in colonial contexts, when it figured as an explicit criterion of civil and occupational discrimination.[19] But as I show in this study, natal status not only retained salience in republican society, it emerged as a key category of liberal law and bureaucracy even as other status distinctions were eliminated. Indeed, it was not until 1998 that discrimination against illegitimate children was abolished from Chilean law. Illegitimacy's remarkable

TABLE 1. Illegitimacy in Chile, 1850–1929.

Years, in quintiles	Percent of illegitimate births
1850–1854	22.3
1855–1859	22.9
1860–1864	24.0
1865–1869	25.5
1870–1874	25.4
1875–1879	22.9
1880–1884	24.1
1885–1889	25.5
1890–1894	32.4
1895–1899	31.9
1900–1904	34.3
1905–1909	36.2
1910–1914	37.6
1915–1919	38.2
1920–1924	36.7
1925–1929	34.5

Source: Dirección General de Estadística, *Anuario estadístico*, años 1929–1930, 4.

social and legal persistence speaks to the resilience of particular prescriptive ideals surrounding marriage and sexuality. But it also speaks to the legal and social structuring of hierarchy, for as I will show, natal status affected individuals' status beyond the family as well as within it, and it marked distinctions among different kinds of families as well as between family members.

Illegitimacy was related to, though by no means synonymous with, a broader phenomenon already referenced: the ubiquity of children whose parents were unable to care for them, children who were orphaned, abandoned, or who had otherwise become unmoored from natal kinship. These were the so-called *huachos*. According to contemporary etymologies, a huacho was "an animal that is not reared by its mother" or "a plant that is born by itself" without human intervention. It also referred to a foundling, orphan, bastard, or someone of otherwise dubious origins.

TABLE 2. Children Abandoned to the Casa de Huérfanos of Santiago, 1850–1929.

Years, by decade	1850–1859	1860–1869	1870–1879	1880–1889	1890–1899	1900–1909	1910–1919	1920–1929	1850–1929
Number of children	4,343	6,060	6,091	5,378	5,786	7,013	7,116	8,481*	50,268

*Estimated.
Source: Delgado, "Infancia abandonada," 103.

Deriving from the Quechua word for adultery and used throughout the Andes, Argentina, and Chile from the colonial period to the present, "huacho" was usually derogatory, by turns affectionate in a paternalistic way, and occasionally a neutral descriptor of orphanhood. A figure primarily of colloquial speech, the term captures the cultural significance of natal ties, the frequency with which these ties were broken, and the stigma attached to this condition.[20]

How exactly were children cut off from natal origins? In a three-week period in the winter of 1878, newspapers reported six separate instances of children found abandoned in Valparaíso. At least three more were found that same month in Santiago. One was a toddler left in a church during mass with a note reading, "I cannot feed him and I hand him over to the charity of whoever will take him."[21] Meanwhile, in the last decades of the nineteenth century, overcrowded orphanages were multiplying across the republic. The largest and oldest was Santiago's Casa de Huérfanos, which a foreign visitor remarked in the 1880s was "so extensive that one is led to inquire how there can be so many orphans in the city of Santiago."[22] In the late nineteenth century, the institution received between 5 and 9 percent of children born in the city. By the turn of the century, according to one calculation, for every 1,000 inhabitants of Santiago, 9 were in the Casa de Huérfanos. All told, more than 50,000 children were left there from the 1850s to the mid-1920s, 18,000 of them in the first quarter of the twentieth century alone.[23] In fact, what elite observers condemned as "abandonment" was merely the most visible dimension of the pervasive cultural practice of child circulation, in which youngsters were reared outside natal kin networks.[24]

TABLE 3. Age Groups, as a Percentage of Total Population.

Age group	1885	1895	1907	1920	1930
0–9	29.4	29.4	25.9	26.2	26.2
10–19	21.6	21.8	22.2	22.4	21.9
0–19	51	51.2	48.1	48.6	48.1

Source: Mamalakis, Historical Statistics, 66.

Regardless of who reared them, one defining characteristic of children's lives in this society was their brevity. At least a quarter of the population was under age nine.[25] But in the early 1890s, more than a third of children died before their first birthday, and by 1920, the number was still over a quarter.[26] Extraordinarily high even by contemporary standards (generations of critics claimed Chile had the highest infant mortality rate in the "civilized world"), the numbers reflect a classic "pre-modern" population pattern of high birth and death rates. As we will see, they also refracted strong political meanings. For elite commentators, plebeian children became the essential expression of the material and moral crisis of their class.

Patterns of illegitimacy, huachismo (the phenomenon of huachos), child circulation, and infant mortality arose out of a fundamental disjuncture: patriarchy without patriarchal households. Chilean legal structures, cultural and religious norms, and highly sex-segregated labor markets were premised on the organization of authority, production, reproduction, and consumption within patriarchal households. Yet in Chile and in Latin America, such households have been, to quote Elizabeth Dore, "imagined," since most people lacked the materials resources to marry and establish long-term, economically viable domestic units as bases of social reproduction. Some plebeians—most obviously inquilinos—did form enduring conjugal units and lasting patriarchal households. But for many others, partnerships and bonds of filiation were fleeting. To argue as much is not to embrace elites' patronizing assertions about plebeians' affective deficits and familial anomie. Poor people developed other kinds of affinities—those based on crianza (the rearing of unrelated children), for example, and compadrazgo (godparenthood or spiritual kinship). In referring to such ties, I avoid the term " 'fictive' kinship" because for the people who developed them, these relationships were no less meaningful

TABLE 4. Infant Mortality in Chile, 1890–1929
(mortality during the first year of life).

Years, in quintiles	1890–1894	1895–1899	1900–1904	1905–1909	1910–1914	1915–1919	1920–1924	1925–1929
Mortality per 1,000	338	290	292	302	285	265	266	233

Source: Mamalakis, *Historical Statistics*, 40; Dirección General de Estadística, *Anuario estadístico*, años 1929–1930, 4.

or "real" than consanguineous or affinal ones. Likewise, other household forms, such as female headship, existed where patriarchal ones did not and may even have afforded plebeian women a degree of autonomy.[27]

Yet it is clear that for poor women the precariousness of patriarchal households could imply not only alternative modes of intimacy, affinity, and perhaps autonomy but also dependency and subordination. For children, they could signal natal alienation and huachismo. More than three decades ago, feminist scholars challenged historical and social science analyses of the Western family that attributed to it a false unity and assumed it to be a harmonious site of uniform interests. Attending to dynamics of gender, they argued that family has harbored dynamics of oppression for women (and children).[28] These insights are undoubtedly relevant to Latin America, except that the patriarchal family must always be read within a broad matrix of social and racial inequality. "Wife" may have been a legally and socially subordinate role, but it was also associated with class entitlement. Where their wealthier counterparts became madres de familia, poor women lacking the requisite social and material resources to establish their own households were often incorporated into others' households as servants.[29] Plebeian children denied the status of hijos de familia grew up as huachos. For poor women and children, in other words, the most acute forms of subordination were not necessarily those of the autonomous, plebeian, patriarchal household. This is not to glorify the patriarchal household or bemoan its precariousness among the poor. It is to highlight its relationship to other, equally significant vectors of subordination and dependency operative in the Latin American context.

Illegitimacy and huachismo harbor particular resonance for Chilean national narratives. Most Chileans know that Chile's "founding father" Bernardo O'Higgins was the illegitimate son of a colonial official who refused to recognize him. His political enemies disparaged him as *el huacho Riquelme*, invoking his maternal surname to emphasize the stigma of fatherlessness. The early republican statesman Diego Portales's multiple illegitimate progeny are similarly common knowledge.[30] If the "birth of the nation" was marked by these high-profile cases of huachismo, so too was subsequent republican history. As I show in this book, poor, marginalized, illegitimate children have repeatedly emerged as harbingers of disorder at moments of heightened class tension.

They have also served as touchstones of some of the most influential critiques of social order and national identity in modern Chile. Augusto Orrego Luco's essay "La cuestión social" (1884), perhaps the most famous of a nineteenth-century genre of social critique, identified the "unsolvable problem of filiation"—the inability of the poor to form families and save their children from the scourge of infant mortality—as a social crisis. More than fifty years later, and an ideological world away, the minister of health, socialist, and future president Salvador Allende penned a study tying Chile's appalling "socio-medical reality" to the world capitalist order. On the book's first page is a photograph of two sleeping street children and the claim, reiterated repeatedly since the 1870s, that Chile's infant mortality rate was the highest in the civilized world. Proletarian child protagonists are a mainstay of twentieth-century Chilean social-realist literature, and concubinage, illegitimacy, orphanhood, and fosterage recur in this genre and in contemporary fiction.[31] Such themes also figure in recent interpretations of national identity, gender, and class politics by leading Chilean scholars. The anthropologist Sonia Montecinos has probed the politics of illegitimacy and mestizaje in the making of Chilean national identity. And in a provocative and influential essay written in 1990 and recently expanded into a best-selling book, the award-winning historian Gabriel Salazar narrates the history of the Chilean poor through the voice of a young huacho.[32]

The patterns analyzed by these writers, while undoubtedly inflected by peculiarities specific to the Chilean historical experience and harboring special social and political resonance within it, are nevertheless not unique to Chile. Concubinage, illegitimacy, low nuptiality, female headship, child circulation, and huachismo are enduring patterns in many

Latin American societies historically. And as in Chile, such patterns have been particularly (though not exclusively) associated with subalterns and have harbored strong associations related to hierarchies of class (and race). As such, while this is a case study grounded in the specificities of Chilean history, politics, and culture, it speaks to broader hemispheric patterns and practices.

States and Families in Chile, Latin America, and Beyond

When a congress on children's health convened in Santiago in 1919, the roster of participants read as a who's who of the political establishment. In attendance were the president of the republic, the ministers of foreign affairs, finance, and industry, the president of the Chamber of Deputies, the intendant of the province, and the mayor of Santiago.[33] The presence of such prominent elite men at a conference whose stated purpose was "propagating knowledge of child care among the lower classes" reflected a growing consensus developed over the preceding seventy-five years about the transcendental public importance of, and acceptability of state intervention in, realms once deemed private or of ecclesiastical jurisdiction. Such ideas were of course not specifically Chilean. In the final decades of the nineteenth century, across the Americas and Europe, the material and moral well-being of the poor became a subject of vigorous public critique. Central to this so-called social question was an impetus to domesticate the lower-class family.[34]

The family patterns described above gave Chilean politicians, philanthropists, and medico-legal professionals ample fodder for recrimination. Illegitimate children were the "disruptive seed of our society," and matrifocal households were said to bring about "the slow debilitation of the race." The fact that poor children were raised amid the "vices and bad examples" of their parents was "the worst of the evils of our society." Chile's high rate of infant mortality threatened the nation itself, since every child who died was "a drop of blood that slowly drains the vigor [and] strength from the arteries of the State." Commentators warned darkly that the fall of the Roman Empire was caused by the corruption of its families.[35] These were the estimations not of conservatives but of nineteenth-century liberals and twentieth-century reformists.

The representation of poor children as *hijos de la patria*, children of the fatherland, was not new. It rehearsed the Bourbon Enlightenment identification of children with modernity and children's welfare with the well-being of the imperial state.[36] Now, however, such discourses were linked to positivist notions of progress and to an altered concept of "the public," in which the nation-state replaced the father-king. And now they were tied to processes of secularization in which the Catholic Church—traditional arbiter of family and sexuality—was gradually subordinated to the state.

An opening salvo of the state's expanded mandate was the Chilean Civil Code, which took effect in 1857 and would become highly influential across Latin America. The Code regulated marriage and inheritance and, as will be discussed in chapter 1, institutionalized a new legal regime that liberalized, secularized, and bureaucratized filiation. Concomitantly, civil courts increasingly heard domestic disputes (such as spousal conflicts) once reserved for ecclesiastical authority. The secularization of marriage (1883) was a particularly obvious, and controversial, manifestation of new state prerogatives over family. As one proponent of civil marriage declared, "Everything that has to do with the organization of the family refers . . . to the organization of the State itself. Consequently, to deny the State the right to legislate about the organization of the family is to deny it the right to constitute itself."[37] A year later, the establishment of the civil registry (1884) ended the Church's supervision of birth, marriage, and death records. The state also engaged with poor children and their families through child-welfare asylums like the Sociedad Protectora de la Infancia and the Casa de Huérfanos, which were either subsidized or administered by public authorities.

Law occupied a particularly significant role in the state's relationship with families and children but not as an instrument of generic regulation and domination. It was, more specifically, a vector of social difference. Because family patterns varied widely among classes, family law had a differential impact on different groups. Legal reforms that disadvantaged illegitimates disproportionately impacted the poor, and requiring parental consent and baptismal or birth certificates to marry, to cite dictates of marriage law, affected the nuptial prospects primarily of a kinless underclass. Lauren Benton has observed that law has served as a site for "cultural boundary marking" and that "particular sorts of laws emerged

as focal points of tension in particular historical circumstances." In
eighteenth-century England, for example, criminal law was a site for the
reinscription of class relations.[38] In nineteenth-century Chile, I argue,
family law played a similar role. Law established rights and obligations
between kin and, in defining the boundaries of family, mandated who
was subject to those obligations and who benefited from those rights.
In so doing, family law managed hierarchies of gender and generation
within the family but also those of class and status beyond it.

Of course, there existed major disjunctures between law and vernacular kinship practices, especially among plebeians. No historical examination of family, gender, or childhood in Latin America can ignore this
often gaping divergence between practice and prescription.[39] But rather
than attenuating the significance of law, these disjunctures were directly
implicated in the legal production of inequality. Some families and kin
relations enjoyed the backing of legal authority and the moral imprimatur of legality while others did not. Lacking natal kin, some children
inhabited the extralegal realm of charity. Law itself severed kin links by
recognizing no legal bonds between fathers and their unacknowledged
extramarital offspring. Moreover, law and popular practice, the legal and
the extralegal, mutually shaped one another. Legal reforms that absolved
fathers of responsibility for illegitimate progeny depended on, and probably encouraged, vernacular practices in which poor children relied on
plural, unrelated caretakers.

In recent years, the relationship between popular culture and nation-
state formation has occupied a privileged role in analyses of Latin American society, culture, and politics. Such scholarship has often emphasized
the role of popular negotiation, appropriation, and resistance in shaping
state power. Through such appraisals, Latin Americanists have contributed to broad theoretical debates about domination versus hegemony,
resistance, the importance of popular sectors to historical outcomes, and
redefinitions of "the political." Drawing on these concerns, scholars of
women and gender have probed states' engagements with family and
sexuality.[40] Likewise, the nascent historiography of childhood has high-
lighted children as subjects of regulation, discipline, and education (a
focus likely motivated as much by available documentation as by analytic
cues) and the articulation of childhood and state formation.[41]

Often implicit, and sometimes explicit, in this scholarship is a particular vision of the way states behave toward the private sphere, summarized in Elizabeth Dore's assertion that states regulate "as many aspects of life as they can reach, including sexual practices, prostitution, vagrancy, contraception, abortion, marriage, and the family."[42] Whether the subject is the Bourbon state in the eighteenth century, the liberal or medico-legal state in the nineteenth century, or the welfare state or revolutionary state of the twentieth century, the emphasis tends to fall on states' ever heightened impetus to regulate gender and "the private" and their increasing capacity to do so. Scholars have variously argued that in early republican Venezuela, "the state intervened in the private sphere by ruling over courtship, marriage, child custody, and divorce"; in Costa Rica, codification "endorsed the legal prerogative of civil authority to regulate domestic morality"; Puerto Rican beneficence officials "invaded the most private of spheres—the family"; and the early-twentieth-century Brazilian Estado Novo witnessed "the gradual expansion of the notion of public interest to encompass realms that had previously been regarded as private."[43] Ultimately, such conclusions are of course not specific to Latin America: they echo a broad postcolonial emphasis on the way imperial authorities have asserted power over what Ann Laura Stoler calls "domains of the intimate," the realm of "sex, sentiment, domestic arrangement and child rearing."[44]

Such analyses of vertical power relations are crucial because they tie gender, sexuality, children, and the domestic to histories of empire, colonialism, nationalism, and state formation. At the same time, as scholars of the state have pointed out, such analyses pose pitfalls. Regulatory policies can appear epiphenomenal and ahistorical if in order to explain them we resort to some generic disciplinary impetus rather than analyzing their specific origins, contents, and trajectories. Narratives of intervention can imply a unitary moralizing "project" where none existed. And an emphasis on top-down projects may overstate their actual impact.[45] Evidence from Chile suggests several additional critiques. First, posing the relationship between public authority and the private sphere as a zero-sum conflict obscures the extent to which these two realms actually drew on a common well of cultural belief and practice. A deeply significant social and cultural category, kinship was also central to the architecture of civil law and legal personhood. This shared significance by no means precluded tension between state and family, but it does suggest this relationship was characterized by more than just diametrical opposition.

A second critique concerns the regulatory impetus itself. If there was any nineteenth-century Latin American state with the wherewithal to impose its will in the private sphere, it was the Chilean one. Legal and institutional developments, as well as the rhetorical identification of childhood and nation, would seem to intimate a narrative linking family and children to state formation and nation building. Yet as I will show, liberal authorities exhibited less a unidirectional impulse to top-down intervention than competing impulses, oscillating between regulation and a calculated circumscription of public action. State rhetoric emphasized intervention. State practice proved distinctly ambiguous.

In fact, these apparent contradictions are fully consistent with the political ideals that Chilean liberals espoused. As Charles A. Hale has observed, liberalism embodies a fundamental tension: its secularizing impulse implies an expansion of state power (at the expense of religious authority), but its emphasis on personal freedom and free will in economic and social life implies state constriction.[46] The history of children and family in Chile lays bare this tension. In the latter half of the nineteenth century, the state systematically appropriated aspects of the Church's traditional dominion over marriage and sexuality. But informed by colonial constructs of public and private, coupled with newer liberal leitmotifs of privacy and personal freedom, it simultaneously withdrew from some arenas it had once regulated. Most conspicuous was the deregulation of pre- and extramarital sexuality. After the 1850s, the courts rarely pursued cases of *amancebamiento*, or illicit unions, which they had once prosecuted with moralistic vigor. Meanwhile, departing from long-standing canon and Iberian legal tradition, the Civil Code refused to recognize *esponsales*, the marriage promise exchanged between partners that sometimes initiated sexual relations.[47]

In the most far-reaching reform, explored in parts I and II, the Code outlawed paternity investigation, and the civil birth registry made the recording of illegitimate parents' identities optional. Invoking older colonial notions of familial honor together with newer liberal ideals of free will, privacy, and personal conscience, public authorities divested themselves of the power to discern illegitimate kin relations, granting to fathers the unfettered freedom to recognize or reject offspring. The distinctly patriarchal form of liberalism in Chile, a liberalism that sacrificed ideals of equality on the altar of privacy and individual liberty, had markedly different consequences for men and for women. It also profoundly affected children.

The impulse to circumscription is similarly evident in the history of public beneficence. As will be discussed in part III, the expansion of a state-funded child welfare apparatus represented as much an abdication of public responsibility for poor children as an assertion of it. Children's asylums privatized social assistance to the poor and parentless by serving as clearinghouses for distributing children to wet nurses and masters. Despite the vociferous rhetoric of its transcendental public significance, in other words, child welfare continued to be outsourced to private households and haciendas as it had been in the colonial era. The expansion of these asylums, which continued through the first decades of the twentieth century, perpetuated and perhaps even enhanced the crucial importance of informal and private provision for poor children. The enduring centrality of private households to state welfare strategy complicates binary models of top-down intervention and popular resistance.

Ultimately, children not only expose the tensions inherent in the liberal state's posture toward the private; they partially displace the prevailing analytic emphasis on the state altogether. As explored in part III, a focus on children and child rearing directs us to informal, extralegal, and vernacular venues of power, including the infrapolitics of class, status, and patronage within households. Such a focus brings to the fore quotidian practices of social reproduction and relations of domination between masters and servants, adults and minors, and elites and plebeians. And it reveals how households both wealthy and humble exploited poor and parentless huachos. In short, children underscore class, gender, and generational power as it operated within and across households, not just as exercised between "state" and "society." As Miguel Centeno has suggested, discipline in Latin America has occurred not primarily in schools, the military, or the penitentiary, as in Europe or North America, but within families and households.[48] Indeed, while the literature of state intervention often references, implicitly or explicitly, the work of Michel Foucault, Foucault himself argued that power was not only, nor even primarily, invested in the state. "Relations of power, and hence the analysis that must be made of them, necessarily extend beyond the limits of the

State," he noted. "The State is superstructural in relation to a whole series of power networks that invest the body, sexuality, the family, kinship, knowledge, technology, etc." In Chile, vernacular kinship, child-rearing practices, and particular forms of domestic servitude constituted some of those "mechanisms of power that function outside, below and alongside the state apparatuses, on a much more minute and everyday level."[49]

Ultimately, shifting our focus from the state to this other level of social power has an additional salutary effect. Analyses of top-down intervention risk regarding gender, family, kinship, and childhood as significant only to the extent that they are sites of regulation and resistance or discursive signifiers of other relations of power. Such a framework is not wrong, but it may disregard the intrinsic significance of these dimensions of human experience.[50] This significance is an underlying premise of this study.

Sources, Methods, Frameworks

Thus, while this book is concerned with the evolution of legal regimes, state formation, and class relations, it is also a historical ethnography of children and filiation in a Latin American society. Adopting a self-consciously social historical approach, I seek to reconstruct a social world, one in which children—nursing on the stoop, running errands in the streets, coming of age in humble *ranchos* and servants' quarters—are ubiquitous. This goal means steering an analytic middle ground between unreconstructed empiricism and wholesale poststructuralism, coaxing my sources to yield practice as well as discourse, social experience, as well as social construction. At the same time, I do not take "state" and "society," "public" and "private," or "family" to be bounded entities with fixed or predetermined meanings. In keeping with a cultural historical approach, I seek to show how the definitions of these categories varied across social groups and over time.

One such category is children. Who or what was a child? As historians and anthropologists of childhood have shown, the answer to this question is far from obvious, varying greatly both temporally and cross-culturally. In English, the term "child" has two different meanings: it refers to minors as well as to progeny (in contrast, Spanish has separate terms for these two concepts, *niño* and *hijo*). This book deals with both kinds of "children." The analysis of filiation in part I probes the changing meanings of children-as-progeny. The category of children-as-minors—what most scholars mean when they talk about a history of children—is more difficult to pin down because for most people, nineteenth-century Chileans included, "childhood" is so self-evident a concept that it rarely necessitates explicit definition.

The chief exception was in the realm of law. Nineteenth-century civil law clearly distinguished between children and adults and between juridical minority and majority, adopting age gradations that often echoed those used in earlier colonial and medieval legal tradition.[51] Legal definitions of minority were not seamlessly transposed into social understandings of childhood, however. Age was but one dimension of the definition of childhood, for as Bianca Premo has noted of colonial Spanish America, "to be a minor was a relational as much as an age-based status."[52] In postcolonial Chile, too, minority was relational insofar as all children were assumed to be socially and legally dependent on adults. On the other hand, to assert that children were "dependent" tells us little because, as we have seen, "dependency" could harbor such starkly different social and status valences.[53]

The relationality of childhood is further illustrated by considering how plebeian children's status as *plebeians* had contradictory effects on their status as *children*. On the one hand, in Chile, as elsewhere, subordinate social status was associated with infantilization. According to her employer's family, sixteen-year-old servant María Caballero was "very lazy" such that "one had to continually scold her to do her work." Once when she disobeyed her mistress she merited three blows with a broomstick. But it was not her mistress who commented on her faults and administered the beating: it was the mistress's eleven-year-old son.[54] Clearly status (and gender) trumped age in shaping perceptions of minority in this relationship. On the other hand, children's plebeian status could compel their precocious induction into social relations, such as those of patronage, we usually associate with adults. When coachman Luis Alberto Ávila was charged with accidentally killing a pedestrian, he presented several patrons who attested to his "honorability," "formality," and "irreproachable conduct." Providing character references from superiors was routine practice for those seeking legal clemency. But Luis Alberto was ten years old.[55] Whether poor children were rendered "younger" or "older" by virtue of their class, their experience of childhood was inseparable from their socioeconomic status. Nevertheless, despite the importance of status in shaping childhood, one can discern a fundamental cultural and legal consensus regarding the existence of the categories "children" and "childhood" in the first place. In Luis Alberto's case, all parties readily agreed "children of a young age" had no business driving coaches and that ethical and criminal responsibility for the accident lay with the adult employers. Luis Alberto, we can discern, was a "child," even if the parties did not express precisely how they defined the term.

This is, then, a history of children. However, it is not explicitly framed around the themes that dominate this historiographic field. I am not primarily concerned with the historical evolution of sentiment, child labor, education, disciplinary institutions, or changing constructions of childhood (though I hope my findings shed light on a number of these themes). Because they reflect the analytic agenda of a field with a distinctly North American and European cast, these issues may not be the most fruitful or relevant ones to pose of children in other cultural contexts.[56] Instead, I have framed this study around two abiding concerns of Latin American history and historiography, namely, state formation and the dynamics of class. These are not, of course, themes specific to this region. Apropos of a recent history of children in the United States, the British historian Hugh Cunningham inquired, "What would the history of childhood look like if we wrote it as part of the history of class?"[57] A case study situated in Latin America, where social hierarchy is so keenly manifest, is particularly well suited to suggesting an answer. In endeavoring to do so, I hope to show Latin Americanist scholars that children offer a productive lens for analyzing the state and class, as well as labor, liberalism, law, patriarchy, and postcolonial societies, and to encourage them to become more active participants in a recently initiated comparative dialogue on childhood. I also hope that this book's explicitly Latin American framework suggests to scholars of other regions alternative questions to ask of the history of children and family.

Writing the history of childhood as a history of class invites an inevitable rejoinder: why not write it as a history of race and ethnicity instead (or as well)? This book focuses on hierarchies of class for the basic reason that the Chilean sources, while extraordinarily rich in many dimensions, speak only rarely to racial and ethnic categories. This limitation, however, can be parlayed to analytic advantage. Race is one category of social differentiation and discrimination and indeed an especially crucial one in the history of Latin America. But it is not the only one. In postcolonial Chile, ethnoracial categories were particularly muted and murky, either because such differences were objectively difficult to ascribe or because the myth of a uniformly mestizo Chile proved expedient to a nation whose most formative armed conflicts were waged against external foes (Peru, Bolivia, and autonomous Mapuche Indians) constructed as ethnic others. In other words, racial difference was often most usefully located outside, not inside, national borders.[58] Inside those borders, meanwhile, other categories of difference proved expedient. One of these was family.

Whatever the analytic questions asked of it, the history of childhood poses distinct methodological challenges. As many historians have lamented, children can be notoriously elusive historical subjects. The sources available for nineteenth- and early-twentieth-century Chile exhibit significant gaps and limitations, perhaps the greatest of which is that virtually all of them were generated by the state. Still, children are surprisingly ubiquitous in this historical record, and as I intend to show, state sources reveal not just law, bureaucratic practice, and prescriptive norms. Read carefully, they can also illuminate vernacular practices toward which the state harbored no regulatory intent.

At the heart of this analysis is a body of more than a thousand judicial cases from civil, criminal, and ecclesiastical courts.[59] As the Puelma case suggests, criminal investigations of abuse, infanticide, and child abandonment lay bare the ever-present perils that stalked poor children. Voluminous paternity suits yield rich narratives, often spanning decades, that chronicle the lives of individuals whose kin ties are in dispute. Custodial battles waged by parents, godparents, caretakers, and masters reveal the value of children, the diversity of child-rearing arrangements, and also, in surprising ways, the agency of children themselves. In all of these cases, as in the photograph of the Puelmas, child subjects are starkly illuminated beneath the high beam of judicial scrutiny.

Yet even when the investigative spotlight does not focus on children per se, as in the turn-of-the-century photographs of street scenes in which barefoot urchins hover at the margins, they are still there, in the penumbra of the documentary record. Often it is when the court's atten-

4. Market sellers, ca. 1890s. *Courtesy of the Museo Histórico Nacional.*

tion is distracted by other matters that judicial investigations prove most revealing about childhood. A divorce case inadvertently reveals a side drama: the ignominious fate of the husband's extramarital progeny. A criminal complaint against a thieving servant brings to light fortuitous details of her childhood. An interrogation of a bigamy suspect prompts the accused to narrate a wide-ranging chronicle of his youth.[60] Taken as a whole, the judicial cases provide frequent glimpses of minors and sometimes make it possible to reconstruct quite detailed accounts of individual lives. This portrait is further enriched by more than 450 wills, drawn from both urban and rural locales. As testators of diverse social backgrounds dispose of their property, they narrate relations of filiation, kinship, patronage, and crianza.[61]

Children and youth, in short, were everywhere, in Chilean households, streets, and haciendas. ("Flies innumerable," wrote a British traveler outside Valparaíso, "children almost emulating the flies.")[62] And they are omnipresent, if sometimes shadowy, figures in the documentary remnants of that world. I adopt the late-nineteenth-century doctor and social critic Augusto Orrego Luco's colorful phrase "the children of fate" (*los hijos del azar*) to refer, as he did, to poor children but also to reference the articulation of children with class hierarchies as well as the kin metaphors through which power relations were so often expressed.

In addition to judicial and notarial sources, I draw on extraordinarily rich materials from Santiago's Casa de Huérfanos. Some children arrived at the orphanage with formal letters of request, and others with barely literate pleas scrawled on scraps of paper. Their departure is documented in the requests of local citizens seeking to "foster" children from the asylum. In public discourse, endemic practices of child abandonment were roundly deplored, but these materials reveal realities considerably more complex than, and often strikingly at odds with, such appraisals. While elite critics denounced the poor for callously abandoning their children, the Casa files reveal individuals like the statesman Benjamín Vicuña Mackenna, as well as two of the asylum's own administrators, actively lobbying to place the infants of women they had hired to nurse their own children. We encounter the feminist journalist and outspoken advocate for women's and children's rights Elvira Santa Cruz Ossa writing on behalf of a poor woman soliciting a child from the Casa, a child likely to become an exploited servant in her household. We can also discern the actions and intentions of poor parents themselves, sometimes filtered through the words of patrons, sometimes expressed in their own shaky penmanship, and evaluate them alongside prescriptive expectations and institutional practices.[63]

It could be argued that a focus on illegitimacy, kinlessness, abandonment, and huachismo overemphasizes nonnormative, even pathological, aspects of social practice. Far from displacing the state, it could be asserted, such a focus adopts the state's own moralizing categories. It is certainly the case that powerful normative valences make it easy to essentialize phenomena whose social meanings were never predetermined. Illegitimacy, for example, did not inexorably lead to familial anomie, as elites invariably assumed. Yet some historical analyses unwittingly accept that appraisal.[64] Indeed, it could be argued that a category like illegitimacy cannot be divested of the normative baggage that is constitutive of its meaning.

There is, however, an analytic rationale for focusing on such phenomena. As scholars of crime know, the nonnormative often throws the normative into particularly sharp relief. A focus on kinlessness serves to reconstruct the cultural and bureaucratic significance of kinship. The experiences of illegitimates and child domestics illuminate the articulation of childhood with labor, of socialization with social hierarchy, and the meanings of dependency. Moreover, while these practices may have been nonnormative, they were hardly exceptional. In this sense, criminality is an imperfect analogy for the phenomena explored here. Illegitimacy was simultaneously "unorthodox" and, among plebeians, endemic. And in households of all social levels, *hijos ajenos*, unrelated children, were omnipresent. Their ubiquity is not just an illusion of the state's blinkered moral vision; these children are in ample evidence despite the state's assiduous disregard for them.

This book traces such phenomena over the course of eighty years of Chile's modern history. The narrative begins in the 1850s, with the transformations in law and legal culture wrought by the new Civil Code, and concludes in 1930, when changes in familial practices, public rhetoric, and law signal an important break in the histories of the Chilean state, class relations, families, and children. This temporal arc captures a transformative period in the country's history. In 1850, Chile was a nation of some 1.4 million people, of whom perhaps three-quarters lived in the countryside. A firmly entrenched landed oligarchy presided over a restricted political sphere and an export-led economy based on mining and agriculture. This was the society whose capital Vicuña Mackenna could characterize as a "city of relatives." By 1930, Chile's population had tripled to some 4.3 million inhabitants, almost half of whom now lived in urban areas. A genteel society of "relatives" had become a fractious polity of citizens. The emergence of a populist, reformist middle class, a rebellious working class, and a militant labor movement transformed the body politic beyond recognition. Once anarchists, socialists, and communists entered the political scene, the old ideological conflicts between nineteenth-century liberals and conservatives appeared patently insular. In the context of mounting class tensions and the heavy-handed repres-

Peru

Bolivia

Chile

Chile Research Locations

○ Putaendo
○ San Felipe
■ Quillota
○ Valparaíso
■ Casablanca   ○ Santiago
San Bernardo ■

Rancagua ○

■ Rengo
○ San Fernando

○ Curicó

Constitución ○
        ○ Talca

○ Linares

Quirihue   ○ Parral
        ○
        ○ San Carlos

0   70 Miles

Northern border before 1879

○ Copiapó

La Serena ○

see inset

■ ○ Santiago

Concepción

Southern border before 1860

Argentina

Atlantic Ocean

Pacific Ocean

○ Court consulted
■ Notary consulted

0   200 Miles

N

Jan Coyne, 2008

sion of labor protest, they also appeared distinctly subdued. The power of the oligarchy was unmistakably on the wane, and the promise, if not quite the reality, of a modernizing, industrial, and more democratic future beckoned.

Significant geopolitical expansion accompanied these demographic, economic, and political changes. In the course of this same period, Chilean national territory tripled in size as the central valley, the country's historic core, expanded both northward and southward. First, Chile wrested the northern desert from Peru and Bolivia in the War of the Pacific (1879–83); thereafter, it subordinated southern territories historically dominated by semi-autonomous Mapuche Indians (1880s). This book focuses primarily though not exclusively on the central valley, the most populous and urban part of the country and the area with the densest evidentiary base.[65] Tracking familiar historical developments through the lens of children and families, the narrative reveals important social changes during this transformative period. But perhaps above all, the story told here is one of striking continuities.

The book is divided into three sections. Part I, "Children and Strangers: Filiation in Law and Practice," explores the transformation of law and legal culture wrought by the Chilean Civil Code, which was not only adopted in Chile but also influenced civil law throughout Latin America. Of the many changes the Code instituted in family law, perhaps the most significant was the abolition of paternity investigation. Chapter 1 describes how the Code reconfigured filiation according to the liberal logic of contract, granting fathers unfettered freedom to recognize or reject their illegitimate children. The contractualization and concomitant bureaucratization of filiation enhanced state authority, but in carving out new and inalienable paternal rights to freedom and privacy, the Code ultimately empowered men at the expense not only of women and children but also of the courts themselves. Chapter 2 examines post–Civil Code paternity suits filed retroactively by people born before the Code. Courts applied a class-based standard of kinship and in so doing became public arenas for the reinscription of social difference. These suits elucidate the everyday process by which children became socialized into particular class statuses. And they reveal how class categories regarded as categorical and axiomatic were in practice contingent and unstable.

Part II, "Children of Don Nobody: Kinship and Social Hierarchy," explores the enduring significance of kinship as a sociocultural, as well as legal-bureaucratic, category in republican Chile. Chapter 3 describes a shadowy, stigmatized "kinless" underclass of poor people who grew up with no knowledge of their parentage or natal provenance. Kinlessness as a form of social marginality helps illuminate the cultural, material, and legal significance of kinship and the ways it helped structure class hierarchies. Chapter 4 argues that ecclesiastical and civil bureaucracies drew on family membership to fix individual identity and constitute legal personhood. Yet the state's deployment of kinship was ironic. For even as legal kinship became increasingly important, welfare asylums, the newly minted civil registry, and civil law systematically dispossessed certain individuals of their natal origins.

Part III, "Other People's Children: The Politics of Child Circulation," describes what became of youngsters detached from the moorings of natal kinship. It explores the demographic and material underpinnings, cultural meanings, and social significance of child circulation, a little-studied practice that has been extremely widespread across Latin America historically. Chapter 5 describes the significance of child fosterage to plebeian family formation and as an informal and extralegal mode of welfare provision for children rendered orphans by law and bureaucracy. Fosterage illuminates the interplay of liberal legal reforms and informal popular practice. Chapter 6 examines another vector of child circulation: the rearing of poor, illegitimate, and Amerindian children as domestic servants. A de facto form of bondage that outlived legal slavery by more than a century, tutelary servitude fed children into adult peonage, demonstrating in particularly stark terms how childhood articulated with labor and class structures. Finally, the epilogue, "Marginals at the Centenary: One Hundred Years of *Huachos*," surveys changes and continuities in the first three decades of the twentieth century. After the turn of the century, legal reforms and new economic realities began to alter the contours of illegitimacy, kinlessness, and child circulation. Yet young huachos ultimately reveal the limits of efforts to secure the social and political enfranchisement of the working class.

While the first photographs taken of the Puelma children depict three young victims of neglect and abuse, a final image shows them once they had been cleaned, fed, and dressed. Delia's wrap is rearranged, and Ri-

5. Children of the fatherland: the Puelma children once they had been washed, clothed, and fed. *Source: Archivo Nacional Histórico de Chile.*

cardo and José Manuel are dressed in caps and button-down suits like miniature soldiers. The "before" and "after" photos narrate the Puelmas' transformation from *hijos del azar*, children of fate, to *hijos de la patria*, children of the fatherland. That transformation, of course, reflected more the aspirations of elite adults than the actual experiences of poor children. The photographs in this sense capture the multiple disjunctures of prescription and reality. They allude to the public furor that surrounded the case and invite us to ponder the motivations of the judge who ordered their creation. But the photographs also challenge us to consider Delia, Ricardo, and José Manuel Puelma as something more than "representations." They prompt us to ask simple but powerful questions about who they were and why they mattered. This book probes elite aspirations, state actions, legal understandings of filiation, and the political meanings of plebeian childhood. But above all, it tells the story of the children themselves and of the adults who they became.

PART I

Children and Strangers

Filiation in Law and Practice

CHAPTER 1

The Civil Code and

the Liberalization of Kinship

The Cook, the Seamstress, and the Baby

For one witness, the proof of paternity lay in the booties. Alejandro D'Huique had given the wet nurse eight *reales* to buy them for the baby Clarisa del Carmen. Now Clarisa's paternity was in dispute in a Santiago court. In her petition for economic support from D'Huique, Clarisa's mother, Mercedes Campos, provided details of a romance gone sour. The couple had met four years before, in 1847, in the household where they both worked, she as a seamstress and he as a chef. Campos, according to witnesses, was poor but from "a very decent and honorable family." But as her lawyer explained, "as a result of a misfortune of which no woman is free," his client had "ceded to the seductions of Don Alejandro," who turned out to be married in his native France. Witnesses were summoned in support of her claim. A midwife declared that D'Huique had paid her for assisting in Clarisa's birth. The wet nurse recounted how in regular visits the alleged father was affectionate with the baby and gave money for her care, once arranging a meeting in the Plaza de Armas to do so. And, of course, there were the booties.

As for Don Alejandro himself, he vociferously denied the allegation. If he had given Campos money, it was as "alms" because she was sick. Noting that she had placed her baby for a time in the city's orphanage, he questioned whether her suit was motivated by maternal sentiment or crass "speculation." Finally, calling attention to the fact that his legitimate wife and children had recently arrived from France, D'Huique argued that adulterous offspring had no right to parental support anyway.[1]

Paternity suits like this one were routine in midcentury Chilean courts, and contemporaries would have been familiar with several recent high-profile suits. The year before, a suit filed against the estate of a wealthy English merchant had featured the testimony of Manuel Montt, who had since become president of the republic. And a few years prior, Santiago had been scandalized when a congressman was murdered by the father of a young woman with whom he was having an affair. His death sparked a spate of paternity suits filed by various children he had fathered with different women.[2] Of course D'Huique did not approach the stature of these men, though in later years he would become a well-known chef and restaurauteur at the Hotel Santiago, where men of their rank would dine on his famed *pudding Nesselrode*.[3]

All of these suits occurred on the cusp of a major legal shift that would dramatically remake kinship in republican Chile. For almost a half-century after independence, medieval Iberian and colonial Spanish legal codes continued to govern civil (and criminal) law, including that pertaining to family and succession. The Chilean Civil Code, promulgated in 1855 and effective from 1857, would sweep away this older legal structure. It reflected the broad trend of codification, a process taking place across nineteenth-century Europe and Latin America that aimed to systematize and rationalize law as a basis for new and consolidating nation-states.

The Chilean Code's impact on cases like that between Campos and D'Huique was particularly direct: it outlawed them. In abolishing paternity suits, the Code revolutionized the gender, generational, and class dynamics of filiation. This chapter charts this transformation by mapping first the older law and legal culture of the 1840s and early 1850s and then the reforms introduced by the Code. Because many of the changes enacted in Chile had been or soon would be implemented across continental Europe and Latin America, this is not a specifically Chilean story. It is a case study of a transformation of family law that occurred on both sides of the Atlantic.[4]

The Chilean Code consisted of over 2,500 articles governing the status of individuals in the family and nation, the dominion and transfer of property, succession, and contracts. It was, and still is, considered a legal tour-de-force, the most influential exemplar of codification in Latin America, and a culminating opus in the prolific career of Andrés Bello, one of nineteenth-century South America's most famous men of letters. A jurist, statesman, philosopher, and humanist, Bello was a native of Venezuela and a naturalized Chilean who spent more than a decade crafting the Code. He drew inspiration from contemporary French, Spanish, and English sources, but his was a unique creation based, in his words, on "our country's peculiar circumstances."[5] The product of a transnational legal milieu, Bello's opus was also an internationally influential document in its own right. The Chilean Civil Code was adopted wholesale by a number of Latin American nations (including Colombia, Ecuador, El Salvador, Honduras, Nicaragua, and Venezuela) and would serve as a model for codes in other countries (Costa Rica, Guatemala, Mexico, Paraguay, Uruguay), leading one jurist to assert that its influence in the Americas was comparable to that of the Napoleonic Code in Europe.[6] The Chilean Code is thus of comparative significance not only as an iteration of broad trends in civil law but for its direct impact on legal structures governing gender and family across modern Latin America.[7]

A central challenge for the architects of postcolonial Latin American societies was the establishment of viable nation-states and structures of political authority in the wake of the Spanish empire's collapse. These contested processes were much in evidence in Chile in the 1840s and 1850s, as the conflict between conservatives and liberals that framed Chilean politics in the nineteenth century reached fever pitch. In the very months the court was scrutinizing Clarisa del Carmen's paternity, the conservative president Manuel Montt was pursuing a repressive campaign against the Sociedad de Igualdad (Society for Equality). The society was an opposition group inspired by ideals of popular sovereignty and egalitarianism that united radical elites with like-minded plebeian elements. But if political conflict seemed far removed from this most intimate of disputes, it was not only because, as a woman and as a foreigner, Campos and D'Huique had no immediate stake in republican citizenship. It was also because, as Andrés Bello himself once observed,

> It is necessary to recognize an important truth: . . . Laws that empower [citizens] to take part in public affairs are infinitely less important than those that secure one's person and property. Nor could it be otherwise: the first are secondary conditions about which we care very little when the affairs that decide our well-being, the fate of our families, our honor and

our life, occupy our attention . . . Rare is the man . . . [who] feels more wounded when he is arbitrarily deprived of, for example, the right of suffrage, than when he is violently dispossessed of his property.[8]

The dispute over Clarisa del Carmen's paternity concerned the very issues Bello flagged: The fate of families, honor, and property. And so too would the Civil Code's reform of family law.

The Code provided the juridical basis for liberal economic relations and a structure of social authority rooted in the patriarchal family, and as this chapter will show, its treatment of filiation reflected both its liberalism and its patriarchalism. The legal regime it established drew on old Iberian elements but reconfigured them according to a new, liberal logic of contract, freedom, and privacy in which fathers could recognize or reject illegitimate children in accordance with their will. At stake was a shift from a paternalistic, colonial patriarchy to a modern, liberal one. This shift would have repercussions for both gender relations and child welfare, altering the balance of power between men and women and parents and children. Above all, as we will see, it occasioned a dramatic erosion of illegitimate individuals' legal and social rights.

The impact of the new legal regime was far-reaching because out-of-wedlock birth was endemic, and people of all social classes—from statesmen and merchants to cooks and seamstresses—were potentially affected.[9] But legal regulations governing kinship affected not only family members. They affected the social and civil order in general. Drawing on a sample of 102 pre–Civil Code paternity suits, a second sample of 90 post-Code suits pursued retroactively, plus dozens of related judicial procedures, this chapter and the next explore how family law managed not just hierarchies of gender and generation but also social status and class formation. The chapter also traces how the Civil Code altered the Chilean state's relationship to families. The Code engendered the bureaucratization, secularization, and centralization of state authority over kinship. But the expansion of state power was crosscut by a countervailing impulse, for the Code deemed illicit sexuality and illegitimate kinship to be "private" arenas subject to the dictates of (male) freedom. Thus, neither an a priori impetus to greater state control nor an epiphenomenal "bourgeois moralizing project" adequately categorizes, much less explains, liberal law's posture vis-à-vis family and filiation.

Filiation before the Civil Code

Illegitimate individuals encountered social, civil, and legal discrimination in the colonial era, attitudes that undoubtedly endured into the
republican period.[10] A series of overlapping and sometimes contradictory Iberian codes promulgated over more than five centuries, including
the Lei de Toro, the Siete Partidas, and the Novísima Recopilación, governed family and inheritance law. A defining feature of the Iberian codes
was their discriminatory taxonomy of filiation types. Legitimate children
of course enjoyed the greatest rights to support and inheritance. Illegitimates, meanwhile, had differing rights based on the marital status of
their parents. The offspring of marriageable couples were natural children (*hijos naturales*) who enjoyed a status far superior to the offspring of
"punishable and damaged unions" (*de dañado y punible ayuntamiento*),
who included children of priests and those born of adulterous and incestuous unions (*espúreos, adulterinos, incestuosos*).[11] Whereas natural
children were entitled to inherit up to a fifth of a parent's estate, those of
"damaged union" could not inherit at all.[12] Meanwhile, the codes established different, sometimes contradictory, standards of proof of paternity, including cohabitation with a child's mother, her exclusive relationship with a man, as well as explicit paternal recognition.

It was the problem of paternity's proof that would attract the most
attention of republican jurists and undergo the most thorough revision
in the Civil Code. Yet pre-Code courts perceived no "problem" at all,
reading kinship through a standard of proof based on prevailing cultural
beliefs and practices. In essence, the courts assigned paternity if certain
acts vis-à-vis a child or its mother created the supposition of filiation.
This explains the court's interest in Clarisa del Carmen's booties. Alejandro D'Huique's financial responsibility for the baby's birth and upkeep, and his open affection toward her, were taken as signs of paternity.
Sentimental and financial ties between women and men were also commonly interpreted to establish paternity of the woman's offspring.

Filiation suits were overwhelmingly filed by mothers or illegitimate
children against fathers or their heirs.[13] The predominance of paternity
(as opposed to maternity) investigations reflects the fact that mothers
took primary responsibility for rearing children, especially illegitimate
ones, and that women were generally economically dependent on men
and hence had greater need for support. As for the class background of

litigants, while some alleged fathers were wealthy and prominent, many were of modest extraction. Alongside politicians, merchants, landowners, and mining magnates, a tailor, a tanner, a provincial scribe, a bakery employee, an orphaned student with a modest inheritance, several small property owners, and of course Alejandro D'Huique, the French chef, figure among pre-Code defendants.[14] Mothers' class backgrounds, while harder to discern, were clearly more modest. They included domestic servants (who were often employed in the households of the alleged fathers) and a "tavern owner and singer" (*chinganera y cantora de tablado*). They also included women deemed poor but *decente*—seamstresses like Mercedes Campos, who carefully distinguished themselves from common maids, women who worked in others' households while simultaneously employing dependents (such as wet nurses) themselves.[15] Sometimes these were women whose single motherhood had reduced them to penury but whose aspiration to marry the fathers of their children suggests a rough social parity with them.

Given the long legacy of discrimination against illegitimates, the degree of success that paternity suits enjoyed in pre-Code Chilean courts is quite remarkable. In a sample of 102 filiation cases, the court ruled in favor of the mother or children 53 percent of the time. In these cases, the illegitimate was legally declared the son or daughter of the defendant and usually granted support (*alimentos*) or some share of the inheritance. Meanwhile, in a third of cases, illegitimates lost. The remaining almost 14 percent of cases either ended in a settlement between the parties or have no recorded outcome (see table 5).[16] Disaggregating these numbers by years reveals further patterns. Plaintiffs filing in the late 1830s and 1840s experienced startling legal success, winning more than three-quarters of their suits, but by the mid-1850s, when the Civil Code had been approved by Congress and its contents were widely known but not yet in effect, their prospects had experienced a total reversal. Now they lost more than three-quarters of suits (see table 6). The Civil Code, in other words, was less a catalyst than the culmination of a shifting legal landscape, one a decade or more in the making.

The numbers are certainly dramatic, but to appreciate the magnitude and the meanings of this shift, we must look more carefully at what exactly went on in pre-Code cases. For one thing, early filiation suits were notably economical and perfunctory, when not downright lacka-

TABLE 5. Paternity Suit Outcomes prior to the Civil Code (1857).

% Illegitimate wins	% Illegitimate losses	% Cases settled	% No outcome recorded	Total cases
52.9	33.3	5.9	7.8	N=102*

*Cases analyzed include full filiation cases, as well as those for "interim support," a judgment on a father's duty to pay support that stood until a definitive legal ruling on filiation took place.

daisical, compared to later ones. Plaintiffs rarely presented more than a handful of witnesses, whereas later in the century it was not unusual for dozens of witnesses to testify in a filiation dispute. Vague and abbreviated witness testimony sufficed to prove an illegitimate's claim, even in the face of defendants' explicit denial of paternity. Indeed, in stark contrast to later practice, when formal manifestations of a father's will would be held sacrosanct, the pre-Code courts treated paternal declarations as just one of many pieces of evidence in deciding paternity—and evinced few qualms about overriding them.[17] The palpable shift in the tenor of paternity suits was the result not of codified reform—which after all only occurred with the Civil Code of 1857—so much as of a changing legal culture surrounding filiation.

As telling as illegitimates' judicial victories was their success in negotiating monetary settlements. The case María Bartola Olivos filed against the estate of her alleged father, the wealthy hacendado Don Mateo Olivos, is illustrative.[18] Six witnesses, mostly servants of the household, testified that María Bartola was the daughter Don Mateo had fathered with the nurse of his legitimate children after his wife's death. His legitimate heirs categorically rejected her petition, claiming her father was a peon and she could "never succeed in proving herself the daughter of the deceased."[19] Abundant witness testimony belied this assertion, however, and three years into the meandering investigation, the defense abruptly changed strategy. The litigants issued a joint statement based on their "mutual consent" in which the destitute Olivos declared she was "persuaded she was not the daughter of the deceased" and renounced her inheritance claims. In return, she received "in the way of a favor or alms" three ounces of gold.[20] The court accepted the settlement, and perhaps attempting to

TABLE 6. Paternity Suit Outcomes prior to the Civil Code, by Year.

Years	% Illegitimate wins	% Illegitimate losses	% Cases that reach legal settlement	Total cases
Prior to 1849	77.1	14.3	8.6	N=35
1850–1854	56.1	36.6	7.3	N=41
1855–1856	22.2	77.8	0	N=18
				N=94*

*Eight cases in which no judicial resolution was recorded are excluded from this calculation.

counter the appearance of what looked distinctly like a bribe, concluded that the sum was "too nominal to oppose."

Had Don Mateo's legitimate relatives simply wanted to end the dispute, which was delaying distribution of the estate? Or were they actually fearful of losing? Either way, the case suggests that illegitimates enjoyed a favorable bargaining position in their bids to establish filiation in pre–Civil Code courts. Illegitimate kinship was a commodity that plaintiffs could "sell" back to families anxious to avoid the despoliation of their name and patrimony. Legal recognition as Don Mateo's daughter would have afforded Olivos much more generous benefits, but both she and the defendants still benefited by avoiding the legal expenses, scandal, and risks of continued litigation. While just under 10 percent of nonappealed suits in the sample end in such settlements, they hint at what was probably a common extrajudicial scenario.[21] Illegitimate plaintiffs succeeded in obtaining settlements of as much as 2,000 pesos from defendants. "Come on, *hijo*," one man reportedly chided his son who intended to file a legal claim. "Enough with suits, it's better if we come to an agreement" (*déjese de pleitos será mejor tengamos un acomodo*).[22]

Courts' reception of illegitimates' claims reflected the broad social and cultural ethos in which filiation disputes transpired. In a society in which marriage enjoyed undisputed moral ascendancy and yet illegitimacy was rampant, communities regularly intervened to enforce standards of paternal behavior. The family that took in Don Mateo Foncea's seven-year-old illegitimate daughter as a servant "scolded Don Mateo for not helping to support [her]." A witness in another suit remembered telling the alleged father "one or two times to support his daughter, and he answered that he would do it." And still another declared, "Before and after María Arias gave birth to [her] daughter, [the witness] told [presumed father] Hilario Fernández that as the man of honor that he was, he should save María from dishonor by marrying her, a duty ever more urgent since they already had a daughter together; and Fernández answered that he would do so as soon as he had the resources to sustain his obligations, because he was poor."[23] Such comments hint at a broad consensus that men of "honor" had a moral "duty" to partners and their illegitimate offspring quite beyond the dictates of law.

Pre-Code jurists more fully elaborated on such notions of duty, asserting an immutable paternal obligation to women and above all to children, regardless of the circumstances of procreation. This obligation was grounded in civil, religious, and natural law. Jurists repeatedly asserted that the duty to feed one's progeny was "sacred."[24] It was also "natural": "wild animals the same as domestic brutes, guided by natural instinct, recognize the duty to rear their offspring, and often they feed motherless babies belonging to other animals of their species." Thus, concluded one illegitimate's attorney, "No one can suppress the voice of nature as my opponent pretends to do." The argument was apparently a powerful one because the defense responded by wholeheartedly agreeing: "It would be to proceed against conscience to deny support to a natural child . . . whose filiation [was proven according to] all the legal requisites." The defense's position was simply that the plaintiff was not the daughter of the defendant.[25] Strikingly, pre-Code Chilean courts repeatedly ruled that even the offspring of incestuous and adulterous unions—those children bearing the most indelible cultural and legal stigma and denied all inheritance rights—enjoyed "natural rights to a minimum level of parental support."[26]

In addition to assertions of natural rights and sacred obligation, community knowledge and "common sense" notions of informal justice frequently informed judges' reasoning. When Juana Arroyo abandoned her infant in the street and disappeared, witnesses testified they had heard her child's father was one Don Tomás Brabo. Called to court by the judge, Brabo neither admitted nor denied paternity (at least on the record). Without comment, the judge assigned him responsibility for the child anyway.[27] Either he found the community testimony credible or he was privy to additional information, gleaned informally, that he withheld

LESLYE Hºs FOTºs
Nº 69, Calle de las Monjitas, Santiago.

6. An unidentified father and his children, Santiago, 1865. While portraits of mothers and their children were more common, fathers also routinely commissioned such portraits. *Courtesy of the Museo Histórico Nacional.*

from the court record. His action reflects how social knowledge of paternity circulated through communities and into courts.

Often a mother's first line of legal action in a filiation dispute was not a judge but a lower-level official such as a subdelegate or inspector, especially in rural and perhaps southern locales. In semiformal, oral proceedings that relied heavily on mothers' claims, local hearsay, and a sense of "customary" justice, local officials routinely assigned fathers to illegitimate children.[28] This level of judicial practice surfaced in court records when men unhappy with these judgments challenged them before higher authorities. Often they or their lawyers complained of local officials' ignorance, irregular practices, and inclination to overstep their authority.[29] In contrast, women, who apparently often succeeded in wresting support through such procedures, never filed complaints. Local officials' sympathetic reception of paternity claims may reflect the weight accorded community interests versus those of individual men. For if children had no fathers, immediate responsibility for them might fall on the shoulders of local authorities. It is this equilibrium between the rights and interests of men, women, children, and community that the Civil Code would radically alter.[30]

If officials saw themselves as defenders of community interests, they also viewed their mediation of paternity disputes as paternalistic intercession on behalf of wronged women and vulnerable children. One lower-court judge agreed to hear the paternity suit between Petronila Baeza and José Contreras after determining that a preliminary hearing conducted by the local subdelegate, which had found in Baeza's favor, had been characterized by a "lack of formality." Yet even as he recognized this informality, he seemed disposed to forgive it because "in these courts, it is not the custom to observe all the required procedures but rather it is enough to establish the fact in dispute [el hecho]." The judge's distinction between strict adherence to formal legal procedure on the one hand, and the common-sense establishment of "the facts" on the other, is telling. What is more, in ruling in favor of Baeza and her two-year-old daughter, he privileged the latter:

> Under no circumstance was it possible to leave the baby in danger of perishing of want, given that she has a father who should support her [;] if he doesn't recognize her, there are all the presumptions of his being the father. . . . With these considerations in mind, the court proceeded with

strict justice, and I am sure that no man with half a conscience would proceed differently in this case or in other analogous ones.

The ruling illustrates how in pre-Code courts paternity might be proven on the basis of what the judge himself characterized as "presumptions." Second, it illuminates the logic through which such "presumptions" were ascertained in the first place. In justifying his verdict, the judge suggested that the "strict justice" of (patriarchal) "conscience" trumped the letter of the law. "No man with half a conscience" could overlook the welfare of the child in question or, for that matter, the welfare of Baeza herself, a young woman who had no family of her own.[31] Assuming the mantle of paternalistic intercessors, magistrates routinely acted as informal matchmakers and counselors who provided not just official verdicts but extrajudicial advice and informal mediation on behalf of disgraced women.[32] The infralegal practices of these "fathers of justice," practices pursued both on and off the bench, suggest a porous distinction between courtroom and community.[33]

Paternalistic infrajustice reflected a distinctly colonial rendering of legal authority, social welfare, and civil dependence. In this rendering, the weakest members of the body politic—fallen women and fatherless children—figured as unfortunates who enjoyed the protection of a benevolent patriarchal state. Illegitimates' strongest claims to paternal support and inheritance were not therefore a function of "rights," and no Chilean jurist advanced the radical assertion that illegitimate and legitimate children were deserving of legal equality, as some French jurists did in the wake of the revolution.[34] Chilean illegitimates' relative judicial power in pre-Code courts was the product of a colonial social vision that rested on a legal commitment to protection and succor, not equality.[35] Such a vision endured for at least three decades after the formal end of Spanish colonialism in Chile, and as we will see, its demise would impact both the unfortunates themselves and the "fathers of justice" who watched over them.

Shifting Constructions of Paternity

Even as illegitimates and their mothers enjoyed remarkable judicial successes, the pre-Code legal and cultural ethos was hardly a utopia for them. The wheels of justice ground painfully slowly, particularly for indigent mothers who sought small monthly pensions to stave off total destitution. It could take years for litigation to be resolved.[36] Mothers and illegitimates faced a slew of practical and legalistic hurdles not only to securing a favorable judgment but also to actually receiving support payments.[37] Above all, women had to contend with the flip side of the paternalistic impetus to protect the vulnerable: formidable patriarchal cultural beliefs about sexual morality. Central to these beliefs was a sexual double standard. A father might be chided to behave as a "man of honor," but his sexual dalliances could also provoke a lively ribbing from peers who "teased him about the fruits of his loves with a *costurerita* [literally, a little seamstress]."[38] Social attitudes toward the sexual behavior of the "costurerita" herself were of course much less ambiguous. Mothers who brought filiation suits were accused of being doubly immoral, because they had had illicit affairs and then made them public in a court of law.[39] Such denunciations of public scandal would only grow more strident, becoming a key argument against paternity investigation. As one lawyer declared in 1851, "All questions of filiation bring with them scandals, dissension, and the ruin of the family, either in terms of its honor or its property, because they reveal immoral incidents that cause defamation."[40] The airing of intimate information in a public theater had a particular meaning in a culture in which the revelation of sin was as reprehensible as its private commission. Jurists' persistent emphasis on scandal suggests that the chief threat paternity suits posed to men and families may not have been economic but social.

Still, the disadvantages and double standards that mothers and illegitimates faced in pre-Code courts pale in comparison to those that would follow. On the eve of the Code's promulgation, the legal shift was becoming palpable. The invocation of children's natural rights began to carry less moral and legal weight in the face of a newly defined set of interests: those of "society." José Vicente Abalos, a law student in the late 1840s who would eventually become president of the Supreme Court, articulated this new interest: "The legislator will always, in dealing with [filiation suits], have to contend with competing interests: those of nature in which the rights of illegitimate children are rooted, and those of society, which does not permit damage to its fundamental institution, marriage; between sentiment and reason, humanity and politics."[41] Abalos then went on to condemn paternity investigation. His placement of illegitimate children's rights in the realm of nature, sentiment, and humanity was not new. What was new was the sharp distinction he drew between this realm and that of society, reason, and politics, with the latter, implicitly identified with men's interests, now accorded clear primacy. Enlightenment thinkers had championed child welfare as a benefit to state and society. The new legal turn placed the interests of children and those of state and society in opposition.

In 1850, a little-known lawyer named Martín Zapata published a seminal essay that laid out the epistemological and procedural shift at stake. The essay, based on his arguments as a defense attorney in an actual filiation suit, called for the abolition of paternity investigation.[42] Zapata argued that the logic of these suits was fundamentally spurious because witness testimony regarding a father's actions could not establish paternal recognition. Such logic was not only erroneous, Zapata declared, it was dangerous: "Ambiguous facts . . . based on the fallacious testimony of . . . unqualified witnesses, are nothing but weapons that are placed in the hands of an unknown [humble] . . . person to assault a status in society that does not belong to him, perturbing the peace of families and usurping a fortune." Whereas in the traditional logic, paternity was an empirical event subject to the scrutiny of witnesses and verifiable by normal judicial methods, now it was constructed as an ineffable mystery beyond the discernment of legal inquiry. This belief became increasingly widespread among Chilean jurists. As one defense attorney put it, "paternity . . . is an act for which it is impossible to give clear proof of any kind." The claim that it was "not an event . . . subject to the rule of the senses [*el imperio de los sentidos*]" implicitly placed it beyond the rule of law (*el imperio de la ley*). For as a "mystery of nature," paternity "cannot be proven through the inductive facts that the judicial method generates"— in marked contrast to maternity, which "involves a material fact, visible, subject to the domination of anyone's senses . . . that is, the birth." Whereas pre-Code Chilean courts interpreted the medieval law codes as establishing a rough parity in the treatment of maternity and paternity investigation, this newly discovered sexual difference would come to justify divergent legal protocols.[43]

Zapata's treatise, which systematized arguments circulating in courts and legal theses and broadcast them to a wider judicial public, made its way into the highest legal echelons of his time and would continue to be quoted for the next fifty years.[44] Yet in the context of international legal developments, his call to abolish paternity investigation was notably unoriginal. The 1804 French Napoleonic Code had prohibited paternity investigation, as did the 1852 Spanish draft code and several other European codes influenced by French law. Chilean jurists were familiar with these legal developments and quoted their French and Spanish counterparts liberally. The idea of paternity as a mystery of nature, for example, was lifted directly from European sources.[45]

Yet Chilean jurists' affinity for such frankly derivative arguments reflected developments specific to the midcentury Chilean political landscape. The growing rejection of filiation suits on the eve of the Civil Code coincided with a seemingly unrelated development: the resurgence of political violence after a decade of relative calm. In 1850, the year Zapata's article appeared in print, the radical cross-class opposition group the Sociedad de Igualdad celebrated its first meeting and within months had attracted some 3,000 adherents. In response, the conservative government declared a state of siege and outlawed this and all popular democratic collectivities. The following year, the controversial election of the conservative Manuel Montt ignited several months of civil war, throwing into doubt Chile's vaunted political stability. The conservative architects of the postcolonial order responded to these events with expansive elocutions on the problem of political disorder. Antipaternity jurists, writing at the same moment, would couch their arguments in the same language.

Montt's presidential address in 1852 reflects this language. In a speech that, like many presidential addresses of the 1840s and 1850s, was shadow written by his close associate, the Civil Code author Andrés Bello, Montt condemned the "spirit of insurrection" of "the ignorant and poor class" that had become "an instrument of subversive plans." Lamenting that "citizens' property and their persons have been exposed to pillage," he heralded his own efforts in "saving the country from anarchy and consolidating internal order."[46] Contemporaneous critiques of paternity investigation tapped into this same vein of political discourse. Zapata asserted that such suits were "subversive and sinister for the tranquility of families and for the security of property." They had rendered law "a real chaos without . . . exit." And they necessitated a legal balance between parental obligations to offspring and the "no less natural and primitive obligation to respect the property of others." Subversion, chaos, and the pillage of property stalked the imaginations of conservative political leaders and antipaternity jurists alike. The discursive overlaps reveal how domestic order was perceived as integral to political order. They also reflect the shared ties between antipaternity jurists and members of the conservative political establishment: the paternity suit for which defense attorney Zapata penned his critique featured the testimony of a notable witness: Manuel Montt himself.[47]

The chaos and subversion of paternity suits were of a particular variety: they were perceived to challenge foundational hierarchies of gender, generation, and class. In the estimation of antipaternity jurists, poor women exploited spurious paternity claims to steal from wealthy men. Putative fathers were "tender and inexpert youth," the innocent victims of female accusers of "humble origin and an immoral upbringing and lifestyle." Women and their families conspired to trap defendants "as women of no worth commonly do with the sons of [good] families, whom they descend on if not [to ensnare] as husbands then in order to have children with them, so as to collect child support, dowries, or penalties." Rather than economic burdens on poor mothers, children were in fact vehicles for their enrichment. As for the children themselves, according to one lawyer, there existed "many examples" of "people who speculate with the benefits of paternity of wealthy individuals."[48] With his flair for melodrama, Zapata warned darkly of a scenario in which "no man of middling fortune will be free from the prospect of some unknown son or daughter appearing at any moment to claim their paternity from him." Significantly, he attributed such fraudulent claims to plaintiffs' desires to ascend to a better social position. Paternity claims were an "assault" by a humble person on a "status in society that does not belong to him [or her]." The implication is that filiation suits were as much about class as about gender or kinship, an argument explored further in the next chapter.

The class fears projected on poor mothers and illegitimate children were also directed at witnesses. Pre-Code filiation suits commonly rested on the testimony of servants and household dependents. It was they who observed the furtive affairs of their masters, shuttled illegitimate newborns to caretakers, and received these children years later when they appeared at their father's back door. Lowly wet nurses, modest midwives, humble individuals who took spurned children into their households—

these were the standard supporting actors in the courtroom drama.[49] For defense attorneys, their participation reflected a cynical conspiracy among the low born: "Some women of a certain social sphere live by trafficking in filiation suits . . . making their female friends and others they know testify in their favor," suggested one.[50]

That these courtroom narratives also appear in popular literature suggests their broad cultural resonance. In his celebrated novel *Martín Rivas*, published in 1862 and set in Santiago around 1850, Alberto Blest Gana portrays a scenario strikingly similar to that narrated by defense attorneys. The ill-fated but honorable Rafael has fathered a child with Adelaida, the daughter of a family of modest circumstances and grand ambitions. Rafael attempts to extract himself from the wrath of Adelaida's mother, who threatens to take him to court, by offering her a portion of his inheritance. At first she rejects the offer. But Adelaida's ne'er-do-well brother persuades his mother to take the money. "Why would you want this case to wander around the courts, when the seven thousand pesos is better?" he chides.[51] Like contemporary jurists, novelist Blest Gana suggests that Adelaida's family regards her disgrace as a convenient source of profit.

This story was of course divorced from judicial reality: as noted above, many father defendants were of quite modest extraction, and mothers were frequently their social equals.[52] Whether in novels or courtrooms, these fictional scenarios served as warnings about the fragility of order and hierarchy in a new republic. They posed carnivalesque cautionaries in which the most powerful members of society—gentlemen of means— were rendered hapless victims of the most powerless—women, children, the poor, and the servile. Significantly, these were not merely the paranoid anxieties of a few outmoded conservatives. Blest Gana himself was a liberal and his novel an often biting critique of upper-class social mores.

The Civil Code and the Liberalization of Kinship

In May 1879, more than two decades after the Civil Code's promulgation, Elisa Wilson appeared in a Valparaíso civil court asking Policarpio Vicuña to acknowledge his paternity of her children. Such recognition petitions were among the most common claims filed in Chilean civil courts in the latter half of the nineteenth century. Wilson was at least the third woman in less than two weeks to appear in the same court with that same object. Her situation must have been particularly dire: she had six children, ranging in age from two months to thirteen years, and she requested that part of the proceedings be conducted verbally rather than in the more costly written format due to her poverty. Justice was uncharacteristically swift in recognition proceedings. Five days later, Vicuña appeared in court, stated that he did not believe himself to be the father of the children, signed his declaration, and went home. Wilson had no right to appeal his statement, offer witness testimony about the paternity of her children, or provide other evidence of what was apparently a fifteen-year common-law union gone sour.[53]

Elisa Wilson's day in court—expeditious in its realization, formulaic in its exposition, categorical in its conclusion—reflected the new face of filiation under the Civil Code. At the heart of the legal shift, of course, was the prohibition of paternity investigation. Parental recognition was now "a free and voluntary act" on the part of progenitors, especially fathers, who exercised unchecked legal freedom to acknowledge and support—or repudiate and forsake—their extramarital children.[54] A mother like Elisa Wilson could call a man to declare his paternity before the court, but if he denied it, as Policarpio Vicuña did, she and her children had no further legal recourse. As the Santiago Court of Appeals declared, paternity depended on "the unequivocal revelation of the conscience of the father . . . a fact that rests only and exclusively on the man's manifest will."[55] The one exception to this rule was individuals born prior to the Code, who were retroactively permitted to bring suits according to Iberian law. Yet these cases, which will be examined in greater depth in chapter 2, merely confirm the plummeting legal prospects of illegitimates. In a sample of ninety post-Code suits, illegitimate plaintiffs won only 23.3 percent of cases, losing 71.1 percent of them.[56] Ironically, those most affected by these reforms were completely absent from the jurists' appraisals: the legions of poor couples like Wilson and Vicuña whose long-term consensual unions were not routinely legalized.

If recognition depended on paternal volition, then witness testimony was moot. The Code stripped everyday acts that were socially indicative of paternity of their legal significance.[57] The consequences reverberated not only in courts but also in households and communities. Paternity suits had involved the imposition of legal judgments, of course, but they had also served as theaters for the public expression of community standards, the application of interpersonal suasion, and social control through shaming. A wayward father's peers could still informally intervene; servants and subordinates could still observe and gossip. But in a reform that surely satisfied the vociferous critics of public scandal, such knowledge could no longer be aired in a courtroom. Thus, the prohibition of paternity investigation was not just a legal reform. It also implied the remaking of filiation's social landscape.

If paternity could never be assumed based on "a carnal, vague, uncertain relationship in which nothing guarantees the fidelity of a woman who has already degraded herself," to invoke Andrés Bello's own characterization, then how would it be determined? The Civil Code's answer was simple: contract. Having abolished scandalous testimony and ambiguous legal deduction, the Code stipulated that paternity could be established only through a formal administrative transaction. Parents wishing to establish kinship with extramarital progeny now had to make an official declaration before a judge or notary, with the offspring required to formally "accept" recognition. Without this procedure, not even written or oral declarations of fatherhood carried legal weight—for, as one lawyer observed, "it could be that [the man] said it as a joke . . . his merely saying it does not constitute an obligatory contract."[58] Legitimation was subject to similar procedures. Whereas under Iberian law children born out of wedlock were automatically legitimated if their parents subsequently married, now newly wedded progenitors had to recur to a formal legal transaction to confer legitimacy.[59]

Such references to free will and formal contract allude to the liberal ideological underpinnings of the new kinship regime. By making paternity dependent on legal procedure, the Code contractualized kin relations formerly cast in terms of natural rights and social knowledge. Filiation exhibited the essential characteristics of all contract relationships: ties between illegitimate parents and children had to be formally and freely made. So great was the emphasis on the voluntary nature of paternity that some jurists initially argued that a father could revoke recognition if he had second thoughts.[60]

Liberalism's great promise was of course equality before the law. But in distributing freedom inequitably among kindred, the Code's liberalization of kin relations engendered inequality. Fathers clearly enjoyed virtually unencumbered free will, and formally, mothers too enjoyed enhanced freedom to recognize or repudiate offspring. But in practice, because mothers were the parents most likely, but least economically equipped, to assume the burden of children's care, the new legal balance implied the expansion of paternal rights at the expense of maternal ones. The result was a situation like that of Elisa Wilson and Policarpio Vicuña. Likewise, illegitimate children enjoyed formal freedom to reject paternity and maternity, but in practice, their liberty and equality was a disingenuous legal fiction. It was virtually never in a child's interest to reject a legal relationship that conferred rights to sustenance and sometimes inheritance.[61] The Code conferred liberty and free will, but it did so to fathers alone.

The inequalities of the new filiation regime found their most pointed expression in the Code's complex new taxonomy of parent–child relationships, in which kin enjoyed different rights and obligations according to the type of legal recognition mediating their relationship. The taxonomy had clear historical precedents in the old Iberian law codes, which as noted above established different categories of children (legitimate, natural, incestuosos, espúreos, adulterinos) based on birth status. But while the Code retained these Iberian designations, its contractarian classificatory logic was new. Take the Code's definition of hijo natural. Whereas medieval Spanish law defined an hijo natural as the offspring of an extramarital union by marriageable partners, in the Chilean Civil Code an hijo natural was one who enjoyed legal recognition—that is, one whose progenitor had appeared before a judge or notary and expressly conferred this special legal status.[62] Natural status was therefore not a right; it was a privilege extended by the good will of the parent. The rationale of free will explains why the investigation not only of paternity but also of maternity was prohibited for the purpose of establishing a child's status as natural.

The status of hijo natural flowed from a legal contract and not from the fact of consanguineous descent, and an illegitimate person did not automatically become natural just because a parent acknowledged his or her biological provenance. "Simply illegitimate" offspring, a new designation introduced in the Code, consisted of those whose parents recognized their biological filiation before a court or notary but chose not to grant them the more privileged status of hijo natural. When Elisa Wilson and women like her called fathers to court to acknowledge their paternity, they were merely petitioning for their children's recognition as simply illegitimate offspring. If men like Policarpio Vicuña chose to recognize children in such proceedings, the children gained the status of simply illegitimate but were not hijos naturales. While paternity investigation was of course prohibited for the purpose of establishing either simple illegitimacy or natural status, investigation of *maternal* origin was permitted to establish simple illegitimacy because maternity was considered an ascertainable empirical fact.

Hijos naturales enjoyed a manifestly superior status to their simply illegitimate counterparts. Both had rights only to "necessary alimentos," a minimum standard of support defined as that "required to sustain life." But natural children also had rights to inheritance—indeed, in some cases rights that were more generous than those under Iberian law—while simply illegitimates had none.[63] Natural status implied membership in a natal family. Simply illegitimates were legally orphans. Like literal orphans, for example, if they wished to marry, they sought out a court-appointed guardian to grant permission in their parent's stead. Equally significantly, they did not benefit from the less tangible cultural associations that accrued to kin belonging, or as one contemporary put it, simple illegitimacy "does not give [children] a name or make them part of a family."[64]

The Code's taxonomy implicitly created a final, residual category of children who were neither natural nor even simply illegitimate. These were children who, legally, had no known or knowable progenitor because they had not been recognized by anyone. Such children had no parent to whom they could direct claims to even a minimal level of support. The children of Elisa Wilson fell into this category vis-à-vis the father who refused to acknowledge them. Ironically, such children probably constituted the largest group of illegitimates of all.[65] The Code's taxonomy reflects how, in this new rendering of kinship, contract trumped blood. Blood might be a necessary condition to enjoy rights of filiation, but it was by no means a sufficient one. Even individuals with legally "certain" paternal origins enjoyed very different legal statuses.[66]

The Civil Code's treatment of natal status is particularly striking given that by the time of its promulgation in 1855, other forms of status discrimination had been abrogated. The republic had abolished distinctions based on ethnicity and noble status in the years following 1810 and declared "equality before the law" to "all inhabitants of the republic" in the Constitution of 1833.[67] Distinctions based on kin status were not only retained in the Code; they were reworked and reinvigorated. What is more, they would endure for another century and a half.[68] The Code's filiation regime thus reflects the striking persistence of ascriptive status distinctions in liberal family law.

Secularization, Bureaucratization, and the Fall of the Judicial Patriarchs

The Civil Code altered power equilibria not only between men, women, and children but also at the level of the state. Most obviously, the contractualization of illegitimate kinship augured its secularization. The gradual displacement of the Catholic Church in matters of family regulation is customarily traced to the laws of civil marriage and the civil registry (1883/4). But the Code curtailed ecclesiastical authority over *illegitimate* kinship decades before. Before its promulgation, baptismal records and the parish priests who oversaw them were the arbiters of legal filiation, both legitimate and illegitimate. The courts interpreted the Code as denying them this power in cases of illegitimacy. A father's name on a baptismal certificate no longer sufficed to prove paternity because it was not necessarily an indication of paternal "presence and acquiescence." Morever, "the baptismal record signed by the father with the object of recognizing [a child] as natural" had no legal validity "because parish priests . . . are not competent functionaries in the case of recognition."[69] In contrast, baptismal records were not only considered valid proofs of *legitimate* kinship, but prior to the 1884 civil registry, no other birth record existed.

In the absence of parish priests, the arbiters of illegitimate filiation were the notaries and court officials who oversaw the new procedures established in the Code and sifted through its regulations involving how, when, and by whom kinship could be established. In this sense, the contractualization of kinship stimulated its bureaucratization. The Code's new administrative procedures were complex—so complex they flummoxed many lawyers and entailed considerable time and expense for petitioners. Ostensibly designed to protect the free will of parents and children, they could in practice have the opposite effect. Juana Arévalo discovered how legalistic dictates could trump even the sacrosanct doctrine of parental freedom when she petitioned to prove her status as natural mother of Nicanor Romero Arévalo, who had died leaving 260 pesos in the bank. She presented her son's baptismal and marriage certificates, both of which listed her as his mother, and offered witness testimony that she had reared and recognized him as her son. But a court official challenged her to verify that the Nicanor of the death certificate referred to the same one as the birth certificate. Impossible to prove one way or the other, the objection seemed almost purposefully contrived to sabotage Arévalo's claim. Two years into her legal petition, a court declared that she had not proven her status as natural mother and heir. The 260 pesos remained unclaimed in the bank.[70]

Newlyweds Ernesto Briones and Juana Covarrubias were similarly stymied in their attempt to legitimate their daughter, Juanitarrosa, born a year before their marriage. In one of the many confounding new directives instituted in the Code, legitimations of premarital offspring had to take place at the time of the parents' marriage or within thirty days. The couple appeared within the designated time period, but a court official wanted to know why they had not requested the procedure sooner. No further action was recorded, and their daughter apparently remained unlegitimated, another casualty of the new regime's onerous formalities.[71] Under Iberian law, children like Juanitarrosa were automatically legitimated by their parents' subsequent marriage, their passage from one natal status to another both silent and seamless. In time no one would know the details of their birth, and the law did not distinguish between the rights of the legitimate and the legitimated. The Civil Code subjected this passage to new judicial and notarial scrutiny. Legitimation and recognition were now public affairs, flagged by new administrative procedures and inscribed in the civil record (and sometimes, as in this case, stymied by overzealous officials). In his message to Congress, Bello characterized these bureaucratic exigencies as "a sacrifice demanded by the social order, the just expiation of a fault."[72] The Code did not close down the "permeable boundaries" between natal statuses that existed in Iberian law. But in bureaucratizing this passage, it made it more difficult to move between them, and it made the state the indispensable gate-keeper of the points of entry.[73]

The secularization and bureaucratization of kinship signaled the apparent expansion of liberal state power vis-à-vis the family. Yet a countervailing tendency is also evident in the new legal regime. For the prohibition of paternity investigation implied the circumscription of the courts' role in relationships now deemed private. Jurists' claim that paternity could not "be proven through the inductive facts that the judicial method generates" reflected a particular understanding of paternity but also of law and its relationship to family. It implied that there were certain realms of social practice—intimate, illicit practice—that the law could not or should not scrutinize. As Bello himself asked, "Will the law penetrate into the shadows of these clandestine connections and confer on them the right to constitute all by themselves the presumption of paternity, which is the privilege of matrimony?"[74] The liberalization of kinship implied the redefinition of the private, a process in which Catholic notions of sexual morality were, perhaps ironically, central. This new definition would compromise not only illegitimates' status but, as chapter 4 will show, the state's own capacity for governance.

Ultimately, the critique of paternity investigation was a critique of law and its perceived role as a vehicle of immorality. "Justice" had become an "instrument of ambition" as poor women and fatherless children "trafficked in filiation suits," their "audacity disguised in the form of a trial."[75] Judges themselves came in for particular blame. According to the anti-paternity crusader Martín Zapata, the problem of the suits was less one of inadequate laws than of their wanton misapplication by judges who "have often been the murderers of the law itself . . . introducing into jurisprudence with their brazen and paradoxical opinions the most sinister of errors." His hyperbole aside, Zapata's critique echoed Bello's own writings, in which he exhorted judges to suppress subjective sympathies and adhere rigorously to the law's letter. The Civil Code itself has been interpreted as an attempt to establish the dominion of codified law over the subjectivities of those who applied it.[76] Certainly its narrow and categorical provisions surrounding paternity did precisely this.

The new legal regime of filiation would entail not only the elimination of judges' interpretive leeway but also an upward devolution of authority over filiation. As noted above, local authorities who drew on a paternalistic model of authority were particularly sympathetic to filiation claims in the pre-Code period. Patterns of judicial decision making confirm these sympathies and also reveal how the judicial system reined them in. During the seven years prior to the Code, lower-court judges were disproportionately responsible for rulings in favor of illegitimate plaintiffs, but their decisions were also increasingly likely to be overturned on appeal.[77] Meanwhile, other low-level judicial authorities such as subdelegados, who had played a key role adjudicating pre-Code filiation disputes, were deemed to lack jurisdiction in such cases. Some men condemned to pay child support by these officials now countered by suing them for abuse of authority.[78] Such scenarios heralded the waning fortunes of illegitimates and their mothers but also the fall of the local judicial patriarchs themselves. The centralization of judicial authority seems to have been a trend across the Chilean legal order. Midcentury jurists repeatedly voiced concerns about the competence and rectitude of low-level judicial officials, and subsequent administrative reforms would devolve judicial authority upward.[79] But while not specific to family and filiation, this trend had a particularly profound impact on these realms.

Rather than a unidirectional expansion or contraction of state power, then, civil law reform catalyzed tectonic shifts among different strata of the state. Even as the bureaucratization of kinship gave greater power to court officials and notaries, it undermined the paternalism of local and lower-level judicial patriarchs. The incontrovertible dictates of the Code imposed bureaucratic rigor but also supplanted the paternalistic posture of colonial law. Above all, the free will of the private paterfamilias was enshrined, though at times the expiatory bureaucracy could weigh heavily on those without resources or access to legal counsel.[80]

Conclusions: Children, Women, Men, and Chilean Liberalism

Clarisa del Carmen and her mother, Mercedes Campos, whose 1851 suit opened this chapter, appear to have beaten the looming legal shift. Reflecting a common pre–Civil Code scenario, a subdelegado declared Alejandro D'Huique to be the child's father and ordered him to pay Campos twelve pesos a month. D'Huique countered by initiating formal judicial proceedings, but a lower-court judge found his testimony to be "evasive" and the evidence "quite in favor" of Campos. Invoking the medieval Iberian Siete Partidas, the judge brushed aside D'Huique's argument that Clarisa had no rights as an adulterina and declared that parents had the obligation "to support their children whether they are natural or spurious." He halved the monthly payments, to six pesos, but confirmed the essential ruling that Clarisa del Carmen was the Frenchman's daughter. In its final phase, Campos's case suffered a sudden setback when a higher court suspended the decision on a technicality, though it is probable that the decision in her favor was ultimately allowed to stand. It was November 1853, and the Civil Code loomed three years away.[81]

The new legal regime of filiation institutionalized by the Civil Code augured many important changes for state practice, the meanings of kinship, and the lives of ordinary people like Clarisa del Carmen, Mercedes Campos, and Alejandro D'Huique. The Code marked a shift from older notions of children's natural rights and judicial paternalism to unencumbered paternal free will through contract. Further reflecting its liberal tenor, it embodied ambiguities about the role of law in the regulation of intimate relations. While the secularization and bureaucratization of kinship heralded an expansion of state power, the abolition of paternity investigation implied state circumscription. The new legal order also signaled an upward devolution of authority over filiation to more powerful officials and to higher courts.

By rescinding illegitimates' right to identify their progenitors and obtain material support from them, the Civil Code rehearsed what would become a recurring practice of civic policies in republican Chile: the generation of an underclass of kinless people. Alienated from their natal origins, kinless individuals suffered a stigmatized status and inhibited life prospects. The ubiquity and significance of kinlessness is the subject of succeeding chapters. The role of patriarchal law in generating it illustrates how the social organization of gender powerfully shapes the social condition of children.

Of course, the sacrosanct principle of paternal free will prejudiced unmarried mothers as much as their illegitimate children. The Chilean Civil Code's treatment of filiation thus confirms recent assessments of women's declining legal status in nineteenth-century Latin America.[82] But here the category of "women" must be disaggregated, since the impact of this reform clearly varied by class. The circumscription of filiation rights may have hurt unmarried mothers, but it favored married ones by protecting wives and legitimate kin from the claims of men's extramarital progeny. Insofar as marriage was disproportionately distributed among higher classes, the reform of family law worked to the detriment not of women in general but of poor women in particular.

Ideologically, the new legal regime of filiation reflects liberalism's clear ascendance in Chilean law and society. Liberal principles pervaded not just land tenure, property rights, economic relations, and eventually political organization but also normative structures surrounding family. In empowering men to apportion their wealth as they wished, the Code's posture vis-à-vis illegitimacy was clearly linked to that touchstone of Latin American liberalism, the liberalization of property regimes. But the new legal order was about more than property rights, inheritance, or testamentary freedom. The liberalization of kinship also constituted an unprecedented freedom, at least for men, to define their families as they saw fit. Finally, the contractualization of filiation anticipated, in perhaps even more striking terms, the transformation of marriage under liberalism. Across nineteenth-century Latin America, marriage, once a sacrament, became a secular contract.[83] In the new legal regime of filiation, parent–child relations, once the domain of sacred, natural law, were likewise contractualized.

Yet for all its legal and philosophical novelty, the liberalization of family law reinscribed a taxonomic logic that looked distinctly colonial. Dressed up in the liberal mantle of contract and free will lay an ancien-regime impulse in which rights were determined by status. Chilean liberalism thus offers a distinct, and highly paradoxical, turn on the familiar transition from status to contract: the new legal regime of filiation was one of status *through* contract. In its hybridity, the Code's provisions exemplify with particular clarity how defining elements of the colonial order could endure not merely in uneasy coexistence with liberalism but in creative complement to it.[84] As such, liberal law did not simply reproduce colonial sensibilities, nor was it a transparent vector of coercion or oppression. Rather, it was an innovative amalgam of old and new that was actively productive of relations of inequality. It is further noteworthy that while the new legal regime was anchored in liberal principles, the arguments against paternity investigation, as we saw, drew on a distinctly conservative political language. Ideological differences between conservatives and liberals in mid-nineteenth-century Chile were acute and sometimes violent. But the hybrid genealogy of the new legal regime of filiation, and the complete absence of public opposition to it, suggests that on issues of gender, filiation, and sexual morality, there existed a fundamental consensus across ideological boundaries.

The new filiation regime was especially pernicious because it operated on a fiction of freedom and equality. If some individuals were legally disadvantaged, it was not because law unjustly mandated inequality based on ascriptive difference. It was because the various contracts mediating kin relations assigned different degrees of rights to different kinds of children. Meanwhile, old moral premises were invoked to legitimate new relationships of power. It was not that some individuals were less equal, merely that some relationships were less moral. In this sense, moral attitudes toward gender and sexuality deriving from Catholic tradition imbued the ostensibly neutral artifice of the liberal contract. But in a key way, the new legal regime differed from the old. In contrast to its colonial variant, the liberal taxonomy of natal status was bled of the paternalistic impulses that had leavened, if not tempered, the colonial-era caste order. In this regard, the law's impact on illegitimate mothers and childen was particularly harsh.

The abolition of paternity investigation was a widespread development in nineteenth-century Atlantic family law, but its consequences were by no means everywhere uniform. In European societies, where the incidence of illegitimate birth was relatively low, the social impact of this reform was probably circumscribed, perhaps even primarily symbolic in some places. In Latin America, where illegitimacy was endemic, the consequences of a legal reform that deprived illegitimate people of kin networks and drastically undermined the basis of their subsistence, especially as dependent children, were potentially explosive.[85] Only at the turn of the century would jurists in Chile and elsewhere in Latin America begin to reconsider the legal regime's "fatal repercussions" on "the society whose order and internal security it perturbs."[86] Even then, legal discrimination against illegitimates would endure well into the twentieth century in most Latin American countries and until the dawn of the twenty-first century in Chile.

Indeed, the Chilean Civil Code was a uniquely radical iteration of the transatlantic legal trend. The Chilean Code took its inspiration from the Napoleonic Code and continental legal developments and, through its wide influence in neighboring republics, broadcast them across the hemisphere. But it also introduced important innovations. For example, the distinction between natural children and simply illegitimate ones was a unique invention of the Chilean Code. That children whose biological paternity was legally acknowledged were nevertheless subject to vastly different legal statuses illustrates particularly starkly the social construction of paternity and the contractual logic of kinship. The Chilean taxonomy reflects how law was understood to *create* relations of filiation rather than simply to *acknowledge* independent biological facts. In this sense Chilean civil law took transatlantic legal principles to their logical extreme. Principles elaborated by French jurists a half-century before were "domesticated," acquiring a distinctly Latin American, and Chilean, cast. Andrés Bello's assertion that his Code was based on Chile's "peculiar circumstances" was correct. In the case of filiation, the "peculiar circumstances" were the distinctive textures of a starkly unequal class society. The next chapter shows how legal categories of kinship were transposed into status categories and social dependencies. Social hierarchy in this liberal, constitutional republic was persistent and profound, and family law would prove instrumental to its management.

CHAPTER 2

Paternity, Childhood, and the Making of Class

A Tale of Two Illegitimates

"Desirous that the public and above all those people who because of their profession have manifested an interest [know] the antecedents of the suit I have filed against the estate of my father Don Francisco Salvador Alvarez [,] . . . I have decided to publish in their entirety [certain] parts of the case . . . [I harbor] the conviction that once in possession of these antecedents, no one will doubt the legitimacy of my rights." By 1876, the year in which Secundino Alvarez filed his petition in a Valparaíso court, the right to present paternity suits such as his was illegal—categorically outlawed, as we have seen, by the Civil Code of 1857. However, people born prior to the Code, like thirty-year-old Secundino, were permitted to pursue suits retroactively. Considerable numbers of adult illegitimates and sometimes even their descendants continued to bring grandfathered cases through the early twentieth century. The social and legal environment in which they did so was very different from the one pre-Code litigants had faced. So too were the material assets at stake in these disputes.

With the gradual solidification of the postcolonial political order, Chile embarked on a remarkable cycle of economic expansion that would endure into the 1870s. This export-led commercial boom generated unprecedented wealth, the principal beneficiaries of which were members of the country's upper classes. The subject of Secundino Alvarez's suit, Francisco Salvador Alvarez, was one of those beneficiaries. Don Salvador, as he was known, was himself the son of a Portuguese immigrant who in the 1830s and 1840s had built a commercial empire based in Valparaíso, the financial capital of Chile and the principal commercial hub of the

Pacific coast. Alvarez-owned ships were among those that carried Chilean wheat to gold-rush California and later to Australia. They brought Peruvian tobacco and Brazilian sugar and coffee back to Chilean shores. At its height, the Alvarez empire stretched to Macao, Sydney, New York, Cádiz, London, and beyond, and Don Salvador himself spent much of his life conducting affairs in the South Pacific and North America, Europe, and the Far East. He served as Chilean consul to California at a time when thousands of his compatriots flocked to the gold fields in search of fortune. During visits home to Valparaíso, the peripatetic merchant dabbled in politics and tended to his extensive properties, including two vast seaside haciendas a few miles north of Valparaíso. According to one estimate, his fortune—valued in the 1840s at some 1,700,000 pesos—was the single largest in all of Chile.[1]

Don Salvador's death in 1873 touched off a noisy legal struggle over this patrimony. Over the course of four years, three interlocking suits involving four different parties worked their way through the Valparaíso courts. One of these suits was the one filed by Secundino. Over seventy witnesses offered testimony in this case alone. They included the humblest of Don Salvador's servants as well as intimate friends and business associates hailing from the port city's upper crust. In keeping with the practice among litigants of publishing parts of high-profile suits, whether because of their interest to jurists or simply to drum up public sympathy, extensive testimony from Secundino's suit appeared in two published pamphlets.[2]

A public dispute detailing the dissolute behavior of a wealthy gentleman was precisely the sort of legal spectacle that antipaternity jurists had condemned. Yet in a key respect, the Alvarez case departed from the jurists' trope of audacious illegitimates who threatened legitimate wives and children. As a lifelong bachelor, Don Salvador had no legitimate succession. The heir against whom Secundino filed his claim was Doña Mercedes Alvarez—Don Salvador's daughter who had been born about five years prior to Secundino, of a different mother, and also out of wedlock. What is more, because Don Salvador had never formally recognized her, Doña Mercedes herself had recurred to the courts to secure her filiation rights. After successfully fending off the inheritance claims of a distant relative, she had been declared Don Salvador's natural daughter and exclusive heir in 1875. Thereafter, before the very same Valparaíso judge, Secundino stepped forward to claim his share of the paternal inheritance.[3]

Thus, both Mercedes and Secundino claimed to be the illegitimate offspring of Don Salvador. Neither had been legally recognized by their father prior to his death. And both recurred to the courts to establish their filiation claims. But if their natal status and initial legal position were identical, there was a glaring difference between the two alleged half-siblings, one patently obvious to the court and to Valparaíso society at large: their class status. In fact, the social positions of Mercedes and Secundino Alvarez could hardly have been more different. Reared by her paternal grandmother in the bosom of an upstanding Valparaíso household, Doña Mercedes had attended the best girl's school in the city and had married into an illustrious lineage. Secundino, meanwhile, had grown up as a servant in a series of modest households and as an adult may have been a shopkeeper on Cerro Barón.[4]

The stark disparity of social position between Mercedes and Secundino was not incidental to the filiation dispute in which they became embroiled. It was of crucial legal significance. For, as this chapter will explore, in the decades after the Civil Code, Chilean courts applied a class-based standard in their reckoning of kinship. The Code's familial taxonomies ("natural child," "simply illegitimate child") and bureaucratic categories ("recognition") acquired meanings referencing social status. As such, Chilean family law came to regulate not just family relations but class relations. While chapter 1 explored the liberal regime of filiation introduced by the Civil Code of 1857, this chapter draws on a sample of ninety post-Code paternity suits, dozens of other post-Code judicial cases, as well as earlier materials where relevant, to map how these changes played out in judicial practice.[5] While these suits resolved concrete legal and material claims among individual litigants, they also had broad symbolic resonance for the collectivity. Like criminal justice in eighteenth-century England, as described by British social historians E. P. Thompson and Douglas Hay, family law in late-nineteenth-century Chile became a public arena for the reinscription of class difference.[6]

Judicial sources illuminate law but also social relations between men, women, and children beyond the courtroom. Kin relations were embedded in a wide social and material matrix, and both courts and everyday individuals "read" kinship within this matrix. Paternity investigations

7. Doña Mercedes
Alvarez, Don
Salvador's daughter.
*Source: Carlos Larraín,
Historia de Viña del
Mar, Editorial Nasci-
mento, Santiago, Chile
1946, p. 241. General
Research Division, The
New York Public Li-
brary, Astor, Lenox and
Tilden Foundations.*

thus entailed systematic inquiries into material exchanges, labor relations, and childhood experiences. On this last score, they yield especially
rich narratives of children's lives and quotidian practices of socialization. I
draw on these narratives to examine how childhood articulated with class
structures. The discussion suggests that children are a fruitful analytic
focus for exploring how status is marked, maintained, and reproduced.

   Indeed, paternity investigation in late-nineteenth-century Chile ultimately illuminates the nature of social hierarchy itself. In a starkly unequal social order, contemporaries tended to treat the categories of rich
and poor, los de arriba and los de abajo, as self-evident, a priori, and
axiomatic. Yet filiation cases, which were in essence protracted disputes
about which status categories individuals belonged to, exposed the fractures of hierarchy. The category of dependency, which organized both
class and kin relationships in ways that could make it difficult to distinguish between the two, helps explain these fractures. This chapter explores how illegitimate individuals reveal the ambiguities of an otherwise

categorical social order. And it shows how, through the regulation of kin relations, law and bureaucracy worked to resolve these ambiguities.

Kinship as "Social Congruity"

The retroactive filiation suits pursued in late-nineteenth-century courts were supposed to be judged according to the old Iberian laws. But the Civil Code's new definition of paternity—as voluntary contract rather than biological fact—proved hegemonic. As one court official put it, filiation suits concerned not the "simple fact of paternity" but the "will or conscience of the father" to recognize offspring.[7] But how could his "will or conscience" be determined, especially in cases when he was dead? The courts could hardly define recognition in terms of the bureaucratic procedures now required by the Code; these had not even existed before 1857. Nor were the notorious ambiguities and lax standards of proof of the Iberian codes considered acceptable guideposts.

In the absence of clear standards for discerning paternal will, the judges took their cue not from written law but from a cultural script familiar to magistrates and litigants alike.[8] Beginning in the 1870s, they began to apply what one court termed the criterion of "social congruity." According to this principle, which emerged in courtroom practice rather than in jurists' writings, paternal recognition of illegitimate offspring was synonymous with the conferring of class position. If a man had made manifest efforts to assimilate his alleged offspring into his social status through class-appropriate education and upbringing, then it was said he possessed the will to recognize, and filiation was established. But if, through material or moral neglect, he had allowed his offspring to sink into poverty, subservience, and social anonymity—to a station "socially incongruous" with his own—then he had not recognized his child, and kinship remained unproven.[9] As a judge summarized the logic of social congruity, to win a paternity suit in a late-nineteenth-century Chilean court, an illegitimate had to demonstrate "acts . . . that cause one to believe the father had the intention of recognizing him as hijo natural," including "support and education corresponding to the different stages of the child's life and *in keeping with the class and social position of the father*."[10]

And it was inevitably the father's social position that was at issue. This was so first because, as earlier in the century, few mothers were subjects of filiation suits, and second because putative fathers in post-1857 Chile were much more uniformly wealthy than their pre-Code counterparts. Indeed, some of the most distinguished members of the Chilean elite became subjects of such litigation.[11] This profile probably reflects the fact that after the Civil Code, filiation investigations became so complex, protracted, and expensive that they were only worthwhile when a significant patrimony was at stake. Secundino's suit was financed by shadowy "sponsors," probably lawyers who agreed to bring the case in exchange for a cut of any eventual award. Meanwhile, mothers of illegitimate petitioners were dependents of the households or rural estates of alleged fathers, or else poorer members of his extended family. While consensual unions between social equals were rampant among the poor, these were not the cases aired as paternity suits in late-nineteenth-century courts. The premise of social congruity, that illegitimate fathers enjoyed a social position superior to mothers, turned out to accurately reflect the suits that made it to court.

In keeping with the logic of social congruity, filiation investigations were inquiries less into petitioners' paternity than into the genealogy of their social condition. The court considered how illegitimates had been raised, by whom and in what conditions, where they had been educated, what provisions had been made for self-sufficiency in adulthood, and the role the persons purported to be their fathers had played in this process. One court found Secundino Alvarez's filiation claim improbable because "Don Salvador Alvarez . . . did not attend to his upbringing in proportion to his resources" and had allowed him to be maintained "in the obscure condition of servant" as a boy. They noted that Don Salvador had chosen a peon and not a social equal as his son's godfather. And they cited the fact that the merchant made no provisions for the young Secundino when he left Chile and spent more than a decade abroad. Rather than placing the boy in the care of "a competent person" during his travels, Don Salvador had "abandoned him in such a way that his mother was obliged to place him as a servant." Finally, the court found it telling that, upon returning to Chile, Don Salvador "did not take care to bring [an eighteen-year-old Secundino] under his care, to maintain him in a school, to present him to his family, and later to give him resources to work."

The justices' argument was *not* that Don Salvador was not Secundino's father. In fact, the court noted that six witnesses had "heard Don Salvador say that the boy Secundino was his son." What was significant is that he had only done so "in one or another isolated and clandestine occasions." His private and grudging admission of paternity did not constitute public and voluntary recognition. Likewise, several witnesses commented on the physical resemblance of the two. Others recalled incidents in which Don Salvador "was affectionate with [Secundino], calling him his son." Such sentimental contact may have been meaningful to witnesses, but it had no legal weight in post-Code courts. Status consistently trumped affect, physical resemblance, or oral admission of paternity. The bottom line was that Secundino Alvarez had come to occupy "a humble condition that is totally incompatible with the formal recognition that a person with the resources of Don Salvador would have made with a son of his." That condition alone belied any claim to kinship.

The court's interpretive approach in the Alvarez case was typical. In another suit, the alleged father had identified the plaintiff as his daughter, but his widow argued that her husband "did not observe with her any treatment other than that accorded to the master's favorite inquilinos [tenant farmers]." A Concepción appeals court concluded that even if the man had admitted his paternity "on repeated occasions," it could not be "deduced that he recognized her as his hija natural through indubitable and explicit acts that implied her recognition, such as presenting her as such to his social relations and giving her the corresponding rank and placement [*colocación*]."[12] Likewise, a court rejected Catalina de la Lastra's filiation claim, citing "the fact that [alleged father, wealthy hacendado Pedro de la Lastra] left her for ten years in the custody of the wet nurse . . . surrounded by the miseries and vices . . . of the social class that a wet nurse belongs to, without thinking about placing her with people who would have instructed her in the principles corresponding to the class to which Don Pedro de la Lastra belonged." Moreover, the court noted, "he did not assist her with the support and care corresponding to his social position, since he only gave her a pension of ten pesos a month."

As noted above, social congruity derived from a cultural script rather than codified law, but it may have been loosely inspired by the Civil Code's regulations regarding child support. According to the Code's taxonomy of filiation, explored in the last chapter, legitimate children had a right to "congruous" support, defined as that corresponding to "the fortune and social rank of the father." Natural children and simply illegitimate ones could claim only "necessary" support, or that required "to sustain life," regardless of either parent's social position.[13] Such differentiation advanced the Civil Code's basic thrust of accentuating the distinctions between legitimate and illegitimate offspring to the disadvantage of the latter. Social congruity altered the taxonomy's logic in a subtle but significant way. Not only did it hold that natural children deserved a caliber of upbringing corresponding to the social status of their fathers but it actually *redefined* the category of hijo natural *in terms of* this standard. The categories "natural" and "simply illegitimate" thus came to refer to children who had or had not been assimilated into their father's social position. In the de la Lastra case, for example, the court observed that sending one's daughter to a wet nurse was "the least that one could do for an illegitimate child who is owed support by law, and therefore these humanitarian acts cannot rise to the category of recognition of a natural child."[14] Such reasoning reflects how, in judicial practice, family law was imbued with significations related to class.

As these anecdotes suggest, social congruity consisted of socially appropriate education, economic support, and placement in proper social circles. Another key dimension of congruous socialization was whether illegitimate sons and daughters had been presented as kin to their fathers' social peers. As one attorney declared, a plaintiff had to demonstrate that "there has been a true recognition before the father's family or his friends and not isolated incidents witnessed by strangers."[15] This notion of successive layers of social familiarity evokes the organization of colonial Iberian society into public and private spheres. Ann Twinam has observed that recognition of illegitimates in Spanish America was "bifurcated" in that parents could acknowledge a child to family members or else within a broader public sphere.[16] To some extent, the Chilean judicial record reflects the persistence of these cultural constructs into the late nineteenth century. Witnesses cited fathers who "presented" illegitimate sons and daughters "to society" and "walked around the streets" with them and children who enjoyed public excursions in their father's coach. Judges distinguished between "public and formal" modes of recognition versus "isolated and clandestine" ones. According to a witness testifying on behalf of Mercedes Alvarez's status as hija natural, "when she was small [Don Salvador] went around with her everywhere."[17]

Yet a closer reading reveals that such layers of social familiarity referenced as much distinctions of class as delineations of public and private. After asserting that recognition had to take place before intimates and not strangers, the lawyer cited above continued: "Pay attention only to the social condition of [the witnesses] . . . The majority of them have not met [the alleged father]; others are servants and workers, and those of the best position are school owners, but without friendship or relations of intimacy with [him]." It was simply not credible that a gentleman would have confided his paternity to "entirely unknown subjects" even as he kept the secret from his "immediate relatives." Individuals high and low might harbor the same knowledge, but the *meaning* of that knowledge differed depending on who was privy to it. The assimilation of an illegitimate child into a class status, and by extension a kin network, necessarily implied introduction into the father's community of social peers.[18]

Perhaps less obviously, it also implied a specific relationship to his *subordinates*. One illegitimate cited as proof of paternity that his father had "ordered his dependents and workers to recognize [him] as master, in the same way that [his father] was." A man who oversaw a mill must be the mill owner's son, noted a witness, because "in the mill the servants respected Don Ramón [the son] as a patrón as well." Another court cited the fact that the defendant had "recommended respect and considerations [for the plaintiff] among his servants" as evidence of paternal recognition, rejecting the defense's claim that the petitioner had merely been one more dependent within his father's domestic entourage.[19] Presumably illegitimates' domination of lowly subordinates proved that they could not logically have shared that station. Inextricable from relative social status, filiation could be read through a person's relationship to individuals both high and low across a broad social hierarchy.[20]

While the standard of social congruity was usually invoked against illegitimates' claims, it could also be marshaled in their favor. One woman's filiation claim was dismissed by the legitimate heirs, who argued that if she had received financial assistance from the wealthy Argentine expatriate she claimed was her father, it was because he was a philanthropic man who wanted to recognize the loyal services of her mother, his cook. Her lawyer countered with the same logic. The plaintiff, he argued, occupied too refined a social position to be the mere daughter of a cook, and the courtesy accorded her in letters from the administrator of the disputed estate proved this.[21] In another case, three women asserted their status as a man's natural daughters. The court rejected the filiation claim of one of them because "it is not conceivable that [the alleged father], if he really had the intention of recognizing her as his daughter, would have left her to live in the sad condition in which she has always lived." But by the same logic it accepted the claims of the other two, concluding that the father "recognized and always treated [them] as his daughters, receiving them in his own house, presenting them in this character to different people, [and] taking care of their upbringing."[22] Social congruity was not the only logic guiding filiation rulings, but it was a key one, and it informed verdicts both favorable and unfavorable to illegitimates.

(Re)defining filiation categories in terms of social status created a mechanism of both familial repudiation and incorporation. The guiding logic of social congruity was thus not to dismiss, a priori, the claims of illegitimates. It was to uphold the will of fathers. Social congruity shielded elite men from unwanted filiation claims, but it also allowed them to selectively assimilate children born outside marriage into their lineages, class status, and social worlds. For men like Francisco Salvador Alvarez who had no legitimate heirs, this mechanism ensured the integrity of their patrimonies and the survival of their lineages. The Civil Code's rendering of family law privileged marriage and legitimacy, but paternal will, which courts endeavored to honor vis-à-vis both legitimate and illegitimate offspring, ultimately trumped both.

Money, Labor, Power: The Ambiguities of Dependency

The historian Luis Alberto Romero has observed that social hierarchy in late-nineteenth-century Chile was "categorical: it is a question of education, of relations, of forms of life, of speech, of everything and nothing at once." Which individuals fell into which status category was obvious: "anyone could distinguish" between rich and poor, divided as they were by "a clear and insuperable breach."[23] These a priori and axiomatic demarcations are echoed in courtroom narratives of filiation, with their references to peers and subordinates, assimilated and unassimilated off-spring, socially congruous and incongruous individuals. Yet paternity suits, which reflected disputes about these categories, simultaneously reveal their fissures. For if such distinctions were so self-evident and categorical, how could they engender such protracted conflicts over interpretation? Filiation disputes reveal how status categories that were outwardly rigid and overdetermined contained elements of contingency and ambiguity. They also illustrate how social condition came to be acquired over time, a process in which childhood proved central.

The fissures of social hierarchy are most obvious in the simplest of material exchanges. Like many filiation suits both before and after the Civil Code, the Alvarez case focused on the material ties that for decades wove the lives of Don Salvador, Secundino, and his mother Carmen Bernal together. Witnesses recounted how, a few days after Secundino's birth, Bernal requested money for herself and the baby. Don Salvador obliged with an ounce of gold, followed by regular payments "for her expenses and those of the child." Witnesses recalled how Don Salvador later paid pensions to Secundino's wet nurse and caretakers and described an encounter years later in which he gave Bernal "a certain sum of money." Finally, they testified that as the young Secundino approached adulthood Don Salvador promised to set him up in business, once vowing "to provide him with three or four hundred pesos in order to work and make a man of him." Such material relations endured for thirty years, until Don Salvador's death. The fact that witnesses remembered the details of these exchanges and that Secundino's lawyers placed such emphasis on them suggests that regardless of the Civil Code's provisions, in social practice material relations between men, women, and children continued to constitute a cornerstone of what it meant to be a father.

Yet such testimony also reflects the difficulties of divining social and familial relations from everyday material transactions. For if these exchanges—an ounce of gold here or a certain sum of pesos there—were eminently concrete, their meaning was not. Such exchanges signified relations of dependence between women and children and their male providers. But what sort of dependence? Plaintiffs and defendants disputed whether these relationships were *paternal* or merely *paternalistic*. Illegitimate petitioners, of course, argued that male economic support of women and their offspring signaled paternity; defendants countered that it reflected charitable largesse. Such competing interpretations extended from lucre to living arrangements. Had a young woman been reared in an extended household as a granddaughter or as a "foundling and out of charity"? Was another the daughter of a couple, as she asserted, or had she simply been "received and given shelter" in their home only to forget "the affection and gratitude that she owes her protectors"?[24] The distinction between paternity and paternalism was obviously much more than semantic: kinship and charity represented two mutually exclusive modes of social relations. Where kinship signaled social proximity, charity marked class distance. Where kinship entailed legal obligation, charity was by definition voluntary. Yet both entailed gendered and generational relations of dependence that in practice could prove stubbornly, and dangerously, similar.

Illegitimates epitomized that uneasy ambiguity. Simultaneously kin and subordinates, intimates and strangers, they blurred the crucial distinctions between status categories, between proximity and distance, between obligation and charity. Attempts to sort out these ambiguities often focused on the household, a space that housed both family members and servile dependents. Interpretive disputes over domestic roles generally, though not always, involved female illegitimates. In a typical argument, a woman asserted she was the daughter of a man who had placed her in the home of his sister. The defense disputed her claim, arguing that she had been known in the aunt's household "not as a person of the family, but as a girl reared and destined by this señora for domestic service." Such a claim was credible because, as we will see in chapter 6, tutelary domestic servitude involving children was very common.[25] In another suit, the defense maintained that an illegitimate petitioner who had lived in her alleged father's house had actually worked there as a servant. If the man had given his consent for her marriage, it was not as a father but rather because "this is a very natural sentiment in any well intentioned person who wishes to see their servants well established."[26] Finally, there was the plaintiff who cited the fact that his putative father, a man of "distinguished social position," had "brought him by his side and kept him in his house until he died," as evidence of his filiation. The court in provincial Rengo disagreed. "Far from giving him the treatment of [a] son," it declared, the man had "maintained him in his house like a servant."[27] As a site of formally distinct but outwardly very similar modes of gendered and generational dependence, the household figures time and again in assessments of illegitimates' status.[28]

Status ambiguities were not limited to households or the "private" sphere, however, because dependence itself was not limited to such spaces. Many filiation disputes, especially though not exclusively in the case of male illegitimates, revolved around the plaintiff's role in the context of family businesses and commercial relations. One plaintiff claimed that property holder and future priest Don Carlos Gac "had recognized Don Juan [the plaintiff's father] as his son by having him under his charge employed in some mills that were of the said Don Carlos's property." While one witness agreed that Don Carlos "himself married [the plaintiff] off and put him in the mills," another declared he "didn't know if [he was employed in the mills] because he was the son of the said Don Carlos or as a private employee [*un particular*]."[29] Payment of a wage was central to distinguishing contractual versus filial labor relationships. José Guillermo Contreras claimed his alleged father had put him to work in his store (*negocio de despacho*) for ten years, "without giving me a salary, but giving me the confidence and considerations of a son." Countering the filiation claim, the heirs asserted that Contreras had worked "as a paid employee." Likewise, a woman asserted that she had worked for years as the overseer (*mayordoma*) of her father's hacienda "without the salary of an unrelated dependent [*sirbiente estraña*]."[30] Where unpaid labor marked the proximity of kinship, a wage signified the social distance of employer and employee.[31]

The nature of work and the degree of authority and trust accorded an employee were further clues as to his or her relationship to the patrón. The woman who claimed she had overseen her father's estate also noted that her husband has been given "tasks and occupations" associated with his status as an "individual of [the owner's] house and family." (That she, or more likely her lawyer, did not feel obliged to identify what sorts of tasks denoted kinship suggests the extent to which these social meanings were self-evident to contemporaries.)[32] Similarly, in his bid to establish his identity as son and heir of Silverio Villalón, Ramón Besoain testified that he had served as an employee of Villalón's Argentine estate and later as bookkeeper for his mill in Santiago. He asserted that in the mill he had actually overseen the business (*corría con el negocio*). Witnesses corroborated that Besoain "was in the mill, not as an employee, but as a member of the family, because he was responsible for the management of the business." When asked to describe "all the acts of recognition of a natural son that . . . Don Silverio has carried out in favor of Don Ramón," another witness noted that "he set him up in a bakery; he gave him flour and everything." But Villalón's heirs disputed these characterizations, producing witness testimony that Besoain had occupied the role of an *empleado de confianza*—a trusted employee, but merely an employee—in Don Silverio's commercial enterprises.[33]

Ultimately it was less the facts that were contested in filiation disputes than their interpretation. Was the monthly pension that a man gave a woman or child a sign of paternal solicitude or paternalistic largesse? Had a young man been employed as a son or favored employee? Did a girl reside in a household as daughter or domestic? Such questions, of course, reflect how kinship was read against a broad social and material matrix. They further reflect how formally distinct modes of dependence could be conflated. Finally, they illuminate the social and economic roles of elite men's illegitimate progeny. Some illegitimates sank to the lowest rungs of the social hierarchy, becoming assimilated into the servile labor force of their fathers.[34] But others occupied a liminal space, somewhere between servant and son, dependent and daughter. This very liminality rendered them valuable to their fathers' economic and commercial pursuits. As the above anecdotes suggest, illegitimate children were trusted to oversee mills, keep books, administer haciendas, and run households, often in their fathers' absence. One woman claimed to have worked for fourteen years as overseer of her father's hacienda near Curicó. While he "passed the majority of his time and even whole years . . . in Santiago," she oversaw "the harvests, sowings, and grape harvest."[35]

Illegitimates' roles in this regard served the economic strategies of elite families in nineteenth-century Chile. Eschewing specialization, the upper classes tended to diversify their interests across a range of productive activities. A single family might be involved in mining, agriculture, commerce, and export activities, straddling urban and rural locales. As José Bengoa notes, elite families exhibited a "division of labor" in which the member with an agricultural vocation remained on the hacienda, the lawyer of the family conducted business in the city, and the politician defended the family's interests before the state.[36] In the context of such arrangements, illegitimate quasi-kin proved particularly valuable. They were trusted intimates without the rights of full kin, who oversaw certain kin-based enterprises while their fathers oversaw others. Contrary to the typical portrayal of illegitimate offspring as threatening legitimate patrimony, their roles in this context benefited not only fathers but paternal relatives generally. Yet such arrangements could prove distinctly exploitive for the "quasi-kin" themselves. Illegitimate sons and daughters sometimes worked for years without formal remuneration, apparently awaiting the day when their labors, filial loyalty, and quiet discretion would be rewarded.

Claims for back wages—filed in addition to or in lieu of paternity suits—suggest that sometimes they waited in vain. One man worked on an estate for two years without a salary, "believing the hacendado to be his illegitimate father." When he sued for back pay, the court ruled that the plaintiff had no right to compensation because he "did not justify the employment contract and [indeed] . . . the plaintiff himself suggested that such a contract did not exist since . . . he provided services to the defendant in the belief he was his father."[37] The prevailing legal and social ethos abetted such exploitation. Occupying an indeterminate status between hijo and employee, illegitimates fell between both the employment contract to which the court alluded as well as the kinship contracts of the Civil Code. So too did the particular texture of agrarian labor relations, which were characterized by oral contracts, payment in kind, and absentee oversight.[38] Like households, haciendas were spaces in which dependents of various stripes coexisted. As such, they were particularly compatible with ambiguous social relations.

In the colonial period, Iberian laws limited illegitimates' entry into civil bureaucracy and artisan guilds. In a republic of equals, such civic discrimination against illegitimates no longer existed, yet natal status continued to shape employment prospects and social status. Indeed, the Civil Code's expansion of paternal prerogatives likely enhanced their vulnerability within these arrangements. Illegitimates' economic and commercial roles illustrate how filiation and family law reverberated well beyond the family, structuring relations of social and economic power.

But if illegitimates' liminality served fathers' economic interests, it complicated in potentially dangerous ways the social categories into which Chilean society was organized. Quasi-kin in the household, hacienda, or mill blurred what were supposed to be the self-evident distinctions between sons and servants, daughters and domestics, heirs and employees, lawful kin and charitable beneficiaries. For how in a society organized around categorical hierarchical differences could there be individuals without a transparent and unequivocal social classification? The anxiety provoked by social liminality is palpable in the court's ruling in the Alvarez case. "Even if [Don Salvador] did not have the same affection for [Secundino] as for his other children," the court surmised, "it is not possible to assume that, recognizing Don Secundino, he would not have any affection for him at all, [to] the shocking [*chocante*] extreme, contradictory with recognition itself, of neglecting his early upbringing and later abandoning him to such a degree that the son ended up as a servant." The prospect of a gentleman's son reduced to servitude was "shocking" and "extreme." Equally shocking—and perhaps even more dangerous—was the reverse scenario: the brazen subordinate who conspired to ascend to a family of higher status. It was a scenario posed by many a defense attorney, including the one in the case of the Argentine expatriate who had made regular payments to the daughter of his cook. When the cook's daughter claimed he was her father, the man's lawyer warned that his philanthropic goodwill was being used as a "poisonous weapon" against his legitimate heirs.[39]

If such scenarios offended sensibilities and imperiled private patrimony, they also threatened the class order itself. Jurists repeatedly cautioned about the dangers of misinterpreting dependency. As the Civil Code–era lawyer Martín Zapata had warned, "There are many people in Santiago who have established quite considerable allowances . . . for poor women; and if all of these women wanted to convert . . . the benefits that they receive in so many weapons to assault a social status and to join the family of their benefactors . . . farewell, benevolence."[40] Three decades later, another lawyer echoed this claim: "If recognition of kinship were deduced from an act of beneficence between he who gives it and he who receives it," then most people would wrongfully be supposed parents of "some or innumerable children" toward whom "they carried out an act of charity."[41] Mistaking paternalism for paternity, in other words, imperiled both individual patriarchs *and* the collective good. Through the idiom of charity, jurists implicitly equated the interests of elite men with those of society in general and identified false filiation claims as a danger to both.

Paternity suits reflected an attempt, through law, to resolve the unset-

86   CHILDREN AND STRANGERS

tling ambiguities of illegitimates' place in a categorical social order. They
achieved this through the judicial application of social congruity. Was
Secundino Alvarez a servile waif, or was he the son of the wealthy and
prominent Valparaíso merchant Francisco Salvador Alvarez? The voluminous court record suggests he was both. But social congruity posed
these as two mutually exclusive identities and assigned him one only.
Meanwhile, the question that should ostensibly have framed this dispute,
namely, the plaintiff's parentage, turned out to be largely immaterial to it.
By contrast, the upbringing, social position, and kin pretensions of the
well-bred Mercedes Alvarez were all mutually congruous. The court
ruled in her favor and then consolidated her social condition by awarding
her a vast patrimony.

Thus, paternity suits were not simply disputes between private individuals over personal interests. They were also public arenas for working
through the nature of class and dependency. And in a suit like the one
involving the Alvarez family, that arena was very public indeed. In a city
of 100,000 people—Valparaíso's population around 1875—news of ongo-
ing litigation concerning such a prominent family and involving more
than seventy witnesses, including two dozen of the city's wealthiest and
most politically powerful members, must have circulated widely. Indeed,
as late as the 1920s, a newspaper article recalled that the Alvarez estate
had been the "object of noisy suits before our tribunals."[42] What people of
all social classes witnessed through such proceedings was the public
reaffirmation of status distinctions. This, ultimately, was what social congruity did: it clarified the class positions of litigants and in so doing
upheld the distinctions between modes of dependency that illegitimacy
threatened to blur. Through such suits, family law, and by extension the
Chilean state, reinscribed social hierarchy.

The Contingency of Filiation
and the Determinacy of Childhood

If status could prove ambiguous, if it was not axiomatic and predetermined, then how was it conferred? In showing how illegitimates came to
be incorporated into or excluded from natal families, filiation investigations richly narrate the process by which social condition was acquired.

In so doing, they illuminate the articulation of childhood and social hierarchy. These narratives suggest that while the categories of rich and poor, los de arriba and los de abajo, were formally self-evident and unequivocal, the process by which young people became assimilated into these categories could be just the opposite: contingent and even fortuitous. What we witness in paternity suits is the usually imperceptible process of individuals acquiring a class status.

The contrasting life histories of half-siblings Doña Mercedes and Secundino Alvarez are illustrative. Merceditas, as she was known, was born and baptized in Santiago, but by the mid-1870s no one seemed to remember exactly when or where or who her godparents were, such details having been either discreetly hidden or conveniently forgotten. Independent evidence, however, suggests she was born in 1839.[43] Likewise, almost nothing is known of her mother, Doña María Antonia Prieto, except that her surname is an illustrious one and she was apparently a member of an upstanding family. Indeed, Mercedes's first few years of life are a mystery; the fact that her attorneys cited no contact with her paternal kin during that time suggests there was none.[44] The girl's incorporation into the paternal household occurred when Don Salvador's mother, Doña Dolores, went to Santiago to fetch her illegitimate granddaughter in 1841 or 1842 and brought her back to Valparaíso. Witnesses remembered that "when she was little [Don Salvador] went everywhere with her" and that he "manifested a very tender affection towards his daughter." Merceditas was perhaps eleven or twelve years old when her father left Chile, first for California and then for Europe, Asia, and Australia. By the time he returned fourteen years later, she had come of age, married, and had her first child.

A series of letters between Don Salvador, Merceditas, and Doña Dolores exchanged during that absence, and later tucked in the pages of her filiation suit, documents the textures of family life and the coming of age of an elite young woman in midcentury Valparaíso.[45] Doña Dolores's missives laud her granddaughter's accomplishments in school ("in drawing she is very advanced . . . English she speaks like an Englishwoman"). Don Salvador's correspondence to his daughter is filled with gentle paternal admonitions to improve her handwriting and apply herself in her studies of languages, piano, and singing, since "these subjects will be of great use to you in life." Merceditas herself laments her father's sporadic

8. Doña Dolores Pérez de Alvarez, Don Salvador's mother. *Source: Carlos Larraín, Historia de Viña del Mar, Editorial Nascimento, Santiago, Chile 1946, p. 233. General Research Division, The New York Public Library, Astor, Lenox and Tilden Foundations.*

9. Don José Francisco Vergara, husband of Doña Mercedes Alvarez, ca. 1879. *Courtesy of the Museo Histórico Nacional.*

correspondence, but at one point she is pleased to tour a frigate that he has named "Mercedes." In later years, the correspondence shifts to her impending marriage to Don José Francisco Vergara, a young engineer from an elite family employed in the construction of the Santiago–Valparaíso railroad. (Vergara would later become a newspaper editor and distinguished Radical Party politician.) Merceditas's marriage to Vergara was the culmination of a multigenerational immigrant success story, for it linked the heirs of a self-made Portuguese newcomer, Don Salvador's father, to one of the most distinguished pedigrees in the country. In this sense, the letters narrate not only the process of Merceditas's class socialization but also the rising social fortunes of her lineage.

The life history of Secundino Alvarez, born in 1846, seven years after Merceditas, could hardly have been more different. But if Secundino wound up marginalized from his paternal family, the testimony suggests his fate was not predetermined. To be sure, certain early events were not promising. On the day of Secundino's birth, witnesses recalled, the door of the Alvarez household was closed early to prevent the newborn being placed in the doorway. ("Abandonment" at the father's residence was a common informal practice by which mothers sought to compel paternal responsibility for illegitimate progeny.) Thereafter, the baby was given godparents of a manifestly low social station (Secundino's godfather was a worker in his father's bodegas).

One major factor working against Secundino from the outset was the lowly status of his mother, the Alvarez family seamstress. Another possible impediment is less obvious: his sex. Once asked why Don Salvador had not recognized Secundino as he had Merceditas, the children's grandmother, Doña Dolores, gave a telling response: Don Salvador "did not want to recognize him because he was a boy, since he feared that once he was grown up he might turn out to be a rascal [tunante] and would waste everything, and that he had taken Merceditas in his care because she was a girl." If Don Salvador in fact made such a consideration, he was not exceptional. Judicial records in general suggest that fathers were more likely to recognize daughters, though why this is so is unclear. They may have been motivated to protect dependent girls because female poverty was associated with moral danger and dishonor. Or perhaps cultural constructions of illegitimates as rogues and scoundrels were implicitly male, making illegitimate sons more threatening. Alternatively, Don Salvador's reference to a son who would "waste everything" may reflect sons' and daughters' differential access to property. Fathers may have balked at enfranchising potentially improvident sons but felt in greater control of their daughters' patrimonial access. Or perhaps daughters were valued insofar as they could "marry up" and improve or consolidate the status of natal kin, as Mercedes did when she married into a long-established elite family.[46]

While both his mother's status and his sex likely influenced Secundino's fate, neither factor was in itself determinant. Indeed, other aspects of his life history appeared distinctly auspicious. Don Salvador apparently had more contact with the infant Secundino, whom he visited regularly in the child's early months and years, than he had had with Mercedes. By all accounts, he also supported the young boy economically. Witnesses recalled how both father and paternal grandmother displayed affection toward the small boy during visits. The fact that an acquaintance asked Doña Dolores why Don Salvador did not recognize Secundino as he had Mercedes implied such a scenario was at least plausible. Secundino's name itself, commonly given to second children, may reflect his mother's (or a godparent's) hope that the boy would be treated as another child, following his older half-sister.[47]

Secundino's social and familial exclusion, it seems, was sealed only at age five or six, when his father left Chile. The caretaker who had reared Secundino until then noted that she had "been charged by Don Salvador with putting the boy . . . in a school so that he would receive a basic education [*a fin de que aprendiera los primeros conocimientos*]" and that Don Salvador had declared "that later on, he would take responsibility for placing him in a good school in order to make a great man out of him [*a fin de que se hiciera un grande hombre*]." Yet whatever his intentions, Don Salvador made no provisions for the child when he departed, and the payments to his caretakers abruptly ceased. It was at this point that Secundino slid abruptly, and inexorably, into servitude. "The boy was treated very poorly," recalled one observer, "because according to what [his caretaker] said, his father was in California." At eight or nine years old, he was placed with the leaseholder of a rural estate on the outskirts of Valparaíso, where witnesses noted that he was "poorly dressed" and worked as a servant. After five years, he ran away in search of his maternal grandfather. At thirteen, he took up residence in yet another household, this time that of a rural subdelegate, where he worked, once again, *en clase de sirviente*. And yet even as Secundino's exclusion as son was being sealed, in these very years another young man was coming to occupy that role. In correspondence to "my dear son-in-law," Don Salvador discussed José Francisco Vergara's impending marriage to Merceditas, directing him to care for her, for his aging mother Doña Dolores, and for his business affairs. (Incongruously, the lifelong bachelor also proffered marital advice!) Vergara, he wrote in one letter, was going to "become one of the family."

Returning to Valparaíso after years of global travels, Alvarez would have occasion to reflect on his choices in the company of old friends and associates. In one casual get-together, according to an acquaintance, he commented that "he was very sorry he could not educate [Secundino] because of his travels." Another witness recounted a conversation in which the merchant told him "that because of his absence from the country he had not taken care of the education of his son Secundino, but that he had given him a certain amount of money so that he could do business with the steamships" that plied the Pacific coast. Don Salvador had apparently come to regret his paternal neglect, and he belatedly sought to fulfill a moral duty to provide for his now-adult son. Yet he also recognized that the time for taking care of Secundino's education was past—and here we may read "education" in the broadest sense to mean not just schooling or professional instruction but the whole process of class and kin assimilation narrated in the letters to, from, and about Merceditas.

Whether or not Don Salvador ever considered making a son and heir of Secundino, whether he ever consciously contemplated his son's future, the narrative suggests that the process of acquiring a lifelong social station and kin circle occurred in childhood and early adolescence. The caretaker whom Don Salvador charged with placing the young boy in school was herself illiterate and of modest station. That she was considered fit to oversee his upbringing during those first five years suggests that the truly decisive years—those in which "great men," to use Don Salvador's words, were made—commenced only thereafter. The merchant's sojourn abroad proved determinant because it occurred during a critical period in Secundino's life, from the time he was five or six years old through adolescence. (Doña Mercedes, in contrast, was safely ensconced in the paternal household, and its broad class matrix, long before his departure.) These were the years Secundino spent laboring in a series of households, badly dressed and poorly treated. By the time his father returned to Chile, the eighteen-year-old had missed the crucial window during which class sensibilities were developed and status conferred.

The life histories of Mercedes and Secundino, reflecting both assiduous cultivation and unforeseen contingency, explain the striking contrast in the two illegitimate half-siblings' social positions, familial status, financial claims, and future prospects. By the time their filiation disputes erupted in a Valparaíso courtroom, such differences would appear axiomatic and predetermined. Yet their life histories show that even out-of-wedlock birth implied no preordained fate. Illegitimacy was a legal category lived on a field of social contingencies.[48] Likewise, social position was less an initial condition determined by birth than an *outcome* shaped by childhood.

The story of José Eleuterio Bustos, which played out in a Santiago courtroom less than a decade later, shares key parallels with that of Secundino Alvarez. In this unusual case, it was the identity of the son rather than the father that was at issue. In 1884, a man identifying himself as José Eleuterio Bustos appeared in court seeking to reclaim his place within his natal family. He was, he claimed, the long-lost son and heir of Doña Carmen Iglesias and her deceased husband Don Celestino Bustos, and brother of the couple's two daughters. Responding to the extraordinary allegation, Doña Carmen admitted that forty years earlier, before their marriage, she and her husband had had a son named José Eleuterio Bustos. They had left him at the Santiago foundling home, but the infant disappeared in the care of a wet nurse.[49] Her admission suggested the distinct likelihood that the plaintiff really was the son and brother of the defendants.

But this possibility was moot in the face of another looming fact: the social distance that separated him from them. The claimant had been the ward of a poor, rural wet nurse and was a self-identified *agricultor*—an ambiguous term that almost certainly masked his lowly status as an inquilino (tenant farmer). As such, he had been reared in a social milieu starkly different from the urban, middling status of Doña Carmen and her daughters.[50] This social dissonance figured as a constant subtext of the judicial proceedings, as when the defendants' lawyer remarked, "He must be a man of the countryside [*un hombre del campo*] . . . who has become enthusiastic about filing the case with the idea of obtaining a fat reward." Bustos further alleged that, for reasons that are unclear, at the age of thirteen and after years of separation, he was brought back to Santiago and reintroduced to his natal family. The reunion was short-lived. As his lawyer explained, "It was natural that the boy . . . would feel detachment [*desapego*] from his parents due to the fact that he had lived far from them for a long time." So he returned to the hacienda and resumed his life there. The lawyer attempted to downplay this "detachment," but in fact it was crucial to the story. And while the implication was that the rift was affective, we can deduce that it was also social. As in the case of Secundino Alvarez's prolonged separation from his father, by the time José Eleuterio was reunited with his natal kin, it was too late. He had become distanced from them by an insuperable social breach.

The Bustos suit ends without a court decision, but it seems likely, given the logic of class congruity, that the judge would have rejected the plaintiff's claim. Certainly his alleged mother had already done so. After revealing she had lost a son in circumstances that made the petitioner's claims distinctly credible, Doña Carmen categorically denied kinship with him. Like the Alvarez case, José Eleuterio Bustos's life story reflects both the contingency of natal status and the determinacy of childhood. While his illegitimate birth explains his initial placement at the Casa de Huérfanos, it cannot explain the course of his life thereafter. After all, his two older sisters were also illegitimate but were not excluded from their family. What is more, all three children were eventually legitimated by their parents' marriage. The boy lost to the wet nurse, no less than his sisters, was thus a legitimate heir. Bustos's socialization in a class environment so different from theirs, however, determined that he could not be that boy.[51]

Law, Bureaucracy, and Illegitimacy in the Social Imaginary

While the legal domain actively produced discourses on filiation, it by no means monopolized this issue. In the final decades of the nineteenth century and first decades of the twentieth, in Chile as elsewhere in Latin America, sexuality, gender, and familial practices increasingly marked the cultural distance between elites and the "alien, strange, and degraded others" that were their poor compatriots.[52] Illegitimacy was one such marker. As paternity suits wended their way through the courts, medical, welfare, and political discussions of illegitimacy were multiplying and expanding. But there was a manifest disjuncture between judicial and other realms. Where paternity suits involved wealthy men, and where social congruity was premised on the inequality of partners, public discussions outside the courts identified out-of-wedlock birth as a specifically *lower-class* phenomenon. According to doctors, welfare officials, and politicians, illegitimacy and concubinage were rampant among the poor, "an endemic evil in the low reaches of society [*nuestra baja sociedad*]."[53] A major argument against civil marriage (established in 1884) was that it would encourage extramarital procreation among the popular classes. Illegitimacy was causally linked to other lower-class scourges, including infant mortality and juvenile delinquency. Long regarded as a moral problem, in the last decades of the century it became a social problem as well.

The association of illegitimacy with the poor posed a potential complication, however. For as paternity suits show, plenty of elite men fathered children out of wedlock. It may be that the class stigma of illegitimate procreation now encouraged more upper-class fathers to hide or repudiate extramarital offspring.[54] But they were not obligated to do so. Law and bureaucracy provided ways for elite fathers to procreate out of wedlock without "having" illegitimate children. Social congruity was a key tool. In its judicial application, it realigned natal and class status in keeping with social expectations. Natural children could "pass" as essentially legitimate members of even very elite families (think Mercedes Alvarez) even as the unrecognized experienced the categorical marginalization of simple illegitimacy (like Secundino Alvarez). Over time, this legal legerdemain could be so successful that the extramarital origins of favored illegitimates, and the very existence of disfavored ones, could disappear from public consciousness altogether. If in elite discourse illegitimacy was the exclusive province of the poor, this was a fiction that the law helped engineer.

The quotidian bureaucracy of filiation followed a similar logic. As described in the previous chapter, the Civil Code established complex new bureaucratic procedures for recognizing and legitimating illegitimates. The Code's author, Andrés Bello, characterized these procedures as the "just expiation of guilt" on the part of those who procreated extramaritally. In practice, however, bureaucratic penance did not fall on all heads with the same cool impartiality. Besides being more public and more elaborate, the new procedures were also more demanding and more expensive. Such factors ultimately placed formal recognition of children out of many parents' reach. When, a few years after the Alvarez case, Mauricio Giannetti recurred to a Valparaíso court to recognize his two young children as hijos naturales, court officials threw up obstacles that very nearly derailed his effort. An Italian immigrant of modest means, Giannetti presented the children's baptismal certificates and arranged for his boss to serve as their legal representative.[55] But a court official was not satisfied and demanded that he "provide [witness] testimony that demonstrates the true convenience of the recognition for the children."

The official's demand can be read as professional diligence or mere legalistic foot-dragging. The economics of judicial and notarial transactions created an incentive for both. Judicial transactions were billed piecemeal, by the page, by the task, by the amount of time they required, and by the kilometer if travel was required.[56] Giannetti attempted to talk his way out of the additional requirements: "As I am not a person of many resources, my object is to avoid expenses," he explained. The court was unsympathetic. So Giannetti produced a list of interrogatories and three witnesses who dutifully and perfunctorily declared the obvious—that the situation of minors with no right to paternal support or inheritance would be much improved by legal recognition, which conferred both. Finally, a month later Giannetti's children were granted the status of hijos naturales.[57]

Other parents and children were not so lucky. When faced with procedural objections that entailed additional time and expense, some simply desisted. The fact that María Arcos had "no resources of any kind to pay for the costs" may explain why her recognition petition ended like many others: with no conclusion.[58] Courts' class biases can be read between the lines of recognition and legitimation petitions. These often stressed parents' social position and property, as when one representative characterized a father as "a gentleman of notable [economic] security [*de relevante prenda*] with an honorable and hardworking character and whose fortune is not less than 10,000 pesos." Likewise, a recently married couple that desired to legitimate their five children was said to possess "sufficient property to support them and educate them comfortably."[59]

Meanwhile, the fact that almost all petitioners in recognition and legiti-mation proceedings could sign their names suggests they were not repre-sentative of illegitimate parents generally.

On occasion, class biases were made explicit. One court outright re-jected a mother's petition to recognize her daughter, citing her poverty and bad reputation.[60] While civil law did not identify status or property as prerequisites for recognition or legitimation—after all, according to the constitution, "before the law, everyone is equal"—the deep social inequalities of Chilean society seeped into, and were reproduced by, the everyday business of family law. Such transactions also reflect the limits of free will in matters of filiation. An inviolate credo in paternity suits involving wealthy men, parental free will was not nearly as sacrosanct when it came to the filiation pretensions of more modest parents, moth-ers as well as fathers.

Circumscribed access to these procedures may explain why, despite high and rising illegitimacy rates in the late nineteenth century, there are surprisingly few recognition and legitimation petitions in the notarial and judicial archives. The vast majority of illegitimate children were never formally recognized by their parents or legally legitimated by sub-sequent marriage.[61] The children of the poor were, and remained, legally illegitimate. It is difficult to say whether access to civil bureaucracy was more restricted after the Civil Code than it had been before. What clearly had changed was the *need* for such access in the first place, since the Code now required formal legal transactions for practices like recogni-tion and legitimation that had once been automatic, informal, and flex-ible. In the very unevenness of its application, quotidian bureaucracy, like social congruity as applied in paternity suits, helped recalibrate class and filiation. It reflects how republican family policy created new vectors of social inequality.

Conclusions: Filiation, Childhood, and
the Making of Inequality

In a society structured by profound hierarchy and dependence, the social practice of class deeply informed the cultural and legal logic of kinship. In elaborate filiation suits as in everyday bureaucratic procedures, family law worked to the economic and symbolic advantage of elites. Ultimately, the legal construction of kinship helped clarify the troublesome liminalities of dependence. Where Chilean social practices surrounding status could be ambiguous, law was categorical. Law helped forge a social reality in which only the children of the poor were illegitimate.

Family law's production and reproduction of status hierarchies in nineteenth-century Chile was not new. A century before, the Spanish Crown's Royal Pragmatic on Marriage (1776–78) had attempted to reinforce hierarchy by preventing marital relations between socially and racially unequal subjects. Republican lawmakers in Chile ultimately rejected attempts to engineer equal status in marriage.[62] And if unequal status was an unacceptable criterion for prohibiting marriage, it was also, formally, unacceptable for the purpose of classifying offspring. According to a jurist writing just prior to the Civil Code, one interpretation of Iberian law held that natural children were those born of parents of socially equal status. In republican Chile, he argued, such an interpretation was unacceptable "for the simple reason that privileged castes are not known in Chile, where thanks to its liberal institutions, equality before the law is a fact."[63] Indeed, this definition of hijo natural (as the offspring of socially equal progenitors) had no currency in republican legal thought.[64]

If the relative social status *of partners* was an unacceptable criterion, social inequality *between parents and children* was a different matter. In the context of filiation, as we have seen, Chilean jurists not only embraced inequality, they elevated it to a widely invoked juridical principle. It was as if the legal management of inequality migrated from marriage to filiation: where the Royal Pragmatic specified who could marry whom, Chilean civil law regulated who could be descended from whom. Why this shift? Perhaps inequality, unacceptable when applied in violation of free marriage choice, became more palatable when it advanced law's self-conscious advocacy of free paternal will.

If filiation became a vehicle of postcolonial inequality, it follows that children will illuminate the nature of hierarchies in this society. Indeed, as the paternity suits show, the prism of childhood reveals how individuals came to acquire status within the social order. Coming of age as a servant or growing up in the household of a humble wet nurse did not reflect an individual's preordained subordination. Rather, such experiences constituted *the very process by which* minors were acculturated into a subordinate social condition. Once established, status was categorical and immutable. But the fact that it had to be cultivated suggests it was not predetermined from the outset. If, as Ann Laura Stoler has observed, in multiracial colonial societies "children had to be taught both their place and their race," in nineteenth-century Chile, they had to be taught their status and social position.[65] The myriad domestic arrangements that characterized child-rearing practices in this society thus turn out to be key to the management and reproduction of social hierarchies, an observation explored in chapters 5 and 6. Ultimately, the life stories of illegitimate people reveal the ambiguity and contingency, as well as the dynamism, of social hierarchies that were actively and creatively maintained by fathers, families, and courts.

As for the Alvarez case, one of the enduring mysteries is why Don Salvador never legally recognized his daughter Merceditas. According to one close acquaintance, it was because the merchant, who died suddenly and intestate at age fifty-nine, tended to "leave everything till the last minute." Or perhaps it was because, as he apparently told several friends, doing so would unwittingly reveal the shameful origins of a daughter so thoroughly assimilated that many people assumed she was legitimate. Whatever the reason for his omission, remedying it would cost his heirs almost two years, hundreds of pages of litigation, concomitant legal fees, and likely mortification before the community. But Don Salvador's omission, while devastating, was not ultimately fatal. Mercedes Alvarez and her husband deflected first the patrimonial pretensions of a distant kinsman and then, before the same Valparaíso judge, the claim of Secundino Alvarez.[66] Ultimately, thanks to the judicial application of social congruity, Doña Mercedes became sole legal and social heir to the Alvarez family estate.

It is tempting to conclude that the stature of the family involved made this outcome inevitable. The witnesses testifying on behalf of Doña Mercedes read like a membership list of high-profile Liberals, Radicals, and Masons in Valparaíso society.[67] Clearly these were political associates of her husband and legal representative José Francisco Vergara, himself a Mason and rising Radical Party politician. As telling as the identities of the witnesses are those of the judges. Among them was Domingo Santa María, who before becoming president of the republic, served as president of the Santiago Court of Appeals and in this capacity presided over—and ruled in favor of Alvarez and Vergara in—the successive suits concerning her family patrimony. Vergara was a personal friend of Santa María and would serve in his administration. In the small world of Chilean elites, the wealthy and well-connected subjects of filiation suits frequently found friends and allies on the bench.[68] On occasion, fathers and judges were actually the same person. Manuel Bernales, who heard numerous paternity suits during his twenty-five years as appellate court justice (including that of Secundino Alvarez), became the subject of a suit by an alleged daughter after his death.[69] Such scenarios raise the specter of blatant favoritism and corruption, of elite men who through cynical legal machinations contrived to protect their patrimonial, patriarchal interests and those of their peers. Yet the judges and litigants in these cases, many of whom (as we have seen in the Alvarez suit) were outspoken Liberals and Radicals, did not need to compromise their ardent commitment to, in José Francisco Vergara's own words, "pay tribute to the law, respect and expand the rights of men, preserve equity and justice for all."[70] The arbitrary manipulation of law was unnecessary because its impartial application alone proved highly effective. Through the doctrine of paternal free will, patriarchal interests had been elevated to a dispassionate, and inviolate, legal dogma.

As for the Alvarez case, the private and civil histories of the litigants after this very public legal battle drew to a close are as revealing as the judicial outcome itself. Twentieth-century accounts identify Doña Mercedes as Don Salvador's daughter and heir and recount that she and her husband José Francisco Vergara had two children. Their daughter, Blanca Vergara Alvarez, married into the elite Errázuriz family, and son Salvador Vergara Alvarez, namesake of his maternal grandfather, completed his studies in Europe, became a military general, and married the daughter of the historian and statesman Benjamín Vicuña Mackenna. Meanwhile, Vergara assumed active administration of his wife's hard-won patrimony. Before the legal dispute with Secundino had concluded, he was engaged in negotiations with public officials to donate part of that property for the establishment of a new town. In May 1878, just months after the litigation drew to a close, Viña del Mar was founded on lands from the Alvarez haciendas. Today the Vergara-Alvarez family is celebrated for their role as illustrious founders of the Pacific coast's premier resort city.[71]

By all measures, Doña Mercedes and her descendants had managed to transcend her illegitimate birth status. As the beneficiary of paternal recognition and the paternal inheritance, she was seamlessly incorporated into her father's social world, becoming a crucial link in an illustrious lineage. Local histories of Viña del Mar trace in careful detail the ownership of the lands that would become the town, the wealth of the Alvarez merchants, and the felicitous hand of town father Vergara. But strikingly, they make no mention whatsoever of Doña Mercedes's inconvenient filiation or the protracted legal battles over ownership of those lands.[72] It is as if she were a legitimate daughter and undisputed heir. Indeed, in a sense she was: both her father, Don Salvador, and civil law determined it would be thus.

Ultimately, the local histories are as revealing for what they do *not* tell us as for what they do. If assimilation was seamless and complete, so too was marginalization. Secundino Alvarez does not appear in the narratives at all, and we can only speculate about the remaining course of his humble and ultimately forgotten life.

PART II

Children of Don Nobody

Kinship and Social Hierarchy

CHAPTER 3

Kindred and Kinless:

The People without History

Autobiography of an Orphan

"It was the year 1868, if my memory serves me, since I was at most four years old. I remember we were a bunch of little kids amusing ourselves in the sun and eating some wafers . . . that the *madrecitas* made. [*Madrecitas* is] what we called the nuns of Providencia, who when all was said and done were our real mothers since we didn't know any others." So begins the extraordinary tale *The Orphan: True Story Recounted by a Foundling of the Casa de Maternidad de Santiago.* Published serially in a provincial newspaper in 1897 and the following year as a book, the narrative recounts the life of Pablo Pérez, who claimed to have been reared in the Casa de Huérfanos, Santiago's massive public orphanage.[1] The author describes his early childhood in the institution, which in the late nineteenth century housed as many as 9 percent of the children born in the city, as well as his subsequent years laboring in private homes as a young servant. The story then follows the shipwrecks, earthquakes, and other swashbuckling adventures of a self-reliant young orphan forced to make his way alone in the world. The narration is intertwined with the milestones of late-nineteenth-century Chilean history. A self-styled "good liberal," Pérez fights in the War of the Pacific against Peru and Bolivia and militates on behalf of doomed President José Manuel Balmaceda in the 1891 civil war. Apropos of his own marital difficulties, his autobiography is also a spirited exhortation in favor of legal divorce, a perennial cause of Chilean liberals.

Part adventure story, part political treatise, Pérez's autobiography evokes another genre as well. It is a mournful narrative of an orphan's search for his natal origins. Pérez longs to know who his parents are, what his surnames are, who he is. Ultimately, his search proves futile. "Thirty-four years have passed," he notes at the end of book, "and I still have not found even a vestige of who gave me life." In addition to generating a profound sentimental disquiet, his natal alienation has concrete consequences for his life course. An intended marriage is complicated by the fact that he has no baptismal certificate and no one to proffer the parental consent required for minors. He writes to the mother superior of the foundling home seeking "any piece of information regarding my existence." The Casa communicates the names of his mother and godmother but also the news that they have no baptismal certificate or further record of his identity. Eventually Pérez is able to marry, but the mystery of his origins continues to haunt him. He appeals to readers who may know his mother or godmother to contact the newspaper that published his tale. The story of near escapes and death-defying adventures closes on this plaintive note: "It may well be that the people who read this story . . . know the said Carmen [his mother] or relatives . . . then by way of the strand, the ball of yarn will be discovered and I will finally find her whom I have desired and sighed over so much: My Mother!"[2]

Was Pérez an *expósito*, a foundling, as he claimed? Had he really grown up in the Casa de Huérfanos? Or was this a purely fictional narrative? To be sure, the pirates and shipwrecks call to mind the adventure stories serialized in newspapers at the time. As the tale of a plucky orphan who overcomes the odds, *The Orphan* also echoes foundling genres popular in Europe, the United States, and Latin America in the nineteenth century.[3] Yet there is reason to believe that Pérez really was an *hijo de la Providencia*, a "child of Providence," as the asylum's wards were known. Specific, idiosyncratic details of his recollections of the foundling home find striking corroboration in the private documentation of the institution.[4] These details suggest that, fictitious liberties notwithstanding, the author had intimate personal knowledge of the Casa de Huérfanos— almost certainly because he had grown up there. If this is the case, *The Orphan* is a rare work indeed, a glimpse into the life of a poor youngster told in the authentic (though by no means unmediated) voice of the individual himself.

While Pérez's memoir is unusual, his lack of natal origins was not.

BIBLIOTECA DE «EL INDUSTRIAL»

EL HUÉRFANO

HISTORIA VERDADERA CONTADA POR UN EXPÓSITO DE LA CASA
DE MATERNIDAD DE SANTIAGO

Y DADAS A LUZ ESPECIALMENTE PARA EL INDUSTRIAL DE CURICÓ

POR

P. N. PINTO

CURICÓ
IMPRENTA DE «EL INDUSTRIAL»

1898

10. Pablo Pérez's autobiography *The Orphan: True Story Recounted By a Foundling of the Casa de Maternidad of Santiago*, published in 1898. *Courtesy of the Biblioteca National, Santiago.*

Diverse sources from nineteenth- and early-twentieth-century Chile hint, obliquely but insistently, at the existence of a shadowy, stigmatized "kinless" underclass. These were poor people who lacked any ties with a kin group and grew up with little or no knowledge of their natal provenance. As a consequence, they had no kin toward whom to direct affective, social, material, or legal claims. Pablo Pérez's experience suggests that the essence of kinlessness entailed what Orlando Patterson has called natal alienation.[5] It was a condition that involved not just separation from one's natal origins but, even more radically, dispossession of a knowledge of those origins. Originless individuals did not know who their parents, families, or godparents were. They did not know where or when they had been born or baptized. As such, while natal alienation affected an individual throughout his or her lifetime, it was effectuated during childhood.

As Pérez's experience suggests, kinlessness could be a product of child abandonment, a common scenario in nineteenth-century Chile. More broadly, it could result from child circulation, the practice of rearing children in nonnatal households. Migration, parental mortality, and illegitimacy also conspired to sever ties between children and their natal kin groups. These patterns of social reproduction in turn arose out of prevailing labor forms, legal structures, and the social organization of gender. Law, labor markets, and cultural norms in nineteenth-century Chile were emphatically patriarchal, yet in the absence of a material base, the patriarchal household enjoyed but a tenuous existence. In a context in which poor women on their own bore sole legal responsibility for offspring they were unable to support, children were routinely cast off from the moorings of natal kinship. Kinlessness, in short, links patterns of filiation to structures of gender, labor, and law and to the reproduction of social and economic inequalities in Chilean society.

This chapter will sketch the meanings, causes, and consequences of kinlessness as a form of social marginality. It will also show how the condition could be perpetuated. As Pablo Pérez's nuptial quest suggests, civil and ecclesiastical regulations governing marriage required that spouses possess a verifiable origin in order to wed. People without kin origins thus found their condition an impediment to creating conjugal ties—and to producing legitimate offspring. In this sense, kinlessness was a legal condition as much as a social and material one. It entailed disenfranchisement from civil and canon law, and law in turn reproduced it.

Kinlessness is a significant phenomenon in its own right, but it also elucidates the cultural, material, and legal significance of kinship in this society. For kinlessness could only have meaning in a context in which kinship itself was socially salient. Nineteenth-century Chile was dominated by powerful families for whom status and subjectivity derived precisely from genealogical identity. By the latter half of the nineteenth century, the most significant symbolic and material trappings of the colonial aristocracy (entailed estates, noble titles) had been abolished, yet ancestry as a form of self-perpetuating, class-based social power persisted. The kinlessness of Pablo Pérez and others played out against the genealogical fetishism of elites. The contrast between the illustrious lineage of a minority and its absence among the majority was an important dimension of status. This chapter thus explores how cultural meanings and social practices of kinship helped structure and reproduce inequality in a republican society of formally equal citizens.

The Power of Pedigree:
Limpieza and Lineage from Colony to Republic

The cultural and legal significance of family origins has a long historical genealogy in Iberian tradition. It is a history reflected in the early modern doctrine of *limpieza de sangre*, or blood purity. Being pure of blood meant that the members of a lineage possessed certain racial and ethnic attributes (namely, that they were unsullied by indigenous and African blood), an acceptable religious heritage (free of Jewish or Moorish taint), and respectable filiation status (legitimate birth). The honor of one's lineage in turn redounded to the honor of the individual. A knowledge of and ability to prove genealogical antecedents was thus a crucial dimension of status in colonial Latin American society.

In Chile, explicit references to limpieza de sangre petered out after the first decades of the nineteenth century.[6] Simultaneously, the republican government abolished noble titles, coats of arms, and other trappings of pedigree. Yet as many scholars have noted, kinship ties constituted the political and economic substrate of the republic and were thus as important as ever. Their significance persisted into the twentieth century.[7] If elites' kin networks structured power relations, the conceit of lineage also informed their identity as individuals and as a collectivity. In rendering tribute to the bishop José Hipólito Salas on the centenary of his birth in 1912, the *Revista Católica* chose to print not a laudatory biography but a genealogy of the Salas family, complete with a family tree.[8] Meanwhile, genealogical histories published in the nineteenth and early twentieth centuries illustrate the centrality of family to elite subjectivity. These mythohistorical narratives abound with men of talent who preside over prestigious public offices and distinguished homes, enriching both the patria and the status of their descendants with their noble exploits.

The mutual construction of family and individual identity is evident in the tendency to portray lineages as anthropomorphic entities possessing the special talents and moral qualities of individual members. "The House of Larraín," declared the author of a genealogy in 1917, "is one of the oldest and most distinguished in the country . . . due to its religious sentiment, its eminent services to the State, [and] its elevated intellectual and social culture."[9] Histories of elite families were portrayed as inseparable from the history of the Chilean nation-state; indeed, in such renderings, it is difficult to discern where the history of *las grandes familias* ends and that of the state begins.[10] Whether the Chilean state, even at the pinnacle of oligarchic power, can be reduced to the exploits and aspirations of elite families is certainly debatable.[11] What is significant is the extent to which elites' own self-narratives situate kinship at the center of both collective identity and the birth of the nation.

While some elites claimed proud descent from the earliest colonizers, the late-nineteenth-century Chilean aristocracy was actually the product of successive waves of relatively recent immigrants. An influx of Basque immigrants in the late colonial period altered the established colonial oligarchy.[12] Subsequently, the early republic witnessed the arrival of French and English immigrants who assumed positions in increasingly lucrative commercial and mining enterprises. Within a generation, the more successful among them were absorbed into the established upper classes through marriage. Their surnames—Subercaseaux, Ross, Edwards, Letelier—would acquire the same aristocratic resonance of earlier Basque names such as Larraín, Errázuriz, Amunátegui, or Ossa. The history of the Alvarez family, traced in chapter 2, reflects these patterns of immigration and assimilation. Francisco Salvador Alvarez, according to one source the wealthiest man in mid-nineteenth-century Chile, was the son of a self-made Portuguese merchant. His grandchildren would marry a Vicuña and an Errázuriz. The Chilean upper classes' remarkable permeability did not diminish the cultural significance of lineage. On the contrary, it may have enhanced it as relative newcomers felt compelled to excavate a usable ancestry for themselves. After all, a lineage could be rendered illustrious through the very act of tracing it.

This was the reasoning behind Nathaniel Miers-Cox's turn-of-the-century genealogical history. Miers-Cox was a wealthy hacendado, one-time Conservative Party senator, and cofounder of the most important landowners' lobby, the Sociedad Nacional de Agricultura. In *Los Cox de*

Chile, which he dedicated to his descendants, the author recounted that his British immigrant father had been a medical doctor, a profession that lacked prestige in early-nineteenth-century Chile. He hoped his book might therefore "compensate for that apparent lack of lineage" implied by his father's occupation. The book traced the Cox lineage, its titles, offices, and exploits, from seventeenth-century Wales through the economic ups and downs of the author's family in Chile. Miers-Cox was so enthusiastic about his British heritage that earlier in life he had dispensed with his Hispanic maternal surname (Bustillos) in order to assume an additional English appellation (Miers), the matronym of his father.[13]

Los Cox de Chile ended with the marriage of the author's only daughter, referred to in a flamboyant display of genealogical memory as Enriqueta Gracia Miers-Cox, Larraín, Bustillos, Ruiz Tagle, Lloyd, Rojas, Maseyra y Larraín. Miers-Cox concluded: "I have written this Narration to my Grandchildren . . . my direct descendants, to whom I have a special obligation to satisfy, and to my siblings and nieces and nephews in general. May it serve to show them who my immediate predecessors are, examples of religious and civic virtues." Hailing from modest immigrant origins, Miers-Cox had acquired the dual trappings of aristocratic power: first, land, which harbored great symbolic value for the Chilean upper classes, and second, ancestry. As his book suggests, a pedigree could be constructed as sure as a rural estate could be purchased. Lineage in turn existed for familial consumption but also for public display: tellingly, while Miers-Cox dedicated his book to his descendants, he presented an autographed copy to the historian and bibliographer José Toribio Medina.[14]

Miers-Cox's genealogical foray is noteworthy for an additional reason. In addition to his political career and activities as an hacendado, the author also served for some fifteen years as administrator of the Casa de Huérfanos in Santiago, a post he still occupied when he wrote his genealogy. His knowledge and veneration of ancestry is all the more conspicuous in the context of his involvement with an institution so intimately associated with kinlessness. Compare Miers-Cox's reverential chronicle of his lineage with the plaintive narrative of Pablo Pérez, who does not know who his parents are.[15] In Chile, elites' conceit of pedigree was the cultural backdrop against which the natal dispossession of individuals like Pérez played out. When an aged Miers-Cox finally resigned

Fotograbado Leblanc

Nathaniel Miers-Cox B.

y

Alejandro N. Huneeus Miers-Cox

11. Nathaniel Miers-Cox and grandson, 1903. The picture appeared on the final page of Cox's genealogy. *Source: Nathaniel Miers-Cox, Los Cox de Chile . . . Imprenta de El Diario Popular, Santiago, 1903. Courtesy of Biblioteca Nacional, Sala Medina.*

as director of the Casa de Huérfanos, the post was assumed by his son-in-law—identified in the Cox genealogy as Alejandro Huneeus García Huidobro, Zegers, Arlegui, Lippmann, Alduante, Montenegro y Gorbea.

The valorization of origins, and the stigmatization of originlessness, was not an exclusively elite value. It extended to plebeian culture, though there it took different forms. Consider the objections voiced to a young man's impending marriage by a father in a provincial court in the 1850s. The father argued that while the intended bride was of a humble background, his son "descends from honorable parents, whose genealogy is very well known in this whole province [Talca]." The father was hardly an aristocrat, however. That he felt compelled to clarify for the court that his son was enrolled in school and was not, as someone had suggested, a shoemaker's apprentice, suggests his modest social position.[16]

Pablo Pérez's dogged quest reflects a parallel valorization of kin identity. So too do the efforts of poor parents to impart a family identity to children deposited at the Casa de Huérfanos, an effort that will be discussed in the next chapter. Finally, Nathaniel Miers-Cox himself made an observation to this effect during his tenure as foundling home administrator. In a letter from 1896 to the archbishop of Santiago, he requested that individuals reared in the Casa be exempt from the traditional banns published prior to marriage, which identified the bride and groom's filiation, in order to avoid revelation of their kinlessness. "The case has arisen in which the groom refuses to be proclaimed, he and his wife, because they do not have known parents," Miers-Cox explained. "In this way, their origin [*procedencia*] in the Casa de Huérfanos is made public and notorious, which is not advisable for their future relations in the society in which they will live."[17] Such comments suggest a deep and abiding concern with natal provenance among plebeian sectors as well.

Kinship was significant not only in terms of status but also as a source of immediate material succor and support, for people of all classes. Both older Iberian law and the 1857 Civil Code carefully defined alimentos, the obligations of material support between kin. The ubiquity of alimentos suits in nineteenth-century courts suggests that people actively appealed to law to enforce these obligations.[18] While the majority of these suits involved wives petitioning estranged husbands and mothers petitioning fathers for support of illegitimate children, myriad other permutations of kindred were also represented. These included abandoned wives petitioning fathers; widows versus sons; daughters-in-law versus mothers-in-law; and sisters versus siblings. Reflecting gendered patterns of famil-ial dependency, women were clearly overrepresented as petitioners. But men too could and did petition for alimentos, soliciting them from brothers, fathers, and sons. In the midst of an economic depression in 1879, Pedro Muñoz declared himself "completely bereft of resources" and unable to find a job "as a consequence of the state of crisis the country is experiencing." He solicited alimentos from "the person who by law is obliged to give them to me": his grandmother.[19] The fairly small sums at stake in these cases bespeak individuals of modest to middling social background. (With the important exception of illegitimate moth-ers, the poorest sectors are absent from these cases as they are from virtually all civil litigation.) The alimentos petitions reflect the impor-tance of kin as sources of support, particularly in moments of crisis (marital abandonment, widowhood, illness, economic adversity) as well as how individuals prevailed on the courts to enforce claims that, as one petitioner put it, were based in both "civil laws" as well as "natural law."[20]

By enforcing alimentos payments among the legitimate members of wealthy families, moreover, the courts observed the principle of social congruity, the legal enforcement of status parity between parents and children discussed in chapter 2. In one case, a son sought alimentos pay-ments from his wealthy father to help him through some economic problems. The father refused, declaring that he had numerous children to support and that the petitioning son, who enjoyed a generous inheritance from his mother, was undeserving because he had married against his father's will. The court ruled for the son, declaring that the father's griev-ance, however well founded, did not excuse him from "the obligation to support in a *congruous manner* the petitioner and [the petitioner's] chil-dren."[21] Such an argument suggests that the purpose of alimentos was not simply to provide succor but to reproduce status cross-generationally.

As the judge's ruling further suggests, another meaning attached to family in this social context is that of material *obligation*, as opposed to mere voluntary benefaction. Kindred were individuals bound by a re-sponsibility, both legal and moral, for mutual support. Family ties were distinguished in this sense from social relationships of assistance medi-ated by charity. By extension, one who lacked natal kin was thrown to the mercy of charity, particularly during childhood. This juxtaposition of kin obligation and charitable largesse is evident in the case of a man described in the following way: "He does not have known parents . . . he is helpless [*desamparado*] and would have died if charity had not come to his rescue."[22] This meaning of kinship explains why determining the nature of a man's support and succor was so critical to paternity suits, as described in previous chapters: while paternalistic largesse could look a lot like paternal solicitude, law and social practice understood these forms of assistance to be distinct. This was because living among kin and living without them, at the behest of charity, implied two fundamentally different social conditions.

The Social and Material Matrices of Natal Alienation

And yet in a society in which kinship conferred both status and legal/moral claims to material support, some individuals became detached from the moorings of natal belonging. The sources hint, subtly but insistently, at an underclass of kinless individuals with no connections to, claims on, or sometimes even knowledge of a natal family. There was a term for such individuals: they were the huachos. As noted in the introduction, a huacho was a foundling or orphan, a waif, a bastard, or someone of dubious origins. The word usually referred to children—but not always, suggesting that the condition it referenced remained relevant in adulthood, as Pablo Pérez's narrative implies. It was generally derogatory, as when Bernardo O'Higgin's political enemies snubbed him as *el huacho Riquelme* (substituting the matronym Riquelme for the patronym O'Higgins), when it was invoked as a term of scorn to refer to poor children, or when disputants lobbed it at one another in verbal altercations. But especially in the diminutive (*huachito*), it could also be affectionate in a paternalistic way. Occasionally the term was a neutral descriptor of orphanhood, as when an individual seeking to place a baby in the Casa de Huérfanos explained that she "had become a huacha" (*ha quedado guacha*) because her mother had died and she had no one else to care for her. The term captures the social and cultural significance of natal ties and hints at the frequency with which they were broken.[23]

The phenomenon of natal dispossession was hardly specific to nineteenth-century Chile. The quintessential kinless individuals, foundlings,

were common fixtures of Latin American societies beginning in the sixteenth century. In some communities, as many as half of all children were
baptized as expósitos (foundlings) or *de padres no conocidos* (of unknown parents).[24] One common term used to refer to them, *hijos de la
iglesia*, children of the Church, reflects the real or assumed absence of a
(human) filiation.[25] To be sure, baptismal status should never be read as
a transparent indication of an individual's familial condition (or lack
thereof): children baptized as foundlings might be quietly reared by natal
kin, just as those registered as illegitimate might lead lives indistinguishable from their legitimate counterparts.[26] Still, it is clear that kinlessness
was a pervasive phenomenon.

The ubiquity of abandoned children in Latin America has often been
read as a byproduct of the rigid dictates of a gendered culture of honor.
To avoid shame, many have argued, unmarried mothers were forced to
give up the fruits of their sin. But kinlessness was also the product of
particular demographic realities, labor practices, and frontier violence.
And everywhere it was inflected by the ethnic and racial politics of colonial and postcolonial societies. For example, the population crises of
Indian communities were associated with widespread orphanhood and
rising numbers of foundlings.[27] Slavery obviously cut people off from kin
networks but so too could other coercive labor arrangements. A census
of household servants conducted in late-seventeenth-century La Paz revealed many Indian servants who "said they did not know either of their
parents, that is had no knowledge of who engendered them." A similar
situation seems to have prevailed among young Indian servants in colonial Lima. Meanwhile, in seventeenth-century northern New Spain,
many children and youth baptized as expósitos were in fact indigenous
war captives.[28] Kinlessness in such scenarios was a deliberate strategy to
cut youngsters off from family, community, and ethnic group, the better
to impose on them servility and dependence.

In some places, plebeian subcultures arose in which lineage "was not
central to self-definition." Poor people in late-seventeenth- and early-
eighteenth-century Mexico City, according to Douglas Cope, "had only a
vague knowledge of their lineage" and little knowledge even of immediate
kin. Surnames were not passed from parents to children in any regular
pattern, and the urban poor tended to rely more on nicknames and
occupational or racial descriptors to identify people.[29]

Meanwhile, in other circumstances, natal dispossession was strategically embraced. In a corporatist colonial order, natal status constituted
an advantageous birthright for some and a social and legal impediment
for many others. In this context, an unfavorable natal status might be
worse than no natal status at all. This was the case for men in colonial
Quito and New Spain who claimed to be expósitos. In casting deliberate
doubt on their ethnoracial provenance, they evaded the tribute obligations borne by Indians and *castas* (people of mixed race). At the other
extreme of socioracial hierarchies, Spanish American elites born of stigmatized adulterous or sacrilegious unions might find it preferable to
embrace the hazy social and legal status of expósito. In these disparate
contexts, originlessness may have been socially stigmatized, but it could
also be a relatively privileged condition to which individuals laid calculated (and often fictitious) claim. The potential appeal of kinlessness was
further enhanced after a royal decree in the 1790s declared all foundlings
to be legitimate, honorable *hijos del rey*, children of the king, exempt
from tribute. In some parts of the empire, the decree was followed by a
suspicious rise in the numbers of "foundlings."[30]

With the republican abolition of legal caste hierarchies, the meanings
of kinlessness became less ambiguous. In late-nineteenth-century Chile,
there existed no legal incentive to obfuscate ethnic background. As for
natal status, while it was common for illegitimates to feign legitimacy,
the status of expósito per se posed no obvious social or legal advantage.
Civil law's categorical emphasis on paternal prerogative made the strategic manipulation of kinlessness moot. The only operative legal distinction was between legitimate and extramarital progeny, and in the latter
case, between the recognized and the unrecognized. I have found no
instances in which individuals of any class or ethnic background purposefully adopted an identity as expósitos; on the other hand, there are
many cases of kinless individuals accused of attempting to "pass" as
members of other people's families.[31] In contrast to the colonial period,
when disfavored castes might embrace natal anonymity strategically and
plebeian subcultures might ignore lineage altogether, the evidence suggests that in nineteenth-century Chile the social stigma and legal and
material disadvantages of natal alienation were categorical and affected
people of all classes.

What caused kinlessness in republican society in the first place? Significantly, it was not coterminous with subalternity. Families of inquilinos—the resident labor force on haciendas—often remained on particular estates for generations and at least according to some accounts harbored a deep genealogical memory. One oft-cited commentator of mid-nineteenth-century agrarian society observed:

> Each hacienda is a population that is more or less numerous, composed of families that have their own surname [*apellido*] and that recognize and respect kin relations. There isn't an hacienda that doesn't have old families of inquilinos, which maintain memories and traditions of their ancestors. Just as Santiago has its great families of Larraines, Errázuriz, Vicuñas, Cerdas and Toros; Talca its Cruces, its Vergaras and its Donosos; Concepción its Mendiburus, its Benaventes, its Zañartu and its Manzanos; la Serena its Munizagas, its Varas and its Solares; so too an hacienda has its large and notable families . . . the Ponces, the Carranzas, the Carocas, the Aguilas, the Montesinos, the Pobletes, etc.

The anonymous commentator went on to contrast the inquilino's relationship to place, kin, and property to that of his rootless alter ego, the peon. While the inquilino was "almost always married, a father of a family [*padre de familia*] and man accustomed to work and to economy," the peon, an unskilled worker who circulated across rural and urban economies in response to fluctuating demand for his labor, was "regularly single, [without] land or family or property that obliges him to adopt a fixed home."[32]

To be sure, this passage says as much about the commentator's valorization of place, property, and patriarchy as it does about the domestic habits of rural dwellers. The notorious lack of documentation on inquilinos in particular makes it difficult to corroborate whether they conserved the "memories and traditions of ancestors" as this author asserts.[33] But if they did, then the contrast between inquilinos and peons suggests it was not poverty per se, but rather the way poverty articulated with particular kinds of labor arrangements and household structures, that inhibited multigenerational kin continuity and generated kinlessness. While peons sold their labor as individuals to a market that valued their unskilled, low-wage mobility and flexibility, the system of inquilinaje relied on a household economy involving the labor of women and children as well as the male head. It is the nature of their engagement with broad economic and labor structures that explains inquilinos' patriarchal households and deep genealogical awareness, and peons' alienation from them.

Whatever genealogical proclivities inquilinos harbored, however, were likely being undermined by the evolution of inquilinaje in the latter half of the nineteenth century. With the development of commercial agriculture and the rationalization of land use, hacendados increasingly turned extra laborers off their lands and augmented the service burdens of those who remained. In the latter half of the nineteenth century, unskilled, landless peons constituted a majority of the labor force. As the sons and daughters of inquilinos left the haciendas in search of other sources of livelihood, the time-honored distinction between inquilinos and peons was blurred.[34] Changing labor arrangements probably impacted associated patterns of social reproduction.[35]

Kinlessness was most prevalent within this propertyless, rootless milieu, in which the threads of lineal descent were tenuous and ever subject to rupture. It is the children of this milieu, the sons and daughters of peons and servants, laborers and laundresses, who were likely to be rendered kinless. In turn, they joined the social and occupational ranks of their progenitors.[36] The nature of labor markets, the migratory patterns they compelled, the grinding poverty of the majority of the population, and the absence of a material base for the formation of enduring kin groups all contributed to prevailing filiation patterns.

Such material realities were in turn always structured by gender. Female headship and illegitimacy were rampant, but poor women on their own were hard pressed to support themselves and their offspring due to limited employment opportunities and miserable wages. As we have seen, civil law reforms only exacerbated this situation by freeing men of legal responsibility for illegitimate offspring. Letters left with children abandoned at the Casa de Huérfanos narrate this gendered crisis of subsistence. "It has cost me almost my life to maintain him from day to day, with no more help than that of my hands, that is, of my work, the work of a poor woman," wrote one mother who, finding herself unemployed, was no longer able to support her one-year-old. Another declared of her newborn, "I cannot maintain him any more because my milk dried up which is how I could work as a wet nurse to pay for him." And a patrón wrote of his servant: "[She is] mother of three children and she has no other means of survival than her poor work as a cook; but because

of her many young children, she can't find work, because no one wants
to admit her as a servant with her children."[37] More than 50,000 children passed through Santiago's orphanage between the 1850s and the
1920s. While a majority of them did not survive infancy, those who did,
like Pablo Pérez, routinely lost basic knowledge of their provenance.[38] A
major casualty of the gendered crisis of subsistence was thus children and
their foothold within kin networks.

The People without History

If we can explain the circumstances of their making, can we also recover
the voices of the kinless themselves? Methodologically speaking, kinless
individuals are extremely difficult to locate. Kinlessness was a stigmatized condition defined precisely by an absence of information or knowledge. Often it was associated with unrecorded birth and hence legal
nonexistence. But because the most definitive ruptures were those that
occurred early in life, it is through a focus on children that the natally
dispossessed most often appear in the historical record.

They emerge, for example, in scenarios of child circulation, the cultural
practice in which children were informally reared in nonnatal, "foster"
households.[39] Personal identities might be altered or lost at any point
along the circuitous routes that children traversed. Kinship did not require coresidence, and natal kin ties could and did endure when children
circulated across households. But in its most exploitive guises, child
circulation entailed a form of bondage associated with natal alienation.
This was so both because children dispossessed of kin networks were
rendered vulnerable to servitude and also because some masters apparently erased children's origins deliberately—and with them, the custodial claims of their kin. The mutability of circulating children's names
suggests the tenuous quality of their identity. One boy around thirteen
whose custody was disputed between two caretakers told a court his
name was Eusebio Flores, "though he was known as José Piñeiro when he
was in Casa-Blanca, in the care of Benjamín Larrosa."[40] Some children
lost natal surnames and over time assumed those of their patrones; as we
will see in chapter 6, this often signaled not incorporation into a new
kin group so much as paternalistic subordination to patrones.[41] Courts

sometimes encountered young servants rendered legally inscrutable by their lack of natal identities, providing a glimpse of a social phenomenon that left only anecdotal traces in the historical record. These were the people without history, and their life stories—or lack thereof—help illustrate the contours of kinlessness and its consequences.

One such person was the adolescent servant María Ramírez. In 1895, Ramírez's mistress accused her of absconding with some jewelry. Ramírez denied the charge and countered that her mistress had physically mistreated her. Ramírez's was a particular form of servitude: as her mistress noted, she had reared the girl since she was ten months old. As such, what knowledge of origins she had was based on what others chose to tell her. Called to make the standard statement of self-identification before the judge, the accused, who thought herself to be around twenty years old and could sign her name but not read or write, declared: "I do not know my surnames because according to what I have heard I was brought from Araucania [to Santiago] and the last name I use is that of my patrones." Her patrona's surname was less a mark of adoptive belonging than an emblem of her alienation. What she did upon leaving the household where she had lived and labored her entire life is revealing: she ceased to be María Ramírez, adopting a new name (not recorded in the transcript).[42]

Ramírez was thus an illiterate, lifelong servile dependent with no kin ties, no surname of her own, and limited knowledge of her provenance. Her plight illustrates how for young servants the loss of identity was part of a larger complex of subordination.[43] Four months after her brush with the law, another young servant appeared in a Santiago criminal court. Prosperina Saavedra's fragmentary statement of self-identification echoed that of Ramírez: "I use my maternal surname because I don't know my father's name, I was born in the south but I don't know where, I don't know how old I am, single, domestic servant, I don't know how to read or write, and first arrest." While her antecedents echoed those of Ramírez, Saavedra's crime was significantly more serious: she stood accused of drowning her infant daughter in a canal. What is more, she readily admitted to the crime, explaining she had killed the child because the baby jeopardized her ability to support herself as a servant. The ensuing judicial investigation focused not on Saavedra's crime but on the court's attempt to elucidate her origins. This was because her lack of identity confounded an essential determinant of criminal culpability: age. The Penal Code stipulated different penalties according to a defendant's status as a minor or adult. In order to mete out punishment, the court needed to know when Saavedra had been born. The very definitions of other crimes, such as sexual abduction (*rapto*) and rape, were dependent on the age of the victim. Thus, kinlessness surfaced in legal proceedings when the age of young defendants and victims proved indeterminate.[44]

Questioned repeatedly about her origins, Saavedra could recall only that her mother's name was Pabla, but she did not know if she was alive, and if so, where she was. "According to her memories," Saavedra had been brought to Santiago from rural Colchagua as a young child. The woman who had raised her had died, and she supported herself as a domestic. It is unlikely that Saavedra had additional information about her background that she withheld, since her kinlessness did not help her legal situation in any obvious way.

With no documentary evidence or witness testimony to go on, Prosperina Saavedra's identity became a medicolegal problem. The court called in doctors to read the defendant's physical person for alternative venues of identity. A medical report concluded, "Given the bone development, the fact of having only four molars, and her physical appearance, we believe she is 17 or 18 years old." Radically alienated from her natal origins, Saavedra had become an inscrutable legal subject, a civil nonperson reduced to a physical body—to bones, to teeth, to a "physical appearance." The court's procedure in the case suggests how the natally dispossessed suffered, if not a social death as in Orlando Patterson's phrase, then a kind of civil one.[45] The court's dilemma further illustrates the significance of natal origins to legal procedure and to the state's reading of legal subjects, an issue taken up in the following chapter.

By the turn of the twentieth century, the phenomenon of rootless, unskilled peonage had reached its high-water mark, to be slowly undone by the expansion of capitalist labor relations and processes of proletarianization.[46] Yet the kinless persist in the historical record through the early twentieth century. Indeed if anything, their condition becomes ever more conspicuous against the backdrop of an increasingly bureaucratized state. In the late 1920s, three decades after María Ramírez and Prosperina Saavedra's criminal imbroglios, a member of the Chamber of

Deputies described to his colleagues an encounter with several members
of the *gremio de suplementeros*, the union of newspaper boys. At once
pitied and reviled, young newspaper boys were a common fixture on the
streets of early-twentieth-century Chilean cities. They were notorious
for having no homes, no parents—in short, no origins.[47] The suplementeros had approached Deputy Abraham Quevedo Vega, a member of the
Communist Party, with the following problem: while municipal ordi-
nances required that they present their birth certificates to ply their
trade, many of them had no such document. This was because, as Quevedo put it, "among them, there are those who never knew their father
nor mother and were never recorded in any registry." In other words,
they were *hijos de Don Nadie*, children of Mr. Nobody. It was a problem,
Quevedo admitted, that "took me by surprise." Describing to his fellow
deputies his fruitless consultations with lawyers and civil registry officials
to determine how to "save the situation of the civil state [legal identity] of
these children," he appealed to authorities to be lenient with the suplementeros lest the regulations "create obstacles for the exercise of this
trade . . . [and] incite the children to delinquency . . . [or] laziness."[48]

Reproducing Kinlessness:
The Making of "Genealogical Isolates"

Natal alienation hindered penal procedure and made it difficult for newspaper boys to make a living. But its most systemic consequence was the
impediment it posed to marriage. It is not by chance that Pablo Pérez
came face to face with his kinlessness in the course of bureaucratic
preparations to wed: both civil and ecclesiastical procedures surrounding
marriage required knowledge of and documentation verifying natal origins. As a result of such requirements, natal alienation systematically
impeded legitimate family formation.

The nuptial quandary of Josefa Torres echoes that of Pérez.[49] As a child
in the 1920s, Torres was interned in the Sociedad Protectora de la Infancia, the asylum discussed in the introduction. Decades later, in 1961, a
patron wrote to the mother superior of the Protectora on Torres's behalf,
requesting information about her baptism. Torres wished to marry in the
Church, but as the patron noted, "for this one needs a baptismal certifi-

cate, which we have looked for everywhere without finding." Both the prospective bride and her patron had already made multiple visits to the Protectora in search of information but had found no one willing or able to help. They could offer only an estimate of when Torres had been placed in the asylum: "more or less in the years 1923–24–25, until 1933." Her condition echoed that of Pérez, Ramírez, Saavedra, and the newspaper boys: "She does not know her date of birth. She does not know the name of her parents. She does not know who placed her in the Protectora." The letter concluded with the patron's entreaty: "Reverend Mother, I understand that you have a lot of work, but please answer this letter with some information, because in so doing, you will contribute to the salvation of two souls." To the legal and material repercussions of originlessness, we can add, in the case of Torres, spiritual repercussions as well.

Someone searched for the requested information, because the letter was tucked into the Protectora's registry on the page recording Torres's entry. As it turned out, Torres's natal dispossession stemmed not from her status as an anonymous foundling but rather from bureaucratic disregard. What the entry books noted, but what Torres herself apparently did not remember and had never been told, was that she had been brought to the Protectora at age seven, together with an older sister. The girls were from Talagante, a small town outside Santiago, and they had been orphaned. Presumably whoever had taken the time to review multiple volumes in search of Torres's information had forwarded these findings to the letter writer, though it is impossible to know for sure. Nor do we know if Torres eventually managed to procure her baptismal certificate or to marry in the Church.[50]

A half-century earlier, in 1911, a papal decree had instituted a formal requirement that brides and grooms present baptismal certificates to marry. Over the next few years, the provision would provoke numerous inquiries from perturbed parish priests and occasionally from prospective spouses to Chilean ecclesiastical authorities.[51] The purpose of the decree was innocuous enough: it was intended to ensure that those participating in the sacrament of marriage had already benefited from the sacrament of baptism. But grafted onto the realities of Chilean social reproduction, as one official from La Serena noted, "This disposition has encountered not a few difficulties in practice.[52] Like Pérez and Torres, many Chilean brides and grooms simply did not have baptismal certificates and did not know where to find them. In effect, the decree made it difficult for people like them to form a family recognized by the Church.

In their quotidian encounters with kinless spouses, Chilean ecclesiastical officials wrestled with the canonical and ethical implications of the papal decree. Was knowledge of one's natal family a prerequisite to marriage? Should kinless individuals actually be prevented from marrying? In fact, these were not new quandaries for Chilean ecclesiastics. While the 1911 decree was the first clear papal directive regarding the matter, it appears that priests had routinely required spouses to present baptismal certificates even before the decree. Moreover, the banns published before marriage typically included information on the filiation of the couple. Proof of kinship was also necessary to prevent consanguineous unions, and minors were obliged to obtain parental consent to marry. Such requirements applied to religious nuptials and, after 1883, civil ones as well. The lack of a legally verifiable family origin, in short, had long posed a potential impediment to marriage.

To be sure, the impediment was not categorical since it was possible to circumvent many of the regulations through alternative procedures. Parentless minors could petition the court for a legal guardian to offer consent.[53] Those marrying in the Church could request dispensations. But while the Church hierarchy always claimed to maintain a flexible bureaucratic posture, on the ground, local priests had wide interpretive latitude. In fact, exchanges between local officials and ecclesiastical higher-ups give the impression that parish priests were often more rigid in applying the rules than were their superiors. In the 1870s, the archbishop of Santiago overruled a parish priest who refused to issue a couple's banns because the groom lacked a filiation.[54] A similar dynamic seems to have been at play in the civil bureaucracy.[55] To the question about whether kinless people should be prevented from marrying, the answer, it seems, depended on whom one asked.

While kinless individuals could circumvent nuptial impediments through specially appointed guardians and dispensations and by lobbying for a generous interpretation of the rules, such measures cost time and money. One parentless bride succeeded in obtaining a legal guardian to give consent for her marriage only after three months of judicial haggling.[56] If the poor were those least likely to possess a verifiable filiation and a valid baptismal certificate, they were also those least equipped to work the system. Their plight was hardly a reality unique to Chile. Latin American societies have historically exhibited low rates of marriage, and in nineteenth-century Brazil, according to Sandra Lauderdale Graham, stringent nuptial requirements were in part to blame: "Those without known parents or whose whereabouts were lost, or those of uncertain birthplace or date could barely construct the necessary proofs of eligibility." Ironically, African slaves, whose alienation from natal origins was particularly brutal and absolute, may have found it easier to marry than the free poor, since ecclesiastical provisions excused slave spouses from presenting the requisite documentation.[57] In Chile, where all citizens were formally free and equal, no special allowances would be made to alleviate the burdens of nuptial bureaucracy. Yet this burden clearly did not fall with equal weight on all spouses.

If bureaucratic impediments were at issue, so too was the fact that nuptial rituals publicly revealed a spouse's stigmatized condition. The prospect of public shame through the marriage banns created an additional obstacle to marriage, social rather than legal. Such was the case of one expósita who, seeking to "avoid the shame of presenting herself at the altar without having her own, known surname" (*un apellido propio y conocido*), falsely claimed kinship in a foster family. And then there is Nathaniel Miers-Cox's request to the archbishop to dispense public proclamations for spouses reared in the foundling home. Spouses who could afford it could purchase dispensations to avoid disclosure of their unfavorable natal condition. For those who could not, the prospect of public revelation may have created an additional disincentive to marry.[58]

As a result of these bureaucratic and social dynamics, a lack of natal origins impeded legitimate family formation. Kinlessness, in other words, became self-perpetuating. If Pablo Pérez's autobiography is the story of a search for origins, it is simultaneously about the pursuit of a legitimate family: "I have concluded my history and adventures up to my present age of thirty-four. Currently, I [am] still alone and unfortunate for not having been able to fulfill my aspirations and desires which are to constitute a family legally."[59] His narrative thus posits the two quests—finding his natal family and forming his own legitimate one—as parallel and complementary.

Finally, beyond the bureaucratic crucible of marriage, there is an even more extreme case of kin dispossession. This is the dispossession, both ascending and descending, of an individual like Prosperina Saavedra, the kinless servant who admitted to murdering her infant daughter. With no family of origin and the obliteration of her own descendant, she represents a particularly stark example of genealogical isolation. Her kinlessness was both a consequence, and a cause, of her highly precarious social and material situation.[60] In a parallel vein, letters left with children at the Casa de Huérfanos sometimes noted that the mothers of the children were themselves parentless. One infant was identified as the child of a *niña de la Casa*, "a girl of the Casa," that is, she was the offspring of a young woman who herself had been reared there. The references to mothers' orphanhood, presumably intended to substantiate their dire need for the asylum's assistance, speak to the general importance of kin ties and the vulnerability of those who lacked them. More specifically, they draw a connection between the absence of ascending kin ties and the loss of descending ones, hinting at the ways kinlessness might be perpetuated.[61]

Conclusions: Alienation and Belonging

The plight of Prosperina Saavedra, the socially isolated mothers of Casa children, and kinless spouses like Pablo Pérez and Josefa Torres evoke Orlando Patterson's notion of natal alienation as an essential characteristic of slavery. Patterson has argued that "the slave's . . . loss of ties of birth in both ascending and descending generations" is a defining feature of bondage across cultures and history. "This alienation of the slave from all formal, legally enforceable ties of blood, and from any attachment to groups or localities other than those chosen for him by the master," he argues, "gave the relation of slavery its peculiar value to the master."[62] The kinless huachos of nineteenth-century Chile were not slaves. Slavery was illegal after 1823, and natal alienation was not imposed by masters acting within a legal structure that systematically denied certain individuals the right to kin ties. On the contrary, a Chilean lawmaker could assert, apropos of the new civil marriage law of 1883, that "the right to form a family is inherent to the status of man and citizen."[63] Nor was the natal alienation of this Chilean underclass as radical as in the case of slaves. An inability to marry and have legitimate offspring surely does not rise to the same level of violence implied by the forced, legally sanctioned separation of parents and children, an experience slaves routinely suffered.

On the other hand, if the servitude of young huachos in Chile was not legal slavery, these social arrangements were still manifestly unfree. Masters had a clear incentive to foment their dependents' natal alienation in order to enhance their custodial claims. Likewise, the kinless women who abandoned their children at the Casa were not usually forced to do so, but given their dire poverty, nor were their decisions regarding their children free in any meaningful sense.[64] And as we have seen, through marriage regulation there existed a systematic relationship between an individual's alienation from ascending and descending generations, such that the Chilean kinless underclass could resemble the "genealogical isolates" that Patterson references.[65] While not legally mandated, then, genealogical alienation was nevertheless tacitly reproduced through law, both ecclesiastical and civil. Finally, in a society that valorized legitimacy, and in which many people subscribed to Catholic notions of marriage as sacrament, the proscription of legitimate or religiously sanctioned marriage and procreation was its own form of social violence. Illegitimate kinship was not the same as legitimate kinship, socially, legally, or spiritually, and some individuals, like Pablo Pérez, clearly perceived it as a form of alienation.

In nineteenth-century Chile, membership in a family constituted an important aspect of subjectivity, self-definition, and status for people of all class backgrounds. This was most obviously true of elites. Kinship and marriage ties structured political and economic power, of course, but as elites' florid paeans to genealogical belonging suggest, they also provided a sense of collective identity. Among more modest sectors, kin belonging also marked social respectability, and as the alimentos cases attest, conferred material entitlements (as well as obligations.)

It is in its absence, however, that the significance of kinship becomes most evident. An underclass grew up with little notion of their parents' or godparents' identities, their natal surnames, or information about their place or date of birth or baptism. In a society without slavery, a republic of formal equality, kinlessness articulated with stigma, civil discrimination, social marginality, and unfreedom. The broad lesson to be drawn from both the slave societies Patterson examines and the different but related case of late-nineteenth-century Chile is that kinship, filiation, and genealogy symbolically and socially structure particular forms of subordination and inequality. This relationship is a central theme of this book.

I have found no further trace of Pablo Pérez following the publication of his autobiography, but it seems unlikely that he ever succeeded in locating his mother or his baptismal certificate. His experience finds a fictional parallel in the story of Gabriela, protagonist of the Brazilian novelist Jorge Amado's celebrated *Gabriela, Clove and Cinnamon*, situated in early-twentieth-century Bahia. A poor migrant from the interior, Gabriela wishes to marry but has no birth certificate, no last name, and no knowledge of her birthplace. The fictional Gabriela and her true-life counterparts in Chile—the prospective spouses, the newspaper boys, and the accused servants—are of course all distinguished by their lack of origins. They share an additional commonality as well: their kinlessness is revealed through encounters with civil and ecclesiastical officialdom, municipal authority, and the courts. This is not by chance. Kinship was a legal and bureaucratic category as well as a social practice. Ultimately, Gabriela is able to wed when an enterprising local notary invents a false entry in the birth registry, thereby resolving her lack of origins.[66] But inherent in the power of legal inscription was the converse power of omission and suppression: if civil authority could grant a natal identity through bureaucratic subterfuge, it could expunge identity with equal facility. As we will see in the following chapter, this is precisely what Chilean civil law and bureaucracy did.

CHAPTER 4

Birthrights:

Natal Dispossession and the State

The War Widow

It was April 1883, in the waning days of the War of the Pacific, when the widow Estefania Lesana wrote in outraged desperation to the president of the republic. Her husband José Jesus López had been killed at the battle of Miraflores, leaving her and their small children destitute. "While I have sold or pawned all my little garments and rags in order to obtain the unpaid salary of my deceased husband and likewise reward and compensation payment, all my hopes have been frustrated," she lamented. Her appeals to officials in the small town of Quillota had proven fruitless. She had sold "the little horse and mount" and relocated to Santiago to pursue bureaucratic recourse, but this too had been in vain. More than two years after her husband's death, Lesana had yet to receive a peso. As a last resort, she appealed to "Your Excellency [who is] the father of all of us poor widows" to provide her with alms, as she had run out of money in Santiago and was returning to Quillota "to die of hunger."[1]

Lesana's experience was by all accounts common. The war with Peru and Bolivia stimulated an unprecedented expansion of Chile's economy and territory. But it proved devastating for the 45,000 soldiers mobilized and their families, the majority of whom were poor. In the wake of the conflict, politicians and the popular press alike denounced *el pago de Chile*, "Chile's recompense," meaning the nation's miserly treatment of its veterans. In December 1881, more than two years into the conflict and with casualties mounting, the Chilean government promulgated a compensation law (*lei de recompensas*) awarding benefits to survivors.[2] But as

Lesana's appeal suggests, mandating benefits was one thing, receiving them quite another. The flurry of petitions filed in the archives of the Ministry of War and the civil courts reflects the difficulties that soldiers' families faced in obtaining benefits.[3] The most common problem was also the most basic: that of proving kinship to the deceased. Unstable names, rampant illegitimacy, migration, and excessively exacting bureaucratic standards all complicated families' efforts to establish their legal identity.

A major part of the problem was the deplorable state of parish records, which served as the documentary basis of identity. "On innumerable occasions death, baptism or marriage were not recorded in the parish archives," observed the Sociedad Protectora, an organization of distinguished citizens organized to assist beneficiaries with their claims. "There have been cases . . . in which a single individual appears with one name in their baptismal certificate, a different one in their marriage certificate, and still another in that of their children's birth certificates. There has been an entire family born on the same day according to those celebrated registries." The crisis of the parish records provided fuel for another epic conflict, this one waged on the home front: the battle between the Chilean state and the Catholic Church over the secularization of marriage, kinship, and legal identity. As the War of the Pacific drew to a close, this other battle reached its culmination. Over the vehement objections of the Catholic Church and political conservatives, civil marriage and a civil registry were introduced.[4] The reforms would engender controversy for decades to come.

The Chilean state that emerged from the foreign and domestic conflicts of the 1880s was very different from that of the 1850s, the starting point of this book. The three interrelated events mentioned so far—the War of the Pacific, the military compensation law, and the civil registry—reflect some of the most significant aspects of Chilean state formation in the final decades of the nineteenth century: territorial expansion, capitalist growth, bureaucratization, and secularization. The war brought under Chilean control lucrative nitrate fields that swelled state coffers and fueled a cycle of boom-bust economic expansion that would last until the Great Depression. Enhanced revenues in turn permitted the development of state-led programs and infrastructure, of which the compensation law was an early, relatively minor example. The state's expansion was also associated with a concerted effort to subordinate the Catholic Church to secular authority, an impetus reflected in civil marriage and the civil registry as well as in the secularization of cemeteries and education.

Estefania Lesana's plight reflects how a poor, provincial widow weathered some of these changes. Her experience also speaks to the growing relevance of civil bureaucracy in the lives of popular sectors. This relationship was often mediated through a key referent of law and administration: kinship. The need to safeguard the transmission of inheritance meant that legal kinship had always been important to propertied individuals. But the dilemma of soldiers' families suggests the need of a critical mass of *propertyless* citizens to establish kinship as a legal matter, perhaps for the first time. Indeed, the growing bureaucratization of a state with new resources at its disposal would make legal kinship an ever more important asset.

While the previous chapter showed how kinship constituted a cultural referent, material resource, and social marker in late-nineteenth-century Chile, the present chapter explores its multidimensional life as a legal and administrative category. For the Catholic Church, consanguinity and filiation were categories germane to the administration of sacraments. For the state, kinship was key because emerging social benefits were based on the gendered and generational dependencies of family. But beyond the obvious example of family-based welfare programs, I will argue that the state drew more broadly on family membership to fix individual identity and constitute legal subjects. Indeed, kinship was central to the architecture of civil law: through the concept of *estado civil*, or civil state, kin relations underpinned civil identity. While chapters 1 and 2 explored how family law reinscribed social hierarchies, this chapter argues that filiation transcended family law, infusing aspects of civil law and bureaucratic practice that had no obvious bearing on family. In short, it elucidates the central place of filiation and kinship to Chilean, and perhaps Latin American, liberal state practice.

The deployment of kinship as an administrative and legal category reflected a paradox, however. For even as filiation was central to sacrament, bureaucracy, and civil law, in practice administrative protocols tended to obfuscate it. This chapter shows how bureaucracies ranging from welfare asylums to the newly minted civil registry systematically omitted or suppressed the natal origins of children born extramaritally.

In this way, the two great milestones of nineteenth-century secularization and liberal state making in Chile—the Civil Code and the civil registry—served to alienate large numbers of people from their legal ties to family. In other words, the problem of kinlessness explored in the last chapter—the existence of people who lacked any kin ties or knowledge of natal identity—was in part a product of state policy.

Moreover, if kinship harbored meanings related to class and status in cultural practice, this was no less true in legal and administrative practice. The state's deployment of kinship and kinlessness reinscribed social and legal hierarchies not only within families but also between them. In liberal practice, filiation systematically and in a broad range of civic bureaucracies functioned as a vector of legal and social discrimination.

Kinship, Legibility, and Legal Personhood

Some of the ways family served as a conceptual referent for state making and ecclesiastical activities have been alluded to already. The state's regulation of support payments (alimentos) between kin was clearly contingent upon its capacity to ascertain how people were related to each other. An incipient system of public benefits was also mapped onto family relations. The wartime compensation law of the 1880s presaged the gradual evolution of other benefits in the twentieth century, including worker's compensation, social security, and the family allowance. Like its wealthier and more expansive counterparts in Europe and North America, the Chilean welfare state structured benefits around familial dependencies.

Ecclesiastical practice, too, was concerned with kin relations. The complex provisions surrounding consanguinity in canon marriage law required that parish priests know how prospective spouses were related to one another. Ecclesiastical law also mandated the routine inclusion of filiation in marriage and death registration—though as the previous chapter makes clear, such information was not always available.[5] Even as Church and state struggled over the prerogative to define and oversee kin relations—the issue at the heart of the conflict over civil marriage and the civil registry—they evinced a parallel preoccupation with this category of social relations.

Beyond welfare benefits or sacramental protocols, kinship proved central to bureaucratic efforts to apprehend individual identity. In his suggestive analysis of modern state power, James Scott has argued that state making is premised on "legibility," that is, the ability of the state to "read" its populace and its environment. Without knowledge of "subjects, their wealth, their landholdings and yields, their location, their very identity," such elementary state-making activities as collecting taxes or forming a draft are impossible. Part of the history of state formation is thus the development of strategies to render intelligible states' subjects and the physical environments in which they live.[6]

One characteristic of a legible populace is that individuals have stable and distinguishable identities. Official documentation fixing identity is thus a crucial tool of legibility. Like the parish records that preceded it, the Chilean civil registry constituted just such a tool, recording births, marriages, and deaths. Established in 1884, the registry fixed identity in order to establish an individual's legal rights and obligations vis-à-vis other people as well as the state. For example, it was used to verify certain attributes of the individual, such as age, which had a whole series of civil effects: age determined punishment in criminal cases, eligibility for the draft and National Guard service, the ability to marry without parental consent, and, among the propertied, voting rights.

Yet even as the registry served as the basis for *individual* identity, most attributes it established were in fact *family*-based. This was obviously true of the marriage registry, but it was also true of birth and death registries. Birth registration established legal filiation, necessary for determining entitlements such as alimentos and inheritance. Death registration established surviving family members' rights and obligations involving inheritance and the ability to remarry. In summary, the information recorded in the registry demonstrates the extent to which attributes of the individual, and their corresponding civil entitlements and obligations, were inseparable from the individual's placement within a kin network. This is not especially surprising in the case of women, whom nineteenth-century polities understood to be dependents (wives, daughters, mothers) rather than citizens and whose civil status was radically altered by marital status. But it was also true of men. The rights and obligations the registry established—whether a widow's pension or service in the National Guard—were clearly gendered, but individual identity was formulated in reference to familial coordinates for men as well as women.

Other forms of bureaucratic documentation further illustrate the kin-based nature of administrative identity. One of the first forms of state-issued identification in Chile was the *libreta de familia*, or family pass-book, which came into usage with the civil registry. As its name suggests, the libreta adopted as its subject not the individual—the standard subject of the twentieth-century national identity card, the *carnet* or *cédula de identidad*—but the family.[7] The booklet was distributed to couples marrying before a civil authority and served to record information about the marriage and the births (and often deaths) of the couple's children.[8] In organizing the populace into families, the libreta reflected how the late-nineteenth-century Chilean state read the identity of individuals as members of kin units.

Kinship was a standard referent of bureaucratic legibility in even more mundane administrative contexts, such as patient records in charity hospitals. Perhaps predictably, hospital logs recorded marital status and husbands' names for female patients. More surprising is the fact that they recorded *parents'* names for both men and women, regardless of the patient's age.[9] The identification of wet nurses employed by the Santiago foundling home reflected similar protocols. At any given time, the asylum monitored hundreds of women distributed across Santiago and its rural environs, who cared for the orphans in their homes.[10] In an effort to track the nurses and their charges, it recorded the woman's name, place of residence, and the name of the landowner or patrón on whose property she lived. As the network of nurses grew, it also began to record the woman's maternal and paternal surnames, and by extension, her filiation. Thus, nurses were typically identified in the form "María Vilches i Armijo" or "Juana Olivos i Quintero." Illegitimate women were listed with only one surname, as in "González i N." ("N." meaning "unknown"), "Peta Cortés (natural) [natural, or illegitimate, daughter]," or even "Juana Reyes, sin padre [no father]."[11] There is no reason to believe the institution was interested in the legitimacy of the nurses or the identity of their parents per se. The recording of such information simply reflected the terms by which it apprehended individual identity.[12]

The ubiquity of familial referents across diverse bureaucracies reflects not only how authorities sought to make the Chilean populace legible but, even more fundamentally, how they conceived of and constituted legal personhood. The kin-based attributes of civil subjects are best reflected in the concept of estado civil. An estado civil, according to the

Civil Code, was "the quality of an individual that empowers him or her to exercise certain rights or contract certain obligations." Or as one jurist noted, it constituted "the essential qualities that define one's permanent place in society."[13] These "qualities" included one's status as a parent or child; legitimate or illegitimate; married, widowed, or single; or an adult or minor still subject to paternal authority. Such qualities or civil states were associated with certain rights and obligations. Indeed, the term *estado civil* was often invoked to refer specifically to marital status (as it is in contemporary usage) and, even more commonly, to filiation. Estado civil thus connoted one's status within a legally recognized kin network. For this reason, illegitimates unrecognized by their parents were said to lack an estado civil.

The concept reflects how the state plotted not only individual identity but indeed civil subjecthood along consanguineal and marital coordinates. In denoting "the legal position a [person] occupies in family and society," estado civil further captures the imbrication of the kin group ("family") and broader social, economic, and political relations ("society").[14] While the rights, obligations, and "essential qualities" that estado civil referenced derived from (and impacted) relations between familial members, it was, as the name suggests, "civil"—that is, legal and public. Estado civil reflects how kinship not only undergirded family law but also constituted a foundational concept of civil personhood generally.

Contrary to liberalism's philosophical emphasis on the autonomous individual, in other words, kinship was central to Latin American liberal statecraft. Critics of liberal theory, most notably feminist scholars, have challenged liberalism's supposition of a neutral subject decoupled from social context and free of ascribed social characteristics. Evidence drawn primarily from the Anglo-American experience has demonstrated how the liberal subject is patently gendered. In Latin America, republican citizenship appears similarly rooted in patriarchy.[15] The concept of estado civil captures additional dimensions of Latin American liberal subjecthood. At its core was ascription of not only gender but also class. For kinship and family were, as explored in the last chapter, deeply invested with cultural meanings related to social status. The state's deployment of family thus implied differentiation and hierarchy not only *within* households or kin groups (between men and women; adults and minors; masters and dependents) but also *between* households or kin groups themselves.

In other words, it constituted a mechanism by which social differentiation was introduced into the ostensibly neutral artifice of civil condition. In keeping with classic liberal theory, the Chilean Civil Code asserted the neutrality of legal personhood, declaring: "All individuals of the human race are people, regardless of their age, sex, pedigree [*estirpe*] or condition" (article 55). But these ascribed characteristics, which according to the Code did not vitiate some essential legal personhood, in judicial practice could become preconditions constitutive of that personhood. More than sixty years after the Civil Code's promulgation, a jurist's subtle rewording of that oft-cited clause turned its categorical assertion of equality on its head: "Before the Law, to be a person, it is necessary to have an age, a sex, a pedigree and a condition, or in other words, to possess an estado civil."[16] The clause asserted a legal personhood existing prior to and regardless of social ascriptions; in this interpretation, personhood was ontologically rooted in these ascriptions.

Precisely this claim was at the heart of a judicial case that worked its way through various courts in the 1920s. In 1921, Doña Elvira Rogat Salas filed suit against her husband of almost fifteen years, Don Manuel Pereira Aránguiz, because, she claimed, he was not who he said he was. "When she married," her representative asserted, Doña Elvira "thought she was doing so with Don Manuel Pereira Aránguiz, and her husband does not have that name, nor is he a legitimate child of the person who supposedly were his parents, nor is he linked through legitimate kinship with the Aránguiz y Fredes family."[17] The precise details of the husband's alleged prevarication are unrecorded. But it is probable that he had grown up in a household of individuals he later falsely claimed as kin, a familiar strategy for concealing kinlessness that we saw in the previous chapter. For Rogat, her husband's "genuine" membership in the Aránguiz y Fredes family was so important because of the status associations, for him and by extension for herself, that such membership implied. Invoking a clause of the civil marriage law that declared unions null and void in cases of errors involving spousal identity, Rogat sought to have her marriage annulled.

But what exactly did a spouse's "identity" consist of? A Santiago judge concluded that annulment was only valid in cases of error involving the identity of the "physical person" whom one wed, not just "the qualities of that person." And then, strikingly, he went on to agree with the aggrieved wife. "The person is not just the individual physically considered," the judge noted, "but . . . the conditions that determine the place that s/he should occupy in society." Or as Doña Elvira's lawyer asserted,

> Just as it is impossible to conceive of a person without age or sex, nor is it possible to imagine one without a pedigree and a condition . . . It is the same to err about the estado civil as to err about the person him/herself, since the one and the other are inseparable, they distinguish the individual, and they give him/her the quality of a . . . legal subject.

In other words, the husband's pedigree—or lack thereof—was intrinsic to his status as a legal subject. In misrepresenting his pedigree, he had fatally distorted his legal identity. Doña Elvira had not married "Don Manuel Pereira Aránguiz," as she believed, and as such the marriage contract was null and void.

The annulment was subsequently overturned by two higher courts. In its reversal, the Corte de Casación invoked among other issues "the democratic spirit of our legislation, which tends toward social leveling." Still, it is striking that as late as the 1920s the argument that pedigree was intrinsic to personhood could be advanced and debated in the highest courts of the nation.[18] Pervasive cultural preoccupations with genealogy and status were firmly ensconced in civil law. There was no neutral legal subject that existed beyond ascriptions not only of age and sex but also of pedigree and concomitant social condition. The etymological root of estado civil in a sense foretells this. The "estado" in *estado civil* derives from "estate," as in the hierarchy of estates. This foundational concept of nineteenth-century liberal law thus references at its conceptual core the ascriptive hierarchies of the ancien regime.[19]

In linking social status and marriage, Doña Elvira's twentieth-century claim evinced eighteenth-century echoes. Specifically, it evoked the Royal Pragmatic on Marriage. Promulgated in the waning days of the Spanish Empire amid endemic racial mixing, the Pragmatic imposed new parental control over children's marriage choices in an effort to enforce endogamy. As a transparent attempt to reinforce race and status distinctions, the Pragmatic reflected the legal manipulation of status that was a hallmark of the colonial society of castes. Republican jurists in Chile rejected social inequality as a rationale for impeding marriage choices.[20] Yet Doña Elvira's suit constituted a kind of latter-day bid for endogamy, petitioned for not by a parent but by a spouse. To be sure, her claim was expressed in conceptual terms far removed from the disputes over marriage choice that parents and children pursued in colonial courts. It revolved around the meanings of concepts like "identity" and "individual." Yet as invoked in this suit, these seemingly innocuous concepts referenced status as surely as did colonial notions of socioracial *calidad* (quality or status). Rogat's petition was arguably more radical than colonial marriage disputes since it involved not averting a prospective union but annulling one already in existence. It shows particularly clearly how legal and civil references to filiation and estado civil harbored meanings related to class and status. As with the taxonomy of filiation, described in chapter 1, and the reinscription of class distinctions in paternity suits, explored in chapter 2, estado civil shows how status hierarchies crept back into ostensibly neutral liberal law by way of the family.

The enduring significance of family as an "associational reference" is clearly not unique to Chile or to Latin America. As Karen Offen has noted, in turn-of-the-century French social and political thought, "the family—not the individual—continued to compose the core unit."[21] The concept of estado civil exists in continental legal tradition, and the libreta de familia was a French invention adopted by Chilean lawmakers. Yet there is a fundamental difference in the invocation of family in these two cultural contexts. Louise Tilly notes that family harbored ideological significance in the French context because of its widespread salience as "an economic productive unit for peasants and craftsmen" and as an "economic resource for propertied and wage earning persons." In other words, family derived its ideological power from the generality of its social relevance.[22] In Chile, meanwhile, invocations of family connoted exclusivity rather than universality. It is not that family was not economically or socially significant to Chileans of all social classes but that its ideological and legal construction was imbued with strong and enduring class significations. In Chile, as in France, the autonomous liberal subject was defined relationally. But the relational matrix within which it was situated differed, for in Chile it was plotted along the coordinates not only of gender and age but also of filiation, genealogy, and status.

Suppressing Kinship: The Orphan as Legal Fiction

In 1885, the year after the civil marriage law went into effect, two young women appeared separately in Valparaíso courts soliciting legal representation. Both were legal minors who desired to marry. Neither had parents or relatives to provide consent, meaning they needed a court-appointed representative to do so. The first woman, Catalina Astorga, provided evidence of her parents' deaths and was assigned a representative. But when the court asked the second young woman, Carmela Arlegui, to verify her orphanhood, she clarified her situation: she was actually an orphan in the legal sense, not the literal one, because she was born out of wedlock. Or as a judicial official put it, Arlegui was "an illegitimate daughter and as such before the law lacks parents and other ascendants to whom to ask for consent."[23]

Arlegui was also assigned a representative, and her condition does not ultimately appear to have prejudiced her nuptial plans. But her legal orphanhood suggests a paradox. Kinship was central to the state's bureaucratic and legal constructs, the basis of both legibility and civil personhood. Yet these same bureaucratic and legal constructs systematically generated legal kinlessness. In depriving illegitimate children of a right to their filiation, the Civil Code denied them legal kinship. A person like Arlegui, who apparently "knew" her parental origin but had not been formally recognized, lacked a family for legal purposes. The kinlessness of illegitimates like her was a legal fiction, and yet the civil and social marginalization it generated could be very real indeed.

The archetypal individual without natal identity or known kin was the foundling. According to classic Western literary and medicolegal portrayals, foundlings were abandoned clandestinely in the anonymous wheels of orphanages by mothers anxious to conceal their identity forever. At least two such wheels, or *turnos*, operated in Santiago in the late nineteenth century, delivering thousands of children to the city's Casa de Huérfanos.[24] Also in deference to parental anonymity, regulations stipulated that no information about provenance or identity was required of children entering the asylum. Personnel were explicitly forbidden to inquire about youngsters' identities with the adults who brought them to the asylum.[25]

Yet the archetypal foundling drama bears little resemblance to the realities of child abandonment in Chile. Placement of children in the Casa de Huérfanos, it turns out, was generally neither anonymous nor clandestine.[26] At least two-thirds of children who entered the asylum arrived with information regarding their family identity and place of origin.[27] Often this information was recorded on an accompanying baptismal certificate, but children were also deposited with letters, notes, and semilegible scraps of paper in which patrons, intermediaries, or kin themselves explained the circumstances of their abandonment. This accompanying documentation, which almost always included specific information about identity, reflects an assiduous concern with communicating the children's origins. Even children left in the turno—a device specifically designed to facilitate anonymity—were generally not anonymous.[28]

The impulse to provide "foundlings" with a familial identity is summarized by one note writer who, after providing information on a child's mother, filiation status, and the person who had reared her thus far, explained: "I give this information so that when the girl is grown up she will know her background [antecedentes]." A small piece of paper accompanying another child read:

> Your name is Margarita del Carmen. You were born in San Fernando the 10th of February 1889. You are the natural child of Manuel Bravo, owner of a wholesale market [abasto]. Your mother is single her name is Lastenia Miranda. Keep this paper and when you are big look for your father who is well off. [Signed,] Your mother . . . [29]

But whatever parents' intentions, the Casa itself had a different set of priorities. In addition to files containing the notes and baptismal certificates left with children, the Casa maintained meticulous ledgers recording each entering child.[30] The painstaking inscription of thousands of names in the nuns' sinuous script suggests they took their bureaucratic duties very seriously. Yet they recorded information selectively. Comparing the documents that accompanied children with the official ledgers makes it possible to evaluate the kind of information parents valued as well as how the Casa filtered this information. This comparison reveals that the asylum systematically suppressed the natal identities of its young wards.

The divergent interests of parents and nuns are reflected in the meanings of baptism. Despite the poverty of most abandoning parents and the expense of the rite, the majority of children had already been baptized when they arrived at the foundling home. The widespread impetus to baptize children before depositing them may reflect the significance of the rite in popular religiosity, as well as fears that a child would die a *moro*—a Moor, that is, a non-Christian—thereby compounding the sin of the usually unmarried parents. But the ubiquity of baptism may also reflect other motivations. By conferring spiritual kin (a godmother and often, though not always, a godfather), baptism widened the circle of people who might one day take responsibility for the child.

Even more fundamentally, baptism was a naming rite that granted the baby a natal or kin identity. As one mother lamented of a child she placed, "He is unbaptized, I cannot even give him a name." In addition to a name, baptismal certificates recorded a child's parish of origin, birth date, parents, and godparents.[31] Once baptized, a child had an identity fixed in geographic, temporal, and above all social space. Her existence and origins were indelibly inscribed, making it theoretically more difficult for her to be lost or inadvertently swapped with another person. The personal name (*nombre de pila*) conferred by baptism further consolidated the infant's link to her kin, both consanguineous and spiritual, since children were frequently named after their parents, relatives, godparents, and favored saints or spiritual intercessors. Perhaps for this reason, parents depositing unbaptized babies sometimes requested that the nuns give their children specific names. More concretely, names also facilitated future retrieval: "I beg you not to take away the name, because I am leaving him *con reclamo* [with the intention to reclaim]," wrote Genoveva Silva, who explained she was placing "this sacred deposit," two-month-old Carlos Alberto, because "I have no way to feed this weak creature who is dying of need."[32]

Meanwhile, the nuns were as preoccupied with baptism as parents and went to extraordinary lengths to ensure that every single child entering the institution was baptized.[33] For the nuns, however, baptism was clearly not about conferring natal ties, a fact evidenced by their tendency to ignore parents' name requests. In a note left with her twenty-day-old infant, one mother explained her baby was not yet baptized because she could not afford the rite. But she requested: "Madre, please do me the service of giving her the name Raquel de la Piedad so that I can reclaim her by that name and by the date [.] [D]o this charity madre don't ignore this poor mother [whose daughter] they are taking from her arms to deposit here. Me, the mother, my name is Mercedes Jiménez." In response to her plea, scrawled on a bit of paper, the foundling home baptized the child

Ignacia.[34] Similarly, Zenobia Ortiz hid a letter to the mother superior in the clothes of the daughter she deposited at the home. It stated: "I put the baby in the hands of Providence because my family is very poor and does not have any way to raise the child, but the affection of a mother calls me to reclaim her in one or two years, paying at that time the cost of her care." She too asked that the baby be baptized with the name she had chosen—Lucía del Carmen Ortiz—presumably to place her under the special protection of the popularly revered Virgin of Carmen, patroness of Chile. The next day, the Casa baptized the baby as Blandina de Jesús.[35] In ignoring the names parents sometimes requested for their unbaptized children, the asylum denied a symbolically powerful connection parents sought to establish with their children. The practice also made it more difficult for parents to identify and reclaim their children.

The Casa severed links between foundlings and their families not only by ignoring name requests but also by screening information about filiation. Both baptismal certificates and other papers recording children as legitimate were routinely altered by the *ecónomo*, or receptionist of the Casa. In patent contradiction to official policy, the ecónomo apparently questioned individuals depositing babies and then corrected any accompanying documentation, amending inaccurate documents to read "*illegitimate*" and crossing out fathers' names when children were identified as extramarital.[36] But the Casa's censorial efforts did not stop there, for the names of illegitimate fathers were routinely omitted when the children were then transcribed in the official ledgers. Ten-month-old Rosa Aubrelia was brought to the Casa accompanied by a scratchy piece of paper noting not only her parents' names but those of her four grandparents as well. No indication was made of her birth status. The ledgers, meanwhile, record her as illegitimate (a piece of information presumably solicited from the person who brought her to the Casa). Her mother's name was recorded but her father's name, as well as those of her grandparents, was omitted.[37] Similarly, the child placed in 1907 and identified in an accompanying note as Humberto Eleuterio Ramírez Muñoz, son of Víctor Ramírez Moyco and Carmela Muñoz Muñoz, is recorded in the entry books as simply "Humberto Eleuterio Muñoz, illegitimate son of Carmela Muñoz."[38] Fathers were omitted even when accompanying documents explicitly stated they had recognized their children. And officials recorded deceased mothers but not illegitimate fathers who were still living.[39] The omission of fathers and the alteration of surnames could mean the total obliteration of kin ties. José Antolín Salinas arrived at the Casa with a paper recording his name, those of his parents, and the fact he had not been baptized. The Casa ignored the name selected by the boy's parents, baptized him as "Angel Custodio," and did not record his father's name at all.[40]

Such editorial manipulation suggests divergent attitudes toward paternity in popular practice and bureaucratic procedure. While illegitimate fathers were apparently still considered part of a child's kin group in popular culture, the Casa adopted prevailing legal conventions, established in the Civil Code, and did not recognize the identity or even existence of illegitimate fathers. In practice, this meant depriving illegitimate children of half of their natal origin. And not just any half. The erasure of fathers' identity was especially meaningful given the importance of paternal provenance in a patrilineal, patriarchal culture. Children unrecognized by their fathers were commonly said to be orphans (even if their mothers were living) or "nameless" (though they used their mother's surname). Thus, the institution imposed on the children in its care an orphanhood that was by turns symbolic, social, and legal.

In this regard, it is instructive to recall the Casa administrator's request to the archbishop that he excuse Casa orphans from public marriage banns. As described in the previous chapter, he explained that the spouses feared they would be stigmatized when "their origin [*procedencia*] in the Casa de Huérfanos is made public." It is telling that he identified the *orphanage* as the origin of those reared there, despite the fact that, as the records indicate, most wards had at least one recorded parent. Even more ironic is the fact that even as the administrator and the archbishop (who ultimately acceded to the request) showed sympathy for the foundlings' kinlessness, the recording bureaucracies they oversaw continued to artificially impose it.

The suppression of illegitimates' natal origins by the Casa de Huérfanos was hardly an exceptional practice. Such conventions reproduced ecclesiastical and civil recording procedures as they applied to the general populace. In a directive in 1853 concerning baptismal records, the archbishop mandated, "The father and mother of the baptized should invariably be recorded when the parish priest is sure that the child is legitimate." A very different protocol applied to illegitimates. In their case, the mother should be recorded if the priest knows her identity, "but if she asks that her name be hidden, it should be suppressed." Meanwhile, "the father's name should only be recorded when he recognizes the child in the presence of the priest, and then he should sign the certificate along with the priest." In cases in which either or both parents' identity was suppressed, "the priest will write on the certificate, *child of unknown parents*, or *of unknown mother or father*."[41] Given that baptismal records from the latter half of the nineteenth century usually include the names of mothers of illegitimates but almost never those of fathers, the directive appears to have been widely observed.[42] Thus, the Church collaborated with mothers who wished to mask an illegitimate child's origins and imposed fatherlessness on such children as a matter of course. In recording the parents of such children as "unknown," baptismal registries cloaked deliberate suppression in the more innocuous mantle of ignorance.

The civil registry that replaced parish records in 1884 adopted a parallel protocol, holding that "in the case of . . . an illegitimate child, no one will be obliged to declare who its parents are." The identity of the illegitimate father or mother would only be recorded if "he or she requests personally or through a legal representative that his or her name be registered." Thus, all children would have their first name, sex, and the time, date, and place of their birth recorded in the civil registry. But only in the case of legitimate children would the substantive elements of filiation—the names and surnames of parents as well as their nationality, domicile, and profession or trade—be required as well.[43] As in parish records, and as with the Civil Code's clauses on paternity investigation, illegitimates had no right to a legal filiation.[44] Civil marriage and death records followed a similar logic.[45] The documentary basis for legibility and legal personhood thus established identity only selectively.

In the case of the libreta de familia, the family passbook civil officials distributed at marriage, the obfuscation of illegitimate identity went even further. Here it was not just parentage or surnames that were suppressed but illegitimates' very existence. Take the libreta de familia of the Abarca-Salinas family, begun in 1890 when Francisco Abarca Santander, a miller from Talca, married Mercedes Salinas Díaz, a woman from Maipo dedicated to "the labors of her sex," in Buin, a community on the rural outskirts of Santiago. The libreta records the seven legitimate children born to the couple in swift succession between 1892 and 1902, including complete information on where and when each child was born, down to the very hour of their births. For the three children who did not survive their first years, it also records the time and place of their deaths. It is, in short, a picture of clarity that is particularly striking given that Abarca and Salinas married just five years after the establishment of the civil registry, amid widespread rejection of civil marriage, the massive under-recording of births in the civil ledgers, and when the recording bureaucracy was still precarious.[46]

But if the libreta was a remarkably lucid portrait of the Abarca-Salinas family, it was a partial one. For as it turns out, another family member was missing from the passbook: Mercedes Salinas's natural daughter, Ignacia, born before her marriage to Abarca. Ignacia's absence would be expected had she been spirited away at birth, unrecognized by her mother and reared by someone else. But this was far from the case. After her mother married, Ignacia had been incorporated into the new household, raised by her mother and stepfather along with a growing bevy of legitimate half-siblings. As Francisco Abarca noted, he had "taken responsibility [for her] since the age of eight." Moreover, when her mother died in 1910, her stepfather asked Ignacia, now an adult, to assume care of her three half-sisters.

Ignacia Salinas may have been a recognized, trusted member of the family, but the state's rendering of her kin network did not record her presence there. It was an absence deriving from the very raison d'être of the libreta as an administrative device designed to surveil the formation and reproduction of legitimate households. The booklet's carefully delineated charts for marriage, births, and deaths did not include a category to which Ignacia Salinas corresponded. Not only did her surname, her origins, or her parentage disappear in this bureaucratic vision of her family. Her very existence did as well.[47]

Secrecy and State Making

Why was Ignacia Salinas missing from the libreta de familia? Why did ecclesiastical and secular authorities deprive extramarital children of an estado civil? Why were foundlings rendered fatherless? Why, in short, given the cultural and civil significance of kin origins, did Chilean authorities deliberately dispossess large numbers of citizens of a natal identity? The civil registry's protocols concerning illegitimate birth sparked heated debates in the Senate, debates that offer some insight into these questions.

A draft version of the civil registry contained somewhat different wording regarding birth registration than the one ultimately enacted. The draft stated that the father, "if he is known and can declare it," and the mother, "if she can declare it," as well as relatives, doctors or midwives, and other third parties were responsible for registering children. Such cryptic phrasing was of course a nod to illegitimacy, which might make parents "unable" to declare their parentage. But debating the draft in Congress, several senators objected to the wording, which seemed to suggest illegitimate parents were *required* to identify themselves. Even more seriously, it appeared to imply that other people (doctors, midwives) were obligated to reveal a newborn's identity even if the parents wished to remain anonymous. "If [this article] only involved declaring the birth of legitimate children, or of those who are . . . already recognized by their parents . . . I would understand it," declared Senator Miguel Elizalde. "[But] in the case of those who are not [either,] . . . it is impossible to fulfill that disposition."[48]

Such critics went on to note that the Civil Code granted parents, and especially fathers, the sole prerogative to recognize children born out of wedlock. Forcing illegitimate parents to identify themselves in the civil registry therefore violated civil law.[49] Significantly, however, the critics spent less time arguing that the clause was illegal than that it was immoral because it forced people to publicly reveal their dishonor. Senator Manuel Valenzuela Castillo explained: "Suppose that it is a case of a birth of an hijo natural. Is it possible to oblige the mother to reveal an event shameful to her? Not only does this procedure seem unacceptable to me, I think it is immoral." He went on to suggest that the prospect of a father forced to reveal his daughter's "infamy" was a "horrific spectacle."[50] Congressman Elizalde suggested that such a legal provision would go "against nature" and hence could never be enforced. His colleague José Manuel Encina agreed: "Here the intention is to make public . . . the dishonor of a family," and he declared, "I cannot agree to oblige people to make their dishonor public . . . knowing that in these cases losing one's life is preferable to losing honor."

Not all senators were comfortable with this reasoning, with its patent privileging of private prerogatives over state interests. In the most forceful rebuttal, Senate vice president Adolfo Ibáñez opined, "The consideration that . . . it is necessary to save the honor of individuals who have given birth to the fruit of illegitimate relations is in my opinion worth very little compared to the importance that recording all individuals in the proper Registry has for the political and civil constitution of society."[51] Other senators sympathetic to family honor were similarly troubled by the prospect of the wholesale omission of a large group of citizens from the registry. Senator Francisco Puelma mused, "On many occasions, due to inconvenience, or due to a transgression or a crime, or out of shame, as in the case of natural and illegitimate children, the State would not be aware of the facts. . . . Meanwhile, sir, it is in the interest of the law that everything be known, and that should be its goal."[52]

Here was a definitive articulation of the state's legibility imperative and its perceived conflict with the private interests of families. Puelma subsequently warned that if illegitimate births were subject to an alternative recording protocol "the Registry will remain . . . incomplete, and scarcely a fourth of individuals will be recorded."[53] He went on to ponder some of the consequences of this omission:

> It is really terrible that this is going to happen when one remembers that the Civil Registry should be the basis of all political and civil rights of citizens, because from it will be derived rights and also the corresponding obligations, such as service in the National Guard . . . [and] electoral rights . . . [We] are going to accept . . . that a third of citizens are not registered and that when their rights and obligations begin is unknown [i.e., because it will not be possible to verify when they reach the age of majority]. This seems very disturbing [chocante] to me.[54]

Even Elizalde, who initially posed the problem of honor and privacy, wondered: "What kind of estado civil does one obtain with a declaration like this: on a certain street and in a certain house a child was born, whose parents I don't know who they are? Such entries do not make a registry from which one can really know people's estado civil."[55]

Yet in the end there was more consensus than discord on the primacy of privacy and the virtues of willful ignorance. Even Ibáñez, who had declared honor to be "worth very little compared to the importance" of a complete record, conceded that it was "rather harsh to oblige the parents to announce their fault." And even as Congressman Puelma characterized the omission of vast numbers of illegitimates from the civil registry as "very disturbing," he sympathized that "it really is true that in the case of a natural child, it will be a little difficult for the parents and relatives to appear in order to declare [the birth], even when they need not say whose child it is, since undoubtedly, taking this step will at least provoke suspicions." Like the opponents of paternity investigation thirty years before, lawmakers debating the civil registry operated on the premise that illicit sexuality should exist beyond legal surveillance. In the "true conflict between natural sentiments of honor and those of obeying the law," law should act in careful deference to sentiments of honor that existed prior to and above it.[56] Significantly, the parliamentarians made no mention of punishing immorality or even of preventing it; they were concerned solely with concealing it.

Ultimately, Puelma captured the spirit of the debates when he characterized illegitimates' lack of a proper estado civil as an "inevitable evil." In the wake of the debate, the Senate appended a last-minute clause that left no doubt about the law's intent: "In the case of an illegitimate child," it stipulated, "no one will be obliged to declare who its parents are." Here was a civil registry, then, that did not require parents to identify themselves when registering a child born out of wedlock nor hold them personally responsible for ensuring their offspring were registered. It was a registry that, according to official illegitimacy statistics, would permit a quarter, and subsequently some 40 percent, of the populace to remain bereft of an estado civil, marginalized for the purpose of vital state activities, to say nothing of the social and cultural salience of kinlessness for the unrecorded themselves. Of course, individuals so excluded hailed disproportionately from popular sectors.

If the lawmakers designed a registry with gaping exclusions, the local officials who administered it sometimes stretched them even wider. Chapter 2 described how exacting bureaucrats could stymie parents seeking to recognize or legitimate their extramarital children. In a similar vein, some civil registrars invoked morality to justify not the protection of parents but rather the obstruction of those who wished to register extramarital progeny. One manual for registrars counseled that when presented with illegitimate children, officials should "inquire, with much reserve" whether they were products of an especially proscribed union. If a child had been born of a "damaged union" (one characterized as adulterous, incestuous, or sacrilegious), parents should be expressly prohibited from declaring their identity "for reasons of morality." The directive is striking since there was no basis for it in the civil registry law itself: at no point had lawmakers suggested that parents should be *prohibited* from identifying themselves.[57] A similar logic is evident in the practice of foundling home officials who erased fathers' identities even when the evidence suggested they had recognized their children. In such instances, the suppression of natal identity did not serve the interests of paternal prerogative, as conceived in the Civil Code, or those of parental privacy and honor, as contemplated by the senators. It appears instead as a deliberate act of retribution, one that echoes Andrés Bello's invocation of the "just expiation" of sexual transgression to justify the Civil Code's burdensome recognition procedures. In liberal law, bureaucratic rigor doubled as moral atonement.

Private and Public: Colonial Conventions, Liberal Innovations

In their abiding deference to family honor, in their willingness to sabotage legibility to protect privacy, Chilean lawmakers demonstrated a marked proclivity to favor private prerogatives over public ones. Their posture is not easily reconciled with the basic demands of statecraft. Vital records are a classic tool of modern state formation, yet the civil registry elaborated by Chilean lawmakers dispensed with the panoptic imperative that James Scott identifies with the modern state. Nor is their posture easily reconciled with liberal Latin American states' ostensible effort to regulate "as many aspects of life as they can reach, including sexual practices . . . marriage, and the family."[58] Rather than extending the reach of the state, the quintessential milestones of secular state power, the civil registry and the Civil Code, assiduously cordoned off a sphere of social relations deemed private. If anything, the political context in which the Chilean civil registry was launched only highlights the apparent paradox. The congressional debates over birth registration occurred at the very moment when soldiers' families were struggling to identify themselves in the parish registries. Motivated in part by their plight, the legislators proceeded to engineer a registry that deliberately stripped a sizable contingent of citizens of legal kin ties.

The Chilean lawmakers' deference to familial honor and their horror of scandal were very much consistent with colonial ideas about sexuality, honor, and shame. Colonial scholars have long explored constructions of public and private and the specific meanings of secrecy and disclosure that accrued to them.[59] As Ann Twinam has shown, family honor was less contingent on actual behavior than on a public image unsullied by disclosure of private immorality.[60] Moreover, because scandal was perceived to threaten public morality and order, religious and civil authorities routinely collaborated with those involved to avoid its public revelation.[61]

Such values are very much evident in the behavior of nineteenth-century Chilean civil and ecclesiastical authorities. As we saw in chapter 1, the prospect of public scandal was repeatedly invoked as an argument against paternity investigation at the time of the Civil Code's promulgation in the 1850s. A similar animus opposed the public airing of parent–child marriage conflicts and legal recognition of marriage promises (*esponsales*). Local officials' treatment of concubinage, or "public scandal," as it was tellingly called, reflected similar sentiments. One rural subdelegado wrote to judicial authorities in the 1850s worrying that the illicit relationship of two community members would produce "a scandal of very great consequence," setting a "bad example . . . in the populous settlement of Pencahue."[62] In another case, a priest enjoined the help of secular authorities to suppress, "without noise," the illicit relationship of a parishioner who "[offers] to the public an immoral example" in the face of the priest's "obligation to watch out for public sins."[63] Judges assumed a similar posture, suppressing scandalous information revealed during the course of testimony in the court transcript. In a custody dispute over an illegitimate child, one judge even suggested that "because of the scandal they cause, these kinds of cases should not follow ordinary procedure with publicity that would have deplorable consequences."[64] By the early twentieth century, the cultural logic of concealment was still alive and well. A distraught bride-to-be wrote to the advice column of the *Revista Católica* that she had been born before her parents married and feared that "when he finds out about my origin, the groom will not want to accept me as his wife." The *Revista*, the Chilean Church's official mouth-

piece, advised her to present her baptismal certificate to the priest or notary "privately," assuring her these officials would readily collaborate in
concealing her status.[65] Discussions of immorality were thus repeatedly
couched in terms of secrecy and disclosure, concealment and publicity.

Did the civil registry, then, simply reflect the triumph of "traditional,"
colonial, Catholic values over "modern," liberal, secular ones? Was liberal
state formation a casualty of the irresistible pull of colonial anachronism?
In fact, the civil registry debates themselves tell a different story. In the
1880s, Chilean politics continued to be dominated by an ideological rift
between conservatives, who were allied with the Catholic Church and
espoused a commitment to order, hierarchy, and colonial values, and
liberals and radicals, who advocated the secularization of state and society and a somewhat more egalitarian vision of social order. But the
legislators who defended family morality against the encroachments of
the civil registry were not conservatives. Almost to a man, they were
members of liberal parties.[66]

Rather than colonial survivals, honor and privacy were woven into the
very fabric of the liberal state project. If the historiography has emphasized Latin American states' interventive imperative in matters of gender
and sexuality, the civil registry episode lays bare another dimension of
liberal state formation: its liberalism. As liberals, these lawmakers sought
to safeguard the privacy of the individual (or more accurately, the privacy
of certain individuals) against the encroachments of the state.[67] They
were broadly committed to "privacy," "freedom from government intervention," a "limited state," and "individual liberty." These were not abstract tenets, however, but principles to which specific culturally and
historically grounded meanings accrued. Cultural notions of honor, secrecy, and scandal clearly inflected them. Meanwhile, the civil registry, as
well as the Civil Code, singled out a particular realm of sentiment and
experience as "private": that involving illicit sexuality and illegitimate kinship. Chilean liberalism accorded a particular set of social relationships—
those between men and the children they engendered out of wedlock—
the liberal imprimatur of individual freedom (and the concomitant right
to contract). I say "men" rather than "parents" because, while lawmakers
represented honor as the collective entitlement of "the family," as we saw
in chapters 1 and 2, it was a prerogative that in practice tended to benefit
fathers at the expense of mothers and children. Moreover, as we have
seen, some men and not others enjoyed these prerogatives.

Liberalism thus implied certain cultural and legal as well as economic and political commitments. The civil registry debates reflected the salience of ostensibly "traditional" considerations of morality, honor, and scandal, but the legislators construed these values through the lens of the "modern" liberal right to privacy. What is more, the way that lawmakers applied liberal ideals to honor and familial morality reinscribed the gendered dynamics of power that undergirded them. The liberal concept of "the individual" was similarly culturally contingent. In Chilean liberalism, as we have seen, the ascribed characteristics of individual identity included not only gender and age but filiation, genealogy, and social condition as well.

Conclusions: War Widows, Street Waifs, the "Children of the King," and the "Children of Don Nadie"

As lawmakers weighed the state's need to know against parents' right to privacy, a third set of interests was conspicuously absent from consideration: those of the unrecorded themselves. At no point did the legislators address the social vulnerability of children rendered legally nonexistent by the registry's provisions. Nor did they fully acknowledge the civil marginalization of the adults they would become. Nonregistration tended to be framed in terms of the problem it posed for the state rather than for the uninscribed themselves.

The very expansion of the state apparatus probably heightened the consequences of natal alienation. A few years after the civil registry's establishment, for example, one official noted that the partial recording of illegitimate children impeded local vaccination efforts, which worked off of birth registries.[68] If it was "in the interest of the law that everything be known," it was increasingly in the interest of individuals as well. The plight of war widows like Estefania Lesana, whose letter opened this chapter, suggests that the compensation law for military families marked an important turning point in the significance of legal kinship. Now individuals with no patrimony or political rights had an incentive to "become legible," perhaps for the first time. And as we saw in the previous chapter, marriage created an enduring incentive to possess a legally verifiable filiation among prospective brides and grooms. Finally, individuals' incentives to be legible are evident in the plight of the newspaper boys, the so-called children of Don Nadie prevented from selling newspapers because they lacked birth certificates. Their dilemma suggests that by the late 1920s even the most marginalized groups were coming into increasing contact with a public bureaucracy that demanded a verifiable estado civil. Bureaucratization exacerbated the plight of the "people without history" to the point that destitute street children could find their livelihood in the informal economy jeopardized for lack of a valid birth certificate. The introduction of family allowances, social security, worker's indemnity, and other kin-based public benefits further enhanced the incentives for a legible estado civil among an emergent working class. It is not by chance that increasing rates of marriage and legitimacy followed the introduction of these benefits in the 1930s and 1940s.

The early-twentieth-century Chilean state was not only expanding. It was also changing, as the burgeoning political power of working- and middle-class sectors tempered its historically oligarchic character. This process likely impacted the state's deployment of kinship. The (contested) outcome of Doña Elvira Rogat Salas's annulment suit, for example, suggests the belated demise of pedigree as an attribute of legal personhood. Meanwhile, the debut of the cédula identity card in the late 1920s marks the emergence of the individual as the principal subject of bureaucratic management. If this narrative is accurate, the late nineteenth and early twentieth centuries probably constituted the high-water mark for kinship's bureaucratic significance. At the same time, these developments did not necessarily affect legal definitions of kinship or the cultural associations that accrued to particular kinds of family. If anything, the development of state benefits contingent on marriage and legitimacy enhanced their association with respectability and social status.[69] Indeed, whatever its administrative or legal significance, lineage continued—and continues—to have extraordinary social and cultural resonance in Chilean society.[70]

Taken together, the war widows, street waifs, and Chilean state's mediation of kin identity yield insights into James Scott's concept of legibility. Their stories suggest the analytic power of legibility even as they offer some refinements of the concept. First, Chilean state practice demonstrates that legibility is not a constant or absolute standard: what is legible to a given state is what is culturally intelligible to its authorities. The Chilean state defined identity in terms of kinship because kinship was a culturally meaningful construct in social practice. Elite kin networks were the basis of political and economic power, and lineage was fundamental to the individual and collective subjectivity of elites. It is therefore not surprising that the Chilean state—embedded in this cultural ethos and dominated by these same sectors—would define legibility in these very same terms. As Maxine Molyneux has suggested, "While states necessarily exert some influence over society, they are also permeated by it through the absorption of prevailing discourses, practices, and social relations."[71]

Second, the Chilean story suggests that legibility is not a condition that states seek to impose categorically but a power wielded strategically and in discriminatory ways. Law and bureaucracy used kinship but selectively imposed kinlessness. The distinction between the legible and the illegible reinscribed the distinction between the legitimate and the illegitimate, the married and the unmarried, the genealogically endowed and the natally alienated. Drawing on the case of eighteenth-century France, James Scott has suggested that the Enlightenment concept of equal citizenship constituted an "abstract grid" that served the state's legibility aims by creating a single, uniform subject, "the French citizen." In this sense, he characterizes the revolutionary French state's "simplification" of its citizenry as "emancipatory," drawing an implicit connection between the imposition of legibility and liberal ideals of equality under the law. Scott's assertion echoes Weber's claim that bureaucracy and democracy advance in lockstep insofar as both are premised on equality.[72] In nineteenth-century Chile, however, bureaucracy and the legibility impulse exhibited distinctly antidemocratic tendencies. Because kinship was a cultural concept invested with hierarchical significations, its civil and legal deployment implied not abstraction but discrimination.

If upon the demise of the colonial political order "the family became the bulwark" of the new republics, as Elizabeth Dore has suggested, the preceding discussion suggests family's enduring civil significance in the late nineteenth century.[73] The Chilean case further suggests that processes of secularization and state formation did not necessarily entail a zero-sum struggle between public and private power, between the state and the domestic sphere. In many contexts the family existed not in contraposition to the state, so much as a key referent of its practice.

Finally, a comparison with the colonial past highlights key cultural continuities as well as changes at work in late-nineteenth-century Chile. In the colonial period, limpieza de sangre and lineage constituted important determinants of legal status. The collapse of the colonial legal edifice did not strip filiation of its civil significance. Instead, estado civil reflected the (re)imbrication of kinship and civil identity. This was not a society of estates based on hereditary privilege, of course. But "birthright" persisted nonetheless. It did so in mundane bureaucratic protocols and in legal constructions of kinship.

Colonial comparisons highlight changes too. The natal dispossession wrought by the civil registry, and the suppression of children's identity in the Casa de Huérfanos, are especially striking in light of social legislation concerning parentless children in the late colonial period. In the 1790s, Charles IV declared all foundlings subject to special royal protection, legally legitimate, and exempt from tributary burdens. The decree reflected the convergence of Enlightenment ideas about childhood innocence, a concern with children's utility to the state, and a corporatist order in which foundlings were envisioned as a group whose social and legal status could be altered by royal fiat.[74]

The contrasts with Chilean social and legal thought almost a century later could hardly be greater. Where the Bourbon "children of the king" were granted a fictive natal status manifestly advantageous to their social and legal condition, the Chilean "children of Don Nadie" experienced the opposite. Systematically divested of kin ties and a natal identity, they suffered civil disenfranchisement and social stigma.[75] As we will see in succeeding chapters, kinless children in late-nineteenth-century Chile were also perceived to have value, but this value was not identified with the state. Rather, the utility of the poor and parentless was "privatized" when they grew up in, and for the benefit of, private households and haciendas. Moreover, if Bourbon legislation privileged child welfare as it converged with state interests, in Chile the inalienable rights of fathers, and secondarily the interests of the state, held sway. This explains how it is that a major legislative initiative concerning parentless children could focus on parents with no mention at all of children. This calculus would change only after the early twentieth century, when the political significance of these children of Don Nadie would be reassessed. Their newly discovered relevance would focus less on their latent utility than on their potential menace. The final two chapters explore the social practices and cultural ideologies surrounding these children.

PART III

Other People's Children

The Politics of Child Circulation

CHAPTER 5

Vernacular Kinships

in the Shadow of the State

The Comadres

Albina Ahumada was thirty-five, the mother of three children, and just days from death when she wrote to her friend Eloisa Carrasco in February 1888 asking her to care for her soon-to-be orphaned daughter, Rosa Amelia. Both women were unmarried and both, while literate, were apparently of modest social backgrounds. In addition to being friends, they were *comadres*, or spiritual kinswomen, possibly because Carrasco was Rosa Amelia's godmother. And they shared an additional tie: as Carrasco later explained, Ahumada "was reared and lived many years in my house." "As you know," Ahumada had written to Carrasco in one of her deathbed missives, "I love you like a sister." Several days later, she made her custody request official in her will, where she also named Carrasco her executor—a role usually reserved for members of a testator's immediate family. The two women shared no relationship based on either blood or marriage and no bond recognized in civil law. Yet they were bound by multiple kin ties, spiritual and secular, based on cultural practices of *compadrazgo* (spiritual kinship or godparentage) and *crianza* (child rearing).[1]

After her death, Carrasco fulfilled Ahumada's final wish and took in her daughter, eight-year-old Rosa Amelia, rearing and educating her, in her lawyer's words, "as if she were of her own family." Thus, the ties of social kinship shared by the two women transcended their immediate generation, just like those of blood. As Carrasco noted, "I can say that both she and now her daughter form part of my family." But when Rosa

Amelia's father filed suit to gain custody from Carrasco, he pointedly argued that she retained the child "without any right whatsoever" since she had "no family relation [*parentezco*] at all with the girl." His case was firmly grounded in the logic of civil law, which defined kinship in terms of consanguineous and affinal bonds. Yet Carrasco and her lawyer could invoke the very same logic. Rosa Amelia's father, they contended, had been married to another woman at the time of her birth. Because the girl was an adulterina, her father "does not have, according to the law, any rights or authority [*potestad*] of any kind." Rosa Amelia was thus doubly orphaned, by the death of her mother and her legal status vis-à-vis her father.

The dispute between comadre and father ended without a recorded decision. But the episode tells us something about the nature of kinship and child-rearing practices in late-nineteenth-century Chile. The relationship between Carrasco and Ahumada reveals how individuals could be bound by networks of affinity rooted in spiritual kinship and successive generations of child circulation, or the rearing of children in households other than those of their progenitors.[2] It also reflects the multiple disjunctures between vernacular kin practices and civil law. Rosa Amelia may have been an illegitimate orphan, but she was no kinless huacho: two adults fought bitterly to assume care of her. And ironically, while neither contender had formal legal rights over her, their dispute was waged in a court of law.

Previous chapters have explored illegitimacy, kinlessness, and the mechanisms by which children were severed from the moorings of natal kinship. This chapter and the next explore what happened to children dispossessed of such ties. Specifically, it examines the ubiquitous practice by which families sent out their own children or took in *niños ajenos,* "other people's children." Child circulation was extremely common in nineteenth- and early-twentieth-century Chile, and we have encountered numerous examples of the practice in previous chapters. Secundino Alvarez, the illegitimate son of Don Salvador, came of age in the households of his father's dependents. Over the course of their early years, kinless individuals like Pablo Pérez lived and labored in the households of adults whom they did not recognize as parents. The child-rearing arrangements and modes of family construction associated with the practice were myriad. Parents called upon relatives, spiritual kin, neighbors, masters and mistresses, and even strangers to rear their children. Households of all social ranks, excluding the poorest and most destitute, took in children.

Such practices were hardly unique to Chile or to the nineteenth century. From the teeming foundling homes of medieval and modern southern Europe, to widespread fosterage in Oceania and West Africa, to "child sharing" in contemporary African American communities, child circulation recurs across cultural and historical contexts. It has also been extremely widespread in colonial, modern, and contemporary Latin American societies. While casual references to *hijos de crianza* and *filhos de criação* ("children by rearing") are abundant in the literature, sustained attention to the practice is much less common, and recognition of its centrality to kinship, social reproduction, and class relations is even less so.[3] Taken collectively, the literature suggests that social arrangements for rearing children in Latin America have often involved households and institutions other than natal families, social affinities other than blood, and relational dyads other than "parent" and "child."

Thus, this discussion, while focused on nineteenth- and early-twentieth-century Chile, represents a case study of a broader Latin American cultural practice. The present chapter describes the ubiquity of child circulation, the demographic and material realities undergirding it, the cultural meanings attached to it, and the social significance of children's movement across households. It examines the motivations, expectations, and experiences of those who took in unrelated minors, of natal families, and of circulating children themselves. The transfer of children among households was associated with the generation of novel vernacular kin relations, such as those between Albina Ahumada and Eloisa Carrasco. It constituted a medium through which relations of friendship, patronage, and intergenerational symbiosis among households were created and strengthened. And it served as an important mode of welfare provision and family formation.

But *crianza ajena*—the rearing of children outside their natal family—was not just a kinship practice. It could also be a particularly exploitive labor practice, in which young children were reared as servants. Chapter 6 will describe the rearing of children in nonnatal households as it articulated with servitude and subordination. No doubt these contrasting valences were not always so starkly demarcated. As Lara Putnam has noted of parallel practices in Costa Rica, "Child fostering combined hierarchy, labor, and love, in degrees that varied from home to home."[4] Kinship and labor, family and hierarchy, were not mutually exclusive categories of social practice. Still, particularly at the extremes of the spectrum, it is possible to discern a clear difference between the status of children reared as sons and daughters and those reared as servants. This was a distinction that parents, caretakers, and children themselves made.

This portrait of child circulation is pieced together from records of courtrooms, notaries, and child-welfare asylums. That the state constitutes the principal source of information on this practice is ironic since codified law neither regulated nor recognized it. The transfer of children among households was an entirely informal practice, and the terms of these arrangements, if they were articulated at all, were established verbally. This disjuncture between law and vernacular practice has characterized households, domesticity, and kinship in diverse Latin American societies historically. Matrifocal households in nineteenth-century São Paulo reflect the salience of "informal roles" and their divergence from the legal and prescriptive norms that "express what ought to be done." In colonial Lima, "the law's overarching emphasis on patriarchal authority over children" contrasted with the "multiple though often extralegal, types of adult authority over children."[5] Filiation and child rearing in Chile reflected a parallel dynamic. The previous chapter explored how the state deployed kinship as a legal and bureaucratic referent. This chapter shows how that civil concept of kinship differed from its vernacular variant. The Civil Code carefully delineated the rights and obligations of parents and offspring and the rules of patrimonial succession. But the rearing of unrelated children corresponded to a whole universe of household and kin relations unacknowledged by the law. It was unacknowledged because, as Elizabeth Kuznesof has observed, "The family as constructed through law [in Latin America] can be seen as the codification of an elite world vision."[6] Law's conspicuous absence from Chilean child circulation reflects the fact that these practices were primarily the province of nonelites and did not involve the transfer of large amounts of property.

Yet law's absence does not imply its irrelevance. Law did not regulate child circulation, but it did articulate with it, in ways that shaped both vernacular practices and law itself, often to paradoxical effect. By nar-

rowing the definition of legal kinship, the state encouraged the pluralization of caretakers and the importance of informal kin networks. Public
modes of welfare provision relied on private caretakers. And the legal
regime of filiation described in preceding chapters relied on extralegal
practices of child circulation. Child circulation ultimately served as an
informal and unacknowledged system of alimentos (child support) for
children whom law and bureaucracy rendered "orphans."

The Ubiquity of Circulation:
Demographic and Material Matrices

The informal circulation of children among households emerges time
and again in documents that, however fragmentary in their coverage
or ambiguous in their interpretation, nevertheless speak to the striking
prevalence of the practice. Because nineteenth-century testators often
left bequests to children they had reared, wills provide one glimpse of the
dimensions of the phenomenon. In a sample of eighty-five wills recorded
in 1850 by Santiago notaries, almost 17 percent of testators made a
bequest to *un niño que he criado*, a child whom they had reared. Meanwhile, in the provincial town of San Felipe in the same year, no less than
one in four testators made such provisions (sixteen of sixty-five wills). In
both locales, will writers hailed from across the social spectrum, ranging
from elites to impoverished widows, raising questions about the class
politics of fosterage that will be examined below.

While high, figures gleaned from notarial records almost certainly
underestimate the presence of such children in testators' households.
Will writers did not always specify their relationship to beneficiaries
mentioned in their testaments. And of course people may have reared
children without choosing to leave them anything. Finally, testators who
desired to name fosterlings as heirs had no incentive to clarify their
adoptive origins since, given the nonexistence of legal adoption, doing so
invited challenges from consanguineous kin.[7]

Census manuscripts provide further insight into the dimensions of
child circulation. Among villagers in the rural department of Los Andes
in the 1840s, 17 percent of the total recorded population of children lived
with people other than their parents.[8] Again, the calculation likely under-

estimates their presence given that census takers on occasion probably recorded unrelated children as sons and daughters. More significantly, the proportion of children in this community who had *ever* lived in such an arrangement, as opposed to those doing so at the moment the census was recorded, was surely much higher.[9] Evidence from Latin American societies in the nineteenth century, from northern Mexico to Mexico City, Caribbean Costa Rica to São Paulo, Brazil, suggests that the Chilean pattern was hardly unique.[10]

The practice of rearing unrelated children also crops up constantly in the narratives of everyday life recounted in late-nineteenth-century Chilean courtrooms. Criminal and civil courts mediated custody disputes over circulating children and considered the nature of rights enjoyed by adults over youngsters whom they reared. Could they represent such minors in court? Could they, like legitimate parents, demand the minors' return to the "paternal" household when they ran away? Courts also heard criminal cases involving the abuse and neglect of children in non-natal households. And even when the investigative spotlight did not focus on issues related to their circulation, judicial investigations often illuminate circulating children's experiences in unexpected ways. A mistress accuses her young servant of theft and casually mentions that the girl has been in her care since infancy. Asked why she consented to her own abduction by a suitor, a twelve-year-old says her intention was not to marry him but simply to escape the household where she was being reared. Circulating children were such a familiar presence in households, neighborhoods, and communities in nineteenth- and early-twentieth-century Chile that they rarely provoked comment from either community members or judicial authorities. From the historian's perspective, what is remarkable about these children is how utterly unremarkable they were.

Child circulation had an important institutional dimension as well, reflected in the movement of children through asylums and orphanages. Not surprisingly, such circuits are much better documented than private, informal ones. Here, too, the evidence points to a phenomenon of massive proportions, with a large and growing number of children passing through charitable institutions in the late nineteenth century. Between 5 and 9 percent of children born in Santiago were deposited at the city's Casa de Huérfanos. While the Casa was the oldest and largest asylum of this ilk, it was hardly the only one. Between 1844 and 1895, at least thirteen institutions for poor children were founded in Santiago alone; by 1912, the capital was home to at least twenty-five orphanages. Meanwhile, such institutions began to appear with increasing frequency in provincial locales.[11]

The circulation of children occurred within a specific social and material milieu, aspects of which have been discussed in previous chapters. Widespread illegitimacy and orphanhood separated children from their natal origins. Orphans from well-off families might be reared by relatives, and the illegitimate offspring of prominent parents—people like Secundino Alvarez—often entered the same circuits of care as those of more humble origins. But numerically speaking, it was overwhelmingly the children of the poor who passed through nonnatal households. Many of those *mandados criar*, "sent out to be raised," were the children of women on their own, whether abandoned, widowed, or single. These women's poorly remunerated labor, coupled with their lack of rights to paternal support, made it extremely difficult for them to support their children.

If the reasons people relinquished children were clear enough, what about those who took them in? Households of all social backgrounds received children, though they did not all do so for the same reasons. Wealthy households frequently fostered poor children, but as we will see in the next chapter, these fosterlings were understood to be subordinates, not kin. Elites reared the children of deceased friends and children within the kin group, especially nieces and nephews. But individuals of means without children of their own rarely sought out hijos and heirs beyond their consanguineous kin circle. A Valparaíso merchant, José Bayoló, and his wife Tránsito Campaña are typical in this regard. The childless couple took in two orphans, at least one of them an abandoned newborn, whom according to one account Campaña reared with "the love of a mother." But in seeking an heir to their sizable estate, the couple recurred not to the orphans but to a nephew from Spain and another distant relative. Ironically, after a dispute with these kin, the couple dedicated their fortune to found an orphanage in Valparaíso, inaugurated in 1856.[12]

Plebeian households, both rural and urban, took in unrelated children as domestic subordinates, but they also did so for the purposes of family formation. A few years after Bayoló's and Campaña's orphanage opened,

another childless Valparaíso couple of a very different social background
took in an orphan. José Tapia, a shoemaker, described how he and his
wife came to adopt four-year-old Victorino del Carmen:

> Privately and in the confessional . . . Friar Pedro Amador Carmete of the
> Order of Jesus asked if he could give me an orphan boy . . . I discussed it
> with my wife who insisted that I accept the offer of the friar, and since we
> did not have children of our own, we would take care of this defenseless
> boy and adopt him as our son.

Five years later, Victorino still lived with Tapia and his wife, who, according to witnesses, treated him "the same as if he had been their son." While
we do not know if the boy ultimately became their heir, in similar situations such children did.[13] Such scenarios were very common given the
prevalence of individuals, both married and unmarried, who had no
(surviving) children of their own. Infant mortality was a scourge that
affected all families but especially plebeian ones. In the 1890s, a third of
children died before their first birthday; in 1925, the figure was still more
than a quarter.[14] Contemporary commentators associated this pervasive
mortality with lax affective ties and an insidious anomie in plebeian families. The sons and daughters of the poor were "children of fate, whose
parents watch them be born without pleasure and die without pain,"
declared the physician and social critic Augusto Orrego Luco in a typical
characterization.[15]

Yet if mortality fractured some ties, it gave rise to others. Child circulation was a major plebeian strategy for confronting these demographic
realities. The 1849 will of Andrea Valenzuela, a widow of modest means
resident in San Fernando, is illustrative. During her first marriage, Valenzuela had borne nine children, all of whom died, probably in childhood
since she could not remember their names. Her second marriage had
produced no children. She named as her universal heir and an executor
of her will Josefa Osorio, "a girl whom I raised." Here child circulation
permitted the generational reproduction of family.[16]

The magnitude of Valenzuela's loss was staggering, but childlessness
itself was common. A striking number of testators declared they had no
surviving legitimate or illegitimate descendants at the time they wrote
their wills. Some 38 percent of Santiago testators in 1850 and 1875 left
no succession; by 1900, the proportion had reached an extraordinary

61 percent. While wills almost certainly overestimate childlessness because people with legitimate or natural children, who were obligatory heirs, had less need to write them, the wills nevertheless suggest that a very significant proportion of the population never had consanguineous succession.[17] Meanwhile, in the period from 1850 to 1900, over one-third of testators in San Felipe had no children.[18]

In keeping with these realities, older testators, above all women who were widowed, never married, childless, alone, or who had adult children, frequently took in youngsters, usually girls, to "keep them company" (*que las acompañaran*) or to serve as "companions" (*compañeras*). A patron recommending the widow María de la Cruz Flores, who wished to take out a child from the Casa de Huérfanos, explained that Flores "has the virtue of protecting orphans, and at her age they serve her as comfort [*consuelo*]." Another woman was said to have taken a girl from the Casa "so that later she would serve as a compañera, because at the time she had no daughter."[19] Besides furnishing "companionship" or "comfort"— which probably also entailed domestic labor in many cases—such children also provided a form of social security for women of modest resources who found themselves alone in their old age.

This was likely the case for Dolores González, who was unmarried, childless, and around forty years old when she took in a young boy named Segundo. Twenty-five years later, she declared in her will that this young man, now around twenty-six years old, "has served me and cared for me like the most faithful of sons . . . maintaining me with the products of his industry and work." She named him executor of her will and instituted him as her sole heir. The young man had also acquired his adoptive mother's last name. In an intergenerational symbiosis, she had provided safe haven to a vulnerable youngster, and he now provided companionship and material support in her old age.[20] While the will communicates with greatest clarity the material dimensions of this relationship, in González's reference to this "most faithful of sons" we can detect a hint of the affective bonds that were also at stake.

Child circulation also intersected with another stage of the female life cycle, that involving the care and especially wet nursing of infants. Poor, single mothers sent their young children to live with wet nurses—often women even more destitute than themselves—while they sought employment. Such arrangements could last long past weaning, however.

The Casa de Huérfanos employed external wet nurses, some of whom petitioned to keep indefinitely the babies entrusted to them. In other cases, nurslings remained in the care of their wet nurses out of circumstance. Around 1880, the adult daughter of an inquilino family on a hacienda in Codegua was hired to nurse the infant Luis Alberto Acevedo. The boy continued to live with his foster family until he died at age five. He was identified as "the illegitimate son of Rozenda Acevedo, who sent him to be *criado* [raised or nursed] about five years ago, leaving one year's anticipated salary, and after that she hasn't been seen since." Acevedo had gone to Santiago, herself employed as a wet nurse by a well-off family.[21]

Acevedo's story reflects how child circulation was intimately tied to the dynamics of the female labor market.[22] The single most important source of employment for women was live-in domestic service, a labor both logistically and ideologically incompatible with caring for one's own children. According to census data, service accounted for almost 26 percent of female employment in 1854 and some 41 percent in 1920.[23] The records of the Casa de Huérfanos indicate that many children were abandoned by mothers working or seeking to work as domestics; frequently those who wrote the petitions were their patrones.[24] In the early 1930s, recognizing that this was an important cause of abandonment, the Casa actually implemented a policy in which it paid servant mothers' salaries if employers agreed to accept them with their children. The director noted that many mistresses of modest economic means were willing to participate in this arrangement.[25] In fact the Casa's payment merely made explicit policy what had been a de facto reality for a century or more. By assuming responsibility for servants' children, the Casa had long subsidized domestic service for Santiago's households.

Child circulation was a response to the demand for female labor, but it also shaped the female labor market by generating caretaking opportunities for women. If babies and young children represented an obstacle to employment for some women, for others they were an economic opportunity. In Santiago in the 1880s, Micaela Ibarra served as wet nurse for Soledad Fuentealba's newborn. She received ten pesos a month, "a salary which, given her poverty, she very much needs." Such arrangements were clearly common.[26] The best illustration of the impact of child circulation on women's employment is provided by the Casa de Huérfanos. At the end of the century, some 600 women were employed by the Casa as nurses, many of them in rural households on the outskirts of Santiago. By the late 1920s, over a thousand children ages two to seven were distributed to rural households.[27] Many of the caretakers were inquilinas, members of the hacienda service tenantry. The extent of inquilinas' wet nursing activities is especially significant given the relatively few wage-earning opportunities for women on haciendas.[28]

Wet nurses employed by the Casa de Huérfanos in 1900 were paid five pesos, sixty centavos monthly for each child they received; dry nurses, who cared for children who were already weaned, earned less.[29] The wage was a pittance, especially considering that urban wet nurses hired privately by women of reduced circumstances earned between five and ten pesos a month in Santiago in the 1880s and 1890s.[30] Yet from the point of view of the cash-poor inquilino household, the sum could be significant. What is more, by taking in more than one child at a time, as wet nurses routinely did—receiving two or more orphans at a time was common, and the Casa administrator cited one woman who had reared five orphans at once—this income could be multiplied.[31] Moreover, some inquilinas became long-term, serial nurses. Dominga Moncada, resident on a hacienda outside of Santiago, received at least eight children from the Casa between 1858 and 1863 and according to a recommendation from her patron had cared for numerous wards before that. Andrea Castañeda, a resident of Isla de Maipo, had taken in Casa orphans for some thirty years, according to a record from 1928.[32]

In the context of chronic female underemployment, wet nursing and fosterage provided additional sources of income for women on haciendas —and a much-needed supplement to the slowly declining economic prospects of the inquilino household. Through inquilina nurses, child circulation overseen by the Casa de Huérfanos introduced essential resources into the haciendas of Santiago's rural hinterland. In this way, filiation and child-rearing patterns reverberated outward, impinging on unexpected dimensions of the social order—in this case, the agrarian economy.

Cash was not the only medium of exchange in fostering relations, however. Not all caretakers were remunerated for their services, and other kinds of debts could be incurred when children were *mandados criar*, sent out to be raised. Self-sufficiency and pride, obligation and dependency, were also at stake. This may explain some mothers' reluctance to avail themselves of seemingly well-meaning caretakers even in the face of great hardship. Carmen Rosa Cuevas, mother of a young son, had experienced, in her words, "miseries and need" since the hospitalization of her husband. But the woman who had given her lodging noted that "even living as she lived, without resources, she did not want to give me her child on one occasion when I asked her for it to raise at my expense." An even more blunt exchange occurred between María del Carmen Díaz, whose baby had just died, and Dionisia Rosales, the sister of the baby's father. Accusing Díaz of having a hand in the baby's death, Rosales asked why she had not accepted her earlier offer to care for the child. Díaz retorted that she "didn't want to have her children reared by others [no quería tener criado su familia]."[33]

Finally, child circulation could precipitate spontaneous arrangements not easily explained by the logic of monetary exchange or social obligation. Strangers and passersby who stumbled upon abandoned children often volunteered to seek out nurses, serve as godmothers, or take foundlings in. Those who did so were usually, though not always, women.[34] One woman who went to wash asparagus in a canal heard cries and, happening upon an abandoned infant, promptly "picked it up and nursed it." A woman who overheard talk of an infant found in a church doorway went to the scene, volunteered to serve as the baby's godmother, and asked to assume care for it.[35] When foundlings turned up—a frequent occurrence in nineteenth-century Chilean communities—local officials might help pay for their support. But often caretakers assumed the burden themselves.

The life history of Celinda Valenzuela's nameless illegitimate infant, born in Santiago in the 1890s, illustrates the promiscuity of caretaking. Shortly after its birth, Valenzuela's mother, the baby's grandmother, asked Rosa Iglesias, a thirty-year-old widow and market-woman, to leave the newborn at the Casa de Huérfanos. "Taking pity on the little thing," Iglesias decided to keep the baby instead. She found a neighbor to nurse it during the night and took it with her to work at the Mercado Central, Santiago's principal market, the next morning. There another market-woman, Filomena Donoso, approached the baby, who was lying in a crate with some rags, picked it up, and noted that it was cold. Iglesias asked if she wanted to take care of it. Donoso consented and took the baby, asking Iglesias to bring her the baptismal certificate. Donoso then gave it to "[another] woman named Rosa [*una tal Rosa*] to nurse it during the day"; later she took it home with her and hired a wet nurse for five pesos. During its first week of life, the infant was thus nursed or cared for by five different women, not including its mother or grandmother.[36] None had any prior relation with the family and all were women of modest economic circumstances.

It is tempting to invoke a romantic but ultimately essentialized notion of plebeian solidarity to explain such behavior. A more compelling interpretation is to consider the centrality of child rearing to women's social roles in this society. The welter of wet nurses and dry nurses, of older women who sought out children and passersby who spontaneously took them in, hints at the existence of a gendered, plebeian culture of child exchange and caretaking labor. This culture was characterized by the exchange of cash and compassion, of interest, affection, and obligation. It reflected the strong cultural identification of women with caretaking. Yet it was hardly a "natural" corollary of biology. The fact that so many women gave up the progeny born to them, and that so many others took in unrelated children, demonstrates the eminently social nature of child rearing.

Plural caretaking was clearly a plebeian phenomenon, and when it occasionally attracted attention from elites, it was caricatured and condemned. In increasingly strident denunciations around the turn of the century, doctors identified the practice with infant mortality and charged that poor women purposefully became pregnant in order to work as relatively well-paid, "mercenary" wet nurses in wealthy households. Their own children were the casualties: "little less than abandoned in the hands of any comadre," they quickly succumbed, for the comadres "pay less attention to them than the dog or the cat: they leave them abandoned in a corner of the room among some filthy old rags."[37] Doctors repeatedly called for women, wealthy and poor, to nurse their own children, reflecting the recent ascendance of the mother–child dyad.[38] The veneration of motherhood placed maternity on a pedestal but devalued vernacular forms of child exchange and plural caretaking. While doctors were the most strident critics, they were not the only ones. The fact that much of the available information on these practices derives from criminal investigations of women suspected of mistreating the children in their care suggests that judicial authorities also harbored deep suspicions of these practices.

Identity, Integration, and
the Multiple Bonds of "Fictive" Kinship

Not surprisingly, medical and legal caricatures failed to capture the diversity of scenarios and outcomes that child circulation entailed. Crianza ajena could involve brief sojourns in foster households, incorporation in new family units, the pluralization of kin groups, and sometimes even social mobility. Some youngsters passed their childhood in a single home while others moved from household to household, in a perpetual state of circulation. Some were eventually reclaimed by their progenitors, while others lost all contact with families of origin. Even individuals who grew up away from their parents might maintain their natal kin as a lifelong reference point. Narciso Flores spent his childhood in households in at least four locales between Talca and Chillán. During that time, he lived less than three years in his father's home in the department of Quirihue, thirty-five kilometers north of Chillán, yet it was still his point of personal orientation. When in his late twenties he was asked to identify his *patria* (place of origin), he named his father's residence, which, he noted, he sometimes visited.[39] Residence notwithstanding, for Flores birth and blood were enduring points of reference.

For others, families of birth and families of crianza were not mutually exclusive. The testator Pedro Jiménes identified himself as the hijo natural of Carmen Jiménes and an unknown father. Jiménes, whose age is not specified but who may have been relatively young when he wrote his will in 1850, was single and childless. His humble possessions included the portion of a house that corresponded to him as part of his maternal inheritance. He had several siblings, among them a brother who owed him fifty pesos and a sister whom he named executor of his will and universal heir. Yet these blood relatives constituted just one part of his family circle. "Given the fact I do not have obligatory heirs [direct, living ascendants or descendants]," he declared, "I leave to Micaela Muños the quantity of 50 pesos, in remuneration for her personal services that she gave me and the love and affection with which she reared me from my tender youth." Here was a typical scenario of a boy sent out to be raised in another household by a single mother who was likely too poor to rear her children herself. But the resulting arrangement implied not familial substitution but pluralization: Jiménes's rendering of his kin network as an adult included both an adoptive mother and blood siblings.[40]

Still other circulating children lost their natal identities only to acquire others. Some children adopted from the Casa de Huérfanos in the 1920s were renamed, even rebaptized, by their new families. When they left the asylum with new parents, Marcelo Jara became Adolfo García Antoine, and Lucía Flores was rebaptized Adriana María Sepúlveda.[41] In contrast to the kinless young servants described in chapter 3, for some children name changes implied incorporation rather than alienation. Through practices of informal adoption, children who became detached from natal kin networks could acquire new identities, kin circles, and affective ties. This was the case of Ignacia Naranjo, whose adoptive mother, Tránsito Figueroa, declared in her will in 1851: "Because of the love and affection that I have had and I have for the girl, whom I reared from her tender years, and aware on the other hand of her constant services, I order that after my death my executor give the said Naranjo the quantity of 30 pesos in silver, a tray, three or four griddles, an image of the Virgen del Tránsito . . . and a little copper pot."[42] While Figueroa's single living son was the chief beneficiary of her will as mandated by law, the items bequeathed to Naranjo were nevertheless of significant value given the very modest size of her estate. Moreover, the religious iconography and everyday objects probably harbored special sentimental value: "small quantities, derisory amounts," Maria Odila Silva Dias has written of similar bequests in Brazilian wills, "but loaded with symbolic meaning and allusions to specific relations belonging to the organization of domestic work."[43]

Children reared in nonnatal households could also become heirs. César Bustamante was an infant when his mother left him at the Casa de Huérfanos, and he spent his first years with the wet nurse Carmen Ulloa, an inquilina on the estate of the García Huidobro family. When he reached age six, Ulloa and her husband petitioned the Casa to adopt him. By this time, Casa regulations required adoptive families to leave a *dote*, a "dowry" or deposit, that adoptees could collect upon marrying or reaching the age of majority. Ulloa, however, did not make the required deposit, "so that the boy does not know he is from this Casa [,] but after they die he will inherit from them."[44]

Occasionally such scenarios implied social mobility in a society with virtually no such outlets. Doña Beatriz Madrid and her husband Don Marcelino Basáez were property owners "with their own honorable and lucrative business" in Valparaíso. While they probably did not qualify as elites, the honorifics "don" and "doña" suggest a measure of financial independence and social status. Without heirs, they hoped to "obtain a little girl of three or four years old, with a nice face, desiring to adopt her as their own daughter," according to a parish priest who recommended them to the Casa de Huérfanos. Aware of the special opportunity the couple presented to a lucky orphan, the administrator of the Casa instructed the nuns that Doña Beatriz "wants [the girl] to be agreeable [simpática], and since this child will have a future and a good education, present her some [children] so she can choose the one she likes." The prospective parents eventually settled on a boy named Several. Though his background is unknown, we can imagine that like other "children of Providence," he came from impoverished and illegitimate origins and had been separated from his natal family as an infant. Becoming the son and heir to Doña Beatriz and Don Marcelino was a rare example of child mobility as a radical improvement on an individual's life prospects.[45]

While wills and the Casa documents tend to speak from the perspective of parents and especially caretakers, a women's mutual aid society provides a rendering of kinship as it might look from the perspective of the fostered. The Sociedad "La Igualdad" de Obreras de Valparaíso, whose members included seamstresses, telegraphers, cigarette makers, and typographers, paid survivor's benefits to members' kin. The Sociedad paid beneficiaries in the following order: first were the member's legitimate and natural children, followed by her husband and parents, siblings, grandparents, and finally "the tia [literally "aunt," but also a generic term of affection or respect for an elder] who, in the absence of parents, provided the member with maternal care." The order of payment obviously favored consanguineous family (although those who had such tias would in many instances have lacked them), but it is significant for recognizing adoptive tias as kin at all. So too is the implication that members not only had such tias but that they might wish to designate them beneficiaries.[46] This plebeian rendering of kinship contrasts with that of the state in a parallel circumstance: the awarding of benefits to families of soldiers killed in the War of the Pacific. Benefits were paid to widows and legitimate children, and in much more restricted form, to natural children. The law made no mention at all of adoptive children. This is not because lawmakers were unaware of their presence in soldiers' households: an asylum for war orphans overseen by Congress accepted children who, "lacking a father or a mother, lose their adoptive father or their only protector in the war."[47] That elite lawmakers provided adoptive children with an orphanage but not survivor benefits reflects the fact that they could imagine them as charitable wards but not, significantly, as rights-bearing kin. A similar logic is evident in the story of José Bayoló and Tránsito Campaña, the wealthy and childless Valparaíso couple who reared two orphans from infancy and then, in a loss for heirs, dedicated their fortune to the founding of an orphanage.

Circulating children passed among households bound by blood, friendship, spiritual kinship, and patronage, creating and strengthening social relations between individuals and among families. A couple might take in an orphan due to the "affectionate memories of friendship" between the wife and the child's deceased mother. A woman might place her daughter in the service of another by way of a "contract of honor," the purpose of which was "not to earn money, but rather out of friendship toward [the caretaker]."[48] As the opening anecdote to this chapter suggests, *compadrazgo*, or ritual coparenthood, was a common vector of child circulation. When one couple petitioned to obtain custody of their orphaned one-year-old goddaughter, they invoked "an obligation contracted on the death bed [of the child's father]" as well as their rights as godparents "in conformity with canon law."[49] Caretakers also strengthened their bonds with adoptive children by serving as their godparents after they took them in.[50]

In addition to operating along the familiar pathways of blood, friendship, and compadrazgo, child mobility generated novel categories of kinship that had no basis in civil or canon law but were richly imbued with meaning in popular practice. The terms *hijo adoptivo* and *padre adoptivo* —adoptive son or daughter and adoptive parent—were frequently used in popular parlance, though, as will be discussed below, adoption did not exist in nineteenth-century civil law. In his will in 1875, the smallholder Pedro Gamboa named his wife and two minors as his universal heirs, explaining that "the latter two are children I reared from their childhood and whom with the present document I adopt as my hijos."[51] Meanwhile, seemingly unambiguous kinship terms that connoted specific legal relationships were imbued in vernacular practice with notably broader meanings. The teenager Filomena Roldán referred to Florinda Inostroza, the woman who reared her, as *mi mamita* ("my mommy") and Inostroza to Roldán as *mi hija*, though she would subsequently acknowledge that "I am not the mother of this girl, but I have served as such since her early years."[52]

Meanwhile, children who had been wet nursed acquired *madres de leche*, or milk mothers, and became themselves *hijos de leche*. Created in infancy, this kinship tie could endure over a lifetime. Felisa de Acevedo was still identified as the madre de leche of Lucinda Guajardo after the latter was an adult woman, married with two children of her own.[53] A natal family also contracted special patronage obligations to their child's madre de leche. One mother who had hired a woman to nurse her daughter was said to harbor "a special interest" in the wet nurse and to have "give[n] her something for the maintenance of her family" years later, when the former nursling was eleven years old. In his will in 1900, Isidoro Moncada, a seventy-year-old father of twelve, left Andrea Dávila fifty pesos "as payment for services since she has nursed all my children for me."[54] In judicial cases, litigants could challenge the testimony of witnesses who shared kinship with their contenders on the grounds they were biased. That milk relationships could be impugned on the same grounds suggests the extent to which they were considered socially or emotionally consequential.[55] Crianza practices thus created enduring ties between natal families, foster families, and children. Laden with affect and social significance, "fictive" kinship relations were fictive only insofar as they were informal and extralegal.

If child circulation produced new "constellations of relatedness," to use Jessaca Leinaweaver's phrase, it could also have the opposite effect, creating distance and even estrangement. Reared by her grandmother in the countryside while her mother resided in Santiago, twelve-year-old María Armijo referred to her mother as her tia.[56] Even more striking is the way circulation could change the status of illegitimate children *within* their natal families. As we saw in chapter 2, biological children born out of wedlock might become "unrelated" dependents in their natal households. Circulation was central to this foil. Romualda Maza was referred to as "a girl whom we raised from childhood" by the couple with whom she had always lived. Only years later was it revealed that she was in fact their blood daughter, born before their marriage, whose identity had been concealed to protect the honor of her mother. Practices of child circulation made it possible to incorporate illegitimate children into the household without having to acknowledge socially problematic consanguinity.[57] Here child circulation implied not physical mobility across households but rather the movement of children across categories of dependency *within* the household, from that of hijo to that of servant, subordinate, or charitable ward.

The result of these broad and mutable categories of vernacular kinship were modes of filiation formed around criteria other than "blood" and kin networks founded on relationships with no basis in civil law. As Lara Putnam has noted of plebeian migrants in Caribbean Costa Rica, kinship and community formed a seamless continuum, a dynamic epitomized by informal fostering.[58] In Chile too, natal, adoptive, and spiritual kinships coexisted and overlapped, giving rise to new modes of affinity. The movement of children across households and kin networks was central to creating these bonds, which existed between adults and children but also between adults. This plurality of "fictive" kinships was apparently specific to plebeian culture. Elites recognized extended kin networks as well as compadrazgo. But they seemed to draw more categorical distinctions between kin and nonkin, to define family more narrowly in terms of marriage and consanguinity, and to avoid "outsiders" for the purpose of family formation and heirship. This was likely because patrimonial succession required specific, stable, and exclusive rules of membership.[59]

Legal Silence and Private Welfare

Law reflected elites' need for such unambiguous kin demarcations. The model of domestic relations propounded by the Civil Code and by nineteenth-century jurists was based squarely on an understanding of family as a unit bound by blood and formal marriage. Through the system of alimentos, the doctrine of *patria potestad* (paternal authority), the institution of estado civil, and the marriage contract, the Chilean Civil

Code carefully delineated the rights and obligations that existed among family members. The complex legal architecture surrounding filiation reflects how the bonds of right and responsibility between parents and children were of particular concern. But in keeping with the emphasis on blood, the Civil Code made no provision for nonconsanguineous kin relations between adults and children. The myriad ties engendered by practices of circulation may have been ubiquitous in vernacular practice, but they had no formal existence in the law.

This was not because such constructions of kinship were unfamiliar to the jurists who designed and applied republican civil law. Drawing on Roman antecedents, Iberian legal tradition had long provided for the incorporation of unrelated children into new families and households.[60] Contemporary codification provided another template: the French Napoleonic Code and the Spanish draft civil code both instituted adoption, albeit in restricted form.[61] The Chilean Code's provisions concerning filiation drew on all these sources but expunged any reference to adoption. This was also true of other major nineteenth-century Latin American codes, including those of Mexico and Argentina.[62] Thus, in contrast to contemporary European trends and Iberian legal tradition, the most influential Spanish American codes eliminated adoption. Why?

The few Chilean jurists who broached adoption rejected it out of hand, declaring it to be a legal fiction "contrary to nature and the principles of civil law that regulate family and succession."[63] As telling as their philosophical hostility was their tendency to dismiss adoption as irrelevant to Chilean social practice. The Civil Code author Andrés Bello referred to the "disuse" into which the practice had supposedly fallen.[64] Three decades later, one lawyer concurred: "The number of those individuals [in Chile] who, possessing resources to maintain a family, are incapable of creating it for themselves and who must resort to unrelated children [hijos estraños], is so small that it is not rational to make an exception to the law for them."[65]

Such comments suggest just how out of touch jurists were with popular practice. While Bello was technically correct about adoption's "disuse" insofar as Iberian legal devices surrounding the practice had not been used in recent memory, informal adoption was of course ubiquitous.[66] As we have seen, a significant number of testators—by definition individuals who possessed at least some resources—were childless, and some "adopted" sons and daughters despite adoption's legal nonexistence. But such practices predominated in plebeian sectors. Civil law, which reflected the family conventions and succession strategies of elites, therefore had little cause to regulate it.

Succession was just one of the legal issues posed by child circulation. The practice also posed questions both philosophical and practical about authority over and responsibility for children. Were minors free to leave the households in which they had been reared, or could caretakers demand their return, as parents could? Could these adults serve as minors' legal representatives in courtrooms or contracts? How was economic responsibility for crianza to be assigned? Who, ultimately, exercised power over and responsibility for the legions of children who circulated? Such questions had no clear legal answers in nineteenth-century Chile. Different clauses of the Civil Code appeared simultaneously to confirm the inalienability of parental rights and to assert that parents who abandoned children could lose authority over them.[67] Meanwhile, juridical devices that might have been applied to crianza relations proved irrelevant to them. Judicial records indicate that legal guardianship, an institution routinely used by masters in Brazil to assert authority over unrelated children, was in Chile used only in cases of propertied minors.[68] In contrast to the contractualization of illegitimate filiation in the Civil Code (see chapter 1), the exchange of children remained entirely informal and extralegal, based on oral agreement. Even when child circulation was envisioned as a permanent arrangement it rarely involved even a notarial contract.[69] Such extralegality could prove a liability for children, for example when caretakers could not serve as their legal representatives in criminal proceedings in which they were the victims.[70]

When conflicts arose within these arrangements, the parties did not hesitate to recur to the courts. But because judicial recourse was slow and expensive, frequently grinding to a halt when there were no financial interests of great magnitude at stake, most disputes over circulating children are incomplete or unresolved. Over half end with no decision on the part of the judge. The scarcity of completed cases, and the myriad issues they dealt with, make it impossible to discern any patterns of juridical decision making vis-à-vis the practice. But this is precisely the point. Courts spoke only intermittently, and obliquely, to it.

If crianza ajena intersected with kinship, succession, and issues of domestic authority, it also implicated the problem of child welfare. As we saw, doctors decried the mortality rates of children who were mandados criar, and a number of (ultimately unsuccessful) proposals were made to regulate wet nursing.[71] But like civil law, welfare legislation too proved fundamentally extraneous to circulating children. The first child welfare law, promulgated in 1912, stipulated that parents found guilty of neglect would be deprived of patria potestad. In other words, it assumed that children necessarily resided with a parent who enjoyed formal, legal authority over them.[72] This was yet another example of how hijos de familia, minor children coresident with their legitimate parents, were the subjects of meticulous legal regulation whereas children inserted in other kin or household arrangements passed below the legal radar.

Yet law's posture vis-à-vis child circulation was characterized by a paradox. Civil law may not have recognized these practices, but in managing kinless children, the state actively recurred to them. This was true of the judicial system itself. When six-year-old Maclovia Peralta was removed from an abusive caretaker, a Santiago judge placed her with the wife of the chief of a provincial railway station—an informal arrangement of crianza ajena indistinguishable from the one from which she had just been removed.[73] This appropriation of vernacular practice is also evident, on a much larger scale, in children's asylums, which routinely farmed children out to private households. The best-documented case is that of the Casa de Huérfanos, which as we saw above managed its enormous population of young children by sending them out to be reared with nurses. In the early 1880s, only 200 of the institution's total population of 1,000 children resided in the Casa itself. The rest lived in nurses' households in arrangements that drew on popular practices of crianza ajena.[74] At age five or six, children who had survived the perils of infancy were remitted to the Casa, but after just a few months, weeks, or even days in the asylum, they entered a second cycle of circulation. This time they were sent to urban and rural households as adoptees, "companions," apprentices, and as we will see in the next chapter, servants. Later in the century, as the Casa and its services expanded, children's stay in the asylum lengthened considerably, and orphans might spend years, rather than weeks, there. But eventually most of these minors too were distributed to private households.

In other words, the Casa and other asylums of its ilk functioned not as orphanages per se but as clearinghouses for distributing children to private households and haciendas. Even as they expanded and multiplied through the first decade of the twentieth century, such asylums never displaced informal crianza practices and private spaces as sites of social provision to poor children. Indeed, they perpetuated them and perhaps even enhanced their importance. The state did not regulate or recognize the informal crianza of poor children as either a kin practice or a welfare strategy, but ironically, its beneficence apparatus amply appropriated such vernacular practices.

Vernacular child circulation in turn helps explain the long-term viability of liberal legal reform. Previous chapters have explored how civil law contractualized illegitimate kinship, deprived children of rights to parental support, and helped generate a kinless underclass. How could a society afford, socially and materially, to systematically exempt large numbers of parents from responsibility for their offspring?[75] This was a question both Latin American and European critics would eventually direct at the ban on paternity investigation. In Latin America, it was not just an abstract ethical question but a pressing practical one: in a context of endemic illegitimacy, excusing progenitors in this way had potentially catastrophic social consequences.

Child circulation explains this wholesale paternal exoneration. Cultural practices of informal fosterage provided for children unmoored from natal kin. Alongside the perennially overburdened Casa de Huérfanos of Santiago and its smaller provincial counterparts there existed an extensive but informal, unregulated, private, and largely silent child welfare "system." Similar cultural arrangements for welfare provision prevailed in Brazil, in Mexico City, and probably all over Latin America.[76] In Chile and perhaps elsewhere, these arrangements permitted the establishment of the patriarchal legal edifice erected in the nineteenth century.

In turn, this legal edifice fomented informal practices. The Civil Code's construction of filiation had the effect of narrowly restricting the universe of kin considered legally responsible for extramarital progeny. It relieved fathers, and in many instances mothers, of legal responsibility for illegitimates, and even natural children recognized by their parents had no right to support from grandparents, aunts, or uncles. This circumscription of kin liability inadvertently encouraged the pluralization of caretaking. Children rendered parentless fell back on the good graces

of spiritual and vernacular kin, friends and acquaintances, and even passersby and perfect strangers. The social synergies between civic policies
and plebeian child circulation illustrate the complex articulation of legal
and extralegal, public and private realms.[77]

Conclusions: Children of the Fatherland,
"Rootless" Masses, and "Fictive" Kin

If eighteenth-century Bourbon monarchs had touted poor and parentless
youngsters as children of the king, their republican counterparts now
touted them as hijos de la patria, children of the fatherland. In Chile, as in
other modernizing societies of the late nineteenth and early twentieth
centuries, political discourses identified children as an urgent national,
and nationalist, cause. Poor children were rhetorically constructed as
"beneficial members" of "the Chilean family" and future "hard-working
citizens eminently useful to their families and the State." The future of
the Chilean nation depended on saving them from epidemic rates of
infant mortality, which observers repeatedly decried as the highest in the
"civilized world," and rearing them as healthy, productive, morally upright citizens. Casa asylee Pablo Pérez adopted the rhetoric of children
and nation when he expressed gratitude to "my patria who raised me"
and "my mother who is Chile."[78] Public ritual also enacted it. When the
municipality of Santiago welcomed home victorious troops from the
War of the Pacific, orphans from various local asylums were mobilized to
participate in the festivities. A few years later, when the Casa de Huérfanos moved to a new facility, the president of the republic and other
high officials were on hand to mark the occasion.[79] The proliferation of
state-subsidized asylums, especially after the turn of the century, suggests that public authorities put their money where their mouths were,
enacting the linkage between children and nation in ways institutional
and material as well as symbolic.

This was the discursive construction, but in actual practice, a different
story emerges. In many historical contexts, children have been socially
and symbolically mobilized for national or imperial purposes, a role Ivan
Jablonka has labeled state utilitarianism. The Portuguese and British
crowns sent "orphans of the king" as colonizers of their far-flung empires.

The Brazilian state funneled abandoned children into the army and navy. Napoleon assembled a regiment at Versailles comprising 6,000 found-lings. In Chile, poor and parentless children had no such public vocation. Identified rhetorically with the nation, in practice they were reared in private households and haciendas.[80] The grandiloquent rhetoric of public utility and nationalist import obscured the quiet reality of private care in mostly poor and mostly female hands. Shifting the focus from state rhet-oric to state practice reveals how the state's posture toward poor children was distinguished not so much by a vigorous interventionist impulse as by the perpetuation of private and informal modes of social provision.

In his celebrated essay "La cuestión social" (1884), Augusto Orrego Luco decried the lot of Chilean peons, that "nomadic mass, without family, without its own home, without social ties." The notion of the poor as itinerant hordes lacking "family" and its concomitant ties of affect and authority was echoed ad nauseum throughout the latter half of the nine-teenth century. Occasionally, child circulation was implicated in these scenarios. Because poor children left home early to live in "different households and even in different locales," their families "do not attribute much importance to . . . paternal rights," observed one lawmaker. The result, he and others asserted, was "weak family ties."[81]

Evidence presented earlier in this book, including the plight of illegiti-mate and kinless huachos, would seem to confirm such assessments. The present chapter presents an antidote to these visions of familial anomie. Illegitimacy, mortality, the structure of labor markets, and poverty did indeed rend family relations asunder. But individuals cut loose from the moorings of natal kinship could, through the informal arrangements associated with child circulation, find safe harbor in new households and kin relations. Such scenarios provide further evidence for the "mecha-nisms of solidarity" that Chilean historians have invoked as features of plebeian culture.[82] And they highlight the centrality of children and child rearing to these mechanisms of mutual aid. This is not to suggest the existence of a morally superior plebeian collectivism, however. Such practices reflected not some essential cultural impulse so much as cul-tural adaptations to prevailing material realities—the need for social pro-vision in old age, for example, and alternative modes of filiation in the face of infant mortality's relentless toll. Among elites, patrimony and its transfer dictated categorical renderings of kinship. But plebeians could in a sense "afford" to adopt plural kinships—and were compelled by the realities of family life and social reproduction to do so. Moreover, as we will see in the next chapter, plebeian and elite households alike were capable of ruthless exploitation of fostered children.

If elites saw anomie, it is because the popular classes so often lacked the ties of legitimate, consanguineous, and affinal kinship that formed the backbone of "decent" households and aristocratic dynasties. It is because patria potestad—a pillar of elites' domestic cosmos that was strengthened in liberal legal codes—was inoperative, at least in the way elites understood it, when children grew up in nonnatal households. What elites could not see is that plebeian sectors drew on alternative bonds and vernacular kinships, often rooted in practices of crianza ajena, to construct families, households, and communities.

Child circulation was a protean phenomenon that served multiple social functions. In a society characterized by high rates of adult and especially infant mortality, it provided children for the childless as well as parents for children like Rosa Amelia, the girl whose dying mother, Albina Ahumada, asked comadre Eloisa Carrasco to adopt her. In a society with high rates of female headship, it was a survival strategy of poor, single, working mothers, even as it provided a form of support for aging women on their own. In a society governed by inheritance laws and notions of honor that served elite interests, it protected the patrimony of legitimate scions from the claims of extramarital offspring, even as it served as an informal mechanism for childless people of modest means to acquire heirs of their own. Finally, in a society characterized by widespread poverty and inequality, child circulation provided for the basic sustenance of many destitute children. But as we will see in the next, and final, chapter, it also served to reproduce the cycles of dependence and exploitation in which these children and their families were trapped.

CHAPTER 6

Child Bondage in the Liberal Republic

The Runaway

In July 1918, fourteen-year-old Ernestina Pérez ran away from home. But the home she left behind, the home where she had spent her childhood, was not that of her parents. Orphaned at an early age, Pérez had been reared in the household of one Luis Siderey Borne in the provincial town of Chillán. When Siderey moved to Valparaíso some years later, he brought Pérez with him. And when as an adolescent she abandoned his household, Siderey petitioned a Valparaíso court to have her returned to him.

At first glance, the relationship between Pérez and Siderey would seem to resemble the vernacular fosterage explored in the last chapter: Siderey was an adoptive father and Pérez his daughter. Except that Pérez referred to the man who had reared her not as a padre but as a patrón. Accusing him of mistreatment, she declared she had run away in order to find an employer who would pay her for her labor as a servant. Siderey did not dispute Pérez's portrayal of her status in his household. The fact that he was literate while Pérez could not sign her name to her court statement corroborates the impression that she had been reared in his household not as a daughter but as a subordinate.[1]

The experience of young servants like Ernestina Pérez reflects another dimension of the crianza arrangements explored in the last chapter. Hers is a much less sanguine story of what happened to the poor and parentless when they moved from kin groups to the largesse of strangers. Many minors in nineteenth- and early-twentieth-century Chile, and in Latin America historically, were reared in adoptive households as servants. Alongside the slave regimes of Brazil and the Caribbean, a variety of labor arrangements based on unfree and paternalistic forms of personal service, indenture, debt peonage, military conscription, penal labor, and forced impressment into public works endured in the nineteenth century and beyond. This chapter identifies the tutelary domestic servitude of poor, illegitimate, and Amerindian children as one of these labor forms.[2] The tutelary service of minors was a customary and extralegal form of bondage cloaked in the "natural" dependence of childhood, one that would endure for at least a century after the abolition of slavery in 1823. This chapter explores how this practice evolved from the early republic to the first decades of the twentieth century, when Ernestina Pérez ran away from "home." It is a story less of change than of striking continuities.

Children's work was valuable to rural and urban households both modest and elite, but the tutelary service of minors was more than just a labor arrangement. It was a complex social relationship to which elaborate cultural meanings accrued, and it sheds light on the social reproduction of subordination and the cultural meanings of dependence. Structured by notions of charity rendered and gratitude owed, everyday relationships between young servants, often called *criados*, and the individuals who raised them generated clientelistic ties of dependency and customary obligation. If friendship, affection, intergenerational symbiosis, and social solidarity could undergird the movement of youngsters across households, so too could patronage, dependence, and subjugation. At their most exploitive, such practices fed minors into lifelong subordination—though as I will argue below, these children were never entirely deprived of agency. The servile tutelage of boys and girls in this sense constituted the formative "prehistory" of adult male and female peonage. Child criados grew up to become the *peones*, *gañanes*, *mozos*, and *sirvientas* that dominated the nineteenth-century Chilean labor market and haunted the elite imagination.

The story of child criados further reveals how, through their sponsorship of charitable asylums, the Catholic Church and Chilean state helped reproduce these dependencies. Some of the richest information on practices of tutelary servitude comes from the Casa de Huérfanos. As described in the previous chapter, the Casa sent children out to private households, arrangements that, as we will see in this chapter, frequently entailed servitude. Indeed, throughout the nineteenth century until at least the 1930s, this was the most common fate of surviving Casa children. Ultimately, however, the state is conspicuous within these practices mostly for its circumscription. The history of Chilean criados is a narrative less of law's heavy-handed intrusion in the "private" sphere than of how, in the context of law's silence, private households of all social levels subordinated poor and parentless minors. Yet law is not for this reason irrelevant to these practices. Servile tutelage was constructed not "outside" law but "against" it. Cultural and legal understandings of the poor and parentless as beneficiaries of charity marked them as something other than bearers of rights. Their status as such sheds light on the way people's place within kin networks and households shaped their status as rights-bearing individuals.

Chinito/as in the Early Republic

If in the latter half of the nineteenth century children's tutelary service was extraordinarily prevalent, the practice neither began nor ended in that period.[3] Throughout the colonial period until well into the nineteenth century, Spanish and then Chilean forces waged a violent effort to subjugate autonomous Mapuche Indians ("Araucanians") in the south. A brisk traffic in Mapuche children destined for slavery or servitude originated along this colonial frontier. It appears to have intensified during the violence associated with the independence wars and together with a traffic in adult women became an officially sanctioned aspect of frontier warfare. According to the English traveler Maria Graham, Bernardo O'Higgins offered rewards to those who "saved" Indian women and children, who would otherwise be killed by the men in order to avoid being taken prisoner. O'Higgins himself reared two young Indian girls obtained in battle who later accompanied him into exile in Peru. During her visits in the early 1820s, Graham was taken with these "wild-looking little girls," whom O'Higgins supposedly addressed in the "Araucanian tongue ... which is soft and sweet."[4]

This traffic was not just a function of warfare, however. In the late 1820s, in the wake of slavery's official abolition, the German naturalist Eduardo Poeppig described a seasonal market in Mapuche children along the southern frontier. In summertime, according to Poeppig, Indians sold children kidnapped from the interior of Araucania to buyers on the other side of the Bío-Bío River. While Spanish officials had ignored this traffic, "the republican government has limited the sale of Araucanian children to the [nearby] province of Valdivia" in an attempt, ultimately unsuccessful, to circumscribe the practice. The long-standing traffic in Amerindian servant children was hardly specific to southern Chile: it echoes practices in the colonial and nineteenth-century Andes, Paraguay, and northern Mexico.[5]

Nor was it an exclusively colonial phenomenon. Young Amerindians in Chile were bartered as servants at least through the mid-nineteenth century and perhaps until the turn of the twentieth. The servant María Ramírez was reared in a Santiago household in the 1880s and 1890s. Having been taken in by her patrona as an infant, Ramírez did not know her parents' identity and had lost her natal surnames. But she did know that she had been born in the south, and a court official referred to her as *la araucana* (the Araucanian)—suggesting that she may well have been of Mapuche origin. Ramírez's case may be an isolated one. Or it may reflect, at the dawn of the twentieth century, the quiet persistence of a traffic in Amerindian children destined for servitude.[6]

Along with Amerindian children, illegitimate youngsters in the custody of their mothers were especially vulnerable to such depredations.[7] Indeed, poor youngsters of any ethnic background or filiation status were fair game, because the poor, like single mothers and Indians, were considered intrinsically unfit parents. In 1829, a republican paper published an exposé of officially sanctioned child abduction. In an open letter to the paper, José Cruz Salinas charged that his ten-year-old son Francisco had been kidnapped by a judge from his home in Cauquenes and passed on to a series of other local and regional officials before eventually winding up in the household of Don Carlos Correa de Sáa, a prominent participant in the independence struggle. The aggrieved father's "letter" was almost certainly penned by someone other than Salinas and had clear political overtones. "Does your child enjoy the liberty that the Nation ensures to all men, in article 10 of the Constitution, as an inalienable and inviolate right?" asked the paper in its "reply" to Salinas. Invoking the abolition of slavery six years before, it continued: "In Chile there are no slaves . . . And what is a man whose will is violated if not a slave? Or do they only consider slaves the blacks who once came to us from the coast of Africa?"

Prompted by the press accounts, the prosecutor of the Supreme Court launched an investigation of the father's allegations. It revealed that the kidnapping of Francisco Salinas was more than a fictional device designed to advance a political argument. Correa de Saá readily admitted to taking the boy. But as telling as the fact of the abduction were the explanations participants offered in defense of their actions. Correa de Sáa declared, "It is not at all strange nor censurable that I would receive a boy because I needed him or out of charity, and when in this area there is hardly a house that does not have the same service." He added that in receiving the boy, he had been motivated more by charity than the need for a servant, since had he wanted such a child, "I would have taken advantage of the many that there are on my nearby hacienda." Correa de Sáa justified his stubborn refusal to return Francisco to his father by noting that the boy, who was "more than ten years old, did not know how to make the sign of the cross" and was so ill-dressed that his benefactors had covered him in castoffs to hide his nakedness. In other words, the ignorance and poverty of his parents justified the boy's abduction. Finally, the recalcitrant defendant argued that he had hardly acted on the margins of custom or law. He noted that the child's capture was "in keeping with the customs of those territories [aquellos pueblos]" and "in accordance with the edict emitted by [military commander Ramon] Freire in his government." On this score, Correa de Sáa was correct: decrees in effect in the south directed local officials to place poor children in masters' households.[8]

The Salinas case was unusual only for the publicity it received and the judicial inquiry it sparked. José Cruz Salinas was a sympathetic symbol of republican aspirations because he was a legitimate father with powerful patrons. He was also, as his statement made clear, not Indian.[9] But the evidence suggests that the abduction, sale, and gifting of poor children destined for servitude was both generally practiced and widely accepted. Indeed, Francisco Salinas was seized together with four other children, yet only his abduction prompted a judicial response. Such practices are most visible in the south, though complaints filed by parents against local officials in the central valley in the 1830s suggest they were more widespread. Regardless of their provenance, many young criados ended up in households in Santiago and Valparaíso. Child trafficking thus linked rural, peripheral, and semiautonomous indigenous territories to the new republic's urban centers.[10]

Child servants in the early nineteenth century were often referred to by the ethnically loaded designation *chinito/a*. Originally, the term referred specifically to children of indigenous parentage or to those who "looked" Indian; it was used in this sense in administrative contexts, as when the Casa de Huérfanos distinguished in its entry records between *chinos* and *blancos* (whites). As racial categories disappeared from republican bureaucratic practice, including the Casa's ledgers, chinito became a generic term for poor children or young servants, regardless of ethnic background. Yet it seems to have retained its ethnic charge, and it also became more derogatory. Other ethnic appellations (*cholito, negrito*) as well as words borrowed from Quechua, Aymara, and Mapundun (*huacho, hueñi*) were also used to refer to poor, orphaned, or servant children. Such etymological evidence suggests that, regardless of their ethnic origins, poor minors were "indigenized" in popular perception.[11]

One function of the chinitos was as markers of their *patrones*' social status. In newly independent Santiago, as in the colonial period, indigenous child servants were considered "a luxury." The "pretty little Indian girls, very nicely dressed" who served Maria Graham mate tea at an acquaintance's home apparently served such a function. Amerindian girls also commonly served as *chinitas de alfombra*, "carpet chinitas," who carried small rugs on which elite women knelt in church. According to the chronicler Vicuña Mackenna, by custom their heads were shorn and they went barefoot.[12] The most enduring significance of child servants, however, was not as symbols of status but as providers of labor. Children both Indian and non-Indian comprised a semicaptive domestic labor force particularly valued for the special degree of fidelity with which they could be inculcated. Poeppig observed that in the south there existed "a special system to prepare good *mozos* [male servants]" whereby mestizo campesinos sold their children to urban dwellers to be reared as servants. Age, sex, and *aspecto* (look, appearance—a reference, once again, to ethnicity?) determined a child's value in the marketplace: "Mestizos from [the southern provinces of] Arauco, Nacimiento, etc, sell their children sometimes for six pesos fuertes," he noted, "and I myself saw how the captain of a merchant ship acquired a rather clever boy for thirteen pesos . . . [who] became an excellent mozo in a short time."[13]

For local and regional authorities, the labor of minors living in one's jurisdiction was a perquisite of public office, and they routinely took children for themselves and gave them to kin. "Don't forget to bring me a chinita" exhorted Viviana Picarte in a letter from Santiago to her brother, the intendant of Valdivia in the 1820s. Likewise, a local military captain gave Francisco Salinas and another child to his mother. It was a venerated tradition that would live on for decades in the Casa de Huérfanos, as administrators distributed children to friends and family. "Esteemed friend," began one solicitant's missive to the Casa administrator in 1862. Another addressed him as "dear *compadre*." Both respectfully sought children from the asylum.[14]

Criados at Work: Labor in Nineteenth-Century Households

By midcentury, the brazen abduction and trafficking of children had subsided—or perhaps were simply more covert.[15] But the use of young criados in Chile was flourishing, in both urban and rural households. Indeed, it was a practice common throughout the hemisphere. In communities in northern and southern Brazil, the labor of young orphans proved increasingly important with the waning of slavery. In midcentury Buenos Aires, children worked as household *conchabos*, or contracted servants. In Lima, highland Indian children known as *cholitos* were an important component of the postabolition domestic labor force. In the Argentine provinces and in Colombia, parents and local judicial authorities assigned minors deemed vagrant, abandoned, or simply poor to masters. Beyond Latin America, this was the era of the U.S. orphan trains, in which poor children from eastern cities were placed with farm families out west, and Britain relocated the children of the urban poor to Canada and Australia.[16] Even as children's industrial labor was coming under scrutiny in these societies, older forms of household-based child labor were quietly thriving, perhaps even invigorated by the abolition of slavery and the formation of "free" labor markets, imperial expansion, capitalist development, and other aspects of "modernity."[17]

In Chilean towns and cities, six-year-olds ran errands in the street and seven-year-olds did housework and cared for infants; nine-year-old boys distributed milk and were apprenticed to artisans; eleven-year-old girls ironed handkerchiefs and washed clothes. In the countryside, young boys worked the harvest, herded donkeys, served as shepherds,

and chopped wood, while girls performed domestic and some agricultural tasks. But while nineteenth-century educational and vocational
programs prescribed strict segregation by sex, in practice the gendered
division of children's labor was not always so marked. At around age nine,
Pablo Pérez, the orphan whose autobiography is discussed in chapter 3,
was charged with caring for his patrones' baby: "I was its nurse in every
way. I washed its diapers, I carried it around and I entertained it when it
cried."[18] Whether it was agricultural, commercial, or domestic, the labor
of both male and female criados was distinguished by the fact that it was
carried out in the context and for the benefit of a household in which
the child was a subordinate dependent—"*like* a son or a daughter," in
the disingenuous idiom so frequently invoked by contemporaries. It
was a metaphor that implied proximity but in fact obliquely referenced
distance.

The fact that the documents frequently portray children engaged in
work is of course neither remarkable nor in itself an indication of their
exploitation. Many children in nineteenth-century Chile, as in many
societies historically, contributed to rural and urban household economies. They did so from as early as age six or seven and regardless of
whether they resided with natal families or not.[19] Nevertheless, it is clear
that those who grew up laboring as criados in others' households were
inserted in a peculiar complex of subjugation. In 1868, the parents of
four-year-old José Tomás Díaz declared before a judge that they wished
to give their son to another couple, "promising not to reclaim him." The
contract, virtually the only one of its kind, contained a telling request:
that their son be given "good treatment, that is, that he not be considered
in the class and condition of a domestic servant."[20] How Díaz's parents
defined "good treatment" speaks to the perils that faced children who
circulated beyond natal kin.

They had reason to be wary. Households routinely received children,
even infants, with the express purpose of grooming them as servants.
María Ramírez, the adolescent servant reared by her mistress from the
age of ten months, provides just one example.[21] Santiaguinos routinely
and openly recurred to the Casa de Huérfanos in search of children as
young as four or five *para su servicio* or *con calidad de sirviente*, suggesting there was nothing objectionable about such arrangements.[22] The
term criado, which derived from *criar*, to rear or nurse, captures the
slippage between child dependents and domestic servants as well as the

association of minority with domestic dependence. The term, with its concomitant ambiguities, is present in peninsular and creole Spanish and in Portuguese, suggesting these social practices and associations were widespread in the Iberian and Iberoamerican world.[23]

Social and legal definitions of work and workers tended to obfuscate the labor that was at the heart of tutelary practices. First, criados' work was obscured by its domestic context. As noted above, the labor of criados was "domestic," regardless of its specific character, insofar as it took place for the benefit of a foster household. And household servants of any age were not considered workers.[24] Young criados' labor was further obscured by their minority. An (ultimately unsuccessful) proposal in 1861 to issue passbooks to all servants in Santiago, for example, required only those over eighteen to register.[25] In other words, children were not recognized as part of the domestic labor force of the city.

And who were the masters that benefited from their labor? A broad cross-section of rural and urban households took in young criados, suggesting both the social reach of crianza practices and the wide significance of children's work. The petitions of individuals taking children from the Casa de Huérfanos in the 1850s, 1860s, and 1870s provide a composite portrait.[26] There were individuals from the lower rungs of rural society, both inquilinos and independent smallholders, such as the man with "some little animals including 3 horses and 6 sheep," another with "8 horses, 5 cows, and 50 sheep," and the wife of a rural subdelegado. Urban dwellers also solicited children. They were often modest property owners or proprietors of small commercial enterprises: a woman with her own house in the plebeian neighborhood of la Cañadilla, a man with a pharmacy on the Plazuela de San Pablo, the owner of a hair salon on Calle Estado. Artisans—shoemakers, tailors, a chocolatier—were well represented. A well-known French immigrant bookbinder and his Chilean wife requested "one of the biggest ones" to "educate" and teach the bookbinding trade.[27] And there was the widow who, with her husband, had served as longtime caretaker of the building that housed the national library, museum, and university. These were individuals considered humble or even poor but who enjoyed a degree of social respectability. Households that could not afford to hire adult servants probably particularly valued child ones, who did not customarily receive a wage. In some households, young criados were the sole servants present.[28]

Elite individuals also solicited children from the Casa, though somewhat less frequently, if only because they represented such a small proportion of the populace. They included a landowner from Curicó, "a woman of a wealthy and honorable social background [*una señora de respeto i fortuna*]," and an individual of a "very well known social position [*mui conocida posición social*]."[29] By the 1920s, Casa sources suggest that households receiving children were more uniformly modest and rural. Some small property owners still figured among solicitants, but they were a clear minority, eclipsed by dependent inquilinos. Meanwhile, elites no longer appear as patrones at all. Such evidence reflects the changing class politics of child servitude, an issue taken up in the epilogue.

A few Casa children returned to natal families or were absorbed into new kin networks, but most who survived their early years became servants. The Casa's population was equally divided by sex, and servitude was the fate of boys as well as girls. After the 1880s, older male asylees were sent to workshops affiliated with the Casa where they received artisan training, but few became skilled tradesmen and most left the Casa as mozos, low-status, unskilled male dependents of households or commercial enterprises—that is, the male counterparts of the female sirvientas.[30] Beyond the Casa de Huérfanos, most beneficence asylums focused their efforts on girls, and for many of these institutions the mission to succor poor females was organized around training for domestic service.[31] As we will see below, Santiago residents of all classes strongly associated charity asylums with the labor of young women and children. The city's welfare apparatus was thus tied to local markets for domestic labor, linking institutional beneficence to the prevailing culture of servitude.

Subordination and Violence, Charity and Gratitude

The deeply paternalistic, bonded labor arrangements young criados entered rarely involved a wage. To the extent young people's labor was recognized at all, it was conceived as compensation for their rearing and "education." Some patrones paid a *dote* (literally, dowry) to take children from the Casa, but this was less a wage than a deposit, refunded to the caretaker if the child was returned to the asylum.[32] Wagelessness distinguished the labor of young criados from even the lowest-paid child

12. Ironing class at the Institute of the Hijas de María Inmaculada for Domestic Service, one of many asylums preparing poor girls for service. Santiago, in the early decades of the twentieth century. *Source: Actividades femeninas en Chile, Imprenta y Litografía La Ilustración, Santiago, Chile, 1928, p. 593.*

workers in the incipient urban industrial sector. It also distinguished them from most adult domestics. And while rural laborers in the nineteenth century rarely received cash wages (especially inquilinos), they were remunerated with land and perquisites.[33] It is likely that with the spread of wage labor, child criados were increasingly distinguished by the peculiarity of their status, especially in urban areas.

In lieu of a wage, some masters willed money and sometimes even land to criados "under the condition that he always remain in the house and that he be faithful and honorable as he has always been" or provided that they "continue the same good behavior and judgment . . . and continue serving me until my death."[34] Here compensation would be granted at some point in the future, contingent on a criado's lasting loyalty, such that wagelessness crept into adulthood. The striking parsimony of some rewards attests to the bleakness of criados' prospects. In one will from 1875, a criada was offered just twelve pesos a year until the testator's death as an incentive to ensure her loyalty.[35] With no other prospects and no kin networks to turn to, some criados accepted such conditions, but they might wait years, even decades, for compensation, only to find it challenged by a patrón's heirs. Unless compensation was carefully spelled out in a will, courts tended to rule that in the absence of a written contract (which of course never existed), criados' claims could not be proven.[36]

Beyond labor exploitation, tutelary servitude could also entail naked violence. At least two adolescent orphans from the Casa died at the hands of violent patrones in the years after 1910.[37] "To recount the thousands of details of the suffering that I experienced," the orphan Pablo Pérez wrote, "would be to never finish."[38] Some of the most telling violence involved the sexual assault of girls living and working in foster households. The perpetrators were sometimes patrones, but aggressors often came from beyond the household, which suggests criadas' vulnerability in the wider communities they inhabited.[39] Significantly, attacks on criadas often occurred while they were unsupervised and engaged in their daily labors in public spaces. One young girl sent to buy potatoes was lured to the home of a neighbor, who offered her a piece of bread. A passerby heard her exclaim, "Leave me alone, señor, I have a lot to do, I have to iron, I'll come back later." The defense argued that the girl, who was ten years old, had a questionable reputation since she "frequently went around the streets asking for alms." In other words, running errands in the street—a common occupation of such children— made her fair game for assault.[40]

Did criadas figure as victims simply because they frequented dangerous public spaces more often? Or were they especially vulnerable because potential perpetrators knew they lacked kin to exercise legal and social authority over them? Did unaccompanied girls' very presence in the street signal this lack of familial protection? The dynamics of public space and social vulnerability remain hazy. What such scenarios suggest is that criados were not simply generic poor children but were somehow "marked" within the communities in which they grew up. No wonder a parent might challenge a patron's practice of dispatching a daughter "habitually to the street with baskets and bundles, as if she were a servant" or of sending her "everywhere alone, going around the streets burdened like a servant."[41] The sexual assault of criadas suggests that these objections did not merely express cultural obsessions with female propriety but in fact reflected well-founded fears of dangers associated with public space.

Yet while violence may have pervaded these arrangements, it was not what sustained them. Caretakers sometimes defended their right to employ physical force against their wards, but extreme violence against young children was socially proscribed. One mistress's lawyer justified her severe beatings of an eight-year-old criada by invoking the girl's "difficult, disrespectful, proud character," but neighbors testified against the defendant, and the judge found her guilty and sent her to prison.[42] Far more powerful in sustaining this complex of subordination between parents, patrones, and children were cultural ideologies of paternalism and Christian charity, such as those proffered in a domestic manual from 1891. The author of *Duties of the Christian Woman* counseled readers that "the mistresses of the household are, in a sense, the parents of their servants, *above all if the latter have been reared by them*; so they should treat them as daughters, look upon them with affection and compassion." As for the servant herself, she "should treat her masters as parents, and regard them with respect, submission, care, and obedience."[43] Relations of servitude were glossed in terms of filial obligation, with obligations contracted in childhood that much deeper.

It is not coincidental that the author of this advice was a priest. Charity between the classes was a central tenet of Catholic social doctrine in the late nineteenth century. In a period of heightened class tensions and the growing mobilization of the working class, charity was to mediate inequalities between rich and poor, generating mutual dependence and social harmony. Such discourses found wide resonance among conservative Chilean Catholics like Archbishop Mariano Casanova, who in countless public addresses exhorted the wealthy to exercise charity among their impoverished brethren.[44] Poor children were the quintessential objects of benevolence, the archbishop declared, for who "does not feel tenderness toward children, who with dry eyes can watch them cry of hunger"? And because "there are not enough treasures to [compensate] . . . an invocation of a child of God who prays for his benefactor," he assured that benevolence toward children would be especially richly rewarded.[45]

Charity and paternalism framed rhetoric about poor children not only among conservative ecclesiastics. The secular administrators of the Casa de Huérfanos referred to those who took orphans as "charitable individuals" and their actions as a "work of charity."[46] Caretakers themselves echoed these terms, describing how they had been "moved by compassion."[47] They also drew on the notion, articulated by the archbishop, that charity and compassion justly deserved recompense. In secular discourse, the currency of compensation was not children's prayers for benefactors but their gratitude, loyalty, and submission to them. Testators conferring gifts to their criados often cited their "fidelity," but many patrones complained of the opposite.[48] One man charged that the daughter of a servant whom he and his wife had reared from childhood had forgotten "the affection and gratitude that she owes her protectors." Accused of abusing the twelve-year-old servant she had received in "an act of charity," another patrona dismissed the charges as the fabrication of a neighbor who tried to "conquer the girl . . . advising her to run away from me."[49]

Notions of charity betrayed are also inscribed in vernacular language, in the insult *huacho mal agradecido*. As described in chapter 3, a huacho was a foundling or bastard. Seemingly incongruously, in popular discourse the word often appeared with the modifier "ungrateful." Variations on the phrase can be traced from at least the 1820s to the 1890s. The juxtaposition of ingratitude with the circumstance of being poor and parentless captures the essence of the huacho's condition: such individuals owed their very existence to a favor and thus lived in a state of perpetual indebtedness.[50]

If such ideologies were from the perspective of patrones frankly self-serving, they should not for this reason be dismissed as cynical or insincere. Masters and caretakers, especially those of some social standing, could harbor a deep sense of paternalistic obligation toward the children brought into their homes. It was a paternalism born of the multiple dependencies, of class, generation, and often gender, in which huachos were inserted. When fourteen-year-old Elena Valdés ran away from the household where she had been reared since age nine, her master ap-

pealed to the police. But he did not want Valdés back in his household. "I
have a moral responsibility over the said minor since she was entrusted
to my wife's care by her grandmother," he explained, "[and] I wish to
return her."[51] Testators also evinced such "moral responsibility" when
they attempted to protect the probity of child wards even beyond their
own lifetimes. One testator left 250 pesos for a young criada but stipulated that "if she marries a person unworthy for his bad conduct," she
would lose the bequest.[52] Relationships with criados were a medium
through which patrones performed particular class identities. Gender
identities were also at stake: as mistresses, Catholic laywomen, nuns, and
later social workers, elite women were deeply invested in child circulation.[53] Undeniably a source of labor for patrones, tutelary servitude was
nevertheless motivated by cultural logics more complex than just labor
exploitation.

The Value of Children

Further down the social ladder, solicitude for poor children took on additional layers of meaning. For more modest households, succoring an
orphan was deserving of recompense not only because it was a gesture of
benevolence but also because it was expensive. As masters and caretakers
repeatedly noted, child rearing involved formidable outlays of time, en-
ergy, labor, and money. It included the obvious material expenses of
feeding, clothing, and sometimes hiring a wet nurse for baptizing a child.
But it also included *formación* and *educación*, the moral and character
education and vocational instruction that prepared a child for adulthood.
Given high rates of infant and child mortality and the modest economic
situations of many fostering households, a child or youth of sixteen,
thirteen, or eight years old—clean, healthy, dressed, fed, educated—was
testament to the "*grandes sacrificios*," the "*mil sacrificios*" of whoever had
assumed the burden of his or her care.[54] Illustrative in this regard is the
spontaneous exclamation of a woman whose three-year-old godchild was
seized by a rival in a custody dispute. As the carriage with the child and
her abductor pulled away, the woman yelled, "Give me back my little girl,
I worked very hard to raise her! [*Entréguenme mi niñita que me ha
costado mucho criarla*]."[55]

Of course, children's value could undoubtedly also be affective, and adults did profess love and affection for children. In the case of the abducted three-year-old, there is no reason to doubt the godmother's emotional attachment to a child she "reared . . . with great care, the same as she would have with her own child." But the would-be patrona, a woman of a higher social status who went to great lengths to engineer the abduction, had never even met the girl. The judicial record is awash in conflicts between parents, patrones, and padrinos that revolved around how much value children embodied and who had a right to control it. These cases sometimes reveal the emotional value of children, but above all they speak to value in terms of the costs of child rearing as well as children's material worth as present or future providers of *servicios*. The two kinds of value, of course, need not be mutually exclusive.

Many legal disputes over criados were initiated when caretakers were challenged by other adults—typically natal family members—who sought to reclaim youngsters after months or years, when the "hard work" of crianza was done. The statement of the shoemaker José Tapia, defending his custody of eight-year-old Victorino del Carmen, is typical: "Today after five years of paternal care in which I have suffered the greatest labors [a woman claiming to be his mother] presents herself asking for his return." Another caretaker, Juana Ferrá, similarly complained, "The petitioner only now claims to be the grandmother of a child [eight-year-old Isidro] educated and reared through my work." Tapia's ward, Victorino, was an apprentice shoemaker, and Ferrá, according to her rival, was "keeping [Isidro] for her service."[56] These and many other caretakers asserted that in their relationships with fostered children, the labor that counted was their own.

In this sense, by virtue of their very existence, the poor and parentless were the living embodiment of an outstanding debt. It was a debt that was implicit, customary, and in practice nonmonetary, but a debt nonetheless, incurred by crianza itself, to be repaid by the children (or by natal kin, if they had any). Significantly, while parents embroiled in disputes with caretakers might argue that such debts had been satisfied by their children's labor to the household, they never challenged the premise of the debt itself. That in certain, specific instances caretakers did in fact receive payment for rearing unrelated children highlights the existence of debt in the many instances where they did not. Children of well-off

parents—illegitimates whose progenitors desired to recognize them socially, as well as the children of parents who were estranged, divorced, or
deceased—were sometimes reared in nonnatal households. But their status there, mediated by the payment of a pension, was clearly different
from that of children taken in "for charity." The distinction between a
niña pensionista versus a "true servant," between an *educanda* (a student
or pupil) and a *sirvienta* was self-evident to litigants.[57] Such distinctions
were also operative in welfare asylums, which routinely distinguished
between different classes of wards, namely, children with resources to
pay their keep (*pensionistas*) and those who earned it with their labor
(*espósitos, abandonados*).[58] The distinction was about living conditions,
but more fundamentally it was about a child's social position within the
asylum or household—as well as beyond. The life history of Secundino
Alvarez, the illegitimate protagonist of chapter 2, reflects this logic. Secundino's father initially paid for his upkeep in the home of a nurse. But
when the wealthy merchant left Chile for California, he made no provisions for the boy, who slid abruptly and inexorably into dependent servitude. The clarity with which witnesses remembered his precipitous fall
from pensionista to sirviente is striking.[59]

The distinction between "the pensioned" and "the abandoned" also
speaks to the role, or more accurately the absence, of money in these
arrangements. Legal claims and counterclaims to monetary compensation occurred in judicial disputes when caretakers insisted on payment
for crianza and opponents demanded back pay for children's services.
But such haggling arose only ex post facto, when custodial conflicts
arose, and perhaps as part of a legal foil. Outside the court, and aside
from the specific scenarios noted above, money seems to have been
almost universally absent from these relationships. The tutelary service
of children was mediated instead by a nonmonetary calculus of labor and
rearing, charity, gratitude, and obligation.[60] This calculus helps explain
why poor mothers were sometimes reluctant to take up charitable offers
to rear their infants (see chapter 5). These "free" offers may in fact have
placed them or their children in future obligation to the volunteer.

Conflict and competition over children played out not only between
individuals but also with institutions. Santiaguinos periodically grumbled
that the city's charitable asylums unfairly restricted access to their young
wards-cum-servants. Madre Bernarda of the Casa de Huérfanos noted

13. Advertised in the classifieds: books, salt, children. The Casa de Huérfanos exhorts "charitable persons" to take foundlings from the asylum. The ad ran over several weeks in various Santiago newspapers in November 1866.

that householders frustrated by the ineptitude of young children they had taken from the asylum "got angry because they thought we had the best ones hidden for our service." The simmering tensions erupted in 1866, when, in response to a complaint by a petitioner denied a child, the Casa was forced to temporarily suspend (the already lax) placement procedures. To the horror of the nuns, the asylum's administrator placed front-page ads in the city papers announcing that orphans were available for the taking. Years later, Madre Bernarda would lament the free-for-all that ensued as the Casa was "invaded by people of all types" who removed children wantonly.[61]

In the 1870s and 1880s, the anticlerical, populist newspaper *El Padre Cobos* regularly aimed its barbs at the nuns and priests who administered local welfare asylums, accusing them of rounding up young vagrants and holding children against their parents' will. They also accused the asylums of overcharging those who sought servants and hoarding their wards in the face of a shortage of domestics.[62] The implication was that not just parents but all the city's householders had a right to children lodged in local asylums. Such denunciations by a populist broadsheet suggest that a broad swathe of society associated poor children dependent on charity with household service. But if the newspaper's vociferous populism took up the cause of modest householders who sought the services of young criados, it did not, significantly, identify with the criados themselves.

Such scenarios played out in Santiago, but nineteenth-century Chile was an overwhelmingly agrarian society and children's work was also a routine aspect of the rural economy.[63] Young criados were part of this labor force. Analyses of household composition in nineteenth-century Chile have found that inquilino and smallholder households alike often included *allegados*, or nonkin dependents, particularly on market-oriented estates. Some of these allegados were children.[64] One was Juan Ybaceta Barrera. Reared in the home of Manuel Carvallo, at seventeen Ybaceta was working as the unskilled peon (*gañán*) of one Eleuterio Carvallo—surely a relative of the family who raised him.[65]

The previous chapter described how the income that inquilinos' wives earned as nurses for the Casa de Huérfanos helped bolster the declining prospects of inquilino households on haciendas near Santiago. Evidence suggests that those infants grew up to provide labor to the households and their haciendas. Inquilinos were required to provide a peon or peons who contributed a set amount of labor to the hacendado each year, but since inquilino families lacked the resources to hire laborers, these *peones obligados* were often members of the household itself. During the latter half of the nineteenth century these labor obligations increased, such that inquilinos were expected, as Arnold Bauer has put it, to "furnish ... any son old enough to 'swing a hoe.'"[66]

14. Children on Hacienda El Huique (Colchagua), 1930s. *Courtesy of the Museo Histórico Nacional.*

But were the youth who "swung hoes" always sons? Because the peon obligado did not receive a wage, the sons of inquilinos themselves often preferred to work as salaried peons on neighboring haciendas.[67] Enter the young criado, a youth reared in the inquilino household, indefinitely indebted to it, and by custom unpaid. In but not of the family, neither hijo nor free agent, such a dependent would be uniquely suited to fulfill this labor obligation. This dynamic may explain why inquilino households, which by all accounts were increasingly impoverished in the late nineteenth century, actively sought children from the Casa de Huérfanos and why they frequently petitioned to keep their nurslings after weaning. As Brian Loveman has noted, the hacienda was characterized by a tension between "the hacendado economy and the [inquilino] economy for use of existing labor resources."[68] By increasing the overall pool of labor, unrelated children reared by inquilinos served the interests of both.

Documentation from the Casa de Huérfanos shows that the asylum provided children to the wine-producing estates of the central valley in the 1920s and 1930s. As José del Pozo has noted, children were an important source of labor in Chilean viticulture, most obviously during the harvest. He finds ample evidence of child labor in the records of one estate, Santa Rita, located in the rural environs of Santiago and owned by Don Vicente García Huidobro. Santa Rita's administrators kept a "careful record" of the number of children living in inquilino households and directed that the application of sulfur on the vines be carried out "only by children." Who were these children? While the surviving documents of the Casa de Huérfanos are inconclusive about its relationship with Santa Rita, they do show that inquilinos from a neighboring estate owned by García Huidobro, El Principal, repeatedly solicited children. Five such adoptions are found among the fragmentary records of the late 1920s, the same years Santa Rita's administrators were counting small heads.[69]

The orphans of El Principal were part of a steady stream of Casa children sent to rural households in the vicinity of Santiago from at least the 1850s to at least the 1930s. While some rural adopters were identified as independent smallholders, the majority were apparently inquilinos. In the 1920s, almost 20 percent of the 239 children recorded were placed on perhaps two dozen estates in San Bernardo, Buin, Talagante, Pirque, and Puente Alto. Many went to large haciendas owned by the wealthy and politically powerful. Six went to Lo Herrera de Tango, the 3,000-hectare hacienda owned by Liberal Party congressman Don Eliodoro Yáñez. Seventeen went to Pirque, almost all to properties of Doña Emiliana Subercaseaux, founder of the Sociedad Protectora de la Infancia and widow of Don Melchor Concha y Toro, of viticultural fame.[70]

In fact, the Casa had long cultivated a relationship with local hacendados. In the 1850s, the institution's administrator sent a letter to landowners describing the activities of the asylum, which had been recently taken over by the Sisters of Providence, and soliciting the "charity of our hacendados." He asked them to donate cows and sheep to provide milk to the orphans and for training in "agricultural manual labor." The likelihood that they would be the beneficiaries of these future laborers was surely not lost on the hacendados, who responded generously to the petition.[71] In succeeding decades, landowners and their wives would write frequent letters to the Casa on behalf of inquilinas seeking to be contracted as nurses or desiring to adopt nurslings on a long-term basis.

15. Children work the grape harvest, 1930s. *Courtesy of the Museo Histórico Nacional.*

Finally, two long-standing administrators of the Casa, Joaquín Valledor and Nathaniel Miers-Cox, were themselves owners of large estates in the vicinity of the Casa; Miers-Cox was also a founder of the hacendados' lobby, the Sociedad Nacional de Agricultura.[72] This is not particularly surprising given that the administrators of public beneficence institutions routinely hailed from the landed oligarchy. But it does reinforce the imbrication of child circulation, beneficence institutions, and the hacienda complex.

By World War I, the intimate paternalism of agrarian social relations was on the wane.[73] But hacendados' petitions to the Casa on behalf of inquilinos seeking orphans suggest that in this realm, such social relations endured. Meanwhile, as the first glimmerings of labor protest began to emerge in the Chilean countryside, the Casa records show no appreciable change in long-term patterns of rural child placement. Access to the labor of young criados was a historic perquisite of inquilinos and hacendados alike, one that was very slow to change.

Status, Patronage, and Life Cycles of Subordination

Tutelary servitude reflects the value and meaning of children and their work, but these practices were about more than child labor. They entailed richly elaborated social relationships that must be evaluated within a broader cultural context. Implicated in the movement of children across households were dynamics of patronage and class power. When parents and patrones fought over children, they were also fighting about status. The mid-nineteenth-century suit Pascuala Armijo brought against the family of Don Pedro Méndez demonstrates how class relations and their attendant tensions were telescoped onto children and their socialization. Armijo had entrusted her twelve-year-old daughter, María, to the Méndez household "not as a servant but rather so that she be subject to the respect and supervision" of the household's mistress while awaiting an opening in a convent school. She asked that María not be sent into the street in order "to preserve her from the vices that she might acquire with such liberty." The mistress, however, had done just that, and when Méndez refused to return her daughter, Armijo filed suit.

Her objections concerned the kind of work her daughter should do and the type of education she should receive. More obliquely, they referenced status. Don Pedro Méndez met this subtext head on, challenging Armijo's contention that her daughter "had . . . entered my house as a *señorita*" with this biting retort: "Given . . . her social condition and humble cradle, [María] is nothing but a criada." But if Méndez and Armijo were at odds about María's status as señorita or sirvienta, they implicitly agreed that her presence in the Méndez household reflected something about the relative social standing of patrón and mother and the obligations that mediated their relationship.[74]

The ties of dependence that child circulation generated were, like kinship itself, multigenerational. Masters and mistresses might rear—and maintain in their employ—the children of their servants. María Armijo was the third generation of her family to work in the Méndez household. Sometimes patrones had even reared servant-mothers from an early age before in turn rearing their children.[75] In such instances, criados were not atomistic individuals radically bereft of natal origins. They had kin ties, and those ties were inseparable from the bonds of service. Such multigenerational webs of patronage safeguarded poor children's survival even as they ensured their subordination. Placing children in service laid the groundwork for the indispensable patronage networks that would yield employment, financial assistance, and other forms of aid in adulthood. Sometimes children themselves found it necessary to call upon a patron's support, as when a ten-year-old coachman who had accidentally run over a pedestrian presented several patrons who attested to his "honorability," "formality," and "irreproachable conduct."[76]

While child circulation usually involved the children of the poor, elites sometimes sent their own illegitimate children to be raised by dependents, a practice that also reinforced patronage ties. In the 1860s, a family of inquilinos on Pedro Antonio Ramírez's hacienda discovered a foundling abandoned near their house. They reared the baby, served as her godparents, and briefly received a stipend from Ramírez, who contributed to the girl's upbringing, following the familiar idiom, "out of charity." Years later, a court determined what the inquilino family had known all along: the foundling was Ramírez's illegitimate daughter. Their ties with their patrón were likely strengthened by the presence of his daughter in their household, the spiritual kinship they shared with him, and the fact they were privy to his long-standing secret.[77] As Grant McCracken has argued of Tudor England, the transfer of children among households served both "to unite and differentiate hierarchical ranks." That is, following on Marshall Sahlins's work on gifting, "even as reciprocity can exercise its power to bind groups, it does so in such a way as to emphasize their distinctness."[78] In Chile, too, child circulation was a quotidian practice that reinforced status distinctions between individuals and households.

The politics of status played out not only with elites but also among plebeians. Allusions to status informed an encounter between Juana Paez, a criada, and Elvira Moreno, a housewife and her neighbor, when they came to blows in San Felipe in 1894. The cause of their altercation is unclear, but when accosted by Paez, Moreno sneered that she "didn't have any reason to get involved in the affairs . . . of servants." When Paez's patrón filed assault charges on her behalf, Moreno further declared, "The court should take notice of the inequality of conditions that exists between herself and the complainant since she is a servant." Moreno was apparently a modest housewife just a few years older than Paez; her allusion to inequality reveals the status hierarchies at work within plebeian communities and the place of criados within them.[79]

Indeed, as noted above, many of those who reared child servants were themselves "masters [and mistresses] of small worlds"—artisans and inquilinos, strapped widows and modest proprietors.[80] Sometimes what distinguished natal families from foster ones was not class status but life cycle stage. The indigent single mothers forced to place children in exploitive relations of crianza aged into penurious older women who took in children as free domestic help.[81] Plebeian patrones, like their elite counterparts, could assert extraordinary rights within arrangements of tutelary servitude. Delfina Galán had reared fourteen-year-old Fortunata Rojas "since she was small," but when Fortunata's father solicited her return, Galán flatly refused: "The minor . . . had been left under her authority as a servant, so she believed she had the right to have her continue living with her." Her claim reflects how even a poor, female caretaker who hardly fit the standard profile of a "patriarch" could harbor a bald sense of entitlement over her criada.[82]

If child circulation illuminates the micropolitics of status and subordination, at a macro level it reflects how prevailing labor forms were associated with particular practices of child socialization. Historians of nineteenth-century Chile have speculated about the formation of peon identity and how labor market migration gave rise to an ambulatory "way of life" associated with loose family ties and rootlessness. Tutelary servitude helps explain the formation of peon identity and, by extension, the social reproduction of a rootless underclass. Such dynamics are evident in the life histories of people like itinerant laborer Narciso Flores. Asked about his previous residences during a bigamy investigation in 1856, the twenty-five-year old Flores recounted the following life history:

> The house of my father is in Ninquihue, department of Quirihue, but when I was very small they brought me to the house of my grandparents in La Vega de Itatá, where I remained until about age 6, and I returned to . . . my father's house where I stayed a year or two and afterwards they took me to Cauquenes towards the mountains where I stayed for a long time and when I was an older youth [*un mozo grande*] . . . I returned to my father's house [for] six months, returning afterwards to Cauquenes, [where] I stayed about a year, and afterwards I came to Talca, where I have been about ten years.

Pablo Pérez narrates a similar experience in *The Orphan*. When he left the Casa de Huérfanos around the year 1870, Pérez was about seven ("I had just lost my first tooth"); by age twelve, he had served as a criado in fourteen households in Quillota, Limache, Olmué, and the surrounding countryside, moving with the vicissitudes of the harvest and the capricious will of his patrones. At twelve, he was hired as a peon and over the next four years worked on two haciendas and in a Valparaíso café before moving on to brief stints in the Peruvian guano mines, the nitrate mines of Iquique and Chañaral, and a steamship that went to Callao, Guayaquil, Panama, and back to Valparaíso. After nine years of itineracy, a seasoned sixteen-year-old Pérez returned to Santiago, where his unstable work life continued.

What is striking about the childhoods of Flores and Pérez is how their circulation as children mirrors the patterns of adult labor itinerary. Child circulation, it seems, constituted a kind of prepeonage.[83] Like his adult counterparts, Pérez recounts moving "in a snap" (*en dos por tres zás*) whenever a new patrón came along who offered him better treatment or, later, a higher wage.[84] His trajectory, which ranged across rural harvests, urban apprenticeships and commercial employment, the northern

mines, and beyond the borders of the patria, retraces with striking preci-
sion the paradigmatic circuits of adult male peons.[85]

As adults, Flores and Pérez continued their peripatetic lives, the former as a self-identified *gañán* (itinerant laborer) and *viajero* (literally, a
traveler), the latter as the servant of a steamship captain, in a Valparaíso
press, and as a soldier in the War of the Pacific.[86] Indeed their life histories suggest an almost seamless continuum from child criado to adult
peon. Almost seamless—but not entirely so. For Pablo Pérez, the transition to adult peonage was marked by a single, well-defined experience:
his first wage. At age twelve, after five years laboring in foster households
and eager to "free myself from so much tutelage [*tutela*]," Pérez left his
most recent patrones and hired himself out to an hacienda for twenty
centavos a day, perhaps two-thirds the going rate for adult male peons. It
was by his own account "the first time I received money for my own
work," and two decades later, he still remembered "how much pleasure it
gave me to receive six *chauchas* [slang for coins], the first chauchas that I
received." Pérez was no longer a criado who labored for a foster household but an autonomous, waged peon who worked for himself. "From
then on, one could say, I was on my own [*quedé por mi cuenta*], since
now I paid for my laundry and my clothes."[87] That the young Pérez
experienced waged peonage as a manifest improvement in his condition
tells us something about young criados' profound experiences of subordination and also suggests the cultural significance of a monetary wage.
Significantly, this wage permitted not leisure or new forms of consumption but simply the ability to provide, independently, for his own basic
needs. Pérez's understanding of domestic dependence as constitutive of
the criado's condition suggests that life stages for poor males were demarcated not by the fact of work or by the kind of work one performed
but by the nature of the labor arrangements in which one was inserted.

Circulation apparently presaged peonage for girls as well, though in
contrast to Flores or Pérez, girls appear much less nomadic. Whether as
infants or adolescents, they were often sent from the central or southern
provinces to foster households in cities, a migratory pattern resembling
that of adult women, who also tended to make a single rural-to-urban
move.[88] What is more, young female criadas were apparently more likely
to remain in a single household for an extended period. While there is no
evidence to suggest that most criadas stayed on into adulthood with the

patrones who reared them, it *is* the case that most of the individuals who stayed on (at least of those encountered in the historical record) were women.[89] The many cases of adolescent girls who ran away from their masters do not necessarily contradict this assertion. Rather than reflecting a female propensity to flight, they may simply reflect masters' expectations that girls would remain longer or indefinitely.[90]

Ultimately, the process by which young criadas grew into adult women peons was even more seamless than for males, because the most common employment for poor women, domestic service, implied laboring under the auspices of a patron's household as did child criados of both sexes. The continuity of domestic tutelage for women probably meant it did not mark female life stages as it did male ones.[91] But the domestic autonomy Pablo Pérez experienced at age twelve, while more difficult for young women to achieve, may have been just as sought after. The adolescent criada Ernestina Pérez's explanation of why she had run away—that the master who reared her did not pay her a wage—suggests that at least by the early twentieth century, poor, young criadas hankered for waged autonomy as much as their male counterparts.

The View from Below: Self-Determination through Self-Circulation

Tutelary servitude delivered children into the repertoires of adult peonage, but criados themselves were by no means passive in this process. As scholars have noted, discerning the agency of children and youth can present stubborn methodological problems, and the Chilean sources are no exception. For one, the protagonists in Chilean courts were consistently adults; in no case in the voluminous judicial record did a child initiate legal proceedings. And while young criados testified as victims or suspects of crimes, they were rarely consulted in disputes over control of their persons. These silences are not simply the unfortunate byproducts of judicial procedure but are in fact richly indicative of social attitudes toward children. As one judge declared, a ten-year-old was too young "to determine . . . the use of his person."[92] Language itself underscored criados' passivity. Children were said to be "loaned" (*prestado/a*) to other households, or else "donated" (*donado/a*), "given" (*dado/a, entregado/a*), "rented" (*alquilado/a*), "contracted" (*conchabado/a*), "placed" (*colocado/a*), or "asked for" (*pedido/a*).

The legal narratives that patrones, parents, and judges wove in disputes over criados also communicate passivity and possession. Luis Siderey filed a kidnapping charge against another man when he found Ernestina Pérez, the criada he had reared, working as his nursemaid. Francisco Días brought charges against Pedro Romero for the return of his eight-year-old godson, José Gregorio Alvear, "whom he has stolen from me [*que me ha sustraido*]." The grandmother of twelve-year-old Juan Cantalicios demanded the boy's return, accusing his patrona of giving him to another woman without her consent. And Constancia Améstica's master filed criminal charges of rapto (sexual abduction) against a young man who had "stolen" the twelve-year-old from his home, where she had grown up. In all of these cases, adults brought legal action against other adults for control of children. Implicit in these judicial actions, and in the very legal categories invoked (rapto, kidnapping), is the conceit of possession: the fundamental assumption that *some* adult had dominion over the person of a young criado.

This conceit obfuscates what on closer examination turns out to be an unexpected degree of volition on the part of the criados themselves. Ernestina Pérez's statement belied the charge of kidnapping: she had left Siderey's household, she declared, because "he treated me very badly and did not pay me a wage." The "stolen" José Gregorio had in fact turned up at Pedro Romero's house seeking to be taken in. Likewise, Juan Cantalicio's mistress had not given him to another patrona; he had gone himself, in spite of her "tenacious" opposition, when offered a better wage. Finally, Améstica told the judge, not only had she consented to her "rapto" but she had done so in the hope her abductor would find her a position in another household where "she would have a better time than in that of her patrón."[93]

These cases suggest that while children never initiated their own legal proceedings, their actions frequently prompted adults to do so. What is more, the legal narratives obfuscate how effective this strategy actually was: strikingly, judicial authorities never returned criados to the households from which they had run away. The judge's intimation that a ten-year-old was too young to "determine the use of his person" notwithstanding, boys and girls this age and younger did precisely that. Again,

Pablo Pérez provides us with a privileged view of criados' own perceptions, observing of his long succession of patrones: "They only wanted me to take advantage of my services and make me work like a donkey . . . So that it was not rare to be in one house today and another one tomorrow. With the goal of having better luck, I went wherever they convinced me [things would be better]."[94] Children like Pérez engaged in a kind of self-circulation among households based on the dictates of their own volition and the hope of a better situation. They treated servitude as a free relationship to be entered and left at will, rather than the perpetual indenture their patrones envisioned.[95]

That these children could leave a bad master in search of a better one reveals at once the possibilities and limits of self-determination. Significantly, most runaways turned up working as servants in the homes of new patrones.[96] No matter how often he changed households, Pablo Pérez met with poor treatment at the hands of exploitive employers. Moreover, as we have seen, the tutelary servitude of children presaged lifelong dependence. Criados were remarkably successful at extricating themselves from specific households, but they were largely powerless to escape the relations of subordination that pervaded this social order.

Law played a perhaps unexpected role in this subordination. In appealing to police and judges to reestablish control over children, patrones implicitly asserted a *legal* claim of authority, but as we saw in chapter 5, those who reared unrelated minors almost never enjoyed formal power over them. As nonprogenitors, they did not possess patria potestad, they rarely enjoyed legal guardianship, and in a republic that had freed its slaves in the 1820s, they could hardly claim ownership.[97] Criados were, in short, dependents who fell beyond the legal categories that structured dependency. Thus patrones were obliged to resort to ill-fitting criminal categories—kidnapping, rapto, flight—to characterize their loss of control over these children. Luis Siderey told the police "that Ernestina Pérez, fourteen years old, whom he had reared since early childhood because her mother and father are dead" had left his home—as if explicating her life history lent weight to his claim. But the law proved largely unreceptive to such petitions. As the judge put it, "The occurrence denounced by Luis Siderey, that the girl . . . whom he reared since childhood left his house, does not constitute a crime."[98] There had been no crime, no transgression of Siderey's rights over Pérez, because the law recognized no such rights in the first place.

Conclusions: Law's Limits, Charity's Reach, and the Demarcation of Public and Private

The German traveler Eduardo Poeppig identified the role of law as a fundamental difference between the lives of child servants he observed in Chile in the 1820s and those of indentured laborers in North America. North American indenture, he argued, was "without a doubt more severe and limits personal liberty much more" since a dependent could be "pursued by the police . . . [and] returned to his patrón."[99] Whether less severe or not, the Chilean state's posture of nonintervention contrasted with prevailing practices not only in North America but also elsewhere in Latin America. No special courts assigned orphans to masters as in Brazil. No notaries formalized the household placement of child servants as in Buenos Aires or child apprentices as in eighteenth-century Lima. No municipal regulations restricted young criados' freedom to circulate among employers, as in nineteenth-century Peru.[100] Undoubtedly state regulation was of limited reach in many of these places, and extralegal practices thrived there as well. Still, in the self-consciously statist, legalistic, and increasingly urbanized society that was Chile, the almost total absence of even notarial contracts mediating the circulation of children is striking. Courts generally rejected pecuniary claims for (masters') crianza expenses or (criados') back wages and also, as we have seen, refused to enforce masters' dominion over the person of their criados.

But even if law did not regulate tutelary servitude, it shaped the social field on which parents, patrones, and children lived and worked. It did so as a kind of foil that, in highlighting what these relationships were *not*, defined what they *were*. In the absence of any formal, legal standing in the household, criados were construed as beneficiaries of a customary charity. And in nineteenth-century Chilean social thought, charity itself was defined against the law, its very essence its distinction from legal obligation. A contemporary jurist's opposition to legal adoption captures with particular clarity how charity and rights were understood as mutually exclusive frameworks for defining social relations. The jurist argued that legal adoption "is nothing more than . . . beneficence converted into an obligation or . . . charity by force," whereas "charity and beneficence are not legally [*en derecho*] a strict duty, nor is it just that . . . the law make [them] a true obligation."[101] As beneficiaries of benevolence, in other words, criados were by definition not bearers of rights; they were *hijos ajenos*, other people's children, as opposed to *hijos de familia*, rights-bearing minors living in the bosom of legally recognized, patriarchal, legitimate families. To draw on Ariela Dubler's characterization of single women's legal status vis-à-vis marriage, young Chilean criados lived in the shadow of family, their status governed by family's normative framework even as they inhabited terrain outside of its formal boundaries.[102]

Private and unregulated, tutelary servitude provides yet another illustration of the broad circumscription of the Chilean state's power over certain kinds of children. Gender, sexuality, households, and private life have been fruitfully cast as sites of domination and resistance between state and popular culture. Criados displace this focus on "state" and "society," highlighting dynamics of class, gender, and generational power as they operated within and across households. Massively practiced and utterly commonplace, tutelary servitude provided labor, reinforced patronage networks, reinscribed status, and reproduced peonage. While compensatory social histories have sometimes portrayed the Chilean poor as solidaristic and morally superior to a rapacious elite, criados reveal that exploitation reached into inquilino households and urban slums. This is, in part, a story of poor people exploiting even poorer children.

Children in turn reveal the multiple articulations between formal and informal, institutional and extrainstitutional, public and private spheres. Comparing such constructs as "hijos de familia" and "hijos ajenos," kin rights versus charity, illuminates the relationship of law, state beneficence, and family. It also speaks to the shifting boundaries of public and private in the shadow of liberalism. Young criados inhabited a terrain beyond law, yet Church- and state-sponsored asylums obliquely subsidized tutelary servitude, and by extension, the costs of social reproduction for households of all social levels.

The tale most often told about states and families in nineteenth-century Latin America is one of increasing regulation and intervention. In Chile, and perhaps throughout the hemisphere, poor children suggest a different, less unidirectional narrative: one of a state that regulated some aspects of private life even as it withdrew from arenas that at other historical moments were considered the purview of state intervention. Children illuminate the role of state institutions that actively, if inadvertently, fomented vernacular kin practices. And they point to the fact that legal reform was contingent on these very practices. In short, they direct our attention to privacy and privatization as enduring characteristics of society and state formation in modern Latin America.

It took three weeks for Valparaíso householder Luis Siderey to locate his runaway servant. Called before the court, Ernestina Pérez narrated her flight from the home of the man who had reared her. After working in a kitchen on the Plaza Central, an acquaintance recommended her for a job as a nursemaid in a home not far from Siderey's. The position, which paid twenty pesos a month, was clearly an improvement over her previous one, where as a criada "reared from early childhood" she had not been paid at all. Nevertheless, twenty pesos was still a pittance in 1918, perhaps a third of what child laborers earned in industrial jobs.[103] As we saw above, the court declined to recognize Siderey's complaint. And so as a result not of the law's forceful intercession but of its active circumscription, Pérez's rupture with the only "family" she knew became definitive.

She had succeeded in gaining autonomy from the crushing paternalism of tutelary servitude but had been delivered into a new kind of dependence. She was fourteen or sixteen years old—tellingly, there was no consensus in the record—illiterate, kinless, and on her own. We can draw from Ernestina Pérez's story an understanding of how child-rearing patterns and ideas of family reproduced social dependencies and status hierarchies. As we will see in the epilogue, much would change in Chile in the tumultuous decades of the early twentieth century, but for young people like Pérez, those dependencies and hierarchies would prove stubbornly persistent.

EPILOGUE

Young Marginals at the Centenary:

One Hundred Years of *Huachos*

The Activist

"My happiness is to have all children as hijos, to guide them, inspire them, because they are spirits that need not only to learn but to create," wrote Elvira Santa Cruz Ossa, the celebrated journalist, writer, editor, outspoken feminist, and activist on behalf of women's and children's welfare. Born in 1886, Santa Cruz Ossa's extraordinarily long and varied career reflected many of the changes occurring in Chile in the 1920s and 1930s. She served as a government inspector of women and children's labor, organized social assistance for poor school children, founded rural summer camps for working-class youngsters, and for almost forty years edited *El Peneca*, a celebrated children's magazine that gained hemispheric circulation.

Most obviously, Santa Cruz Ossa's wide-ranging social, intellectual, and literary labors reflected new public initiatives concerning children. While charitable assistance to poor children (and women) was nothing new, Santa Cruz Ossa's democratic vision of childhood as a birthright of rich and poor alike certainly was. Her career also reflected the marked political transformations occurring in early-twentieth-century Chile. Populist, middle-class reformist parties had begun to challenge traditional oligarchic forces and by 1920 had elected their first president of the republic. Feminists like Santa Cruz Ossa were among the new constituencies to participate in this widening political sphere. Meanwhile, her activism on behalf of workers' rights reflected perhaps the single most striking political development in early-twentieth-century Chile and Latin

America: the rise of working-class and popular-democratic movements in response to intensifying capitalist development. Beginning in the 1890s, Chilean mines, cities, and ports witnessed a surge of labor mobilization, and leftist political parties emerged to represent the interests of an increasingly militant working class.

Yet the political system seemed incapable of confronting the social, economic, and political challenges of the new century. Social and labor legislation stalled in a do-nothing parliament even as class tensions intensified. At the centenary of the republic's birth in 1910, critics of various ideological persuasions denounced the political and moral "crisis" of the Chilean republic and the venality and incompetence of its traditional political class.[1] The power of the oligarchy was unmistakably on the wane, but what would replace it was as yet unclear.

How did this shifting political landscape shape family and filiation, realms of social practice that, as we have seen, were so intimately related to class relations? To what extent did these transformations affect the social condition of children? At the turn of the twentieth century, Latin America had the lowest rates of marriage and probably highest rates of extramarital birth in the world.[2] In Chile, where nuptiality was low and illegitimacy high even by regional standards, familiar patterns of child circulation, kinlessness, and illegitimacy persisted at least into the 1930s. Thereafter, the region would witness a striking shift in historic patterns of family formation as illegitimacy declined and marriage surged. Nowhere was that change more dramatic than in Chile. The ever-elusive legitimate, patriarchal family appeared to become a tangible reality for more people, though the causes, consequences, and meanings of this shift can only be hinted at here. This epilogue sketches in broad strokes some of the ways social practices and normative frameworks surrounding filiation changed as well as the ways they did not.

The twentieth century also witnessed a transformation in the Chilean state's relationship with family and filiation. After the turn of the century, critics of diverse ideological stripes seized on illegitimacy as a vehicle of social and political critique. Reform of filiation law emerged as a major focus of juridical interest and for the first time since the Civil Code's promulgation in the 1850s, the legal regime that had alienated so many individuals from kin networks came under attack. As political elites groped for solutions to *la crisis*, nineteenth-century liberal law suddenly looked distinctly archaic. Ultimately, however, legal efforts to remake filiation proved tentative, partial, and protracted. It was not until the eve of the twenty-first century that the nineteenth-century legal tradition explored in this book came under frontal attack, signaling a very different posture of the Chilean state toward poor children and their families.

Huachos at the Centenary

In 1927, Monica Donaire petitioned the Casa de Huérfanos to give her *un chico*, a boy. In a time-honored tradition of clientelism, she presented a patron's letter describing her as a married woman with grown children, a resident of the hacienda of Santa Rita with "a good house" (*buena casa de campo*), and a member of a morally upright family (*gente de conducta correcta*). The relationship of Donaire to her "chico," and that of the patron to Donaire, recapitulate a modes of social relations we have seen throughout this book. Here was another rural denizen recurring to the Casa for a kinless child who, very likely, would occupy a servile position in her household. Here was a letter writer who, while not specifying the precise nature of her relationship with Donaire, was clearly a social superior. The persistence of these social forms is particularly striking given the identity of the patrona: writing on behalf of Monica Donaire was Elvira Santa Cruz Ossa.[3] Her fleeting appearance in the Casa records reminds us that against the convulsed political and social landscape of the early decades of the twentieth century, many of the patterns and practices involving poor and parentless minors documented in this book persisted.

The child Donaire sought from the Casa de Huérfanos was in fact part of a surging orphan population. For years the Casa had witnessed a steady increase in admissions, receiving more than 18,000 children during the first quarter of the twentieth century alone. At its peak in the late 1920s, it was managing the care of some 2,000 children at a time.[4] Beyond the numbers, internal documentation from the Casa attests to the persistence of familiar vectors of child circulation: poverty, illegitimacy, and the inability of women on their own to support young children. Indeed, illegitimacy rates reached new highs in the 1920s, fluctuating between 35 and 40 percent of all births. Infant mortality also remained epidemic, with more than a quarter of children dying before their first birthday.

The fate of the Casa's children did not change appreciably either: this asylum and others continued to produce a steady stream of labor destined for urban households and rural haciendas. As Mother Superior Bernarda Morin observed in 1899, "The same thing that happens now happened then [in the 1860s]. In times of scarcity or want, the petitions to obtain . . . [an orphan] multiplied, with each [petitioner] having the idea of shaping [the orphans] in their own way and making use of their services."[5] Placement records from the 1920s, including Donaire's petition, reflect the survival of traditional patterns of child transfer. According to official protocols, children were now placed in private homes only once they were "capable of fending for themselves," at age fifteen or older, a policy made possible by the expansion of the Casa and its services. But in the 1920s some eight-year-olds still left the Casa as servants. As late as the mid-1930s, household placements were still the modus operandi, though they were now monitored by the Casa's newly established social service department.[6] Meanwhile, judicial records confirm that young criados continued to be common fixtures in Chilean households.[7]

As we saw in chapter 4, kinship was central to civil identity, but Church and state bureaucracies, including welfare asylums, systematically erased origins and rendered people kinless. The enduring vigor of children's institutions, at least fourteen of which were founded after the turn of the century, implied the continued bureaucratic production of kinlessless. Indeed, the suppression of children's kin identities in the Casa de Huérfanos records is most systematic in placements after the turn of the century. The surging numbers of interned children meant that a contingent of kinless adults existed through the greater part of the twentieth century.[8] Meanwhile, expanding state services and regulatory capacity in the early twentieth century only exacerbated the consequences of kinlessness. The "children of Don Nobody," the kinless newspaper boys prevented by municipal regulations from working without a birth certificate, illustrate the consequences of bureaucratization for those lacking kin origins.

But if huachismo persisted, there were also intimations of change, especially in terms of the normative matrix in which it was embedded. In 1899, the mother superior of the Casa de Huérfanos observed that once upon a time "many people affirmed that the purpose of the Casa . . . was to prepare servants for the comfortable class of society." If this historic function was slow to die, in some quarters child servitude now provoked a distinct unease. Both the mother superior and the administrator of the Casa went so far as to characterize the destiny of the asylum's children as "slavery." Of the female orphans, the latter declared:

> Placement in domestic service is the best option we have. [But] for this one has to close one's eyes to the sufferings to which those who must do it are exposed. With the awareness that it is really slavery, one must submit to the hard necessity of giving away some girls who are older and who are of an age at which they can take care of themselves, to make room for so many others in the Casa.[9]

On the other hand, there existed no hegemonic consensus about such matters. Several years later under a different administrator, discussions were under way to formalize rather than eliminate these practices by establishing a School of Domestic Service within the Casa.[10] Ultimately, these tensions are captured in the Casa de Huérfanos's rebaptism in 1929. Arguing that the children reared there "should not have to carry a stigma that complicates their future," an administrator prevailed upon the Junta de Beneficencia to excise the word "orphan" from the asylum's name. One hundred and seventy years after its founding, the Casa de Huérfanos became the Casa Nacional del Niño. The new appellation echoed the identification of poor children with the nation even as the nation continued to outsource them to private foster parents–cum-patrones.[11]

Amid the shifting terrain of class politics, the old paternalistic ethos was slowly changing. Tensions of change and continuity are further documented in wills. In 1850, 25 percent of testators in provincial San Felipe and 16.5 percent in Santiago made bequests to unrelated children whom they had reared. Twenty-five years later, in 1875, such bequests had declined dramatically. By 1900, testamentary references to criados had disappeared entirely.

Here is one of the most compelling indications of change, but one that on the face of it appears to contradict evidence from the Casa de Huérfanos and the judicial record. Were criados disappearing from Chilean households, or weren't they? What the wills appear to document is not the disappearance of tutelary servitude but a shift in its class distribution

TABLE 7. Percentage of Testators Leaving
Bequests to Child Criados.

	1850	1875	1900
San Felipe	24.6	9.8	0
Santiago	16.5	11.3	0

Source: ANSF, ANS. The calculation is based on a sample
of 400 wills. See also the methodological appendix.

and class meanings. In a word, child servants were no longer the symbols
of conspicuous paternalism they had once been, and elites changed their
engagement with these practices. By the turn of the century, the households taking children in were more modest, their members less able to
pursue paternalistic largesse vis-à-vis dependents and indeed less likely
to write wills in the first place. The steadily rising cost of living beginning
in the 1890s probably made young, unpaid domestics disproportionately
attractive to modest households. The Casa's child placements also reflect
this shift. In the 1850s, 1860s, and 1870s a broad spectrum of households
solicited children. By the 1920s, foster households had become primarily
rural and more homogeneously poor. Of 239 placements in the 1920s
and early 1930s, for example, in only 6 cases was the solicitant identified
as an independent property owner.

Criados' disappearance from elite houses did not portend elites' with-
drawal from practices of child circulation, however. It simply meant the
nature of their participation had changed. Elite women no longer took
poor and parentless children into their own houses, but they were as
active as ever as intermediaries who negotiated placements in other
households and asylums. Elvira Santa Cruz Ossa's intercession on behalf
of Monica Donaire reflects this role. So too does Emiliana Subercaseaux's
involvement in the 1894 Puelma affair, described in the introduction.
Fifty years earlier, Doña Emiliana might have taken the waifs into her
own household and remembered them in her will. Now she placed them
in the children's asylum she had recently established. The asylum itself,
which was subsidized by public funds, institutionalized this mode of
patronage: every child who entered was sponsored by a *protector*, many

of whom were women hailing from the rarified echelons of the Chilean oligarchy.[12] Another important shift was the advent of social work in the 1920s, which signaled the professionalization of women's roles as child brokers. Many hospitals and welfare institutions established social service units headed by social workers who moved children among families and asylums. Clientelistic modes of operation had not disappeared from elites' cultural repertoire. They were simply being displaced outside of their own households, and they were becoming professionalized.

Middle- and upper-class mobilizations on behalf of poor children in the early twentieth century were unprecedented in size and scope, and in Chile as elsewhere children's industrial labor was a particular source of critique and condemnation. But the doctors, lawyers, politicians, and philanthropists who championed the cause of child welfare were either oblivious to tutelary servitude or, more likely, tacitly approving of it. As one outspoken proponent of regulating child labor asserted, children should be restricted to light work in the countryside or "in the home, together with their parents or guardians, as assistants to them." Perhaps this reasoning explains why Santa Cruz Ossa, who inspected child labor conditions in workshops and factories, was willing to arrange placement of a child in domestic tutelage. Tentative child-welfare legislation likewise ignored the subordination of child criados.[13] If anything, the attention accorded modern, industrial forms of child labor rendered older and more widespread domestic modes all the more invisible.

Illegitimacy: Anatomy of a Crisis

If tutelary servitude went largely overlooked, the opposite was true of illegitimacy. The first three decades of the century witnessed a veritable explosion of interest in the topic. Augusto D'Halmar's well-known novella *Juana Lucero* (1902) presaged the contours of this discourse. Juana is the illegitimate daughter of a seamstress and an aristocratic congressional deputy who refuses to recognize her. When her mother dies, she is taken in by a great aunt who expects her to earn her keep by replacing the maid. When Juana goes to live in another home, she is raped by her patron, becomes pregnant, and descends into madness and prostitution. The novella, the original subtitle of which was *Los vicios de Chile* (Chile's

16. One of the families constituted by the Social Service, 1927. The social worker pictured assisted the couple in marrying and legitimating their children. Servicio Social no. 1/2, marzo/junio, 1927. *Courtesy of the Biblioteca Museo Nacional de Medicina Enrique Laval.*

vices), exemplifies the genre of *la crisis del centenario*, which explored Chile's perceived social, political, and moral malaise at the centenary of independence.[14] D'Halmar—the illegitimate son of a French merchant and a Chilean mother, who would go on to win the first National Prize for Literature—used Juana's story to indict class exploitation and, as his subtitle suggests, the decadence of the Chilean social order.

Illegitimacy worked as a literary trope because of its tremendous social and political resonance. Many works on child welfare and social medicine addressed the issue, but above all it was a topic of juridical interest. Between 1897 and 1931, at least eighty-five legal publications appeared on the topics of filiation and illegitimacy. The vast majority—seventy-five—were theses of law students from the University of Chile's Faculty of

Law, the premier proving ground for Chile's political class. By way of comparison, the number of theses on illegitimacy roughly equaled those written on labor law, unions, housing, and related topics *combined* in the same period. Some of the country's most respected legal and social thinkers wrote about illegitimacy.[15] Chilean jurists echoed a hemispheric preoccupation. Legal discrimination based on natal status was a perennial topic at the Pan-American Child Congresses held regularly beginning in 1916 and a subject of legal theses from Mexico to Peru to Brazil to Argentina.

At the heart of this upwelling of juridical interest were calls for reform of the nineteenth-century legal regime of filiation. For most jurists, the single most important issue was the reestablishment of paternity investigation, and at least two bills were proposed to this end (in 1916 and 1928). Critics condemned the Civil Code's treatment of filiation as anachronistic and identified its reform with progress and legal modernity. Many couched their critiques in terms of nationalism—epidemic rates of illegitimate birth were a stain that "our Chile shamefully flaunts before the other nations of the civilized world"—but above all, reform was a question of sound public policy.[16] Rather than promoting morality, the Civil Code was said to exacerbate illegitimacy, discourage marriage, and foment all manner of associated ills, including infant mortality, infanticide, juvenile delinquency, poverty, and the decadence of the "Chilean race."

During this time, of course, the only individuals with the right to file paternity suits were those born prior to the Civil Code. As discussed in chapter 2, these retroactive suits were adjudicated in the late nineteenth century according to the principle of social congruity, in which an illegitimate's status parity with his or her father was considered a precondition of legal kinship. In 1923, the Supreme Court rejected social congruity as a basis for ascertaining paternity, on the grounds that no such standard had existed in Iberian law.[17] The ruling explicitly repudiated more than a half century of Chilean judicial practice, yet its practical impact was limited since few retroactive paternity suits still found their way to court. The only illegitimates with the right to sue were approaching age seventy (at the youngest), and virtually no witnesses to their early childhood were still around to testify.[18]

Writers on illegitimacy were almost unanimous in their call for re-
instating paternity investigation, though many favored restrictions to
avoid "abuse" of the practice.[19] They also differed about whether children who proved their paternity in court would have rights to inheritance or merely to basic support. Beyond this reform, jurists variously
called for abolishing the category of adulterous and incestuous offspring,
collapsing the distinction between natural and simply illegitimate children, simplifying the Civil Code's byzantine procedures for recognition
and legitimation, and (that perennial favorite) moralizing and educating
the poor.[20] Given the transcendental significance attributed to concubinage and illegitimate birth, overall the proposed reforms tended to
be fairly modest. Still, they represented a significant departure from legal
precepts in force since the 1850s.

Critiques of illegitimacy reflect how family law in early-twentieth-
century Chile continued to implicate relationships not only of gender and
generation but also of class. Chapter 2 discussed the late-nineteenth-
century identification of illegitimacy with the poor. This association retained currency for a later generation of jurists, for whom degenerate
families were a core theme of the "social question." But as *Juana Lucero*
indicates, illegitimacy also proved a rich vein of antioligarchic sentiment.
One law student declared, "We know various cases of highly placed
persons who lived publicly with young women of the poor classes, and
called by their children to provide support they had previously given
voluntarily[,] . . . denied, under sworn oath, their obvious paternity."
Another denounced the restriction on paternity investigation as "a privilege for the white-gloved macho scoundrel."[21] For legal and medical
professionals who often identified as a middle-class reformist vanguard,
illegitimacy reflected as much the decadence of the traditional political
class as it did the depravity of the poor.

Given that in the 1850s elite men who fathered children out of wedlock
were defended as "tender and inexpert youth," the "white-gloved scoundrel" of the early decades of the twentieth century reflected a striking
about-face in the class and gender politics of illegitimacy. Poor women
and wealthy men had reversed the roles of perpetrator and victim. Yet
there were definite limits to this shift. Jurists who advocated the ame-
lioration of illegitimates' legal status still declared their defense of "the

family," by which they meant legitimate, patriarchal marriage. Illegitimate children may have been innocent victims, "but it is not possible to
accept that the other group of children in society, legitimate children, be
sacrificed by extending their rights to those who, in the crude reality of
life, do not have moral origins," asserted one writer. Even as they advocated reform, few jurists openly challenged the fundamental distinction
between progeny born in and outside of marriage: "The law is just when
it creates . . . different categories of children according to the legal status
of their parents at the time of conception," went a typical critique.[22]

Indeed, some of the most outspoken advocates of reform did so for the
most conservative reasons. Illegitimate children and vicious family structures had long been associated with criminality, delinquency, and vagrancy. Now they were also associated with political subversion, and
proposals to modify their legal status were couched in terms of that
threat:

> Our century . . . has created . . . a residue . . . of human beings within which
> all those disinherited by fortune [*desheredados de la fortuna*] are grouped
> and become restless . . . And it is precisely this nucleus, as the most danger-
> ous for collective peace and well being, that modern social action [ad-
> dresses] . . . Laws that prohibit paternity investigation in the end do noth-
> ing but exacerbate this social ferment, awaken in [its] victims . . . hatred for
> the system that . . . distances them from their unknown parents.[23]

In a speech titled "The Orphan" delivered at the recently founded School
of Social Work, the noted philanthropist Ismael Valdés Valdés agreed: "Is
it not dangerous to produce a race of discontented ones, who later on
will go out and struggle against society?" A conservative congressman
echoed this sentiment: "Children who come from illegitimate homes are
always full of hatred against the social order . . . This is natural because
they are on the margin of society." And the authors of a well-known study
of a plebeian family in turn-of-the-century Santiago warned that those
left "outside the law" in concubinage and illegitimacy presented a "goldmine" that "socialist doctrines [would] exploit."[24]

Illegitimates were, literally and metaphorically, the quintessential dis-
inherited ones, exemplars of the plight of the working class in general.
As such, they inspired moral outrage, pity, charitable solicitude—and
also a distinct unease. No wonder some jurists saw in the equalization of

legitimate and illegitimate children a distinctly Marxist project. One law student who criticized discrimination against spurious and adulterous children and denounced the prohibition of paternity investigation as "arbitrary and iniquitous" was nevertheless quick to defend "the secular institution of the family which Communist and revolutionary socialism seeks to destroy."[25] Illegitimacy outlived the ideological struggles of the nineteenth century to be seamlessly absorbed into those of the twentieth. Preoccupations with the legal status of extramarital children were never just about children but about the adults they would become. Whether in 1850 or 1930, these children reflected the enduring imbrication of hierarchies of filiation and the politics of class.

The early-twentieth-century impetus to legal reform also extended to adoption.[26] As we saw in chapter 5, a range of vernacular kinships, including informal fosterage, were widespread and juridically unacknowledged in the nineteenth century. After the turn of the century, lawmakers "discovered" these plebeian practices. A bill in 1929 to institute adoption reversed the standard nineteenth-century argument that adoption was alien to Chilean family practice, declaring the need to "give legal life to a universal institution that is in fact practiced among us and will become an indispensable complement to the protection that the law affords poor children." Like those directed at illegitimacy, proposals to formalize adoption reflected the recrudescence of Iberian legal tradition, such that the colonial became modern. As the author of the adoption bill observed, "The fundamental principles of [this] proposal are the same ones that . . . prevailed in Chile when the Siete Partidas were in effect [that is, prior to the Civil Code]."[27]

Yet even as this proposal boldly challenged certain strictures of nineteenth-century civil law, it remained wedded to an understanding of family as a unit bound by ties of consanguinity and legitimate marriage. The bill permitted only those without biological children to adopt, created a narrow juridical relationship between adopter and adoptee that did not extend to other members of either natal kin group, and conferred inheritance rights inferior to those of legitimate children. Indeed, "because it is not possible to destroy links derived from blood," the adoptee was still considered a member of his or her natal family. Finally, reflecting long-standing cultural attitudes toward hijos ajenos, the adoption contract could be broken in instances in which the adoptee showed "ingrati-

tude." The adoption bill, which ultimately did not become law, also reflected the unpredictable politics of family law: the congressman who
authored it was a Conservative.[28]

Meanwhile, even as it attracted broad ideological constituencies, the
impulse for legal reform was hardly universal. One law student, a future Supreme Court justice, argued in 1909 that paternity investigations visited upon the social order "evils much greater than those borne
by the child . . . [who is not] supported by its father."[29] Given that the
nineteenth-century regime of filiation was an eminently liberal project,
perhaps it is not surprising that the most influential opposition to its
reform can be traced to liberal redoubts. In 1924, one of the last retroactive paternity suits in Chilean tribunals pitted two formidable jurists
against each other. Arguing before the Supreme Court on behalf of illegitimates' rights was Arturo Alessandri Rodríguez, son of the president
of the republic and a rising civil law star. His opponent was the noted
jurist, journalist, and Liberal politician Eliodoro Yáñez, whose lengthy
and spirited defense of paternal prerogative recapitulated many of the
arguments of the 1850s. Adapting these arguments to a contemporary
context, he asserted that mistaking acts of charity for paternity (that old
bugaboo of Civil Code–era jurists) was especially harmful in "modern
societies," in which charitable impulses toward the needy had only intensified. Where many fellow jurists condemned nineteenth-century civil
law as retrograde, the sixty-four-year-old Yáñez offered an eloquent plea
for the timeless verity of the Civil Code: "This is our law, this is our
juridical tradition, these are the fixed precepts of social life; this is peace
and public order, the stability of families and the stability of fortune."

A champion of public education, the separation of Church and state,
electoral freedom, and the separation of powers, Yáñez was in many ways
a classic representative of an older generation of liberals. In the social
climate and political landscape of early-twentieth-century Chile, his liberalism would seem distinctly conservative, not least in the context of
filiation law. Yet his was hardly the lone voice of an obsolete legal tradition: the Supreme Court voted eight to one to dismiss the paternity
claims against Yáñez's clients. The court in the 1920s was dominated by
jurists of Yáñez's generation, men who had received their law degrees
in the 1870s, 1880s, and 1890s, when the Civil Code's filiation regime
reigned supreme and uncontested. In subsequent years, a consensus in

favor of reform would gradually gain traction, but significantly, it would take decades to implement. Opposition to illegitimates' rights clearly ran deep and cannot be dismissed as the idiosyncratic position of the last generations of nineteenth-century jurists.[30]

Traditional elites and emerging middle-class professionals were not the only participants in dialogues about family and filiation, however, as seismic shifts in the early-twentieth-century political landscape opened the field of social critique to groups previously marginalized from it. One such group was feminists. In the 1920s and 1930s, feminist and women's groups in Chile and elsewhere in Latin America lobbied actively in favor of civil law reform.[31] They condemned the civil incapacity of married women, their lack of control over property, and their inability to exercise patria potestad over their children. As for the patriarchal structure of filiation law, however, in Chile their collective voice was conspicuously muted.[32] Individual feminists at times articulated positions in favor of illegitimate children, as did the writer and Nobel laureate Gabriela Mistral. A list of children's rights she composed in the 1920s included the right to be born under laws "that do not make [the child] bear during his whole life the sins of his parents." The feminist Amanda Labarca apparently also articulated a reformist position.[33] But middle-class Chilean feminists were not at the forefront of their country's early-twentieth-century reform movement. In this they apparently differed from some of their counterparts elsewhere in Latin America. In Cuba, according to K. Lynn Stoner, filiation reform became one of the most contentious issues confronting the early-twentieth-century women's rights movement, one that drove a fatal wedge between radicals and conservatives that weakened the movement as a whole. Initially, the reform of natal status was simply too radical for moderate feminists to stomach, but by the late 1930s, they too had embraced it.[34]

In Chile, meanwhile, ideological conservatism does not seem to explain early-twentieth-century feminists' conspicuously muted participation in the cacophonous debate over filiation reform. For as we have seen, the reformist stance—advocated to varying degrees by a broad spectrum of commentators—was not necessarily considered radical. Instead, Chilean feminists' stance may reflect the class politics either of feminists themselves or of their targeted constituency. By holding fathers accountable for their extramarital children, filiation reform benefited poor, single mothers, but in exposing legitimate families to the economic claims of illegitimates, it posed a potential threat to married women and their legitimate children. As such, it reflects how family law in Chile has implicated relations of class as much as those of gender and generation. The decoupling of filiation from the otherwise active movement for expanded women's civil rights could be striking. Two years before he successfully argued against paternity investigation before the Supreme Court, Eliodoro Yáñez had publicly advocated full civil rights for women and had introduced an (unsuccessful) bill to that effect in congress.[35]

Compared to middle-class feminists, leftist parties, nationalists, labor activists, and proletarian novelists articulated more forceful positions on issues of children, family, and law. In his caustic nationalist critique *La raza chilena* (1904), Nicolás Palacios drew on the same metaphor as his bourgeois and conservative opponents: "The poor class [*el pueblo pobre*] of Chile . . . is today the Great Orphan, disowned [*desheredado*] within its own country."[36] Meanwhile, center-left parties propounded some of the most far-reaching filiation reforms. As early as 1896, the Radical Party ideologue and social-democratic intellectual Valentín Letelier asserted that nineteenth-century civil law was the creation of "bourgeois jurists" and that the prohibition of paternity investigation benefited "the superior classes from which derive the seducers who repudiate their children . . . to the detriment of the inferior classes that provide victims and fodder for aristocratic depravity." By 1912, both the Convention of Liberal Youth and the Radical Party convention called for the reform of filiation law, and both the 1916 and 1928 proposals to (re)establish paternity investigation were sponsored by Radical Party legislators.[37] One law student arguing for civil law reform in 1928 went so far as to assert that orphanages "contribute to forming peons for the capitalist regime and servants who give illegitimate children to the new generations."[38] By the mid-1930s, the center-left Partido Radical Socialista had issued the most radical call of all: full equality for all children before the law.

It is tempting to narrate a chronicle in which the emerging popular-democratic movements of the early twentieth century mounted a successful challenge to bourgeois jurists and the oligarchic social order, revolutionizing the status of the poor and parentless. The reality is considerably more complicated. Even as left-wing parties championed filiation reform, labor and the left exhibited a pointed ambivalence toward these children, an attitude reflected in fiction. In early-twentieth-century

Chilean social-realist literature, *el niño roto*, or working-class child, was a favorite vehicle for social commentary.[39] In a short story published in 1917, Baldomero Lillo, perhaps the most famous writer of this genre, narrates the plight of Gabriel, an orphan who lives with and labors for a cruel patrona. Tormented by happy memories of his deceased parents and the sisters from whom he has been separated, he commits suicide. The boy's fate is clearly meant to provoke outrage, but it has another message as well. As Berta López Morales has pointed out, Gabriel's blind obedience, which ends in tragedy, contrasts with the defiant stance of Lillo's other plebeian protagonists.[40] The child criado is an ambivalent symbol: an object of compassion but one whose ignominious destiny bespeaks the dangers of dependency and submission.

Lillo's ambivalence vis-à-vis Gabriel characterized attitudes toward such children in labor and working-class politics in general. Activists denounced capitalist exploitation of women's and children's labor but, like elite and middle-class critics, scrutinized only certain kinds of labor—namely, that which took place in factories or workshops. Conspicuously absent from these critiques was a consideration of domestic labor in general and of child criados in particular.[41] This absence reflected prevailing understandings of who was a laborer and what constituted labor. But it may also have reflected the fact that criados were a politically inconvenient reality for popular politics because by the early twentieth century their primary exploiters were not capitalists or oligarchs but urban working-class and inquilino households. In this sense, early-twentieth-century labor activists were heirs of the political and cultural attitudes expressed in the late-nineteenth-century populist press. As described in chapter 6, this press defended the interests of the modest households who took in poor and parentless children but did not identify with the children themselves.

If labor and the left proved ambivalent about tutelary servitude, they could also exhibit a pointed ambivalence toward the sexual politics implicated in filiation reform.[42] On the one hand, working-class women were repeatedly portrayed as victims of seduction by patrones in factories and workshops.[43] Yet the debut of the "white-gloved scoundrel" and his twentieth-century counterpart, the lecherous foreman, did not signal the exit of that stock figure of the nineteenth-century filiation drama, the

dissolute woman of "humble origin and immoral upbringing." The vili-
fication of poor women would prove one of the most enduring themes in
the sexual politics of illegitimacy. "It is a well-known fact that the poor
woman . . . presents no great difficulties for conquest," asserted one law
student, who actually supported legalizing paternity investigation. The
causes of the "gangrene" of concubinage and illegitimacy were thus not
"economic" but "simply moral." Such invective was not new, articulated
as it had been by "bourgeois jurists" since the promulgation of the Civil
Code. But in this case it dated from 1918, and its author was Eugenio
Matte Hurtado, a future founder of the Chilean Socialist Party.[44]

Could They Be Our Children?
Filiation, Class, and the State in Modern Chile

In the first decades of the twentieth century, the patriarchal household
would continue to be an enduring normative ideal and an elusive plebeian reality. Poor mothers still found it impossible to support their
children, and some of these children continued to live and labor beyond
kin networks in the shadow of popular-democratic mobilization. With
the important exception of the calls for filiation reform, they were as
marginalized in leftist and labor politics as they had been in "bourgeois
civil law." But over time these political transformations had an *indirect*
effect on them, both in eroding the intimate paternalism of class relations
and in heightening the incentives to enfranchise those whose radical
marginality rendered them "dangerous." Subsequently, the rise of the
family wage system would also impact working-class men, women, and
children.

As we have seen, such children had long harbored symbolic meanings. At moments of class strife, poor, marginalized, illegitimate huachos
emerged as harbingers of disorder. In the 1850s, amid political violence
and the specter of popular mobilization, the construction of illegitimates
as threats to gender, generational, and class hierarchies helped usher in
legal reforms that redrew the boundaries of kinship and radically deprived
them of rights. Fifty years later, as labor agitation and working-class
movements convulsed the country, illegitimacy again became a Ror-
schach test of national politics and class conflict. And again, family law

emerged as a subject of public scrutiny and a strategy for mediating class conflict. These reformist episodes reveal the striking persistence of certain social and legal attitudes toward children, dependency, kinship, and hierarchy. They also exhibit manifest differences. In marked contrast to the 1857 Civil Code's posture of radical legal marginalization, the reformist impetus of the 1920s ushered in a halting measure of social enfranchisement for the poor and parentless. It also implied the legalization and formalization of long-standing vernacular kin practices. If huachos and criados, the children of fate and the children of Don Nadie, were to become children of the patria, they would have to be given a stake in that patria by way of the families that were, as jurists never tired of repeating, its building blocks. Twentieth-century reformers sought to reinsert the disenfranchised into families both by restoring the legal kin ties abolished in nineteenth-century civil law (through paternity investigation) and by creating new modes of legal kinship (through adoption).

Political projects embracing "modernization" in twentieth-century Latin America were often associated with efforts to remake working-class families in the image of a legitimate, nuclear, patriarchal ideal. Through a mixture of repression and economic incentives, a populist-developmentalist state and capitalist employers worked to domesticate a working class perceived as restive, rootless, and disorderly.[45] The rise of the family wage and state-sponsored benefits implemented in the 1930s and 1940s, including family allowances, social security, as well as smaller programs ranging from disability insurance to housing services, created compelling material incentives for marriage and legitimacy.[46] Such inducements began to achieve what law and perennial moralistic cajoling had failed to bring about: By the 1950s, illegitimacy rates had dropped by half and marriage rates were increasing.[47] Capitalist development both required and made possible a plebeian patriarchal household that in the nineteenth century had proven for many poor people a normative fiction.

Such developments obviously had profound effects on men and women, but they also impacted children. While it is tempting to see the domestication of poor families as a timeless and epiphenomenal bourgeois impulse, the history of children reveals what was novel about it. In the realm of family law, domestication heralded an emphasis on enfranchising people whom earlier legal regimes had propelled beyond the family fold. Children thus reveal a discernible shift in the state's posture toward

plebeian kinship, from marginalization and disenfranchisement to formalization, legalization, and incorporation. Also evident is a changing
valuation of child welfare more specifically. The first decades of the
twentieth century witnessed the (re)identification of child welfare with
societal welfare reminiscent of the eighteenth-century Bourbons, after an
extended interval in which children's well-being was regarded as the
lamentable but inevitable price of protecting privacy, property, and the
social order. Finally, children reveal changing understandings of law's
role in society. The history of family law in Chile illustrates particularly
clearly the enduring tension between two different visions of law's role: as
the expression of an aspirational ideal that works to the detriment of
those who do not live up to it, or as a pragmatic attempt to acknowledge,
and thereby lend a degree of legitimacy to, the full range of prevailing
practices.[48] In governing family relations, Chilean law exhibits a palpable
(though extraordinarily contested) shift from the aspirational model to
the pragmatic one.

It would take the whole twentieth century to institutionalize this re-
orientation. Decades of public discussion of filiation culminated in the
mid-1930s in the establishment of a limited form of adoption and, more
than eighty years after its abolition, the partial reinstatement of paternity
investigation. A second round of reforms in 1943 and 1952 expanded
adoption, extended paternity investigation, and simplified recognition
and legitimation.[49] Yet taken as a whole, these reforms proved extremely
tentative, tempering rather than eliminating discrimination based on
natal status and shifting slightly the line between legal and extralegal
modes of filiation. As late as the 1990s, adoptive children did not necessarily enjoy the legal status of legitimate ones, and the right of illegitimates to know their progenitors was so narrowly defined as to be
"illusory."[50]

The exclusionary essence of family law would endure until the dawn of
the twenty-first century. In 1998, the New Filiation Law more fully liberalized paternity investigation and eliminated the historic distinction between illegitimate and legitimate children from civil law.[51] A century
after Pablo Pérez chronicled his search for natal kin in his autobiography
The Orphan, the reform affirmed "the right of all persons to know their
origins."[52] In extensive debates over the reform, supporters and critics
invoked new arguments as well as old ones. Supporters framed it as a

question of equality before the law, an important step forward in post-dictatorship Chile's process of redemocratization. The reform was introduced by the Servicio Nacional de la Mujer, the government office concerned with women's affairs, and in a departure from patterns earlier in the century, feminists proved instrumental to its passage.

Meanwhile, the law's opponents—right-wing sectors and conservatives within the Catholic Church—employed several arguments that harked back to the nineteenth century. Championing an exemplary model of family law, they invoked the natural differences between children born in and out of wedlock and maintained that falsely imposing natal equality undermined marriage. Such invocations demonstrate the extraordinary staying power of certain aspirational ideals of family in the face of pervasive and enduring divergence from them. According to one interpretation, Chile's tardy reform of family law, which lagged behind its hemispheric neighbors, reflects the inordinate political power of the Catholic Church in Chile.[53] A broad historical perspective partially revises this interpretation by showing how Chile's modern regime of filiation derives as much from liberal commitments as from Catholic ones. As we saw, the nineteenth-century revolution in family law enshrined principles of individual will, freedom, and privacy from government intervention. Strikingly, these ideas continued to inform contemporary filiation debates. Some opponents of reform argued that obligating parents to support extramarital progeny represented "an assault on freedom." Parents might have a moral obligation to support their children, but the government could not compel them to do so.[54] Such arguments suggest that it is the power of (neo)liberal tenets as much as of Catholic ones that explains the tenacity of filiation structures in Chile.

Ultimately filiation reform passed the lower house of congress in 1994 but due to intense resistance in the Senate did not become law until 1998. The protracted and highly conflictual path toward natal equality in Chile is particularly striking in a society known for its venerable democratic tradition, its strong republican political institutions, and its relatively open electoral politics. The history of family law, and the history of children, highlight the quiet and enduring exclusions of a society often characterized as "one of the most stable, reformist, and representative democracies in the world."[55]

The point is not that Chile is more exclusionary and less democratic than its champions have assumed. It is rather that in modern societies, hierarchy and status dwell in sometimes unexpected redoubts. This book has argued that in Chile, and probably in Latin America, inequalities have been reinstantiated through legal understandings and social practices surrounding family and filiation. We have seen how kinship structured elite political and economic power and conferred symbolic and material benefits to people of all social classes. We have also seen how civil bureaucracies devised in the latter half of the nineteenth century helped create a "kinless" stratum of people deprived of these benefits.

But what counts as kinship, and who count as kin, is of course neither obvious nor unchanging. It is the very process of delineating these relationships that proves crucial. The fate of extramarital progeny and children reared in foster arrangements elucidates how the boundaries of belonging were constructed. Such scenarios reveal kinship as a strategic source of power for the male household heads who enjoyed the prerogative to define its borders. They further reveal how, in demarcating social propinquity, kinship simultaneously demarcated social distance. Filiation thus implicated class hierarchy and status differentiation. The British social anthropologist Edmund Leach famously observed that people distinguish social boundaries by asking "Do we intermarry with them?"[56] Nineteenth-century Chileans asked a different, but related, question: could they be our children? If this question strikes modern readers as strange, it is because ideas of kinship, so culturally and historically contingent, appear so natural to their adherents.

The answer to that question was for no one more consequential than for children themselves. This book has adopted a focus on childhood to probe the social boundaries operative in modern Chile. If children expose the workings of hierarchy, they also expose its paradoxes, contradictions, and contingencies. They show the staying power of status, but also the ways it must be actively constructed and maintained. Child rearing and socialization thus prove rich veins for exploring definitions of class, the acquisition of status, and the reproduction of social inequality in modern Latin America, and perhaps in colonial and postcolonial societies more generally.

In his celebrated social critique written in 1884, Augusto Orrego Luco characterized the children of the poor as hijos del azar, "children of fate," condemned to illegitimacy, rootless families, neglectful parents, and premature death. The hijos del azar were emblematic of all that was wrong with the moral and material condition of the Chilean poor. Yet their status as such was fraught with a fundamental contradiction. Elite discourse harped on the need to domesticate poor families as a blight on the social order. But these children, and specifically the social and civic practices surrounding their identity, rearing, sustenance, and socialization, were constitutive of that social order. In this sense, they were not children of "fortune" or "chance" at all, but children whose lives were intimately and decisively intertwined with the households, communities, and society in which they grew up.

APPENDIX

Sources and Methods

Most of the source materials for this study derive from the central valley of Chile, a geographically and culturally coherent area that forms the middle third of present-day Chile (see map, introduction). I adopted this focus in the supposition that family and kinship, class structures, and the state manifested themselves in very different ways in the mining communities of the north and the frontier regions of the south. A disproportionate share of my material is drawn from Santiago, Valparaíso, and San Felipe, a rural department some ninety kilometers north of Santiago. This reflects the availability of documentation as well as a conscious attempt to include both urban and rural areas within my frame of investigation.[1] The bibliography provides a full list of the judicial and notarial archives consulted.

Judicial Sources

The historiography of gender, family, and more recently children in Latin America has profited from an incredibly rich heritage of judicial records. This study draws on a corpus of more than 1,000 judicial cases from civil and criminal, secular and ecclesiastical courts. These include some 550 cases found in the judicial archives of some sixteen different locales, as well as a small sample of 32 cases from the ecclesiastical court of Santiago. It also includes 450 cases excerpted and summarized in two jurisprudential publications, the *Gaceta de los Tribunales* (published continuously from 1841) and the *Revista de Derecho y Jurisprudencia* (published from 1903). I also consulted a dozen published filiation suits (such as the one Secundino Alvarez filed against his father).

Because I reviewed a very wide range of judicial cases over an eighty-year period—including custody disputes, child support cases, legitimation and recognition proceedings, as well as cases of abuse, insults, seduction, bigamy, infanticide, and theft—my source materials did not lend themselves in any obvious way to quantitative evaluation. Instead, I seek to exploit their qualitative richness. As for sampling methodology, the limitations of the courts' classification systems conspire to confound the most conscientious and systematic of sampling designs. There is a huge quantity of catalogued materials in the Chilean judicial archives, and it is possible to go through indices and identify cases based on *materia*, the criminal or civil subject of the suit. But these categorizations are often extremely broad, vague, or downright inaccurate. Cases involving *derecho a herencia* (right to inheritance), to give just one example, can involve any number of different legal issues, most of which have no bearing on the themes of interest. There is no way to identify which cases will prove useful other than by reviewing them one by one. Meanwhile, because individual cases are bound more or less randomly in bundles, *legajos*, I found it useful when requesting a given case to peruse at least briefly all the other cases in the legajo—thereby widening the documentary net (cases very casually perused were not counted in my tally of cases consulted, however). In addition, I reviewed a significant body of uncatalogued materials. These consisted of stacks of legajos piled on the floor of the basement of the Archivo Nacional to which the staff graciously gave me access.

This admittedly haphazard and somewhat indiscriminate methodology (if it can even be characterized thus) had several important virtues: it was reasonably random, it required copious reading and hence yielded a broad sense of the archives' general contents, and it made it very difficult to predetermine the subjects to be pursued. Instead, what I found in the archives determined in large measure the topics explored in this study. Paternity, kinlessness, and child circulation, for example, did not figure at all in my original research proposal about gender and family in Chile, but these are issues I found, over and over again, in the judicial archives. The only cases I have attempted to quantify are paternity suits before and after the Civil Code (see chapters 1 and 2). The body of cases analyzed (102 pre-Code cases, 90 post-Code ones) consists of all the cases located, but given the scattershot methodology and the impossibility of predicting which of the thousands of support or inheritance cases deal with this particular issue, this body clearly represents just a sample of a much wider universe of suits, the dimensions of which are impossible to estimate.

Chilean judicial archives contain abundant materials for the latter half of the nineteenth century but become increasingly scarce after 1900, since twentieth-century judicial records have yet to be systematically compiled and catalogued. Accordingly, I have attempted to supplement the dearth of materials in this period by consulting published jurisprudence, nonjudicial sources, as well as uncatalogued materials in the basement of the Archivo Nacional. Nevertheless, certain aspects of family relations—such as the circulation of children—

are necessarily somewhat hazier after the turn of the century than they are for the earlier period.

As for the *Gaceta de los Tribunales,* for some years there exist indices by subject. These years have been more thoroughly mined but with the caveat noted above, that the materia of a suit is only a rough indication of what it actually deals with. The sample of cases culled from the *Gaceta* is thus by no means exhaustive, but I hope it is representative. The cases appearing in juris-prudential publications consist only of those suits heard by appellate courts or by the Supreme Court because litigants appealed the decision in the first instance (*primera instancia*). Thus, the *Gaceta* and the *Revista* necessarily exclude those cases that were incomplete or interrupted or in which litigants reached a settlement. Certain kinds of cases, most notably those in which no great financial interests were at stake, were likely to end without a decision from a lower-court judge when contenders, unable to sustain the cost of pro-longed litigation, reached out-of-court settlements or simply desisted in their legal petitions. As I discuss in chapter 6, around half of all cases involving the custody, status, or treatment of circulating children ended with no decision from the judge, probably for this reason. These kinds of cases, therefore, are almost certainly underrepresented in the *Gaceta* and the *Revista.* However, as long as the jurisprudential publications are not interpreted to reflect the kinds of cases filed in Chilean courts, this lack of representativeness should not pose a problem.

In this brief appendix, I do not pretend to offer new insight into the uses and abuses of judicial records as historical sources. Other authors have taken up this subject, and I defer to them for a more thorough discussion of the issue.[2] But several brief observations about the body of materials analyzed in this study are in order. Approximately two-thirds of the materials consulted involve civil litigation and are therefore exempt from the criticism most commonly leveled at criminal records, that they privilege nonnormativity, deviance, and violence. At the same time, civil disputes, like criminal ones, privilege conflict (and they also reflect only that subset of conflicts that actually ended up in court). No less than criminal cases, they involve contending parties who present interested stories in an effort to convince judicial officials of their version of the conflict. Consequently, legal testimony should rarely be read literally, and these sources require a keen attentiveness to the power dynamics inherent to their creation. It seems to me that there is no special methodological "trick" for getting around these pitfalls. However, one conclusion I have reached after reading hundreds of suits is that when the subject of historical interest is tangential to the legal investigation at hand, it may be less subject to deliberate distortion than when it stands squarely in the blaze of the judicial spotlight. Or put another way, judicial records are particularly valuable when the court's attention is directed toward an issue different from the one that concerns the historian. This is why some of the most valuable cases for reconstructing child-rearing practices or kinship patterns turn out to be not custody disputes or paternity proceedings but, say, investigations of theft or even of a traffic accident (see introduction).

Notarial Records

I surveyed some 400 wills, sampled in roughly twenty-five-year intervals: from 1850, 1875, and 1896 for the provincial department of San Felipe; and from 1850, 1875, 1900, and 1925 for the city of Santiago. I also consulted an additional fifty to sixty wills from the rural locales of Quillota, Rengo, and Curicó in the 1850s. In looking at wills, I was primarily interested in two issues: the presence of unrelated minors reared by testators and that of illegitimate kin. I had no information for any of these locales about individual notaries and whether their constituencies were skewed in some way. I chose notarial volumes randomly, based on availability for the target years.

While nineteenth-century Chilean testators' economic situations varied widely, will writers are not necessarily representative of the community at large, deriving from that segment of the populace that had at least some patrimony to pass on. What this means for wills as indicators of the dimensions of child circulation or illegitimacy is difficult to say. Households of all social stations took in children, though the poorest people, who would not be represented among testators, were more likely to send children out to be reared than to receive other people's children. So wills provide a portrait of receiving households and not of sending ones.

In turn, the poorest households were also more likely to engender illegitimate offspring (indeed, the absence of property explains both why people might not bother to marry and procreate legitimate heirs as well as why they might not bother to leave a will). This probably means that wills underestimate illegitimacy. On the other hand, perhaps individuals *with* property who had procreated out of wedlock were more likely to write wills precisely in order to provide for these children.

The incidence of illegitimacy and child circulation in wills varies across locations and over time in intriguing ways. To summarize very roughly, illegitimates and niños criados appear more frequently in testaments from San Felipe than from Santiago. And the frequency of both illegitimate children and niños criados declines steadily over the course of the late nineteenth century. While clear enough, these patterns are, once again, difficult to interpret. The principal issue is whether trends across time and space can be attributed to substantive variation in the phenomena themselves (for example, actual variation in

the numbers of illegitimates or niños criados, or changes in attitudes toward
them) or whether they reflect instead changes in the characteristics of the
populace, the pool of testators, or the protocols of will writing itself. For
example, if more individuals make bequests to niños criados in San Felipe than
in Santiago, does this necessarily imply that the rearing of unrelated children
was more widespread in provincial communities? Or might it imply that, say,
testators in San Felipe were simply better off compared to their counterparts in
Santiago and therefore more generous toward dependents in general? If there
are more illegitimate children in San Felipe, is it because more individuals bore
children out of wedlock in San Felipe, because these children were more socially accepted there, or simply because poor individuals were more likely to
have illegitimate offspring and the testators in San Felipe are poorer as a group
than those in Santiago? Parallel problems plague the analysis of change over
time: are the pools of testators in 1850 and 1900 comparable in terms of their
composition by age, sex, level of wealth, and so on? Do testamentary customs
remain constant?

   In short, the number of variables that must be considered in analyzing this
source is such that an extremely large sample size is necessary to generate
credible hypotheses. Since this study does not exclusively, or even primarily,
focus on wills, such an analysis is beyond its scope. Thus, while I do note
several tentative patterns as outlined above, I chiefly treat wills as a qualitative
source rather than a quantitative one. When I make quantitative statements
based on wills (such as in the epilogue), I do so in conjunction with other
source materials.

Institutional Documents: The Casa de Huérfanos

Thanks to the meticulous recordkeeping of the Hermanas de la Providencia,
the congregation of nuns that ran Santiago's Casa de Huérfanos for almost a
century, a voluminous documentary record narrates the lives of the tens of
thousands of children who passed through the institution. Among these materials are a series of registries, the Registros de Entradas, that record all children
entering the Casa, including information on their origins, age, family identity,
natal status, and ultimate fate. The historian Manuel Delgado has conducted a
very thorough quantitative analysis of patterns of admission, provenance, and
identity of Casa children based on these registries, and his analysis proved an
indispensable resource.[3]

   Meanwhile, my own study probes another Casa source: documents relating
to the entry and exit of asylees. As noted in the acknowledgments, these
documents, which have not been analyzed before, are located in the Casa

Nacional del Niño, the present-day incarnation of the Casa de Huérfanos. They include several different types of materials. The Libros de Entradas, or Entry Books, contain baptismal certificates, letters, and even good luck charms that accompanied children left at the institution. Among these materials are reports penned by officials, such as police officers, members of charitable societies, and later social workers; letters of "recommendation" or "sponsorship" written, usually at a parent's request, by patrons arranging a child's acceptance into the Casa; as well as letters and notes of children's kin or caretakers. Such documents were probably retained because they included baptismal certificates. Libros de Entradas survive for the years 1871–74, 1873–82, 1883–89, 1896–98, 1899–1901, 1907, 1909, 1912, 1918, and 1928, though they are disorganized and the actual contents of a given volume may not correspond to the designated year.

In addition, the Libros de Salidas, or Exit Books, contain information relating to the transactions by which private citizens received children from the asylum. Depending on the time period, the Libros de Salidas include letters of recommendation presented by those seeking children and/or the contracts they signed detailing their obligations to these young wards. Only two Libros de Salidas survive, either because most were lost or because this information was never systematically maintained. The first is for the period 1854–71 and the second for 1922–30. From time to time, I also draw on the Registros de Entradas, the entry registries mentioned above, for further information regarding individual children mentioned in the Libros de Entradas or Salidas.[4]

A final source from the Casa de Huérfanos is the Libro de Amas, the Wet nurse Book, a registry of the nurses who cared for young children outside the institution. Only a single volume survives, covering the period from 1857 to 1861. From this volume it is possible to discern not only a profile of the nurses but also the complex trajectories of circulation that nurslings followed during their first years of life.

While Casa children are obviously not representative of children (even poor children) in general, they did constitute a numerically significant group, accounting for some 5 to 9 percent of all children born in Santiago in the late nineteenth century. Moreover, the Casa materials are especially valuable for the glimpse they provide of the landed estates where many children were sent. Haciendas dominated rural society, but because of the state's weak legal and administrative presence, social and labor relations within these private estates are often difficult to reconstruct. The absence of hacienda service tenants (inquilinos) in the historical record is especially conspicuous.[5] The Casa materials are thus particularly valuable for the light they shed on social and economic relationships within inquilino households and between these households and the hacienda. Indeed, there is no better example of the value of children in illuminating often unexpected social realms.

ABBREVIATIONS

AAZ	Archivo del Arzobispado de Santiago
AGLA	Archivo de la Gobernación de Los Andes
AGLU	Archivo de la Gobernación de La Unión
AIC	Archivo de la Intendencia de Colchagua
AJB	Actas de la Junta de Beneficencia de Santiago
AJC	Archivo Judicial de Concepción
AJCo	Archivo Judicial de Copiapó
AJCu	Archivo Judicial de Curicó
AJL	Archivio Judicial de Linares
AJLS	Archivo Judicial de La Serena
AJS	Archivo Judicial de Santiago
AJSF	Archivo Judicial de San Felipe
AJSFer	Archivo Judicial de San Fernando
AJR	Archivo Judicial de Rancagua
AJT	Archivo Judicial de Talca
AJV	Archivo Judicial de Valparaíso
AMG	Archivo del Ministerio de Guerra
AMH	Archivo del Ministerio de Higiene, Asistencia, y Previsión Social
AMI	Archivio del Ministerio del Interior
AMJ	Archivo del Ministerio de Justicia
AMS	Archivo de la Muncipalidad de Santiago
AMV	Archivo de la Municipalidad de Valparaíso
ANC	Archivo Notarial de Curicó
ANQ	Archivo Notarial de Quillota
ANS	Archivo Notarial de Santiago
ANSF	Archivo Notarial de San Felipe
AUCH	*Anales de la Universidad de Chile*
BE	*Boletín Eclesiástico*
BHM	Biblioteca de Historia de la Medicina, Universidad de Chile
CamDip	Sesiones de la Cámara de Diputados
CamSen	Sesiones de la Cámara de Senadores
CC	*Código Civil*

CHLA	Casa de Huérfanos, Libro de Amas
CHLC	Casa de Huérfanos, Libro de Correspondencia
CHLE	Casa de Huérfanos, Libros de Entradas
CHLS	Casa de Huérfanos, Libros de Salidas
CHM	Memorias de la Casa de Huérfanos, Ministerio del Interior
CHRE-BHM	Casa de Huérfanos, Registros de Entradas, Bib. de Historia de la Medicina
CHRE-CNN	Casa de Huérfanos, Registros de Entradas, Casa Nacional del Niño
ESC	Expediente sin catalogación, Archivo Nacional
Figueroa	Virjilio Figueroa. *Diccionario histórico, biográfico, y bibliográfico de Chile*
Gaceta	*Gaceta de los tribunales*
Ravest, *Diccionario*	José Ramon Ravest. *Diccionario de jurisprudencia de las Cortes de Justicia*
RC	*Revista Católica*
RDJ	*Revista de Derecho y Jurisprudencia*
SPIA	Sociedad Protectora de la Infancia, Actas
SPIRE	Sociedad Protectora de la Infancia, Registro de Entradas

GLOSSARY

adulterino—the offspring of a union in which one of the partners was married to someone else

ajeno—belonging to someone else (as in *hijo ajeno*, someone else's child; *crianza ajena*, child rearing performed by an unrelated caretaker)

alimentos—child support, or material assistance owed to a family member

ama—nurse, especially a wet nurse; synonymous with *nodriza*

Casa de Huérfanos—the foundling home of Santiago

chinito—poor child or child servant; term carries an ethnic charge

comadre—kinswoman; woman with whom spiritual kinship is shared

compadrazgo—cogodparenthood or ritual coparenthood

criado/a—servant or dependent; young person reared in a nonnatal household

crianza—rearing; upbringing

curador—legal representative appointed to represent the interests of minors in official transactions; legal guardian

espúreo—spurious offspring; extramarital progeny born of a proscribed union (such as of a priest or an adulterous union)

estado civil—civil state; in the Civil Code, family-based attributes of the individual that entailed certain rights and obligations toward others

estirpe—lineage

expósito/a—foundling

filiación—relations of descent between parents and children or genealogical origins; also, one's birth status as illegitimate or legitimate

formación—education in the broad sense not only of instruction in a trade or skill but also of moral or character education

gañán—itinerant, unskilled laborer; peon

hacendado—the owner of a hacienda

hacienda—large, landed estate

hijos del azar—literally, "children of fate;" the phrase used by Dr. Augusto Orrego Luco to refer to the plight of poor children in an 1884 essay titled "The Social Question"

hijos de crianza—"children by rearing"; children defined as part of the family by virtue of rearing, not blood kinship

hijo natural—"natural child"; in the Chilean Civil Code, an illegitimate child legally recognized by his or her parents

huachismo—the phenomenon of abandonment, illegitimacy, and kinlessness

huacho/a—usually pejorative term for an illegitimate, orphaned, or otherwise kinless individual

incestuoso/a—the product of a relationship deemed incestuous according to canon or civil law

inquilino/a—tenant farmer on a hacienda

limpieza de sangre—Iberian concept of blood purity; defined in reference to certain racial, ethnic, religious, and familial attributes

los de arriba/los de abajo—literally, "those above" and "those below"; a common nineteenth-century phrase to denote wealthy and poor social sectors

mandar (a) criar—"to send out to be raised"; the practice of sending a child to an unrelated caretaker

mozo—male servant, often young

parentesco—kinship; family relation

patria potestad—in the Chilean Civil Code, the authority fathers exercised over the property and persons of their minor children

patrón/patrona—master; mistress; patron

simplemente ilegítimo—in the Chilean Civil Code, an illegitimate child who enjoyed only a limited form of legal recognition by his or her progenitors

torno—a wheel-like contraption in which infants could be anonymously abandoned to the foundling home

NOTES

INTRODUCTION *State, Class Society, and Children in Chile*

1. I consulted the trial transcript of the Puelma case among uncatalogued materials at the Archivo Nacional. It has since been provisionally catalogued: [Puelma case, November 1894], AJS, Caja 16 corresponding to the year 1895, sistema de catalogación provisional. The children's entry into the Protectora is recorded in SPIRE, 1894–1902. Their case was followed carefully by the press and became part of the city's collective memory. In an unrelated 1898 case, for example, a defense lawyer rhetorically compared the plaintiff to the blood-thirsty relatives in the Puelma case: José Acevedo con Mannhein Aguiles sobre nulidad de lejitimación, ESC, Agosto 1898, Segundo Juzgado del Crimen de Valparaíso. A note on citations: a significant number of uncatalogued judicial cases located in the basement of the Archivo Nacional in Santiago were consulted for this study. They are denoted ESC (*expediente sin catalogación*). Because no catalogue numbers are available for such cases, in citing them I have provided as much identifying information about them as appears on the transcript's cover page.

2. This is the definition given in nineteenth-century versions of the Real Academia Española.

3. *Constitución política*, art. 12. By midcentury, entailed estates (*mayorazgos*), an institution serving the economic interests of elite families, had also been abolished.

4. As a church authority noted in 1853: "Since there is no longer any need to ascertain who are the real Indians and blacks, we believe that the reason for maintaining separate books of baptismal registries for people of different castas no longer exists. For this reason . . . we approve the practice that was introduced some time ago of consolidating [the two] into a single baptismal book. Valdivieso, "Ordenanza sobre libros," 18. On mestizaje in the Chilean imaginary, see Waldman Mitnick, "Chile: Indígenas y mestizos negados."

5. Romero, *Qué hacer*, 92 and chapter 4; Salazar, *Labradores, peones y proletarios*.

6. On landownership, see Bauer, *Chilean Rural Society*, especially chapter 7. Recent appraisals have suggested histories of the oligarchic Chilean state have neglected the significance of popular politics to state formation. Mallon, "Decoding the Parchments."

7. Brian Loveman has estimated that "substantially less than ten percent of the enumerated actively employed" men in the 1875 census (which calculated a population of 2,100,000) corresponded to either a nascent middle class or the "numerically tiny" elite. Loveman, *Hispanic Capitalism*, 152. Archival records, in which the same elite individuals appear again and again in different contexts, reinforce the impression of a remarkably circumscribed group.

8. Salazar and Pinto, *Historia contemporánea* II, 32, citing Sagredo Baeza.

9. On kinship and independence, see Felstiner, "Family Metaphors"; on kinship among twentieth-century elites, Zeitlin and Ratcliff, *Landlords and Capitalists*. The Errázuriz calculation derives from Gabriel Marcella's thesis, cited in Loveman, *Hispanic Capitalism*, 139. See also Vicuña, *La belle époque chilena*; Yeager, "Club de la Union"; Balmori and Oppenheimer, "Family Clusters." Vicuña Mackenna cited in Vicuña, *La belle époque chilena*, 24. Familial identity is evocatively rendered in Maria Rosario Stabili's oral history of "aristocratic sentiment" in Chile in the 1990s, *Il sentimento aristocratico*. On nineteenth-century elite kin networks elsewhere in Latin America, see Balmori et al., *Notable Family Networks*, and other works cited in Caulfield, "History of Gender," 467.

10. Lastarria, "El manuscrito del diablo," [1849], 107.

11. For example, the foundling home administrator distinguished between hijos de familia and those raised in the asylum. CHM, 1900; CHM, 1897.

12. Milanich, "Whither Family History," 455–56.

13. Bauer, *Chilean Rural Society*; Johnson, "Internal Migration"; Salazar, *Labradores, peones, y proletarios*.

14. Orrego Luco, "La cuestión social."

15. This figure, which also includes weavers, derives from census data. Cited in Loveman, *Hispanic Capitalism*, 132–33. As Loveman notes, such data almost certainly underestimate women's work in agriculture. Female peonage and gendered migration are discussed in Salazar, *Labradores, peones, y proletarios*, chapter 5, and in Johnson, "Internal Migration."

16. Johnson finds that up to 40 percent of households in some provincial communities in the central valley at midcentury were headed by women, "Impact of Market Agriculture."

17. This calculation is based on a sample of seventy-five wills dictated in San Felipe around 1850. See the methodological appendix for more on this source. One indication of underregistration is the extraordinary frequency with which I encountered illegitimate children falsely registered as legitimate.

18. Kertzer, *Sacrificed for Honor*, 21–22. National statistics of course obscure subnational variation; for example, urban rates of illegitimacy, especially in France, were significantly higher. But this is also true of Chile, where certain areas (for example, the northern provinces) had illegitimacy rates well above the national average. For a provocative global perspective on family structures that identifies a Latin American family culture (characterized by low nuptiality,

high illegitimacy, etc.) distinct from other world areas, see Therborn, *Between Sex and Power.*

19. On illegitimacy in colonial society, see Dueñas Vargas, *Hijos del pecado*; Kuznesof, "Sexual Politics"; Mannarelli, *Pecados públicos*; Nazzari, "Concubinage in Colonial Brazil"; Twinam, *Public Lives, Private Secrets.* A work exceptional for its coverage of the modern period is Lewin, *Surprise Heirs, II.*

20. "Apuntes sobre chilenismos"; Rodríguez, *Diccionario de chilenismos*, 235–36. The term *huacho* is discussed further in chapter 3.

21. Six incidents of abandonment are reported in the Valparaíso *El Mercurio* in a one-month period spanning July and August 1878. The Santiago cases are reported in judicial records.

22. Russel, *A Visit to Chile*, 93

23. 5–9 percent: Delgado, "Marginalización e integración," chapter 2; 9 in 1000: Meyer, *Guía médica de higiene*, 213; 51,600: *Congregación de las Hermanas*, 45. This last statistic roughly corroborates Delgado's calculation, cited in the table. Delgado's thesis deserves particular mention as an exhaustive quantitative analysis of the Casa's entry logs.

24. On the relationship of abandonment and circulation, see Milanich, "Casa de Huérfanos."

25. As Mamalakis points out, this figure is probably an underestimate given the propensity to underreport young children. Mamalakis, *Historical Statistics*, 65.

26. Ibid., 40.

27. Dore, "Holy Family." Female headship is discussed in Dore and is analyzed in Kuznesof's seminal work, including "Role of Female-Headed Household." Milanich, "Women and Gender," surveys interpretations of female headship as a reflection of, alternatively, women's vulnerability or autonomy.

28. A classic statement of this argument is Hartmann, "Family as Locus."

29. On this distinction, see Milanich, "From Domestic Servants to Working-Class Housewives," and on domestic service in Latin America generally, Kuznesof, "A History of Domestic Service."

30. O'Higgins also sired an illegitimate son himself and fostered two young Amerindian orphans. On Portales, see Bunster, "Los amores de Portales."

31. Allende, *Realidad médico-social.* On the plebeian child protagonist in Chilean literature, see Pearson, "El niño roto." Literary representations of these themes in the first half of the twentieth century include Alberto Romero, *La viuda del conventillo* (1930); Eduardo Barrios, *Gran señor y rajadiablos* (1948); José Luis Fermandois, "Diablofuerte" (1905); Baldomero Lillo, "Era él solo" (1917); Federico Gana, "La señora" (1890s); Augusto D'Halmar, *Juana Lucero* (1902). More recently, illegitimate children and orphans populate the fiction of Isabel Allende, including *La casa de los espíritus* (1982) and *Hija de la fortuna* (1999), and José Donoso's *El obsceno pájaro de la noche* (1970).

32. Montecinos, *Madre y huachos*; Salazar, "Ser niño huacho" and *Ser niño "huacho."*

33. *Antecedentes, Actas, y Trabajos.*

34. On the social question in Chile, see Morris, *Elites, Intellectuals, and Consensus*; Grez Toso, *Cuestión social*; and Romero, *Qué hacer.*

35. Disruptive seed: Alamos González, CamDip, 30a ordinaria, 9 agosto 1883; matrifocal households: Mancilla Cheney, *Investigación de paternidad ilegítima*, 119; vices: SPIA, Acta #4, sesión del 2 de diciembre de 1894; blood: Vergara L., *Población de Chile*, 102; Roman Empire: Alessandri Rodríguez, *Precedencia del matrimonio civil*, 19.

36. Premo, *Children of the Father-King*; Lipsett-Rivera, "Introduction."

37. Ricardo Letelier, CamDip, 33a ordinaria, 16 agosto 1883.

38. Benton, *Law and Colonial Cultures*, 14; Hay et al., *Albion's Fatal Tree.*

39. Vivid explorations of plebeian familial practices that engage with their divergence from prescription include Dias, *Power and Everyday Life*; Premo, *Children of the Father-King*; and Putnam, *Company They Kept.* Dore's "Holy Family" provides a compelling interpretation of the disjuncture between prescription and practice.

40. Alonso, *Thread of Blood*; Besse, *Restructuring Patriarchy*; Bliss, *Compromised Positions*; Caulfield, *In Defense of Honor*; Caulfield et al., *Honor, Status and Law*; Chambers, *From Subjects to Citizens*; Dore and Molyneux, *Hidden Histories*; Díaz, *Female Citizens, Patriarchs and Law*; Findlay, *Imposing Decency*; Guy, *Sex and Danger*; Hunefeldt, *Liberalism in the Bedroom*; Klubock, *Contested Communities*; Meade, *"Civilizing" Rio*; Rosemblatt, *Gendered Compromises*; Tinsman, *Partners in Conflict.* See also Caulfield's review essay, "History of Gender."

41. On regulation and education, see Kuznesof, "Puzzling Contradiction," Szuchman, *Order, Family, and Community.* Children appear in works on schooling and disciplinary institutions though they are not an analytic focus: Arrom, *Containing the Poor*, Vaughan, *Cultural Politics.* Works emphasizing the articulation of childhood and nation-state formation include Blum, "Conspicuous Benevolence"; Schell, "Nationalizing Childhood"; Wadsworth and Marko, "Children of the Pátria"; Windler, "City of Children." A number of essays in Potthast and Carreras, *Entre la familia, la sociedad y el estado*, and Hecht, *Minor Omissions*, also emphasize the state. Premo summarizes this orientation: if the incipient field of Latin American children's history has any "overarching thematic concern," she notes, it is "the interaction between nation-state and family." *Children of the Father-King*, 3.

42. Dore, "One Step Forward," 8.

43. Venezuela: Díaz, "Women, Order, and Progress," 72; Costa Rica: Rodríguez, "Civilizing Domestic Life," 87; Puerto Rico: Martínez-Vergne, *Shaping the Discourse on Space*, 158; Brazil: Besse, *Restructuring Patriarchy*, 3–4.

44. Stoler, "Tense and Tender Ties," 829.

45. These critiques are summarized in the contributions by Corrigan, Sayer, and Scott in Joseph and Nugent, *Everyday Forms of State Formation.* Drawing

on rich empirical evidence from Costa Rica, Lara Putnam has also offered a compelling critique of state-centered analyses of gender, domesticity, and sexuality; see *Company They Kept*, especially introduction and conclusion.

46. Hale, "Political Ideas and Ideologies."

47. Amancebamiento was apparently prosecuted when it involved adultery. Regarding esponsales, the Code held that "the mutually accepted marriage promise is a private act, that the laws submit entirely to the honor and conscience of the individual, and that produces no obligation whatsoever before the civil law." *CC*, libro I, título III. For the contrasting case of Venezuela, see Díaz, "Women, Order, and Progress."

48. Centeno, "Disciplinary Society," 304.

49. Foucault, *Power/Knowledge*, 122, 60.

50. Lara Putnam makes a similar statement to this effect: "Practices surrounding gender, kinship and sexuality at times became central to class struggle and state formation. But it was not always so, and the legitimacy of these practices as objects of study should not rest on this claim alone" (*Company They Kept*, 19). See also Milanich, "Whither Family History."

51. Civil law distinguished between minors (*menores*), defined as those below age twenty-five, and adults (*mayores de edad*). Minors were in turn categorized as *infantes* (those under age seven), *impúberes* (girls under twelve, boys under fourteen), and *menores adultos* (females aged twelve to twenty-five and males fourteen to twenty-five). But various rights and obligations commenced at other ages (sixteen, eighteen, twenty-one, etc.), suggesting a graded understanding of development. Criminal law, of course, also relied on age distinctions, for example in defining criminal culpability (see chapter 4).

52. Premo, *Children of the Father-King*, 23. Her point is particularly clear in colonial law, which defined Indians as legal minors. In republican Chile, such explicit legal discrimination was obviously not in effect. But social definitions of minority were also relational, particularly as minority articulated with class.

53. The ways dependency defined and demarcated childhood, in ways that differed for girls and boys, is discussed further in chapter 6.

54. María B. Güemes por homicidio de María L. Caballero, 1915, AJS, Leg. 1657.

55. Contra Wenceslao Plaza, Alejandro Moraga, y Luis Avila por el homicidio de la niña Elena Valencia, ESC, Octubre 1895, Primer Juzgado del Crimen de Santiago.

56. Milanich, "Whither Family History." 449–53.

57. Hugh Cunningham, review of Steve Mintz, *Huck's Raft: A History of American Childhood*, February 2006.

58. These two nineteenth-century conflicts—the War of the Pacific with Peru and Bolivia and the war with Mapuche peoples on Chile's southern frontier—are discussed briefly below and are referenced as well in chapters 4 and 6.

59. These include more than 550 cases culled from the judicial archives, 450

cases published in the *Gaceta de los Tribunales* and the *Revista de Derecho y Jurisprudencia*, some 30 cases from the ecclesiastical courts, and a dozen or so published cases from civil and criminal courts. See the methodological appendix for more on these sources and on selection criteria.

60. Divorce: Doña Juana Josefa Madariaga con Don Pedro Antonio Ramíres por divorcio perpetuo, 1867/8, A A Z, rollo 1855307, Leg. 813–14; thieving servant: Contra María Ramírez por hurto, 1895, E S C, Primer Juzgado de Crimen de Santiago; bigamy: Narciso Flores por doble matrimonio, 1856, A J T, Leg. 738, 16.

61. See the methodological appendix for additional details.

62. Russel, *A Visit to Chile*, 79.

63. The Casa materials are further described in the methodological appendix.

64. In this I depart from Gabriel Salazar's stimulating explorations of huachismo (Pinto and Salazar, *Historia contemporánea*, 48; Salazar, "Ser niño huacho"). Drawing on illegitimacy statistics, he argues that 80 percent of Chilean children were huachos "without fathers and sometimes without mothers." His conclusion assumes (as did the dominant normative discourse) that out-of-wedlock birth inevitably led to certain social scenarios. While illegitimacy was obviously related to huachismo, and many illegitimates were indeed "fatherless," many "illegitimate" families were sociologically indistinguishable from their legitimate counterparts.

65. For more on the regional courts and notaries consulted, see the bibliography and methodological appendix. While regional comparison falls largely beyond the scope of this project, chapter 6 briefly explores distinct patterns of child circulation in the south.

CHAPTER 1 *The Civil Code and the Liberalization of Kinship*

1. Dona Mercedes Campos con D Alejandro D'Huique sobre filiacion y alimentos, 1851, A J S, Leg. 1130, 15.

2. The merchant was Santiago (James) Ingram, who was friends with Diego Portales. The murdered congressman was Manuel Cifuentes. The man accused of his murder was represented by the Argentine expatriate Juan Bautista Alberdi.

3. Palma Alvarado, "*De apetitos y de cañas*," 394. D'Huique also appears in the historical record in later decades as the beneficiary of a government concession to produce bread.

4. I compare the Chilean experience of filiation reform with several European cases in Milanich, "Perfil local."

5. Bello, "Presentation of Bill to Congress," 271.

6. Brazilian and Argentine codifiers also cited the Chilean Code as an influence. Guzmán, *Codificación civil en Iberoamérica*, especially 467–68; Mirow,

"Borrowing Private Law," especially notes 1 and 2. Mirow characterizes the Code as "perhaps the most influential civil code in Latin America," *Latin American Law*, 137; Lira Urquieta compares it to the Napoleonic Code, *Código Civil chileno*, 27.

7. Curiously the Chilean Civil Code has remained absent from important recent discussions of gender and law, including Dore, "One Step Forward," and Caulfield et al., *Honor, Status, and Law*. Deere and León, "Liberalism and Married Women's Property Rights," do discuss the Chilean Code in·a comparative analysis of marriage law.

8. Bello, "Responsabilidad de los jueces de los jueces," 195–96. On Bello's concern with civil law, see Jaksic, "República del orden," and on his broad intellectual concern with order in his introduction to Bello's *Selected Writings*.

9. See my introduction for a discussion of illegitimacy's ubiquity in nineteenth-century Chile.

10. A rich scholarship has documented colonial beliefs and practices surrounding illegitimacy: Dueñas Vargas, *Hijos del pecado*; Mannarellli, *Pecados públicos*; Johnson and Lipsett-Rivera, *Faces of Honor*; Nazzari, "Concubinage in Colonial Brazil"; Twinam, *Public Lives, Private Secrets*. Additional bibliography is cited in Milanich, "Illegitimacy and illegitimates." On Chile, see Cavieres F. and Salinas Meza, *Amor, sexo, y matrimonio*, and Cavieres F., "Consensualidad, familia e hijos naturales."

11. The precise combinations of categories varied from code to code, though the logic was more or less constant. On the significance of these distinctions in the Luso-Brazilian context, see Lewin, "Natural Children," and *Surprise Heirs*.

12. A Chilean law promulgated on November 22, 1838, limited natural children's share to a sixth of the estate, and this was the standard size of their petitions. However, on occasion they asked for—and were awarded—the fifth even after that date. See also note 63.

13. The mother's identity was in dispute in less than 5 percent of cases (5 out of 102 cases).

14. Prominent alleged fathers include Ramon Goyenechea, member of a prominent aristocratic family whose daughter Isidora married the commercial and industrial scion Matías Cousiño; Miguel Gallo, founder of the fabulous silver mine of Chañarcillo who was dubbed Chile's first millionaire (Collier and Sater, *History of Chile*, 80); Francisco Arriagada, one of the 145 wealthiest landowners in nineteenth-century Chile (Bauer, *Chilean Rural Society*, 30–31); José Vicente Aguirre, a prominent independence-era official and member of the Supreme Court; and Manuel Cifuentes, a deputy whose murder by the father of a woman he had "seduced" became a cause célèbre. Modest fathers: María Larrieu v. Hipolito Caut por filiación y alimentos, 1855, AJS, Leg. 1302, 5; Doña Mercedes Campos v. D. Alejandro D'Huique, 1851, AJS, Leg. 1130, 15; D. Manuela Latapia c D. Adolfo Gastón por alimentos, 1854, AJS, Leg. 1305, 5;

Doña Mariana Granifo contra Don Andrés José González sobre alimentos, 1852, AJS, Leg. 1255, 3; Agustín Gamboa con Javier Zamorano por alimentos, 1853, AJS, 2a serie, Leg. 1223, 13; Petronila Baeza c J. M. Contreras sobre alimentos, 1852, AJS, Leg. 912, 22.

15. Mothers' backgrounds are more difficult to discern because their financial circumstances were not subjects of careful scrutiny as were men's. Also, occupation is key to discerning male class position in these suits, but as a rule only poor women had identifiable occupations.

16. This sample includes suits from Santiago, Valparaíso, and several provincial courts, as well as cases appearing in the *Gaceta* or published on their own. A note on how the tally was determined: plaintiffs could petition for a temporary ruling in order to obtain immediate support while a more lengthy filiation case was pursued. Judges in interim alimentos cases ruled on the merits of the plaintiff's filiation claim and awarded (or withheld) alimentos accordingly. At that point, the plaintiff or defendant could pursue a full judicial investigation to rule definitively on the question of filiation, which would affect both the alimentos ruling as well as any eventual inheritance rights. In instances where I have records of both an interim alimentos petition and a formal filiation case for a given individual, I count only the latter, final sentence. If I have only the alimentos petition, I count that instead. In addition, I have categorized as successful for illegitimates two sentences that were actually suspended by higher courts due to procedural errors (namely, because minors had not received a formal court-appointed legal representative). While the decision in their favor did not technically stand, I counted these as illegitimate "wins" because the higher court did not challenge the substantive finding that filiation had been proven.

17. Dn Ceferino Avila por su esposa Da Lorenza Foncea, con el albacea de Dn Mateo Foncea sobre filiación, 1849, AJSF, Caja 2; Dolores Mena contra Manuel Mena (testamentaria) sobre filiación, 1841, AJS, Leg. 1343, 6; Da Luiza Iturrieta sobre lejitimarse, 1843, AJS, Leg. 519, 6.

18. The hacendado's estate, which included properties in the province of Rancagua and in Santiago, was estimated at 20,000 pesos.

19. According to witnesses, Olivos had been reared in the humble *rancho* (rural dwelling) of a woman with whom she still lived "out of charity" as an *agregada*, or unrelated household member.

20. The amount was far less than the sixth of the estate she originally demanded but was a respectable sum nonetheless, particularly for a woman living in "notorious poverty." María Bartola Olivos con Mateo A de los Olivos por alimentos, 1851, AJS, 2a serie, Leg. 1193, 23.

21. This figure represents the five settled cases among fifty-one total suits culled from the judicial archives. Only cases taken from the judicial archives were counted because these are representative of all suits filed in court. Cases appearing in the *Gaceta de los Tribunales*, a journal whose purpose was to

publish judicial sentences, were eliminated because by definition they had not reached a settlement.

22. 2,000 pesos: Domingo Caballero por Carmen Galdames con el albasea de la testamentaria de Dn Toribio Galdames sobre filiación, 1852, AJSF, Caja 7. The quote is from Ugolino y Manuel Jesus Guzman con Fernando Guzman por alimentos, 1846, AJSFer, Leg. 126, 2. In another case, an illegitimate son awarded a fifth of his deceased father's estate by a local official opted to settle with his father's widow, since the modest estate did not justify the expense of the inventory and appraisal. He accepted a payment of twenty-five pesos instead. Overseen by a local subdelegado, the case never made it to a court. AIC, Vol. 36, Expedientes administrativos y judiciales, 46–49. Extrajudicial outlets for filiation disputes are discussed below.

23. Dn Ceferino Avila por su esposa Da Lorenza Foncea, con el albacea de Dn Mateo Foncea sobre filiación, 1849, AJSF, Caja 2; Clara Guzmán c Ramón Tagle por filiacion y alimentos, 1851, AJS, 2a serie, Leg. 1268, 9; Virjinia Fernández Arias c Juan, Salvador, y Manuela Fernández, 1850, AJT, 7a serie, Leg. 393, 3. Interestingly, in the first case the head of the family that scolded Don Mateo was himself subsequently the subject of a filiation investigation. Don Benancio Escobar con los herederos de don Patricio Mecinas, sobre filiación i alimentos, *Gaceta*, 1855, 674, p. 5998.

24. Domingo Caballero por Carmen Galdames con el albasea de la testamentaria de Dn Toribio Galdames sobre filiacion, 1852, AJSF, Caja 7; Doña Dolores Escobar con doña Dolores Romo sobre entrega de una nieta, 1853, AJS, Leg. 1193, 7; Don Napoleon Charpin con Doña Ervina Cantos sobre entrega de un niño, 1853, AJS, Leg. 1550, 18. Doña Manuela Latapia con D. Adolfo Gaston por alimentos [y filiación], 1854, AJS, Leg. 1305, 5; Abalos, "Memoria sobre filiación," 316.

25. Domingo Caballero por Carmen Galdames con el albasea de la testamentaria de Dn Toribio Galdames sobre filiacion, 1852, AJSF, Caja 7. The invocation of zoological models to make arguments about what constituted "natural" relations between parents and children had a long genealogy, dating back to classical legal and philosophical traditions: Boswell, *Kindness of Strangers*, 84–87. Revolutionary French jurists also invoked natural law arguments about illegitimacy: Brinton, *French Revolutionary Legislation*.

26. Don José María Prast con don José María Maturana, sobre filiación i derecho a una parte de los bienes del finado presbítero don Juan José Prast, *Gaceta*, 1845, 178, #606, p. 247; Doña Mercedes Villarroel con don José Miguel Villarroel, sobre filiación i alimentos, *Gaceta*, 1853, 584, #5649, pp. 4615–16; Don Manuel Cortez Araya con don Manuel Antonio Berguecio sobre filiación i alimentos, *Gaceta*, 1850, 420, #2130. Dona Mercedes Campos con D Alejandro D'Huique sobre filiacion y alimentos, 1851, AJS, Leg. 1130, 15. In his 1849 will, one father left two adulterous children a trust of 400 pesos to generate funds for their support, plus an additional 100 pesos each, "in order to avoid

all suits after his death." Whether the bequests reflected the father's benevolence toward his offspring or simply legal hedging, they suggest the expectation that even adulterous children could pose a legal challenge to an estate. AIC, Vol. 36, Expedientes administrativos y judiciales, 46–49.

27. Criminal de oficio contra Juana Arroyo, ausente, por haber votado a su hijo a la calle pública, 1856, AJT, Leg. 738, 3.

28. As a judge from Chiloé noted, for example, this procedure was "a generalized custom in the province." *Gaceta*, 1861, #1254, p. 534.

29. Filiation disputes involving local authorities include Leaplaza Manuela con Merino Nicolas sobre filiación y alimentos, 1829, AJS, 2a serie, Leg. 1308, 1; Magdalena Leiva con D Fausto Fuentes sobre que le de alimentos a su ijo natural Francisco Castro, 1838, AJSF, Leg. 32, 20; Cuevas Juan Francisco con Santiago Castro (testamentaria) sobre alimentos y servicios de su esposa, 1845, AJSFer, Leg. 115, 7; AIC, Vol. 36, Expedientes administrativos y judiciales, 46–49; AGLA, Vol. 6, Solicitudes 1813–69; Juan Bargas contra don Joaquin Ilavaca como albacea de Dionicio Duarte sobre derecho a la sesta parte de los bienes que quedaron por muerte de dicho Duarte, 1849, AJSFer, Leg. 158, 8; Dna Carmen Vargas contra Faustino Fuente, 1850, AJS, 3a serie, Leg. 1576, 14; Dona Mercedes Campos con D Alejandro D'Huique sobre filiacion y alimentos, 1851, AJS, Leg. 1130, 15. In all of these cases, men challenged judgments by local officials. I have found no cases in which women did so.

30. Hull, *Sexuality, State, and Civil Society*, comes to a similar conclusion about the abolition of paternity suits in Baden, Germany. I compare the politics of filiation in Baden and Chile in Milanich, "Perfil local."

31. Baeza was described as having been reared by an unrelated caretaker, and no family member appeared on her behalf in the proceedings. In contrast, Contreras was represented by his stepfather. Petronila Baeza c J.M. Contreras sobre alimentos, 1852, AJS, Leg. 912, 22.

32. Other cases of illicit relations in which local authorities attempted extrajudicial remedies by encouraging the parties to marry or otherwise counseling wayward women include Contra Cruz Basoalto i Cornelia Sespedes por rapto, 1854, AJT, Leg. 728, 8; Narciso Flores por doble matrimonio, 1856, AJT, Leg. 738, 16; Tadeo Baeza c Rosario Ortiz sobre entrega de una niña, 1851, AJS, 2a serie, Leg. 1094, 6; Milanich, "Children of Fate," 50–52.

33. The phrase "father of justice" is invoked by a woman in a petition to a local authority: AIC, Vol. 3, Solicitudes recividas de funcionarios y particulares, [18]29–63.

34. Brinton, *French Revolutionary Legislation*.

35. On colonial judges as paternalistic protectors, see Premo, *Children of the Father-King*, chapter 1.

36. One paternity suit lasted over seven and a half years; another meandered through courts for twelve years. In the course of both investigations, the presumed fathers died and the Civil Code went into effect. Not coincidentally,

both plaintiffs lost their suits. D. Manuela Latapia c D. Adolfo Gastón por alimentos, 1854, AJS, Leg. 1305, 5; Dna Mercedes Pizarro c D Juan José de la Fuente sobre alimentos, 1850, AJSF, Caja 4.

37. Because mothers did not enjoy legal authority, or *patria potestad*, over their children, their very right to represent offspring in court could be challenged. An illegitimate might emerge victorious only to be awarded a pittance, the actual payment of which was often difficult to enforce. Alternatively, the court might withhold any award for a number of reasons: because the illegitimates in question were old enough to work to support themselves; because, in the case of married women, husbands and not fathers were responsible for their maintenance; or because, in the case of deceased fathers, the moral obligation of a father to support offspring was deemed not to extend to his heirs.

38. Alvarez, *Antecedentes del juicio*. While this suit was heard in the 1870s, the incident of the man teased by his peers had occurred decades before.

39. Women sometimes seemed at pains to justify their legal action. One mother invoked her poverty to justify her suit: "If it were not for this fact, there would be no consideration at all that would convince me to recur to a judicial solution." Denuncia puesta por Aurora Morales, contra Juan Francisco Jaña respecto a dos hijas naturales, Santiago, 1862. BHM, Fondo: Varios, Caja 1, doc. 18. Attacks on the immorality of female plaintiffs was nothing new; Cavieres F. and Salinas Meza, *Amor, sexo, y matrimonio*, 95, mention a late-eighteenth-century case in which a parallel argument is made.

40. Tadeo Baeza c Rosario Ortiz sobre entrega de una niña, 1851, AJS, 2a serie, Leg. 1094, 6.

41. Abalos, "Memoria sobre filiación," 332–33. The essay was the author's law school thesis.

42. Zapata's essay was published anonymously in the principal jurisprudential organ, the *Gaceta de los Tribunales*. Its authorship is deduced from the fact that the essay reproduces verbatim long passages of the defense's arguments in a contemporaneous paternity suit against the estate of Santiago Yngram (James Ingram), a wealthy Englishman and friend of Diego Portales resident in Chile. A transcript of the defense's arguments in the Yngram case was published as a pamphlet the same year as the *Gaceta* essay, and both appeared with the title *Discusión jurídica sobre la prueba en materia de filiación natural*. Zapata's critique thus appeared in two published versions. (Zapata, *Alegación en derecho*, and Zapata, "Discusión jurídica.") I have found little information about Martín Zapata himself, other than that he was a lawyer in civil practice in mid-century Santiago.

43. Clear proof: Dna Mercedes Pizarro c D Juan José de la Fuente sobre alimentos, 1850, AJSF, Caja 4; imperio de los sentidos/maternity: Ramon Besoain c Atila Villalon sobre filiación, 1893, AJS, serie B, Leg. 228, 23; mystery of nature: Egaña, *Alegato pronunciado*, and Abalos, "Memoria sobre filiación," 321.

44. The Biblioteca Nacional's copy of Zapata's statement in the Yngram case has a handwritten dedication to Supreme Court justice Santiago Echevers. Zapata's essay was quoted forty-five years later by a lawyer who praised it as an *estudio precioso* in Ramon Besoain con Atila Villalon sobre filiacion, 1893, AJS, serie B, Leg. 228, 23 (the lawyer's statement is dated 1895).

45. Brinton, *French Revolutionary Legislation*; Hull, *Sexuality, State, and Civil Society*. Zapata himself quoted liberally from Spanish jurists, including García Goyena (author of the draft Spanish Civil Code), Aguirre, Bermúdez de Castro, and others.

46. Bello, "Discurso del Presidente," 160, 171, 161, 171.

47. Montt appeared in the case because he had assisted the putative father in drawing up his will. *Alegación en derecho*. At the time, he was serving on the Supreme Court and on the Civil Code's drafting committee. He would be elected president a year later.

48. Women of no worth: Dna Mercedes Pizarro c D Juan José de la Fuente sobre alimentos, 1850, AJSF, Caja 4. Speculation: Clara Guzmán c Ramón Tagle por filiacion y alimentos, 1851, AJS, 2a serie, Leg. 1268, 9.

49. Hunefeldt makes a similar observation about the role of servants in filiation cases in nineteenth-century Lima. Hunefeldt, *Liberalism in Bedroom*, 203.

50. D. Manuela Latapia c D. Adolfo Gastón por alimentos, 1854, AJS, Leg. 1305, 5.

51. Blest Gana, *Martín Rivas*, 246.

52. Moreover, economic differences between male and female litigants could reflect the general economic dependency of women on men in all social classes. In this sense, paternity suits were taken as metaphors for class relations when in fact they sometimes reflected the economic contours of gender relations.

53. Elisa Wilson c Policarpio Vicuña sobre reconocimiento de hijos, 1879, AJV, Leg. 1306, 17. The duration of their relationship is surmised from the age of the oldest child. For a similar case of a couple who had been together eleven years and had six children together, in which witnesses actually testify they thought the couple was legally married but the father denies paternity anyway, see Agripina Briones c Blas Ricardi sobre reconocimiento de hijos naturales, 1893, AJS, serie B, Leg. 174, 25. Apparently, many women only turned to the courts to solicit legal paternal recognition when relationships with partners collapsed or because fathers had suddenly ceased to lend support voluntarily.

54. *CC*, art. 271, 272.

55. Don Secundino Alvarez con la sucesión de don Francisco Salvador Alvarez, sobre filiación natural, *Gaceta*, 1790, 1877, #1772, pp. 586–89.

56. These cases were decided after January 1, 1857, when the Civil Code went into effect. Illegitimate petitioners lost sixty-four cases and won twenty-one. An additional five cases were incomplete or ended without a substantive ruling on filiation.

57. As Bello observed, "Testimonial proofs . . . are so easy to forge, if not during the parents' lifetimes at least after their deaths." "Presentation of Bill to Congress," 273.

58. Dna Mercedes Pizarro c D Juan José de la Fuente sobre alimentos, 1850, AJSF, Caja 4.

59. In Iberian law, children were automatically legitimated as long as they were not products of "damaged unions." According to the Civil Code, only children previously recognized as natural by both parents would be automatically legitimated by marriage. Another reform of the Code was the abolition of *lejitimación por rescripto*, an extraordinary legitimation granted by the Chilean state for the benefit of wealthy, well-connected, or publicly esteemed individuals (in other words, the republican version of the Spanish Crown's *gracias a sacar*). The best-known beneficiaries of this procedure were the three extramarital children of Diego Portales, who were legitimated several months after their father's assassination. In the 1850s, President Manuel Montt apparently conferred legitimacy with some frequency (AMJ, 1856, Vol. 207, Solicitudes Particulares; D. Napoleon Charpin con Doña Ervina Cantos sobre entrega de un niño, 1853, AJS, Leg. 1550, 18). The practice would subsequently be denounced as "a monstrous prerogative of absolutist monarchs that could not be exercised by the heads of a constitutional and republican government." The critic was a lawyer in an inheritance dispute stemming from the Portales legitimation who represented family members seeking to annul the legitimation. Herederos de doña María Portales con don Juan Santiago Portales, *Gaceta*, 1885, 2155, #2361, pp. 1413–14.

60. Although there was debate on the issue of irrevocability early on, by the end of the nineteenth century most jurists argued that once paternal recognition had been formally extended, it could not be rescinded. Badilla Acuña, *Filiación natural*; Astaburuaga Cueto, *Reconocimiento de hijo natural*; Concha, *Clausula testamentaria*; Orrego Concha, *Cuestiones sobre reconocimiento*; Rudolph, *Estudio sobre estado civil*; and Ravest, *Diccionario*, 1881, p. 727, no. 1197, Corte de la Serena: "The status of hijo natural, once conferred by the father, is not revocable."

61. On the freedom to legitimate and be legitimated, Bello declared, "Supposing that the man believes that the illegitimate child is his, would he be forced to legitimize a son or daughter of bad habits, and would he be placed in the position of either not marrying or introducing a source of immorality and depravity into his family? And would the child, on his part, participate against his will in a debased union, and place the administration of his property in the hands of a dissolute man?" Bello, "Presentation of Bill to Congress," 273.

62. Although the parents' ability to marry was technically a prerequisite for recognition as an hijo natural, parental marriageability was not the centerpiece of the status. Indeed, other parts of the Civil Code explicitly contradicted the marriageability prerequisite because the recognizing parent was not required

to name the other parent (*CC*, art. 272). As long as one parent's identity remained concealed, the court obviously could not ascertain whether the progenitors could be married. What is more, wills sometimes treated children who were born of adulterous unions as hijos naturales, though this was technically illegal.

63. *CC*, art. 323. Legitimate children, meanwhile, were entitled to "congruous alimentos," or "those that permit the beneficiary to subsist modestly in a way corresponding to his social position." The significance of these distinctions, and the meanings that accrued to them in juridical practice, will be discussed in chapter 2. Regarding inheritance, it is impossible to offer a concise overview of the rights of hijos naturales (or indeed anyone), since these rights varied considerably according to whether the deceased had left a will or not, whether there were legitimates descendants or ascending heirs, etc. This was true both in Iberian and republican law. For a thorough analysis of inheritance laws involving extramarital offspring in Portuguese America, which shares many parallels with Spanish American law, see Lewin, "Natural and Spurious Children."

64. Francisco Javier Arancibia c Eloisa Carrasco por entrega de una hija, 1889, AJS, serie A, Leg. 105, 21. As another jurist put it, "Illegitimate children . . . do not belong to the family." Iturrieta Sarmiento, *De los hijos ilegítimos*.

65. Many poor parents in consensual unions did not bother to formally recognize their offspring. While petitions like Wilson's are numerous, they should be much more so given the soaring rates of out-of-wedlock birth in late-nineteenth- and early-twentieth-century Chile. Moreover, like Vicuña, many fathers denied paternity such that children remained unrecognized.

66. A parallel development was the elimination of the customary rights that "spurious" children had enjoyed in pre-Code judicial practice. Whereas we saw pre-Code jurists defended the natural rights of such children to basic paternal support, now courts declared that, for example, "the children of clerics" have no rights "to inherit nor to have anything from the property of their fathers." Doña Ascension Trincado con testamentaria de don Manuel Ascencion Trincado, sobre alimentos, *Gaceta*, 1860, #848, p. 461.

67. *Constitución política*, art. 12. See introduction for more on this trend.

68. See the epilogue.

69. "Presence and acquiescence": Doña Rosario de la Maza con doña Josefa Novoa, sobre petición de herencia, *Gaceta*, 1863, #1106, p. 1850; "competent functionaries": Ramon Formas con herederos de Ramon N. Formas, sobre nulidad de testamento, *Gaceta*, 1885, 2149, #1834, pp. 1102–3; also Claro Solar, *Explicaciones*, 424. Baptismal certificates were rejected even when the father had expressly requested to be recorded. María Riboulet con Lorenzo Astorga por reconocimiento de hijos/nombramiento de curador, 1867, AJV, Leg. 1137, 3.

70. Juana Arévalo sobre que se le declare madre natural, 1884, AJS, serie A, Leg. 43, 26. A parallel case of a mother seeking to prove her kinship with her natural son, deceased in the War of the Pacific, is Espediente de Margarita Saavedra, sobre filiación, *Gaceta*, 1887, #1325, p. 821. The widespread problems encountered by soldiers' survivors in attempting to prove their filiation are discussed in chapter 4.

71. Ernesto Briones y Juana Covarrubias por legitimación de hijos, 1884, AJV, Leg. 1419, 29. Similarly, when one father sought to legitimate his son on the last day permitted by law, the court demanded to know the cause of the delay. Only after he explained illness had prevented earlier action did the court oblige his request. Francisco Balbontín sobre legitimación de hijo, 1892, AJS, serie B, Leg. 139, 8.

72. Bello, "Presentation of Bill to Congress," 274.

73. Twinam uses the descriptor "permeable" to characterize "the boundaries between legitimacy and illegitimacy" in Catholic/Hispanic law. Twinam, *Public Lives, Private Secrets*, 40.

74. Bello, "Presentation of Bill to Congress," 273. Abalos also refers to the need to "bury these matters in mystery," "Memoria sobre filiación," 326.

75. Ambition: Abalos, "Memoria sobre filiación," 320; traffic: D. Manuela Latapia c D. Adolfo Gastón por alimentos, 1854, AJS, Leg. 1305, 5; audacity: Zapata, "Discusión jurídica."

76. Bello, "Observancia de la lei"; Lira Urquieta, *Código Civil chileno*, esp. 58–61.

77. In fact, higher courts, especially the Santiago Court of Appeals, began to overturn lower-court decisions in favor of illegitimates at a striking rate. Of fifteen rulings against illegitimates in the period 1850–54, in six cases the lower-court ruling had been favorable but was overturned on appeal. Of fourteen rulings against illegitimates from 1855–56, six were again favorable lower-court decisions overturned by higher courts. That is, during the seven years prior to the Code, of the twenty-nine cases illegitimates ultimately lost, twelve had originally been decided in their favor by lower courts. Of course it would be helpful to compare this pattern to other kinds of civil suits in order to determine whether it is specific to filiation cases. I know of no study that would permit this comparison.

78. The courts rejected local authority over filiation in Eujenio Concha con el subdelegado de Santa Fé, sobre entrega de una hija, *Gaceta*, 1859, #1905, p. 782; Doña Antolina Mery con don Antonio Mery sobre alimentos, *Gaceta*, 1863, #376, p. 107; Doña Margarita Bravo con testamentaria de don Luis Bravo sobre alimentos, *Gaceta*, 1864, #1151, p. 415. See also Claro Solar, *Explicaciones*, 425. Subsequently, procedural reforms would institutionalize this circumscription of local power. The 1875 Lei de Organización i Atribuciones de los Tribunales removed the judicial functions of subdelegados and inspectores, investing these powers in a newly created corps of lower justices (*de menor*

cuantia). The law carefully delineated the judges' jurisdiction, preventing them from ruling in, among other matters, filiation disputes. Guerra, *Instrucciones para jueces*; Vera, *Manual para jueces*. Examples of subdelegados accused of abuse of authority (*torcida administración de justicia*) include *Gaceta*, 1861, #1254, p. 534, and *Gaceta*, 1859, p. 922.

79. Critiques of low-level justices include Vidal, "Reflexiones sobre administración"; Bello, "Responsabilidad de los jueces."

80. It is interesting to note that this trend seems to mirror in reverse legal patterns in the nineteenth-century United States. Michael Grossberg has argued that antebellum judges challenged traditional paternal rights in child custody cases, but rather than awarding these rights to mothers, usurped them for themselves. Through the doctrine of child welfare and parental fitness, the judges assumed "the mantle of patriarchs." In Chile at more or less the same time, local judges lost this mantle. Grossberg, "Who Gets the Child?"

81. The higher court noted that Clarisa del Carmen, a minor, needed a legal representative in order for the case to proceed. The case was sent back to the court of first instance.

82. Dore, "One Step Forward." An alternative interpretation is Deere and León, "Liberalism and Married Women's Property Rights," who find certain improvements in married women's legal status—a finding not necessarily in contradiction with my own.

83. This process is analyzed in comparative perspective in Deere and León, "Liberalism and Married Women's Property Rights."

84. On "hybrid 'conservative liberalism,'" see Joseph, "Preface," xiv.

85. For a comparative discussion of illegitimacy rates, see the introduction.

86. Claro Solar, *Explicaciones*, 466.

CHAPTER 2   *Paternity, Childhood, and the Making of Class*

1. The sum is quoted in Figueroa, *Diccionario*, 426. The commercial pursuits of the Alvarez family are chronicled in Larraín, *Viña del Mar*; Martínez Baeza, "Cinco documentos"; Garrido, "Orígenes de Viña del Mar." Alvarez was supposedly a rather eccentric character. In his chronicle of the gold rush, Vicente Pérez Rosales remembers that he led an unsuccessful mutiny on the ship to California and later had to be rescued by his countrymen when he was accused of theft and almost lynched. Pérez Rosales, *Recuerdos del pasado*, 232–34. Based on private business correspondence in his possession, Martínez Baeza suggests Alvarez was an inveterate gambler who squandered much of the family fortune.

2. Alvarez, *Antecedentes del juicio* and *Resumen de algunos puntos*.

3. Doña Mercedes's claim is detailed in Francisco M Rivera con Herederos de Francisco Salvador Alvarez sobre derecho de herencia, 1873, AJV, Leg.

1185, 2. Secundino's case is reconstructed from the two published pamphlets cited above as well as from Don Secundino Alvarez con la sucesión de don Francisco Salvador Alvarez, sobre filiación natural, *Gaceta*, 1877, 1790, #1772, pp. 586–89. A third petitioner, Francisco Salvador Segundo, came forward in 1876 also purporting to be Don Salvador's illegitimate son. The case turned on a clause that provided the only exception to the Civil Code's ban on paternity investigation: the case of rapto, or the kidnapping of a woman by a male suitor. The plaintiff claimed a right to support because Don Salvador had kidnapped his mother. The court denied his petition, at which point Secundino filed suit. Curador del menor Francisco S. Segundo Alvarez con sucesión de Don Francisco Salvador Alvarez, sobre alimentos, *Gaceta*, 1876, 1750, #1393.

4. Rich in details about his past, Secundino Alvarez's suit provides virtually no information about his life at the time of the trial. In a single, cryptic reference, a witness observes that two years before, he had been invited "to go by Barón to see Secundino, where . . . he had a small shop [*estaba con un negocito*]." I have interpreted this as a reference to Secundino's employment. Six years later, a Secundino Alvarez signed a petition on behalf of miners near Copiapó who as "Catholics and patriots" denounced the new civil marriage law. The petition was published in a newspaper. "Adhesión de Punta del Cobre," *El Amigo del País*, #1317, 24 noviembre 1883. Was this miner the same Secundino Alvarez? It is impossible to know.

5. See methodological index for a discussion of how these cases were collected.

6. Hay et al., *Albion's Fatal Tree*. My wording here draws on Benton's characterization of this work: "criminal law became an arena for public redefinitions of class boundaries." Benton, *Law and Colonial Cultures*, 14.

7. Eloisa Bernales de N. con Manuela Bernales y otra sobre declaración de hija natural, 1881, AJS, serie B, Leg. 58, 6.

8. Ironically, of course, this meant that courts resorted to interpretive standards with no basis in codified law—precisely the judicial posture that antipaternity jurists, including Bello himself, had condemned.

9. In such cases, the petitioner might be deemed "simply illegitimate," a legal status that accorded limited rights to support and no right to inherit. In practice, however, no plaintiffs were awarded support through this reasoning. The natural/simply illegitimate distinction is discussed further below.

10. Zoila Flores con sucesión de Don Pablo Flores sobre filiación i alimentos, *Gaceta*, 1881, 1969, #946. Italics are mine. A very similar summary was articulated in Domingo Santa María's dissenting opinion in an 1876 case. He argued: "While it is true that [the Iberian codes] do not establish a special formula for the recognition of a natural child, it is undoubtable that . . . the proof that must be presented must include constant, precise, and determined acts that, encompassing the different situations of the child, according to his age and develop-

ment, show that the father has intended [*ha tenido en mira*] to give him his name and social position, introducing him into the bosom of his own family." Doña Carlota Sotomayor de Reveco con sucesión de Don Trifon Sotomayor sobre derechos hereditarios i filiación, *Gaceta*, 1877, 1788, #1035. This is one of the first articulations of the social congruity principle I have located. The logic, expressed here in a dissent from the majority's decision in favor of the illegitimate petitioner, would be invoked two weeks later by the same court— this time by the majority in the ruling against Secundino Alvarez.

11. In addition to Francisco Salvador Alvarez, they included Adolfo Blanco Gana, son of independence-era naval admiral Manuel Blanco Encalada; Manuel José Balmaceda, father of future president José Manuel Balmaceda; noted philanthropist José Joaquín Luco; wealthy viticulturalist Pedro de la Lastra; and Manuel Bernales, longtime justice of the Court of Appeals in Santiago. In contrast, as noted in the previous chapter, alleged fathers in pre-Code suits represented a range of social stations.

12. Doña Carmen Lavín de E. con doña Manuela Villalobos, sobre reforma de testamento, *Gaceta*, 1885, 2149, #1861.

13. *CC*, art. 232; libro 1, tit. XVIII.

14. Doña Catalina de la Lastra con los herederos de Don Pedro de la Lastra, sobre derecho a herencia, *Gaceta*, 1885, 2160, #2819, pp. 1691–92. See also Ramón Besoain con Atila Villalón sobre filiación, 1893, AJS, serie B, Leg. 228, 23, in which the plaintiff's father had given him "certain attentions that could be appropriate for a simply illegitimate son," but the court concluded none of them (schooling, an allowance, a modest business as a young adult) "clearly expressed the desire to confer the status of hijo natural."

15. Eloisa Bernales de N. con Manuela Bernales y otra sobre declaración de hija natural, 1881, AJS, serie B, Leg. 58, 6

16. Twinam, *Public Lives, Private Secrets*, 140, and on recognition in general, 137–57.

17. Society/streets: Egaña, *Alegato pronunciado*; public excursions, Doña Cármen Ibañez con doña Natalia del C. Ortiz, sobre reinvindicación, *Gaceta*, 1878, 1830, #1460; forms of recognition, Don Secundino Alvarez con la sucesión de don Francisco Salvador Alvarez, sobre filiación natural, *Gaceta*, 1877, 1790, #1772, pp. 586–89; Mercedes Alvarez: Francisco M Rivera con Herederos de Francisco Salvador Alvarez sobre derecho de herencia, 1873, AJV, Leg. 1185, 2.

18. See also Ramón Besoain con Atila Villalón sobre filiación, 1893, AJS, serie B, Leg. 228, 23; Doña Isabel Cifuentes con herederos de Don Manuel Cifuentes, *Gaceta*, 1882, 2088, #3514; the dissenting opinion in Doña Carlota Sotomayor de Reveco con sucesión de Don Trifon Sotomayor sobre derechos hereditarios i filiación, *Gaceta*, 1877, 1788, #1035. In the Alvarez case, the Santiago Court of Appeals noted, "The proof provided in this trial . . . does not fulfill the required standards . . . since of forty-one witnesses who testify, only

fifteen know how to sign their names." This proved the witnesses were "obscure persons" who did not share the confidence of Don Salvador enough to know his "conscience." Don Secundino Alvarez con la sucesión de don Francisco Salvador Alvarez, sobre filiación natural, *Gaceta*, 1877, 1790, #1772. In contrast, the testimony on Mercedes's behalf was invaluable, noted her lawyer, because of "the character and condition of the witnesses." Francisco M Rivera con Herederos de Francisco Salvador Alvarez sobre derecho de herencia, 1873, AJV, Leg. 1185, 2.

19. Dependents and workers: Manuel Blanco con Ismenia Blanco sobre derecho a herencia, 1901, AJS, serie B, Leg. 293, 9; mill: Ramón Besoain con Atila Villalón sobre filiación, 1893, AJS, serie B, Leg. 228, 23; respect: Don Antonio del Canto con doña Rufina del Campo, sobre filiación i alimentos, *Gaceta*, 1853, 562, #5110.

20. This social logic clearly preceded the Civil Code, as pre-Code cases also make reference to illegitimate plaintiffs' relationships to fathers' subordinates. This suggests that while the Code changed the *legal* weight accorded acts of recognition, the social meanings of these acts did not necessarily change. Juan Francisco Cuevas con Santiago Castro (testamentaria) sobre alimentos i servicios de su esposa, 1845, AJSFer, Leg. 115, 7; Doña Petronila Vargas con los herederos de Don Juan Justo Vargas, Cobro de la sexta parte de unos bienes, 1846, AJSF, Leg. 3, 19.

21. Egaña, *Alegato pronunciado.*

22. Mercedes Echevers i otros con el Iltmo. i Rmo. Arzobispo, sobre filiación, *Gaceta*, 1882, 2036, #3165. Another case where the court finds for the illegitimate using the logic of social congruity is Doña Cármen Ibañez con doña Natalia del C. Ortiz, sobre reinvindicación, *Gaceta*, 1878, 1830, #1460.

23. Romero, *Qué hacer*, 167.

24. Foundling: Don Pedro Ahumada contra Don Juan Clímaco Aguirre sobre derecho a la sexta parte de los bienes . . . , 1848, AJSF, serie 2a, Leg. 9, 7; shelter: José Ramón Vidaurre con Beatriz Vidaurre sobre impugnación de lejitimidad, ESC, julio 1901, Segundo Juzgado del Crimen de Valparaíso.

25. Doña Lucia Cifuentes con Doña Rita Cifuentes, sobre petición de herencia, *Gaceta*, 1881, 1989, #2255.

26. Zoila Flores con sucesión de Don Pablo Flores sobre filiación i alimentos. *Gaceta*, 1881, 1969, #946.

27. Don Bernardo Floridor Besoain con sucesión de Don Ramón Besoain sobre petición de herencia, *Gaceta*, 1882, 2032, #2835.

28. Don Narciso Tapia con la testamentaria de Don Narciso Perez, sobre filiación i espensas, *Gaceta*, 1849, 350, #140; Doña Cármen Ibañez con doña Natalia del C. Ortiz, sobre reinvindicación, *Gaceta*, 1878, 1830, #1460; Don Francisco Orquera con Don Damián Vásquez, sobre petición de herencia, *Gaceta*, 1882, 2015, #1415. In another case a father who no longer wanted custody of his illegitimate daughter appealed to her mother to accept her into

her home, "if not as a daughter than as a *criada* [maid]." Carmen Contreras con Rosauro Mellafe sobre filiación y alimentos para su hija Nicolasa, 1851, AJSF, Caja 6.

29. Don Pedro Marurim con el Sr Don José Vicente Sánchez como albacea y heredero de Doña Mercedes Gac sobre filiación y cobro de la sesta parte de una herencia, 1846, AJS, Leg. 1337, 154.

30. José Guillermo Contreras con Aurelia Contreras y otras, *RDJ* 6, #2, nov 1908, 67–71. Juan Francisco Cuevas con Santiago Castro (testamentaria) sobre alimentos i servicios de su esposa, 1845, AJSFer, Leg. 115, 7. Her husband, who represented her in the suit, made the same claim about his own labor for the man whom he considered his father-in-law.

31. The logic of the wage worked only with jobs of a certain rank since low-level dependents in households and haciendas did not customarily receive a wage and were compensated in kind.

32. Juan Francisco Cuevas con Santiago Castro (testamentaria) sobre alimentos i servicios de su esposa, 1845, AJSFer, Leg. 115, 7.

33. Ramón Besoain con Atila Villalón sobre filiación, 1893, AJS, serie B, Leg. 228, 23.

34. An example of an hacendado's illegitimate children being given to his inquilinos is Doña Juana Josefa Madariaga con D. Pedro Antonio Ramires por divorcio perpetuo, 1867/8, AAZ, 1855307 (Leg. 759–816), Leg. 813.

35. Juan Francisco Cuevas con Santiago Castro (testamentaria) sobre alimentos i servicios de su esposa, 1845, AJSFer, Leg. 115, 7.

36. Bengoa, *Poder y subordinación*, 96–97.

37. Ravest, *Diccionario de jurisprudencia* (the case is from the Corte de Concepción, 1880, p. 833, 1204).

38. This characterization applies not only to inquilinos' labor conditions but also to those of second-tier administrative employees, such as *capataces* and *mayordomos*. The court's ruling that a man needed a contract to collect payment is thus disingenuous. Bauer, *Chilean Rural Society*, 136–37.

39. Egaña, *Alegato pronunciado*.

40. Zapata, *Alegación*.

41. Eloisa Bernales de N. con Manuela Bernales y otra sobre declaración de hija natural, 1881, AJS, serie B, Leg. 58, 6.

42. Hernández C., "Mirando al pasado," 12. (The article appeared in *La Unión*.)

43. At the time of the litigation, Mercedes Alvarez's lawyers looked for her baptismal certificate but were unable to locate it. The Mormon Church's genealogical database contains a record for her baptism, dated 1839 (www.family search.org). While it cannot be verified with other sources, the other information listed for her in the database, all of which is drawn from parish records, is accurate. I hedge only because most of the witnesses in the case (perhaps even Doña Mercedes herself), as well as her father in letters around the time of her marriage, seemed to assume she was born around 1841, not 1839. The discrep-

ancy may be significant: perhaps for all intents and purposes, she did not "exist" for her paternal family until her paternal grandmother took her into her household in 1841 or 1842.

44. In the context of the filiation suit it was, after all, in her interest to demonstrate as close and early a connection to paternal kin as possible.

45. This extraordinary cache also includes correspondence with Doña Mercedes's suitor and then husband, José Francisco Vergara, with cousins, and with an Alvarez business associate. In total, some sixty-seven letters are included in the case.

46. The judicial record indicates it was quite common for illegitimate sons who had not been recognized to sue illegitimate sisters who had been. In contrast, I found no cases in which sisters sued brothers. This evidence and potential explanations for it are explored in Milanich, "Merceditas and Secundino."

47. It may also be that Bernal and Alvarez had already had a child together who subsequently died. This was certainly a frequent scenario, though there is no evidence of such a child in the available sources.

48. The wide variety of life experiences of illegitimates in Latin America is explored in Milanich, "Illegitimates and Illegitimacy."

49. Her story is credible given that registries of wet nurses in the 1850s and 1860s show the asylum lost track of some 10 percent of its charges. Bustos would have entered the Casa in the 1840s, but there is no reason to believe surveillance practices were any better in this earlier period.

50. Many wet nurses who worked for the foundling home were members of inquilino households in the rural environs of Santiago. Bustos's wet nurse lived on the Hacienda de Lampa and was almost certainly an inquilina. Since it is unlikely he would have superseded the social status of his caretakers, it is probable Bustos was too. (The class politics of fosterage are explored in chapters 5 and 6.) The impression that the two sides were separated by a significant social breach is further confirmed by the fact the plaintiff could not sign his name, whereas the two sisters could, and even the mother, who as an older female was less likely to be literate, could scratch out a passing signature.

51. José Bustos con Carmen Iglesias i otros sobre filiación, 1884, AJS, serie B, Leg. 123, 27.

52. This is Luis Alberto Romero's characterization, *Qué hacer*, 11.

53. Echavarria, CamDip, 34a ordinaria, 18 agosto 1883. See also Abel Saavedra, CamDip, 48a ordinaria, 25 septiembre 1883, and Alessandri Rodríguez, *Precedencia*, 17, for similar comments. If only because the poor so vastly outnumbered the wealthy, unions between working-class parents almost certainly did account for the lion's share of out-of-wedlock births, which by the 1890s exceeded 30 percent of all births. But given that this had long been the case, elites' new construction of illegitimacy as lower class probably reflected less their keen powers of observation than the way they now seized on domestic practices to express class differences.

54. While wills and other notarial records do appear to suggest a decline in

the volume of late-nineteenth-century recognitions even as illegitimacy rates increased, the sources are too ambiguous to be decisive. One does have the impression that illegitimacy was perhaps more acceptable among elite men earlier on. In the early republican period, a number of high-profile men were openly known to have fathered children out of wedlock; see the introduction on the public cases of Bernardo O'Higgins and Diego Portales, for example.

55. In keeping with the Code's stipulation that children "voluntary accept" recognition, as described in the previous chapter, such representatives were required in order to formally receive recognition on the minor's behalf.

56. These fees were set in the *Lei de organizacion i atribuciones de los tribunales* of 1875.

57. Mauricio Giannetti sobre reconocimiento de hijos naturales, 1882, AJV, Leg. 1367, 9.

58. María Arcos sobre reconocimiento de hijo natural, 1882, AJV, Leg. 1364, 14.

59. Ten thousand pesos: Recognition petition of Francisco Sciolla of the minor Humberto Rainieri Manuel Sciolla, ANS, 1900, Vol. 1940, fj 451; sufficient property: Estanislao Pizarro y Lastenia Salinas sobre legitimación de hijos, 1884, AJV, Leg. 1402, 7.

60. *Gaceta*, 1885, #1228, p. 737.

61. While "many" is obviously a vague characterization, it is clear, for example, that there are many more petitions from illegitimate mothers seeking alimentos from fathers than there are recognition or legitimation transactions.

62. The Bourbon Pragmatic regulated unequal unions by giving parents greater power over children's marriage choices. In 1820, Chilean officials instituted a republican marriage Pragmatic, which would be derogated by the Civil Code's provisions. The Code departed from both colonial and republican Pragmatics in eliminating inequality as a legitimate reason for opposing a son's or daughter's marriage. In discussions surrounding the Code, Bello apparently rejected the inequality criterion. Claro Solar, *Explicaciones*, 390. Andreucci Aguilera, "La Pragmática de Carlos III."

63. Ravest, "Memoria sobre filiación natural," 399.

64. This jurist's explication and rejection of this definition of hijo natural is the only reference I have found to it among Chilean jurists.

65. Stoler, *Carnal Knowledge*, 84.

66. As noted in the introduction, they also won a suit brought by a second individual claiming to be Don Salvador's illegitimate child.

67. Witnesses included Francisco de Paula Taforó, Juan Brown, Mariano E. de Sarratea, José Tomás Ramos, Agustín Edwards, José Cerveró, and Domingo Arteaga Alemparte. Several of these individuals figure in the highest echelons of the Chilean elite. Each of them was also identified with Liberal-Radical or Masonic activities or as firefighters (affiliations that were tightly interwoven). Gazmuri, *El "48" chileno*.

68. On the relationship between Vergara and Santa María, see Aránguiz, "Cartas políticas." The Alvarez case was decided in 1877; in correspondence in 1878, Santa María was addressing Vergara as "mi querido José Francisco" and signing as "su amigo afectísimo." Santa María also presided over a filiation case concerning the patrimony of Liberal political ally José Manuel Balmaceda's deceased father. Balmaceda gave a speech to Liberal Party faithful in favor of Santa María's presidential candidacy just one month before the Santiago Court of Appeals ruled in favor of his father's estate.

69. Eloisa Bernales de N. con Manuela Bernales y otra sobre declaración de hija natural, AJS, serie B, Leg. 58, 6, 1881. Bernales voted against Secundino Alvarez. An earlier case in which a well-known judge became the subject of a paternity suit is Manuel Aguirre contra Rodríguez Mercedes sobre entrega de bienes hereditarios como hijo natural, 1837, AJS, Leg. 13, 7.

70. This was Vergara's characterization of *radicalismo* as described in a letter to a political ally, cited in Amador Fuenzalida, *Galeria contemporánea*, 227.

71. Blanca Vergara's husband, Guillermo Errázuriz Urmeneta, was a congressman whose uncle would become archbishop of Santiago. For more on the Errázuriz clan, see the introduction. This is the pedigree provided in Figueroa's *Diccionario histórico*, in Larraín's authoritative local history, *Viña del Mar*, as well as in histories of Viña available on patrimonial websites, including that of the Archivo Histórico Patrimonial de Viña del Mar.

72. The sole ex post facto reference to the litigation that I have located is a newspaper article from the 1920s that recalled the Alvarez estate had been the "object of noisy suits." The article did not, however, allude to the nature of those suits. Hernández C., "Mirando al pasado," 12.

CHAPTER 3 *Kindred and Kinless*

1. The narrative ran serially beginning in August 1897 in the liberal popular newspaper *El Industrial* of Curicó.

2. Pinto [Pérez], *El huérfano*, 96–98.

3. David Kertzer has noted that "European literature was . . . rife with references to foundlings in the nineteenth century." *Sacrificed for Honor*, 11. Think, for example, Oliver Twist.

4. For example, Pérez discusses a caretaker he was especially fond of, a woman named Dolores, who was not a nun and who would not have been known in public circles (in contrast to most nuns, who came from elite society families). In private correspondence at the turn of the century, the administrator of the Casa de Huérfanos mentions the disciplinary problems that have arisen since the passing of a longtime caretaker who was herself reared in the institution and was much loved by the children. The woman's name is Dolores.

CHLC, 6 diciembre 1901, Al Sr Don Ventura Blanco Viel, Administrador de los Talleres. Even more strikingly, Pérez claims that he and several other children were "adopted" by José Vicente Izquierdo, a priest from Quillota. The institution's internal documentation shows that a priest from Quillota named José *Isidoro* Izquierdo took children out of the asylum. Pérez further recounts that Izquierdo removed him shortly after returning one of his playmates, a boy named Francisco Solano, whom the priest had adopted some time before. Casa records show that on September 24, 1867, the priest Izquierdo did indeed take a boy named Francisco Solano whom he subsequently returned. What is more, a note scribbled to the mother superior two years later on a document relating to Izquierdo directs her to give the priest a boy named "Paulito"—a reference to Pablo Pérez himself? CHLS 1854–71, #282, 24 septiembre 1867, and an unnumbered letter from "Eyzaguirre," dated July 1869, in the same volume.

5. Patterson, *Slavery and Social Death*. Patterson argues that natal alienation is a condition specific to slavery, which did not exist (as a de jure institution) in republican Chile. I use the concept to highlight the oppressive aspects of kinlessness in a society where all individuals were formally free. Natal alienation and slavery are further discussed in the chapter conclusion.

6. Lira Montt notes that an 1818 decree of O'Higgins considered legal declarations of limpieza de sangre to be valid, but apparently this was not true for long. "Estatuto de limpieza de sangre," 101. In an 1839 case, the plaintiffs refer to their *limpiesa de sangre i buena comportación*: Juan de Dios Ramírez (sus hijos naturales) contra la sucesion de Juan Dios Ramírez, 1839, AJT, 127, 8. Here limpieza de sangre is invoked as a general characterization of status or respectability rather than a specifically legal or civic classification, as it was used in colonial society. After this date I have found no references to limpieza.

7. The literature on kinship and elite power in Chile is cited in the introduction.

8. del Campo, "Datos genealógicos."

9. de Fleury, *Casa de Larraín*, 9

10. Stabili offers this characterization in her oral history of Chilean elites, *Il sentimento aristocratico*. I believe it applies to their nineteenth-century forebears as well.

11. Florencia Mallon offers a pointed critique of this tendency in "Decoding the Parchments."

12. Barbier, "Elites and Cadres."

13. Had he followed typical naming practices, he would have been Nathaniel Cox Bustillos, as were his siblings. In adopting both the patronym and matronym of his father, he presumably enhanced his English pedigree. He characterized the name Miers as a *legado*, a legacy or gift, of an English cousin, Molly Anne Miers. The practice of choosing among family surnames was common in the colonial period, as Miers-Cox himself noted in his history. It seems he was consciously emulating this custom, which was unusual enough in the nine-

teenth century that it provoked comment in a biographical sketch of Miers-Cox. Figueroa, *Diccionario*.

14. The book, with Miers-Cox's dedication, is in the Medina collection of the Biblioteca Nacional.

15. A parallel example is the genealogical awareness of Doña Alicia Amunátegui de Ross, president of the Sociedad Protectora de la Infancia, described in the introduction, and the natal alienation of Protectora ward Josefa Torres, described below.

16. Cited in Salinas Meza and Corvalán, "Transgresores sumisos," 22.

17. CHLC, 13 mayo 1896, Al Ilmo y Rmo Señor Don Mariano Casanova, Arzobispo de Santiago de Chile.

18. Chambers, "A Right to Support."

19. Pedro Muñoz con María Rojas por alimentos, 1879, AJV, Leg. 1306, 10.

20. Agustina Rosales c. Rosales, Manuel, 1840, AJS, 2a serie, Leg. 1442, 2. The alimentos cases reflect only some dimensions of prevailing kin practices, however. As will be discussed in chapter 5, plebeian constructions of kinship were considerably broader than those recognized by law.

21. José Rosa Veloz con Santiago Veloz, sobre alimentos, *Gaceta*, 1887, #1129, p. 667. Italics are mine. A parallel case before the same judge is Francisco Romero con Emilia Romero, sobre alimentos, *Gaceta*, 1887, #1008, p. 588.

22. Ma [María] Mesías con Ildefonso Tagle, Divorcio perpetuo, Leg. 796, 1859, AAZ, 1855307, Leg. 759–816. Likewise, in the case of the wealthy father and his estranged son, cited above, the court noted that the son's economic situation was "so critical that on occasion he has to recur to the protection [*amparo*] of charitable persons."

23. As a colloquialism, the term properly belongs to oral speech but surfaces in written documentation nonetheless. For examples of the term *huacho* applied to children: [Morin], *Historia de la Congregación*; Pinto [Pérez], *El huérfano*; CHLE 1870s–80s, [1882] #4937; [Puelma case, November 1894], AJS, Caja 16 corresponding to the year 1895, sistema de catalogación provisional; Vowell, *Campaigns and Cruises*, 471. References to the term applied to adults, as either nickname or insult, include Tornero, *Guía ilustrada*, 385; José Manuel Armijo con José Ignacio Silva, por calumnias e injurias, *Gaceta*, 1889, 2956, p. 2903; Smith, *The Araucanians*, 177.

24. Some communities of northern New Spain in the seventeenth century exhibited such rates. Cramaussel, "Ilegítimos y abandonados." Dueñas Vargas, *Hijos del pecado*, finds many children registered as *de padres no conocidos* in mid-eighteenth-century Santa Fe de Bogotá, and a rich Brazilian literature has explored the ubiquity of child abandonment in the eighteenth and nineteenth centuries. Marcílio, *História social*; Venâncio, *Famílias abandonadas*.

25. This term was used in various parts of New Spain. Calvo, "Familia y registro parroquial"; Cramaussel, "Ilegítimos y abandonados"; Gutiérrez, *When Jesus Came.*

26. This distinction between natal and social status is a recurring theme of Twinam's analysis, *Public Lives, Private Secrets*. The tendency to read baptismal or official natal status as a transparent indicator of social or familial condition is evident in, for example, Salazar and Pinto, *Historia contemporánea* V, where the authors assume that all children registered as illegitimate were necessarily fatherless. See introduction for a discussion of this issue.

27. Minchom cited in Milton, "Wandering Waifs," 119.

28. Glave, "Mujer indígena," 55; Charney, "Negotiating Roots"; Cramaussel, "Ilegítimos y abandonados."

29. Cope, *Limits of Racial Domination*, 58, 66.

30. This was the case in colonial Quito, as described by Milton, "Wandering Waifs." On New Spain: Reyes, "Expósitos e hidalgos." On Spanish American elites: Twinam, *Public Lives, Private Secrets*, especially chapter 5.

31. For example, Ma [María] Mesías con Ildefonso Tagle por divorcio perpetuo, 1859, AAZ, rollo 1855307, Leg. 796; Miranda v de Euth con Miranda, *RDJ* 1, #1/2, oct/nov 1903, 55; Rogat con Pereira, *RDJ* 22, 1925, 538–47. The Penal Code punished the usurpation of another person's identity, a transgression that was sometimes investigated by the courts. Such cases are explored in Milanich, "Children of Fate," chapter 3.

32. Atropos, "El inquilino," 100, 603.

33. See the appendix on inquilinos' elusive presence in the historical record.

34. These changes are further described in the introduction. This discussion draws on Bauer, *Chilean Rural Society*, Johnson, "Internal Migration," Romero, *Qué hacer*, and Salazar, *Labradores, peones y proletarios*.

35. On patriarchy in inquilino households in the twentieth century, see Tinsman, *Partners in Conflict*. Despite the difficulty of locating inquilinos in the historical record, dislocations in the patriarchal inquilino household occasionally surface. For example, an inquilino who moved to another hacienda "where they give me better guarantees as an inquilino" filed suit when his wife, who did domestic work for the hacienda, refused to move with him because their patrón "is pleased with her service and advises her not to follow me." Cabrera Juan de Dios declaración que demandada debe irse a la residencia del marido, 1921, AJL, Civiles, Leg. 658, 1. In another case, an inquilino accused the brother of his patrón of seducing his daughter in complicity with his wife and then jailing his son when he stood up to the abuses. Hilario Pino contra Gumercindo García por violación y rapto, ESC, diciembre 1895, Primer Juzgado del Crimen de Santiago. Were such conflicts between patriarchs large and small related to changes in the system of inquilinaje? Or do they cast doubt on whether the idyllic inquilino patriarchy painted by observers ever existed in the first place? The source materials are simply too limited to answer these questions.

36. The reproduction of peonage will be explored in chapter 6.

37. Work: CHLE 1873–82, [1879] #2908. Wet nurse: CHLE 1873–82, [1880]

#3569. In these two instances, the mothers attempted to give the children to a paternal grandmother and a father, respectively. These individuals apparently rejected the children, who were picked up "abandoned" outside their residences by municipal guards and remitted to the Casa de Huérfanos. Cook: CHLE 1912, #6414. A parallel letter is CHLE 1873–82, [1877] #1686. The letters remitted with children are discussed in Milanich, "Casa de Huérfanos."

38. As we will see in chapter 4, this was because they sometimes arrived anonymously, but also because the asylum itself routinely suppressed the kin origins of its young wards.

39. Child circulation will be explored at length in chapters 5 and 6.

40. Espediente de don Benjamín Larrosa sobre entrega de un niño, *Gaceta*, 1862, #2072.

41. *Gaceta*, 1862, #1620, p. 602. A case of a child known by the surname of her patrona until her sister appeared to reclaim her is Contra Andrea Martínez por heridas a Elena Martínez, menor, ESC, mayo 1892, Primer Juzgado del Crimen de Valparaíso. See also the case of fourteen-year-old Fortunata Rojas, reared as a servant since she was small, whose father reappeared to claim custody of her. During the conflict that ensued between father and patrona, Fortunata declared she "cannot remember who her parents are." Antecedentes sobre entrega de la menor Fortunata Rojas a su padre Ramón Rojas, ESC, septiembre 1894, Primer Juzgado del Crimen de Santiago.

42. Contra María Ramírez por hurto, ESC, abril 1895, Primer Juzgado del Crimen de Santiago.

43. Ramírez's ethnicity may have played a role in her subordination; her "Araucanian" provenance suggests she may have been Mapuche. This aspect of her case is discussed in chapter 6.

44. One court held that in cases in which the age of a rapto victim could not be determined, it was obliged to absolve the accused "because without that circumstance it is not possible to establish the existence of the crime": Ravest, *Diccionario*, 1887, p. 921, n. 525, C de Concepcion. A rape case in which the victim's age is at issue is Contra Manuel Salas y Domingo Soza por violación de Filomena Roldán, ESC, febrero 1894, Primer Juzgado del Crímen de Santiago. Other cases of young servants of indeterminate age accused of crimes include Contra Nicolas Muñoz i María Santos Cid, por hurto, *Gaceta*, 1855, 653, #2408, p. 5690, and Con Camilo Machuca Leon i otro por robo i homicidio, *Gaceta*, 1878, 3759, p. 1563. In the latter case the young, male defendant claimed to be about eighteen but was examined by medical authorities because "neither the baptismal certificate nor relatives or persons who could declare about the matter were found."

45. Patterson, *Slavery and Social Death*. Ultimately, Saavedra was found guilty and sentenced to ten years of incarceration after her original death sentence was commuted. Contra Prosperina Saavedra por parricidio, 1895, AJS, Leg. 1638, 6.

46. Romero, *Qué hacer*, emphasizes this change around the turn of the century, as do Salazar and Pinto, *Historia contemporánea* V. Klubock explores efforts, beginning in the 1920s, to root itinerant miners by encouraging patriarchal households: *Contested Communities*. See also the epilogue of this book.

47. A devilish young suplementero, who actually spends his first years in the foundling home in Santiago, is the subject of *Diablofuerte*, a popular novel by the well-known writer José Luis Fermandois ("Jotavé"). The story first appeared serially in 1902–3. With the establishment in 1915 of the Asilo de Suplementeros, these children became the subjects of charitable/disciplinary efforts led by the Church. "Asilo de Suplementeros," RC 29, 1915, 321.

48. Speech by Diputado Quevedo, CamDip, 27a ordinaria, 6 agosto 1928, 1258–59. The congressman assumed that the suplementeros' ambiguous situation was a result of their illegitimacy, and he went on to call for a reform of civil law, specifically, an end to the prohibition of paternity investigation.

49. The woman's original name has been changed on the assumption that she or her immediate descendents could still be alive.

50. Their father's name was recorded but their mother's was listed as unknown. The sisters had been brought to the institution by a nun from a charity hospital in Santiago (perhaps where their father had died). SPIRE, 1920–27, #7406, and Letter from "MS" dated December 10, 1961, inserted in the volume.

51. Priests' and spouses' questions to ecclesiastical authorities were published in the *Revista Católica*, the principal organ of the Catholic Church in Chile: "Nuestras consultas: Sobre remoción de Curas y avisos de matrimonios contraidos," RC 20, 1911, 849–54; "Nuestras Consultas," RC 21, 1911, 106–8; "Nuestras Consultas," RC 21, 1911, 542–43; "Sobre las partidas de bautismo exigidas para el matrimonio," RC 22, 1912, 94–95; "Nuestras Consultas: Partida de bautismo en las informaciones matrimoniales," RC 28, 1915, 408; "Nuestras Consultas: Sobre el bautismo y el matrimonio," RC 33, 1917, 752–53; "Nuestras Consultas: Ambos novios deben presentar la partida de bautismo antes del matrimonio," RC 34, 1918, 8; "Nuestras Consultas: Todo matrimonio debe anotarse en la partida de bautismo de ambos novios . . . ," RC 37, 1919, 6–7; "Circular a los párrocos sobre la presentacion de la partida del bautismo, antes del matrimonio," RC 37, 1919, 787–88.

52. "Circular a los párrocos . . . ," RC 37, 1919, 787–88.

53. Examples of parentless minors' petitions for *nombramiento de curador* include Carmela Arlegui, ESC, 1885, Primer Juzgado Civil de Valparaíso; Catalina Astorga, ESC, 1885, Primer Juzgado Civil de Valparaíso; and the case cited in McCaa, *Marriage and Fertility*, 56. Legislators also alluded to such problems in the debates over civil marriage. One deputy made reference to the plight of individuals who sought to marry but could not because they had an "absent father." He suggested that in such instances, priests appeal to civil authorities for assistance, though it is unclear what help they might be able to offer. CamDip, 32a ordinaria, 14 agosto 1883.

54. The archbishop, Rafael Valentín Valdivieso, argued that ecclesiastical law did not actually require the recording of filiation in the banns: BE 6, #656, 1875–78, 364–65. There existed great leeway in the interpretation and practical application of the rules, and priests may have had an incentive to interpret rules narrowly in order to collect dispensation fees. Uniform fees for baptism, marriage, and death rites were not established until 1914; until then, individual parishes apparently determined their own fee schedules. See BE 7, #867, 1878–80, 823–25; BE 19, #352, 1914–16, 225–29. McCaa cites a related case involving a priest who petitioned his superiors to deny dispensation to a poor parishioner, *Marriage and Fertility*, 52.

55. An example is the civil registry official whose protocol for registering illegitimate births was considerably harsher than the lawmakers who designed the registry apparently intended, discussed in chapter 4.

56. McCaa, *Marriage and Fertility*, 56.

57. Graham, *House and Street*, 73.

58. The quote is from Miranda v de Euth con Miranda, RDJ 1, #1/2, oct/nov 1903, 55. A spouse marrying into a wealthy Petorcan family who pays to avoid public revelation of his illegitimacy is cited in McCaa, *Marriage and Fertility*, 56. McCaa notes that such procedures could cost the equivalent of half a year's wages for a day laborer.

59. Pérez's difficulties do not, however, stem from bureaucratic hurdles associated with his originlessness. He is unable to marry his present partner because he cannot obtain a divorce from his first wife, whom he claims he was forced to marry by an unscrupulous priest and a scheming mother-in-law. Thus, he is stuck in a marital limbo that prevents him from forming a legitimate family with his new partner.

60. Another case of a woman reared as a servant who murders her infant is Flora Peralta. It is unclear whether the defendant was kinless, since she was clearly over the age of majority and the court consequently had no interest in her origins. The fact that as an adult she continued to live alongside and labor for the family of her patrones strongly suggests that she did not have natal kin. Sumario sobre la muerte de un recien nacido en el Bosque contra Flora Peralta por infanticidio, 1899, AJCO, Leg. 1150, 13.

61. Mothers who were themselves orphans or otherwise without parents of their own and who sought to place children in the Casa include CHLE 1873–82, [1874] #424, [1879] #3030, and CHLE 1918, #12754. There are also numerous generic references to mothers as "alone in this world" (CHLE 1896–98, [1896] #12285) or as "completely alone" (CHLE 1928, #30—(ripped); letter from Palmyra O'Ryan de Cardenas, 7 diciembre 1928). One mother wrote, "I am alone I don't have any help [*amparo*]" CHLE 1896–98, [1897] #12749. See also the mother *sin padres* in Contra Vicencia Salazar Manriquez, por abandono de un niño, *Gaceta*, 1878, 1858, #4489. That mothers were alone or even parentless does not necessarily imply radical kinlessness, of course. They may have been orphaned or geographically distant from kin or estranged from them.

While I believe that a lack of knowledge of origins reflects an especially stigmatized condition, in this particular circumstance, the cause of mothers' isolation was obviously less important than the fact they were deprived of kin ties and the assistance those ties afforded.

62. Patterson, *Slavery and Social Death*, 7.

63. Diputado Ricardo Letelier, CamDip, 33a ordinaria, 16 agosto 1883.

64. In fact, actual coercion was sometimes evident in children's placements. See the cases cited in Milanich, "Illegitimacy and Illegitimates," 87.

65. Patterson, *Slavery and Social Death*, 5.

66. Amado, *Gabriela, Clove and Cinnamon*.

CHAPTER 4 *Birthrights*

1. Letter from Estefania Lesana, April 24, 1883, #71, AMG, Vol. 898, solicitudes particulares, 1880–83.

2. These benefits included pensions for surviving family members and the establishment of educational and charitable institutions for soldiers' children.

3. Such petitions are filed in the Ministerio de Guerra under "Solicitudes particulares." Parallel petitions to the courts are found in the archives of local civil courts interspersed with other kinds of cases.

4. La [Sociedad] Protectora, *Cuarta memoria*. The Sociedad's founding member was Benjamin Vicuña Mackenna, the prominent historian and liberal statesman. Of course, the so-called *leyes laicas* (which included, in addition to civil marriage, the secularization of cemeteries and liberal educational reform) were the product of long-standing conflicts with the Church and a broad process of liberal state formation. The war pensions controversy created yet another immediate impetus for these reforms, one as yet unexplored in the historiography. As the Sociedad Protectora argued, a civil registry had become an "urgent and imperious necessity" as a result of survivors' needs.

5. On the Chilean Church's often unsuccessful attempts to prevent proscribed consanguineal unions, see Cavieres F. and Salinas Meza, *Amor, sexo, y matrimonio*, chapter 4. With the establishment of civil marriage, which adopted the Church's marriage regulations essentially without revision, the state assumed this concern. The persistent inability of Chilean parish officials to establish basic information about parishioners' filiation is described in Milanich, "Children of Fate," chapter 3, especially 144–53.

6. Scott, *Seeing Like a State*, 2, 64–71.

7. The carnet continues to serve as the official currency of personal identification in Chile; other countries in Latin America use equivalent identity cards.

8. According to an "Important Notice" on the back of the booklet, "The Libreta de Familia serves to avoid errors in the recording of births and deaths

after marriage, which can only be rectified through judicial decisions, occasioning expense and a loss of time for families." It was retained by the family and presented to civil authorities when births or deaths occurred. The Chilean libreta was likely modeled on the French *livret de famille*, which came into use around this time as well.

9. Late-nineteenth-century logs from the Santiago hospitals of San Juan de Dios and San Francisco de Borja follow this pattern.

10. Annual reports for the Casa show that just two inspectors were charged with overseeing hundreds of nurses who lived in the capital, dispersed across its rural hinterland, and on occasion in southern provinces. According to wet nurse logs from the 1850s, the Casa lost track of about 10 percent of the children in the care of nurses. See also Milanich, "Casa de Huérfanos."

11. CHLA, #8064, #7972.

12. Indeed, there were few other markers the institution could employ, though it is interesting to note it did not opt for the obvious one—recording the nurses' husbands—even though it tended to hire married nurses and even though married women of means were routinely identified by way of their husbands.

13. CC, art. 304; Rogat con Pereira, RDJ 22, 1925, 538–47; 545. The concept of estado civil in Chile was apparently first defined by the Civil Code. By this time, it was already in use in French law.

14. Rogat con Pereira, RDJ 22, 1925, 538–47.

15. Particularly influential feminist critiques of liberalism include Brennan and Pateman, " 'Mere Auxiliaries to the Comonwealth' "; Fraser, "Rethinking the Public Sphere"; Nedelsky, "Reconceiving Autonomy"; Pateman, *Sexual Contract*. On the gendered nature of republican citizenship in Latin America, see Dore, "One Step Forward," and essays in Dore and Molyneux, eds., *Hidden Histories of Gender*, and Chambers, *From Subjects to Citizens*.

16. Rogat con Pereira, RDJ 22, 1925, 538–47.Or as the jurist Luis Claro Solar noted in his classic *Explicaciones de derecho civil chileno y comparado* (1898), "Identity . . . encompasses not just the physical person but the civil person" (322).

17. While I have been unable to trace the individuals in this case, the surnames of these spouses (Salas, Aránguiz, Pereira) are those of prominent families. Moreover, one of the informants in Maria del Rosario Stabili's oral history, Gloria Errázuriz Pereira, who was born in the 1920s, was married to Guillermo Arthur Aránguiz (see her rendering of the Pereira lineage in Stabili, *Il sentimento aristocratico*, 93–94). Given the strong propensity of Chilean families to intermarry repeatedly with one another, it is likely the husband in this legal dispute was a member (or as his wife claimed, a false member) of this clan.

18. Rogat con Pereira, RDJ 22, 1925, 538–47. A parallel, though much earlier, annulment case brought before an ecclesiastical tribunal is Ma [María] Mesías con Ildefonso Tagle por divorcio perpetuo, 1859, AAZ, rollo 1855307, Leg. 796.

The wife sought the end of her marriage, claiming of her husband that "far from belonging to a respectable family, and having wealth . . . he does not have known parents, as the fruit of an accident, he is poor and would have died if charity had not helped him."

19. See the definitions of "estado" in such dictionaries as Escriche, *Diccionario razonado* and the Real Academia Española.

20. See the conclusion of chapter 2 for a brief discussion of the Royal Pragmatic in Chile.

21. Offen, "Defining Feminism," 10. The familism of French social thought is evident in how the welfare state was conceived as well as how feminists framed their arguments.

22. Tilly, cited in Offen, "Defining Feminism."

23. Catalina Astorga, Nombramiento curador, ESC, 1885, Primer Juzgado Civil de Valparaíso; Carmela Arlegui, Nombramiento curador, ESC, 1885, Primer Juzgado Civil de Valparaíso.

24. Embedded in the wall of a building, the wheel provided a space on the outside where a baby could be placed and then spun around to be received by a person inside. The device was designed so that the person leaving the child could avoid being seen.

25. Internal regulations stated that an official *ecónomo* or receptionist would "keep a book in which the abandonments are daily noted, expressing in the entry all the circumstances that serve to distinguish the exposed child. If the person or persons who bring the child wish to give information regarding his/her family, they will be recorded in the book. In no case will the ecónomo or any other employee of the Casa demand this information." The Junta de Beneficencia articulated a similar rule. "Reglamento provisorio para la Casa de Expósitos," in *Colección de ordenanzas*; Junta de Beneficencia, sesión del 10-XI, 1860, cited in Delgado, "Marginación e integración," 93.

26. Indeed, there clearly evolved the expectation on the part of the asylum's officials that children would arrive with at least some information about their identity and provenance. Thus, the bookkeeper noted on the rare occasions when, as in the case of a two-year-old boy, "the person who brought him refused to give information about the child." And even in this case, the child was hardly anonymous: "It is only known that he was from el Principal, the fundo of Sr Vicuña, and that his mother was named Ernestina" (CHLE 1918, #13028). The suppression of information is even clearer in the period before the Hermanas de la Providencia assumed charge of the city's foundlings, when the public maternity hospital doubled as an orphanage. The only surviving records of children entering this older institution, which date from the early 1850s, show that information about a child's origins was not routinely recorded. This was not because children arrived anonymously, since officials apparently knew much more about the identities than they recorded. One entry recounts that when the baby Mercedes was placed in the wheel with a

note saying she would eventually be reclaimed, the Casa sent a message back to the individual who had left her there explaining that this was against policy. Clearly the officials knew who had brought the baby and where the person lived, presumably because such information was included in the note accompanying her, yet they did not record this information in the ledger (CHLA, #7329).

27. Delgado, "Marginación e integración." For an analysis of similar kinds of documentation in Brazilian institutions, see Venâncio, *Famílias abandonadas*.

28. The principal wheel servicing the Casa de Huérfanos was located very close to the public maternity hospital, which opened in the 1870s. The majority of the babies placed in the wheel had been born in the hospital and were abandoned with baptismal certificates issued by the hospital chaplain.

29. Antecedentes: CHLE 1899–1901, [1899] #13890 (the letter was written by a patron who noted that the parents had asked him to write the statement); Margarita del Carmen: CHLE 1883–89, [1889] #8215. Another note writer who included information on the birthplace and baptism of a child whose parents were unknown declared, "I want all this to be kept by the Casa so that afterwards she will know." CHLE 1873–82, [1874] #510.

30. These documents are discussed further in the methodological appendix. Both the ledgers and the entry documents were maintained by the Hermanas, but they were clearly weighted very differently. While the ledgers were the basis for official record-keeping purposes and the source for the all-important monthly statistical compilations that were forwarded to government ministries and published in annual reports, the entry documents were evidently considered less critical. The ledgers were kept carefully up to date, but the entry materials were haphazardly bound long after the fact (such that papers from the 1870s wound up with those from the 1900s, for example). While the entry documents were probably kept because they included original baptismal certificates, they do not appear to have served as the primary source of information about children's identity. The ultimate fate of these two sources further reflects the value accorded them. I located the bound volumes of entry documents in a closet at the Casa Nacional del Niño (the contemporary heir of the Casa de Huérfanos), whereas most of the ledgers have been archived at the Biblioteca de Historia de la Medicina of the Universidad de Chile.

31. CHLE 1873–82, [1878] #2243.

32. CHLE 1873–82, [1878] #2518. A week later the baby died. CHRE-BHM, Vol. 2, 1877–81.

33. Those who were known "moros" were baptized within a few days of arrival. Cases in which babies were said to have been baptized but for whom no documentation existed were more complicated. A few years into their tenure at the Casa de Huérfanos, the nuns began to verify every single instance of unverified baptism. In practice this meant writing hundreds of letters a year to parish priests requesting information about baptisms among parishioners. If

the baptism could not ultimately be verified, the Casa baptized the baby conditionally (*sub conditio*).

34. CHLE 1896–98, [1897] #12555.

35. CHLE 1896–98, [1898] #13639. The baby died several months later. CHRE-CNN, 1898–1902.

36. Italicized letters would have been in boldface. Thus, Rosa Luisa arrived with a note identifying her as the "illegitimate daughter of Margarita de las Mercedes Martínez and Pedro León." Before the paper was filed, León's name was scratched out in the tell-tale pencil of the ecónomo. CHLE 1912, #8439. See also CHLE 1912, #8814, #8825, and CHLE 1928, #2527 for an example of when a priest makes the corrections.

37. CHLE 1907, #5271.

38. CHLE 1907, #5438.

39. CHLE 1918, #13123.

40. CHLE 1918, #13034. Examples of such selective recording and the omission of illegitimate fathers' identities and surnames abound in the documentation: CHLE 1907, #5099, #5134, #5413, #5455, #5566; CHLE 1909, #6815; CHLE 1918, #12754.

41. [Valdivieso], "Ordenanza sobre libros," 22. Italics are his.

42. This observation is gleaned from a general perusal of baptismal records from the Santiago parishes of San Saturnino, El Sagrario, and Apóstol dating from the latter half of the nineteenth century.

43. "Reglamento para la ejecución de las leyes de Rejistro i de Matrimonio Civil. 24 octubre 1884," in Gaete, *Estado civil*; "Lei de Rejistro Civil" in *Códigos chilenos.*

44. Of course, in giving illegitimate mothers and fathers equal opportunity to conceal their identity, the registry was more egalitarian than parish records or the Civil Code, which treated illegitimate paternity and maternity differently.

45. An official of the Civil Registry in Talca noted on the back of a marriage certificate that parents of spouses were only recorded when the bride and groom declared they were legitimate. Novoa Garrido v sucesión de J.M. Garrido, 1894, AJT, Leg. 691, 9. Similarly, in civil death records, the name and surname of the deceased's parents were recorded only when they were legitimate. *Guía comercial de Valparaíso*, 41–45.

46. The libreta is additionally impressive given that the marriage and many of the births took place in rural locales, where civil registry offices were particularly rudimentary. In addition, the family moved frequently among different *circunscripciones* (civil jurisdictions), which would surely have further complicated the procedures.

47. Francisco Abarca c Ignacia Salinas por entrega de hijos, 1912, AJS, serie A, Leg. 375, 15. The libreta was included in the pages of a judicial suit that took place years later between the widowed Abarca and Ignacia Salinas over the care of two of the legitimate children, her half-sisters. Later revisions of the libreta

would offer a broader vision of family by adding a special space for children of the couple who had been legitimated by their marriage. But illegitimates like Ignacia continued to be omitted.

48. CamSen, 8a ordinaria, 20 junio 1884, 84.

49. Because the registry stipulated that doctors and midwives were similarly responsible for recording births, senators argued that the article also violated provisions of the penal code that punished professionals for breaching client privacy (ibid., 52; 85). Professionals were in fact sued for such transgressions, as was one midwife when she threatened to reveal a client's clandestine birth to extract payment: María R de Blancart contra Gregoria Labbé, matrona, por violación de secreto, ESC, 17 agosto 1888, Primer Juzgado del Crimen de Santiago. Elizalde proposed that third parties be required to report only legitimate births.

50. It is interesting to note that Valenzuela Castillo had in the past heard paternity cases as a judge on the Santiago Court of Appeals.

51. CamSen, 6a ordinaria, 16 junio 1884, 50. Ibáñez likened the public registration of an illegitimate birth to the public instruments of recognition and legitimation provided for in the Civil Code. He noted that after "considering the evils that result from announcing or not announcing" the scandal of illegitimate birth, the Code's authors "opted for the first."

52. CamSen, 3a ordinaria, 6 junio 1884, 30.

53. CamSen, 5a ordinaria, 13 junio 1884, 44.

54. CamSen, 6a ordinaria, 16 junio 1884, 49.

55. CamSen, 6a ordinaria, 16 junio 1884, 51.

56. CamSen, 8a ordinaria, 20 junio 1884, 80; this quotation is Elizalde's.

57. Molinare, *Manual para oficiales*, 75. The author of the manual was a lawyer and official of the Civil Registry in Santiago. He may have derived the protocol from the Civil Code's provision that barred parents from recognizing or legitimating such children or from baptismal protocols that suppressed parents' names when children were of damaged unions. For example, in 1917, a priest asked the *Revista Católica* about the procedure for recording the baptism of a child whose parents were "publicly known adulterers." The *Revista* responded that "the custom with adulterous children is to record simply 'of unknown parents.'" "Nuestras Consultas. Consultas varias," RC 33, 1917, 819–21.

58. Dore, "One Step Forward," 8.

59. Indeed, the titles of works on gender and the family reflect the centrality of this theme: Mannarelli, *Pecados públicos* (Public Sins), Twinam, *Public Lives, Private Secrets*, Nazzari, "An Urgent Need to Conceal," Chambers, "Private Crimes, Public Honor."

60. Twinam, *Public Lives, Private Secrets*. In particular, she describes how elite women could bear children out of wedlock but still maintain an honorable reputation if knowledge of the transgression was limited to their private family

circle. See also Patricia Seed's characterization of the culture of honor in colonial Mexico: "More important than private morals . . . was the lack of public disclosure. Seed, *To Love, Honor, and Obey*, 63.

61. Seed, *To Love, Honor, and Obey*, 64. Steve Stern shows how parties to domestic disputes might manipulate the threat of scandal to force the intervention of authorities. Stern, *Secret History*, 108–9.

62. Contra Orcaistegui Francisco por relaciones ilícitas, 1852, AJT, Leg. 727, 18.

63. Contra D. Manuel Cordero por escándalo público, 1853, AJC, Leg. 75, 6.

64. Tadeo Baeza c Rosario Ortiz sobre filiación y paternidad, 1892 [*sic* 1851], AJS, serie B, Leg. 47, 30. The judge's opinion is especially ironic in this case because several decades later, the father, a lawyer, would represent soldiers' family members attempting to clarify their kinship to receive military benefits. AMG, Vol. 292, solicitudes particulares, 1881–87, fj 53. See also Cruz Bascuñán Guerrero con Jerónimo Meléndez sobre entrega de una niña, 1875, AJS, serie B, Leg. 38, 8 and Julio Brignoli con Lucinda Guajardo sobre entrega de hijos, 1907, AJS, serie B, Leg. 599, 1 for similar comments.

65. "Presentación de la partida de bautismo para el matrimonio," RC 23, 1912, 766–67.

66. Senators appearing in the debates had the following party affiliations: Adolfo Ibáñez, Partido Liberal; José Manuel Encina, Partido Liberal; Manuel Valenzuela Castillo, Partido Liberal Radical; Francisco Puelma, Partido Nacional (originally a conservative party that after the 1870s shared many points of agreement with their one-time liberal rivals. Puelma was the congressman who spoke out against the exclusion of illegitimates). Miguel Elizalde's party affiliation is unknown.

67. Okin, "Gender, the Public, and the Private" provides a cogent analysis of privacy in liberal theory.

68. Yrarrázabal, *Circular a los oficiales*. This consequence of the registry is ironic given the growing public concern with infant mortality, particularly as it affected illegitimate children.

69. On working-class notions of gender and respectability, see Rosemblatt, *Gendered Compromises*.

70. Stabili's evocative oral history, *Il sentimento aristocratico*, explores the genealogical fixations of contemporary Chilean elites.

71. Molyneux, "Twentieth-Century State Formations," 38.

72. Scott, *Seeing Like a State*, 32. On Weber's association of democracy and bureaucracy, see Caplan and Torpey, "Introduction," 5.

73. Dore, "One Step Forward," 15.

74. The foundling decree is discussed in Premo, *Children of the Father-King*, 163–67; Twinam, *Public Lives, Private Secrets*, 298–306; Twinam, "Church, State, and Abandoned."

75. As many authors have pointed out, the potential radicalism of the Bour-

bon foundling reform was defused by local officials' resistance to its more radical provisions. Still, the decree apparently had real effects in some places, as when individuals took advantage of it to cast doubt on their unfavorable racial or filiation status (Milton, "Wandering Waifs"). Moreover, beyond the actual impact of the Bourbon legislation, it seems significant that its philosophical impetus contrasted so starkly with republican law and bureaucracy.

CHAPTER 5 *Vernacular Kinships in the Shadow of the State*

1. Their family configurations as well as the limited details provided about Ahumada's modest estate suggest that the women, while literate, were not elite.

2. As Claudia Fonseca has noted, child circulation is "a generic term that permits the comparative analysis of different forms of child placement found throughout the globe and at different moments in history." Fonseca, "Inequality Near and Far," 398.

3. Important recent exceptions to this general dearth of scholarship include the work of anthropologists Claudia Fonseca and Jessaca Leinaweaver. Historical and anthropological studies that deal with child circulation, either explicitly or, more commonly, through implicit reference, include Blum, "Child Circulation"; Bridikhina, "Criadas y ahijadas"; Cadet, *Restavec*; Calvo, "Warmth of the Hearth"; Cardoso, "Creating Kinship"; Dias, *Power and Everyday Life*; Fonseca, "Pais e filhos," "Inequality Near and Far," and *Caminos de adopción*; Fonseca and Rizzini, *As meninas no universo*; Kuznesof, "Puzzling Contradiction"; Leinaweaver, *Circulation of Children*; Mannarelli, *Pecados públicos*; Marcílio, *História social da criança*; Meznar, "Orphans and the Transition"; Milanich, "Casa de Huérfanos"; Premo, *Children of the Father-King*; Putnam, *Company They Kept*; Restrepo, "Concertaje laboral"; Rizzini, "Pequenos trabalhadores do Brasil"; Rodríguez, "Iluminando sombras"; Sabato and Romero, *Trabajadores de Buenos Aires*; Shelton, "Like a Servant"; Szuchman, *Order, Family and Community*; and Walmsley, "Raised by Another Mother." A number of these works focus on child servitude, an aspect of circulation discussed in chapter 6.

4. Putnam, *Company They Kept*, 54.

5. Dias, *Power and Everyday Life*, 27; Premo, *Children of the Father-King*, 44. Other cogent statements of this disjuncture include Dore, "Holy Family," and Kuznesof, "Home, Street, Global Society."

6. Kuznesof, "House, Street, Global Society," 859.

7. These observations are based on documentation from the Archivo Notarial de Santiago and the Archivo Notarial de San Felipe. The methodological appendix discusses the nature of this sample and the challenges of attempting to discern macrolevel patterns from testaments. Cases of adoptive chil-

dren whose status as heirs is challenged include Doña Mercedes Salinas con don Jerónimo Concha sobre nulidad de testamento, *Gaceta*, 1884, #2381, pp. 1928–30; Mercedes Moreno i otros contra Eloisa Zelaya por supuesto parto, 1902, AJSF, Caja 128.

8. Salinas Mezan, "Familia y hogar," 199. Such findings remain inconclusive, however, because few nineteenth-century census manuscripts have survived in Chile. Moreover, as Igor Goicovic has suggested, the identity and origin of unrelated children, like that of other agregados (household residents who are not members of the nuclear family), are difficult to interpret in this source. Goicovic, "Familia y estrategias."

9. The census provides a synchronic snapshot of where individuals were living at the moment their residence was recorded but obviously does not record how many children had at some point lived in a nonnatal household. In addition, Salinas Meza points out that children in general are notoriously underestimated in this type of source. It is difficult to say whether children in nonnatal households would be more likely than others to be passed over by recorders, but the marginal status of many of these children (discussed in chapter 6) would likely make this the case.

10. Shelton, "Like a Servant," Blum, "Child Circulation," Putnam, *Company They Kept*, Dias, *Power and Everyday Life*.

11. The introduction provides additional statistics from the Santiago Casa de Huérfanos. 5 to 9 percent: Delgado, "Marginación e integración," chapter 2; 1912 statistic: Poblete Troncoso, *Lejislación sobre hijos ilejítimos*. The author indicates that he received this information from the Oficina Central de Estadística, although it is unclear how the number was calculated. It surely does not include smaller asylums that operated privately or autonomously. There were surely others, which due to their small size, ephemeral existence, or autonomy from ecclesiastical and state support left no documentary trace. The relationship of informal and institutional modes of circulation is explored in Milanich, "Casa de Huérfanos."

12. An example of an orphan from a wealthy family reared by his parents' friends is Amador Quinteros con Carlos A. Rodríguez sobre cobro de pesos, *RDJ* 17, 2do semestre, 1920, 551–54. I found no wills in which elites adopted unrelated children as heirs. Examples of propertied testators without children who name other blood relatives as universal heirs or major beneficiaries include Ignacia Vargas, ANS, 1850, Vol. 215, fj 284, vta.; Mercedes Alvares de Toledo, ANS, 1850, Vol. 215, fj 289, vta.; María Loyola, ANS, Vol. 214, fj 447; Vicente Uribe, ANSF, 1876, Vol. 93, fj 672. The story of Bayoló and Campaña is recounted in Correa, *Crónica del Asilo de la Providencia*.

13. José Tapia con Cruz Altamirano sobre entrega de un niño, 1867, AJV, Leg. 1135, 6.

14. Mamalakis, *Historical Statistics*, 2: 40.

15. Orrego Luco, "Cuestión social," 50.

16. Andrea Valenzuela, Testamento, AIC, Vol. 39, expedientes administrativos y judiciales, 1846–49.

17. These figures include parents without legitimate or extramarital offspring. For a similar pattern in Lima, see Hunefeldt, *Liberalism in the Bedroom*, 22–23. The explanation for the rise in childlessness is unclear. There is some indication that whereas in 1850 people wrote their wills at the end of their lives, people in 1875 as a matter of course wrote them earlier, when their reproductive lives were not yet complete. But this theory is impossible to test because testators' ages, routinely recorded in the 1875 wills, are not included in those from 1850. This speaks to the problem of discerning whether the pool of testators in a given place or time is comparable to that in another. See the methodological appendix.

18. The proportion of childless testators in San Felipe remained strikingly constant at between 35 and 36 percent over the course of the latter half of the century.

19. Company/companions: this language is generalized in the documentation; Flores: CHLS 1854–71, unnumbered documents, marzo 1859; Don Buenaventura Miranda con don Emilio Muñoz sobre filiacion, *Gaceta*, 1865, #192, p. 76.

20. Dolores González, ANQ, 1875, Vol. 153, fj 46. Note that the references to Segundo González's services, industry, and work should not be read as indications of his servile status. Nineteenth-century testators often used the language of "servicios" to refer to the merits of their beneficiaries, whether they were sons and daughters, spouses, adoptive children, or others.

21. Indagación sobre la muerte de un niño encontrado en el canal Rafaelino [?] en Codegua, 1885, AJR, Leg. 911, 490.

22. The relationship of child circulation and women's labor is discussed in greater depth in Milanich, "Service and Circulation."

23. Gálvez Pérez, "Siete décadas de registro del trabajo femenino," 33, 20–21. On the difficulties of interpreting censal data on women's labor, see Hutchison, "La historia detrás de las cifras," and idem, *Labors Appropriate to Their Sex*, chapter 2. On the incompatibility of service and child rearing, see Milanich, "From Domestic Servant."

24. CHLE 1873–82, [1875] #848, [1874] #57; CHLE 1894, [1895] #11854, [1895] #10772; CHLE 1896–98, [1897] #12994; CHLE 1899–1901, [1900] #553, [1899] #162, [1899] #14052, [1900] #518; CHLE 1907, #4931, #5111, #5151–52, #5447; CHLE 1912, #6414, #8529, #8780, #8978, #9079.

25. From the point of view of the Casa, it cost less to subsidize a servant's salary for around forty pesos a month than to raise her abandoned child at a cost to the institution of more than a hundred pesos. This was an important consideration at a time when the Casa found itself overwhelmed by demand for its services. Calvo Mackenna, *Memoria de la Casa Nacional del Niño*.

26. Homicidio de un párvulo contra Micaela Ibarra, ESC, 188?, Juzgado del

Crimen de Santiago. Evidence on wet nursing is also drawn from Sobre la muerte de una niña, 1858, AJC, Leg. 158, 2; Por infanticidio conra Ysidora Maureira, 1848, AJT, Leg. 364, 14; Muerte del párvulo Juan Bautista Ramírez Arriagada contra Mercedes Ossa, ESC, 30 julio 1884, Juzgado del Crimen de Santiago; Contra Fabian Guerrero y Juana M. Villagra por Infanticidio de Mercedes Laura Pinto, ESC, 8 de enero 1893, Primer Juzgado del Crimen de Santiago; Luisa Guibert vs. Candelaria Peralta, ESC, 11 de septiembre 1896, Primer Juzgado del Crimen de Santiago; Abandono de un menor contra Rosa Iglesias y Celinda Valenzuela, ESC, 9 de octubre 1895, Primer Juzgado del Crimen de Santiago. All of these cases involved wet nurses investigated when their young charges died—a common occurrence in the context of high infant mortality. In all cases, the autopsies revealed causes of death unrelated to the nurse's treatment.

27. Calvo Mackenna, *Memoria de la Casa Nacional del Niño*. It is unclear if the asylum was still sending nurslings out during this period as well.

28. *Boletín de la Sociedad Nacional de Agricultura*, 1871, cited in Johnson, "Internal Migration in Chile." This lack of job opportunities for women was cited by hacendados as one cause of rural poverty. Historians have suggested that it accounts for the strong female out-migration from haciendas witnessed in the late nineteenth century.

29. CHM, 1900.

30. Wet-nursing salaries are drawn from the judicial cases cited throughout this discussion.

31. CHM, 1897. In addition, working for the Casa at least guaranteed a steady source of income, whereas private arrangements with low-wage mothers could prove precarious in that such mothers often defaulted on their payments. This impression derives from the internal records of the Casa de Huérfanos, which reveal that many children were deposited there by wet nurses who had not received payment from their mothers. In addition, wet nurses sometimes went to court to file complaints for nonpayment of wages.

32. Dominga Moncada: CHLA and CHLS 1854–71, #23, 2 enero 1858; Andrea Castañeda: CHLS 1922–30, #673, 10 marzo 1928. In addition, both women adopted at least one of their child wards on a more permanent basis. By the late 1920s and 1930s, wages had increased to forty pesos, though it is unclear if the nurse received the full sum or if part of it paid for medical and other services for the children. Calvo Mackenna, *Memoria de la Casa Nacional del Niño*.

33. Contra Carmen Rosa Cuevas por abandono de un menor, ESC, 10 de septiembre 1894, Primer Juzgado del Crimen de Santiago; Causa criminal por infanticidio contra María del Carmen Díaz, 1860, AJR, Leg. 701, 15.

34. Examples of women passersby or community members who solicit foundlings or agree to care for them: Causa criminal por abandono de un niño contra Florencia Espinola, 1882, AJSF, Caja 39 (14); Sumario por hallazgo de un párvulo/infanticidio contra Zoraida Castillo, 1899, AJL, Leg. 79, 10; Suma-

rio sobre la esposición de un niño, 1870, AJT, Leg. 912, 238; and of men who do so: Sumario por hallazgo de un párvulo, 1901, AJLS, Leg. 12, 49; Por abandono de una creatura recien nacida, 1881, AJL, Leg. 24, 14.

35. Asparagus: Indagación sobre el abandono de un párbulo, 1885, AJR, Leg. 911, 489. Godmother: Sumario sobre el abandono de un párbulo, 1885, AJSF, Caja 53.

36. Abandono de un menor contra Rosa Iglesias, ESC, 9 de octubre 1895, Primer Juzgado del Crimen de Santiago. Iglesias was prosecuted for "abandonment" when the baby's mother asked for the baby back. The precise nature of her allegation and why she recurred to the police is unclear.

37. Dávila Boza, "Mortalidad de los niños en Santiago," 310–11; Sierra and Moore, *Mortalidad de los niños en Chile*; Vergara Keller, "Nodrizas mercenaries."

38. On women as mothers, see, for example, Zárate, "Proteger a las madres," 165.

39. This mobility permitted him to remake his identity and to marry twice. Narciso Flores por doble matrimonio, 1856, AJT, Leg. 738, 16.

40. Pedro Jiménes, ANSF, 1850, Vol. 50, fj 295.

41. CHLS 1922–30, #737, 17 septiembre 1929; #686, 22 julio 1928. See also #694, 22 diciembre 1928.

42. Tránsito Figueroa, ANS, 1851, Vol. 51, fj 53.

43. Dias, *Power and Everyday Life*, 26.

44. CHLS 1922–30, #676, 2 april 1928. Other contracts and wills that express the intent to make an adoptee an heir include #203, 8 febrero 1928; #732, 23 agosto 1929; CHLS 1854–71, #1138, 8 agosto 1867; Dolores González, ANQ, 1875, Vol. 153, fj 46. An example of a son and heir whose adoptive origins are not mentioned in a will is Doña Mercedes Salinas con don Jerónimo Concha, sobre nulidad de testamento, *Gaceta*, 1884, 2381, pp. 1928–30.

45. CHLS 1854–71, #284, octubre 1867.

46. *Estatutos de la Sociedad "La Igualdad,"* 9–10.

47. The orphanage was known as the Asilo de la Patria. CamDip, 37a estraordinaria, 23 diciembre 1881; *El Ferrocarril*, 24 diciembre 1881.

48. "Affectionate memories": *Gaceta*, 1920, 2do semestre, #127, 551–53; "contract of honor": Secundina Brito contra Paulina Carrasco, 1899, AJSF, Caja 115.

49. Dionisio Toro con Rita Orellana sobre entrega de una niña, ESC, 1893, Primer Juzgado del Civil de Valparaíso. Similarly, Margarita Aguilar asked that a young orphan boy be handed over to her in her "character as the godmother that I am." Margarita Aguilar con Andrés Cornejo sobre entrega de niño, 1880, AJV, serie reciente, Leg. 1322, 4. A godmother might also take in a child whose parents separated and invoke her status as such to assert custody rights superior to those of the legitimate father. Juan Clausen con Rosa Espindola sobre entrega de una menor, ESC, 1912, Segundo Juzgado Civil de Valparaíso.

50. Francisco Díaz con Pedro Romero sobre entrega de un niño, 1884, AJV, Leg. 1408, 30. Pedro Vergara contra Filomena Aguirre v de Otárola por violación de domicilio, golpes y rapto, 1894, AJSF, Caja 89. Wet nurses employed by the Casa de Huérfanos also routinely served as godmothers to their nurslings. Casa wet nurses who served as godmothers and then petitioned to keep children permanently include CHLA, #8144, #8205. On compadrazgo in Mexico City's Casa de Expósitos, see Blum, "Public Welfare."

51. He went on to name the executor of his will as tutor and guardian "of my two adoptive children whom I declare above." Pedro Gamboa, ANSF, 1875, Vol. 93, fj 368. See also Manuela Baras, ANC, 1859, Vol. 11, fj 17.

52. The creation of adoptive kin relations between Roldán and Inostroza is especially noteworthy given that at least one member of the girl's natal family, her grandmother, was alive and apparently in contact with her. Here was another example of a youngster who was simultaneously a member of her natal family as well as of her family of crianza. Contra Manuel Salas y Domingo Soza por violación de Filomena Roldán, ESC, febrero 1894, Primer Juzgado del Crimen de Santiago.

53. Julio Brignoli con Lucinda Guajardo sobre entrega de hijos, 1907, AJS, serie B, Leg. 599, 1. See also Ramón Besoain con Atila Villalón sobre filiación, 1893, AJS, serie B, Leg. 228, 23.

54. Isidoro Moncada, ANS, 1900, Vol. 1124, fj 48. Only three of the twelve children were surviving at the time Moncada left his will. Intriguingly, a man with the same unusual name, Isidoro Moncada, received a child from the Casa de Huérfanos some forty years before. At the time, he was apparently married but childless. The name of the child he took from the Casa was, like the wet nurse in the will, Andrea. CHLS 1854–71, #145, 6 agosto 1862. Might the child he took from the Casa have grown up to nurse his children?

55. Tadeo Baeza c Rosario Hortiz sobre entrega de una niña, 1851, AJS, 2a serie, Leg. 1094, 6. Doña Mercedes Campos v D. Alejandro D'Huique, 1851, AJS, Leg. 1130, 15.

56. Leinaweaver, "On Moving Children," 178. Doña Pascuala Armijo c. Don Pedro Méndez por entrega de una hija, 1852, AJS, serie 2a, Leg. 1079.

57. Romualda Maza con Josefa Aros sobre alimentos, 1855, AJS, serie 2a, Leg. 1341, 8. Nazzari and Twinam discuss identical scenarios in colonial Brazil and Spanish America. Nazzari, "Urgent Need to Conceal"; Twinam, *Public Lives, Private Secrets*.

58. Putnam, *Company They Kept*, 137–38.

59. The major exception to this more categorical mode of kinship, of course, was illegitimate children. As I argue in chapter 2, it was their very liminality as simultaneously insiders and outsiders that made extramarital progeny socially and legally problematic, particularly in elite families.

60. Medieval Iberian codes and Roman law featured a number of juridical devices for creating adoptive kin ties. They included adopción, crianza, prohi-

jamiento, and arrogación, which provided for different rights and responsibilities between "adopter" and "adoptee." See Dougnac Rodríguez, *Esquema del derecho*, chapter 12.

61. On adoption in the Napoleonic Code, see Gager, *Blood Ties*, epilogue. On the Spanish draft code, see "García de Goyena y el Código Civil chileno," in Lira Urquieta, *Código Civil chileno*, 82–83.

62. It was also, of course, true of the many Latin American countries that adopted Bello's code as their own. Other codes, such as those of Peru and Costa Rica, retained adoption.

63. Valenzuela, *Adopción*, 42; Chacón, *Esposición razonada*, 219. Jurists' objection to adoption as contrary to nature or natural law stands in contrast to their acceptance of the Civil Code's distinction between hijo natural and hijo ilegítimo, which they also understood to be a "legal fiction." See chapter 1.

64. This comment is found in Bello's notes on a draft of the Code dating from 1841–45. He wrote, "Nothing in this draft is said about adoptive children. Adoption appears to have fallen into disuse; but maybe it would be good to reestablish it." Of course, he did not ultimately act on these musings. Guzmán Brito, *Proyecto no completo*, 107–8.

65. Valenzuela, *Adopción*, 52. The suppression of adoption in the Chilean Civil Code after it had been accepted in medieval Spanish law parallels the earlier disappearance of adoption in early modern French law. Also, nineteenth-century Chilean jurists' argument that adoption was contrary to natural law and had fallen into disuse echoes legal scholars in early modern France and Spain, who made similar claims about its social extinction. See Gager, *Blood Ties*, chapter 1, Vassberg, "Orphans and Adoption." The epilogue discusses the reintroduction of adoption into Chilean civil law in the 1930s.

66. Dougnac Rodríguez finds no evidence of legal adoptions in the late eighteenth century. *Esquema del derecho*, chapter 12.

67. CC, art. 237 and 239. For a more detailed discussion of the Civil Code's ambiguities, contradictions, and silences regarding circulating children, see Milanich, "Children of Fate," 255–60.

68. Adults who reared unrelated children almost never enjoyed the legal status of *curador*, or guardian, though on occasion they moved to obtain this status when their rights over a child were challenged. In Brazil, patrons used guardianship to secure legal authority over poor and illegitimate minors and the free children of slaves and ex-slaves. García Alaniz, *Ingênuos e libertos*, Kuznesof, "Puzzling Contradiction," Meznar, "Orphans and the Transition." Cases in which caretakers solicit legal guardianship during the course of litigation include Clorinda Yáñes con Elisa Cox sobre entrega de una niña, 1862, AJV, Leg. 1107, 11; José Tapia con Cruz Altamirano sobre entrega de un niño, 1867, AJV, Leg. 1135, 6; Rosa Roba [su curador] con María Contreras sobre entrega de pupila, 1877, AJV, Leg. 1238, 7.

69. I have found only two written procedures involving adoption: one was a

procedure overseen by a judge involving the permanent transfer of a child from his mother to an adoptive couple. Causa civil sobre entrega de niño a doña Petronila Méndez, 1868, AJT, serie 7a, Leg. 422, 3. The second also involves the transfer of a child from her mother to another woman, "authorizing her to legitimate her as her own daughter" and "promising not to reclaim her for any reason." It appears to have been overseen by a judge or other local official, although inexplicably the document was found with papers related to the entry of children to the Casa de Huérfanos. CHLE 1912, [1919] #8713. Finally, in one instance the Casa itself oversaw an "adoption" CHLS 1922–30, #752, 16 diciembre 1929.

70. Juana Figueroa contra Alberto Camus por violación, 1897, AJSF, Caja 104, discussed in Milanich, "Children of Fate," 262.

71. Zagal Anabalón, *Lactancia y nodrizas asalariadas*; Vergara Keller, "Nodrizas asalariadas"; AMS, Vol. 189, solicitudes y oficios, 1860–61; AMS, Vol. 217, solicitudes y oficios, 1866–67.

72. The law was the Ley sobre Protección a la Infancia Desvalida. Critics immediately recognized this deficiency. Barros O. and Calvo Mackenna, "La beneficencia." The shortcomings of this legislation and of the law's posture vis-à-vis children in general are discussed in Milanich, "Informalidad, extralegalidad y niñez." See also Rojas, "Derechos del niño."

73. Sobre lesiones a la niñita Maclovia Peralta, ESC, agosto 1901, Primer Juzgado del Crimen de Santiago. Children in mid-nineteenth-century jails were sometimes placed with private citizens who solicited the youngsters. A routine inspection of the Santiago jail mentions a young inmate who is given to a "gentleman." "Visita de Cárcel de Santiago," *Gaceta*, 29 septiembre 1849, 379. Such informal practices continued in the case of child abuse victims or minors whose custody was disputed by adults. Gino Baudrán con Echeverria sobre entrega de menor, ESC, 1916, Segundo Juzgado Civil de Valparaíso. The practice mirrored the long-standing procedure of placing adult women in *casas de respeto* (respectable homes) while their judicial fate was decided, except that in the case of women the practice seems to have disappeared around midcentury, whereas for children it continued into the twentieth century.

74. *Memoria de la Casa de Huérfanos*, 1882. The Casa continued to outsource wet nursing into the early 1930s, and possibly later. This argument is articulated in greater detail in Milanich, "Casa de Huérfanos."

75. In early modern Europe, authorities faced with the problem of illegitimacy adopted just the opposite tack. A poor law in England in 1576 called on justices of the peace to pressure illegitimate mothers to identify the fathers of their children, so that they and not the parish would assume material responsibility for the children. The French *déclarations de grossesse*, which also originated in the sixteenth century, had a similar purpose. Hoffer and Hull, *Murdering Mothers*, 13–15.

76. This is the essential thrust of Marcílio, *História social da criança*, 136, and Blum, "Public Welfare and Child Circulation," 251.

77. For more on this dynamic, see Milanich, "Casa de Huérfanos."

78. CHM, 1886; *El Mercurio*, 26 junio 1855. See also Morin's assertion that the Casa de Huérfanos would "give useful citizens to the patria." Letter from Bernarda Morin, August 1867, reproduced in Morin, *Historia de la Congregación*, 250–66. Officials of the Casa, meanwhile, frequently noted that in saving poor children, the institution was helping alleviate Chile's much-lamented demographic deficit. Pinto [Pérez], *El huérfano*, 78, 149.

79. War festivities: AMS, Vol. 299, Secretaria Municipal, 1881. Casa inauguration: *El Mercurio* (Valparaíso edition), 28 mayo 1885.

80. Jablonka, *Ni mère, ni père*; Venâncio, "Os aprendizes da guerra"; Ramos, "A história trágico-marítima"; Marcílio, *História social da criança*; Jablonka, personal communication.

81. Don Abel Saavedra, CamDip, 48a ordinaria, 25 septiembre 1883.

82. The phrase is Igor Goicovic's, "Mecanismos de solidaridad." See also Salinas Meza's reference to *solidaridad comunitaria* in "Lo público y lo no confesado."

CHAPTER 6 *Child Bondage in the Liberal Republic*

1. Denuncio de Don Luis Siderey sobre secuestro de una menor, ESC, julio 1918, Tercer Juzgado del Crimen de Valparaíso. Gender does not explain his ability to sign and her inability to do so since early-twentieth-century literacy rates for males and females in Chile were roughly the same. While the court record provides no information about Siderey or his class background, his brother was probably the Roberto Siderey Borne who appears in the historical record as a subteniente of the Chillán batallion, gravely wounded in the War of the Pacific. The brother's middling military rank would indicate a family of modest social status. Vicuña Mackenna, *Historia de la campaña*, 1006.

2. A comparative analysis of children's tutelary servitude in Latin America is developed in Milanich, "Degrees of Bondage."

3. On servitude, including that involving children, in eighteenth-century Chile, see Araya, "Sirvientes contra amos," and Dougnac Rodríguez, *Esquema del derecho*. Vicuña Mackenna describes the presence of young Amerindian servants or slaves in colonial Santiago: "The *chinas* and *chinitos* of Arauco," he notes of Mapuche women and children, "were given as gifts as little horses from Chiloé are given today." *Historia crítica y social*, 428.

4. Graham, *Journal of a Residence in Chile*, 73–74.

5. Poeppig, *Un testigo*, 199–200. The British captain Richard Longeville Vowell also observed a traffic in children in the 1820s: *Campaigns and Cruises*, 394. On Amerindian child servants in other colonial Latin American societies, see Glave, "Mujer indígena," Charney, "Negotiating Roots," Cramaussel, "Ilegítimos y abandonados," Súsnik, *Indios del Paraguay*.

6. This case is discussed in chapter 3 as an instance of natal alienation.

Ramírez was around sixteen in 1895, meaning she was born around 1880. Contra María Ramírez por hurto, ESC, 1895, Primer Juzgado de Crimen de Santiago. An earlier instance of the kidnapping of an indigenous youngster is Criminal contra Gregorio Pradines por urto de un niño, *Gaceta*, 1844, 123, in which a man is accused of trying to sell ten-year-old Pedro Yaitul, identified as *un indíjena*.

7. See the examples cited in Salazar, *Labradores, peones, y proletarios*, 288–91. On the tenuous custody claims of single mothers later in the century, see Milanich, "Illegitimacy and Illegitimates," 85–87; for comparative parallels, Guy, "Lower-Class Families," and Meznar, "Orphans and the Transition."

8. A decree from the Intendant of Concepción in the 1820s held that "the children of beggars who are seven or older will be handed over by the respective inspectors, prefects, or subdelegates to artisans of honor and good judgment or to honorable homes, such that in exchange for their service, they will be fed, clothed and taught; for those younger than this age, [the authorities] will make appropriate arrangements." Quoted in Salazar, *Labradores, peones, y proletarios*, 288. Such proclamations were not new: Araya cites an edict from 1783 regarding the impressment of vagrant children, "Sirvientes contra amos," 168. The abduction and indenture of children echoes the fate of poor, single women, who were also routinely forced into domestic service in the early nineteenth century. Poor men, meanwhile, were conscripted as military recruits. Salazar, *Labradores, peones, y proletarios*, 286–87.

9. In his "letter," Salinas describes how his family fled from the "incursions of the barbarians [rebellious, royalist indigenous communities] of the south," thereby distinguishing himself from their ranks. Having served in the independence battles, he was able to marshal statements on his behalf from high-ranking officials, including Ramon Freire himself. Carlos Correa de Sáa sobre infracción de la constitución (por entrega de hijo), 1829, AJS, serie 2a, Leg. 1159, 3.

10. Examples of child abduction in the central valley include the separate incidents denounced by Juan Consuegra and Manuel Rubio in the mid-1830s in communities in San Fernando, both in AIC, Vol. 3, solicitudes recibidas de funcionarios y particulares, 1829–63. On Santiago as a destination for trafficked children: Manuel Rubio claimed that seven-year-old Juana had been abducted by the subdelegado of Quiriagua (department of San Fernando) and remitted to Santiago. See also Viviana Picarte's reference to *chinitos* below. Richard Longeville Vowell notes that the children loaded onto a ship at the southern port of Talcahuano along with adult military recruits were destined for Valparaíso to be "either distributed among the men of war or given as servants to private families." *Campaigns and Cruises*, 394.

11. The Casa de Huérfanos classified entering children as "chino" or "blanco" until the mid-1830s, when it ceased to record ethnic designations. AMI, Vol. 162. Thereafter, people sometimes used the term to refer to foundlings: CHLE

1883, [1888] #8039. Several words that referred to indigenous people in the diminutive form referred specifically to child servants (chino/chinito, cholo/cholito). According to Rodríguez, *chino* derives from the Quechua/Aymara for servant. Bernarda Morin makes reference to the derogatory connotations of the term *chinito/a*, *Historia de la Congregación*, 234. A case in which *china* is deployed as an insult is González Nicanor contra Elvira Moreno y otra por lesiones, 1894, AJSF, Caja 88. *Cholito* is cited in Poeppig, and *negrito* appears in the Casa records (cf. CHLE 1883, [1887] #7548). *Huacho* is discussed in the introduction and below. According to Rodríguez, *hueñi*, the Mapundun word for child, was used by Spanish speakers in southern Chile to refer to child servants, *Diccionario de chilenismos*.

12. Poeppig, *Un testigo*, 200, remarks on the chinitos' association with luxury. Graham, *Journal of a Residence*, 77. This particular observation was from 1822. By the 1870s, commentators remembered the chinitos de alfombra as the quaint custom of a bygone era: Vicuña Mackenna, *Historia crítica y social*, 428; and Tornero, *Chile ilustrado*, 457. The Swedish American traveler C. E. Bladh also made reference to an encounter with a French naturalist outside Santiago in the 1820s who was accompanied by a dog, two guanacos, and a barefoot eight-year-old Amerindian girl, who "had been given voluntarily by her parents as a goddaughter . . . and seemed to love [her guardian] profoundly." Bladh, *La república de Chile*, 151.

13. Poeppig, *Un testigo*, 198–99.

14. The Picarte letter, from 1827, is cited in Vergara Quiroz, *Cartas de mujeres*, 183. Casa requests include CHLS 1854–71, unnumbered letter to Miguel Dávila from Santos Prado, 2 diciembre 1862, and from M. Campino, #132, 18 julio 1862. Also illustrative: the letter to Dávila from Melchor Martines, #4441, 27 abril 1858, and to Tedeon Huberdault, #8, 17 marzo 1854. Dávila was the Casa's administrator from the early 1850s until 1867; Huberdaught was the asylum's chaplain. A parallel case of a priest who uses his missionary work on a hacienda to procure a young servant for his sister-in-law in Santiago is Antecedentes sobre la remisión de la menor Adelaida Martínez, ESC, mayo 1894, Primer Juzgado del Crimen de Santiago.

15. At the turn of the twentieth century, the Casa de Huérfanos administrator Nathaniel Miers-Cox called repeatedly for the closing of foundling wheels located around the city that collected babies and remitted them to the Casa, citing "denunciations that children received in the wheel had been given to people who had requested them, paying for them." CHM, 1899.

16. Meznar, "Orphans and the Transition"; Kuznesof, "Puzzling Contradiction"; Marcílio, *História social das crianças*; Dias, *Power and Everyday Life*; Szuchman, *Order, Family and Community*; Aguirre, "Patrones, esclavos y sirvientes"; Sabato and Romero, *Trabajadores de Buenos Aires*; Restrepo, "Concertaje laboral." The literature of the orphan trains and British imperial child placement is enormous. Of course, these latter policies were not only or per-

haps even primarily about child labor. British "waifs" were sent to Australia as part of an imperial "whitening" strategy, and the removal of poor, urban children was a strategy for managing the effects of urbanization.

17. Milanich, "Degrees of Bondage," makes this argument.

18. This characterization of child labor is based on placement records from the Casa de Huérfanos as well as the following judicial cases: Contra Esteban Barraza por la muerte de la niñita Filomena Castro, ESC, junio 1895, Primer Juzgado del Crimen de Santiago; Contra Manuel Mancilla por maltrato al niño Eduardo Calderon, ESC, julio 1919, Tercer Juzgado del Crimen de Valparaíso; Samuel Mancilla por Melanea Mancilla por violación y estupro, 1895, AJSF, Caja 96; Contra David León por violación, 1894, AJSF, Caja 89; Pinto [Pérez], *El huérfano*, 32.

19. It was only around the turn of the century that child labor was "discovered" in Chile and then only certain kinds of labor were identified as problematic. Rojas, *Los niños cristaleros*. On earlier developments in Europe and North America, see Heywood, *Childhood in Nineteenth-Century France*; Mintz, *Huck's Raft*; Zelizer, *Pricing the Priceless Child*.

20. Despite its uniqueness, there is no reason to believe the parents' aspirations were unusual. Causa civil sobre entrega de niño a doña Petronila Méndez, 1868, AJT, serie 7a, Leg. 422, 3.

21. Contra María Ramírez por hurto, ESC, 1895, Primer Juzgado de Crimen de Santiago.

22. One woman solicited a "little orphan girl four or five years old for her service." CHLS 1854–71, #190, 25 febrero 1863. Other examples of requests explicitly requesting children for service include, from the same volume, #132, 19 julio 1862; #135, 21 julio 1862; #152, 2 septiembre 1862; #161, 7 octubre 1862; #184, 18 enero 1863; #201, 22 marzo 1863; #204, 8 abril 1863; unnumbered letter from Gonzáles re Ana Teresa Baso, 24 junio 1870.

23. The definition of *criado* in the RAE dictionary (beginning with the 1803 version) included "he who serves for his salary" and "he who has received from another initial care [*primera crianza*], support and education." The latter part of this definition only disappears in 1950. As the definition suggests, *criado* was also a generic term for servants of all ages.

24. On popular and elite understandings of domestic service in this period, see Milanich, "From Domestic Servant." On conceptions of women's labor in general, see Hutchison, *Labors Appropriate to Their Sex*, and on domestic service in Latin America, Kuznesof, "A History of Domestic Service."

25. Pursued for several years, the idea of the registration system was never ultimately put into practice. AMS, Vol. 189, solicitudes y oficios, 1860–61; AMS, Vol. 217, solicitudes y oficios, 1866–67.

26. Some petitioners undoubtedly sought adoptive children, as described in chapter 5, and I have excluded from this portrait those whose intentions appear to lean toward adoption, with the recognition that of course true motives are often difficult to discern.

27. The bookbinder was Pedro Isidoro Combet, who wrote a memoir of his adventures in gold-rush California a decade before.

28. Cases involving criado who were sole servants include Contra Bernardina Carrera por hurto, ESC, 20 abril 1916, n. 7976, Juzgado del Crimen de Santiago. I am grateful to Soledad Zárate and Ivonne Urriola for sharing this reference. Contra María Ramírez por hurto, ESC, 1895, Primer Juzgado de Crimen de Santiago; CHLC, 26 octubre 1899, Nathaniel Miers-Cox al Sr Intendente.

29. Other solicitants include the administrator of the women's Casa de Corrección and his son, the director of a school in provincial Colchagua, and the widow of an army official. Elite individuals may well be underrepresented in Casa records either because, in the narrow circle that was Santiago society, they were already known to the administrator and did not need to undertake this vetting process, or because they had informal networks for obtaining child criados and did not need to recur to the Casa. Examples of the latter include the sisters of the intendant of Santiago and of the statesman Diego Portales, both of whom fostered children. Cruz Bascuñán Guerrero con Jeronimo Meléndez sobre entrega de una niña, 1875, AJS, B38, 8; Doña Dolores Portales, ANS, 1850, Vol. 211, fj 299, vta.

30. The Casa memorias from the 1890s include data suggesting boys left the workshops to work as artisans, but a critical retrospective published decades later called into question that pattern. Citing evidence from the files of the Casa's social service department, Zorrilla Moreira noted in *La Casa Nacional del Niño* that boys went on to "menesteres inferiores" (as mozos, shoe shiners, or "simple vagabonds") and not the trades for which they had ostensibly been trained. Meanwhile, nineteenth-century administrators periodically complained that apprenticeships with local employers invariably involved menial work that did not teach children skills.

31. Milanich, "From Domestic Servant" discusses the role of charitable asylums in preparing domestics.

32. In any event the dote was a paltry sum. In the 1920s, it ranged from 30 to 200 pesos, according to the caretaker's ability to pay, and was normally set at 100 pesos or less. Many petitioners promised to pay the deposit but never did. CHLS 1922–30. By way of comparison, the mean daily wage in the mid-1920s was 10.80 pesos for men, 4.95 for women, and 2.88 for children. DeShazo, *Urban Workers*, 31.

33. While some adult servants did not receive a wage, it appears that these individuals had often labored as child criados. Thus wagelessness marked criados as children but sometimes also as adults, a fact that points to the legally and socially liminal status of these individuals even in adulthood.

34. José Domingo Luco del Castillo, ANSF, 1850, Vol. 50, fj 51, vta.; Luis Ballester, ANS, 1850, Vol. 214, fj 145. Such clauses lend further credence to the thesis, discussed in chapter 5, that young dependents served as old-age security for those without offspring or other family support networks. Many testators

who made such clauses were childless, including Luco del Castillo and Ballester (cited here) and Varas (below).

35. María Varas, ANSF, 1875, Vol, 92, fj 235. Around the same time, five pesos per *month* was the going rate paid by a hacienda to a twelve-year-old peon. Pinto [Pérez], *El huérfano*.

36. Ravest, *Diccionario*, 1883, p. 371, n. 701, C de Stgo, 1a sala; Agustina Olmedo y María Cordero con Don Pablo Herrera y Don José Marcoleta sobre servicios personales, 1854, AJSF, Caja 11.

37. María B. Güemes por homicidio de María L. Caballero, 1915, AJS, Leg. 1657, 10; the case of Ester Valdivia, reported in *El Chileno*, 17 noviembre 1915, 2 [*sic*], cited in Brito Peña, "Transformaciones," 39.

38. Pinto [Pérez], *El huérfano*, 36. Judicial cases narrate similar scenarios. The most notorious one was that of the Puelma siblings, described in the introduction: Puelma case, November 1894, AJS, Caja 16 corresponding to the year 1895, sistema de catalogación provisional.

39. Cases in which criadas accused patrones of sexual abuse include Antecedentes sobre la remisión de la menor Adelaida Martínez, ESC, mayo 1894, Primer Juzgado del Crimen de Santiago; Contra Bernardina Carrera por hurto, ESC, 20 abril 1916, n. 7976, Juzgado del Crimen de Santiago; Contra María Ramírez por hurto, ESC, 1895, Primer Juzgado de Crimen de Santiago.

40. Samuel Mancilla por Melanea Mancilla por violación y estupro, 1895, AJSF, Caja 96. The victim lived with her aunt and uncle, for whom she worked, in her own words, "doing errands in the street and ironing handkerchiefs at home." See also Contra Manuel Salas y Domingo Soza por violación de Filomena Roldan, ESC, febrero 1894, Primer Juzgado del Crimen de Santiago. Roldan was allegedly raped while delivering food to some workers. Contra David Leon por violación, 1894, AJSF, Caja 89, in which a six-year-old was raped during an errand to a store and a twelve-year-old was attacked as she washed clothes in a grove. All of these girls were living in the homes of masters and mistresses. Foster parents' legal right to file rape charges on behalf of such children could be challenged, as in Juana Figueroa contra Alberto Camus por violación, 1897, AJSF, Caja 104.

41. Ruperto Herrera con Dolores Figueroa por entrega de hija, ESC, 1894, Primer Juzgado del Crímen de Valparaíso; Doña Pascuala Armijo c. Don Pedro Méndez por entrega de una hija, 1852, AJS, serie 2a, Leg. 1079.

42. Contra Andrea Martínez por heridas a Elena Martínez, menor, ESC, mayo 1892, Primer Juzgado del Crimen de Valparaíso. Other cases of patrones convicted of abusing children include María Güemes B. por homicidio de María L. Caballero, 1915, AJS, Leg. 1657, 10, as well as the case of the Puelma children. In other cases, the court did not convict the defendant but did remove the child from the household: Sobre lesiones a la niñita Maclovia Peralta, ESC, agosto 1901, Primer Juzgado del Crimen de Santiago.

43. The italics are mine. Venegas, *Deberes*, 425, 328.

44. Casanova, "Pastoral sobre propagación de doctrinas irreligiosas," in Grez Toso, *Cuestión social*, 405. Other representative addresses by Casanova include "Discurso pronunciado al bendecir solemnemente las nuevas salas del Hospital de Caridad de Valparaíso, el 20 de abril de 1872"; "Discurso pronunciado en la apertura del Asilo de San José de Valparaíso, destinado a educar sirvientes, 15 de febrero 1874"; "Discurso pronunciado en el acto de la solemne inauguración del Hospicio de Viña del Mar, 21 de julio 1878," all in *Obras oratorias*.

45. Casanova, "Discurso pronunciado en la apertura del Asilo de San José de Valparaíso," *Obras oratorias*, 700. In keeping with this philosophy, Casanova actively participated in efforts to support asylums for needy children. Note too the numerous works that Grez Toso locates within conservative, Catholic intellectual currents that make reference to children (*Cuestión social*).

46. "Espósitos," *La República*, 23 noviembre 1866, 1; the contracts caretakers signed used this language, CHLS 1854–71.

47. Contra Andrea Martínez por heridas a Elena Martínez, menor, ESC, mayo 1892, Primer Juzgado del Crimen de Valparaíso. Other references to charity in fosterage include Florindo Miranda con Federico Díaz sobre entrega de hijo, ESC, 1912, Segundo Juzgado Civil de Valparaíso; Francisco Díaz con Pedro Romero sobre entrega de un niño, 1884, AJV, Leg. 1408, 30; José Tapia con Cruz Altamirano sobre entrega de un niño, 1867, AJV, Leg. 1135, 6. Petitions to take children from the Casa de Huérfanos also make frequent reference to charity.

48. María de la O., Mercedes, y Ursula Ballester, ANS, 1850, Vol. 211, fj 37, vta.

49. José Ramón Vidaurre con Beatriz Vidaurre sobre impugnación de lejitimidad, ESC, julio 1901, Segundo Juzgado del Crimen de Valparaíso; Contra Felisa Mallea por maltrato de Victoria Cavieres, ESC, 1918, Tercer Juzgado del Crimen de Valparaíso.

50. Observing the tendency of child servants to abandon the households where they had been reared, British observer Richard Longeville Vowell noted that "a common phrase in Chile is 'tan ingrato como un huacho' [as ungrateful as a huacho]," *Campaigns and Cruises*, 471. The phrase appears in a slander suit, José Manuel Armijo con José Ignacio Silva, por calumnias e injuries, *Gaceta* 1889, 2956, #2903, and in the Puelma case in the 1890s.

51. Gino Baudrán con Echeverría sobre entrega de menor, ESC, 1916, Segundo Juzgado Civil de Valparaíso.

52. Tomás Clifton, ANS, 1850, Vol. 214, fj 312, vta. The bequest would then be incorporated into the inheritance of Clifton's children. Neither Clifton nor any other testator stipulated such a nuptial clause for their own children, though the law provided for the disinheritance of children who married against parental wishes. A similar clause is found in Dolores Portales, ANS, 1850, Vol. 211, fj 299, vta.

53. These roles are revealed with particular clarity in the frequent letters they wrote on behalf of subordinates seeking to place children in the Casa de Huérfanos and in their active participation in charitable institutions. Elite women's roles in this regard form an interesting parallel with crianza ajena as a social domain of plebeian women, described in chapter 5.

54. Sobre lesiones a la niñita Maclovia Peralta, ESC, agosto 1901, Primer Juzgado del Crimen de Stgo. Concepción Berrios contra José del Carmen Loaiza por entrega de una muchacha, 1860, AJS, serie B, Leg. 8, 30.

55. Pedro Vergara contra Filomena Aguirre v de Otárola por violacion de domicilio, golpes y rapto, 1894, AJSF, Caja 89.

56. José Tapia con Cruz Altamirano sobre entrega de un niño, 1867, AJV, Leg. 1135, 6; Juana Ferrá con Gabriela Cisternas sobre entrega de un niño, 1885, AJV, Leg. 1430, 19.

57. However, litigants sometimes disputed which category applied to a particular child. Niña pensionista vs. true servant: Ruperto Herrera con Dolores Figueroa por entrega de hija, ESC, 1894, Primer Juzgado del Crímen de Valparaíso; educanda vs. servant: Concepción Berrios contra José del Carmen Loaiza por entrega de una muchacha, 1860, AJS, Leg. B8, 30. The patrona referred to herself as an *aya*, a governess, rather than as a mistress.

58. Espósito/abandonado vs. pensionista: Francisco B Covarrubias con Zoila R Donoso sobre presentación de una menor, ESC, 1908, Juzgado de San Felipe. In this case, a "guardian," who may have been the illegitimate father of the child in question, objected when his pupil was "placed in the monastery of the Buen Pastor in the [condition of 'abandoned'], so that I immediately went to [her] aid, changing her condition from espósito to that of pensionista."

59. Alvarez, *Antecedentes del juicio.*

60. Additional cases revolving around children's value, status, and labor include Florindo Miranda con Federico Díaz sobre entrega de hijo, ESC, 1912, Segundo Juzgado Civil de Valparaíso; Francisco Díaz con Pedro Romero sobre entrega de un niño, 1884, AJV, Leg. 1408, 30; Ravest, *Diccionario*, 1887, p. 1379, n. 2248, C de Concepcion; 1882, p. 1106, n. 1994, C de Stgo, 2a sala; 1883, p. 1382, n. 2486, C de Stgo, 1a sala; 1887, p. 606, n. 1036, C de Stgo, 2a sala; 1887, p. 1227, n. 2175, C de Stgo, 1a sala; 1883, p. 371, n. 701, C de Stgo, 1a sala; 1887, p. 1214, n. 1994, C de Stgo, 2a sala. These conflicts, all of which involve control of children, form a contrast with those involving babies. On the contrast between (costly) infants and (useful) children in circulation practices, see Milanich, "Casa de Huérfanos."

61. She recounts the episode in *Historia de la Congregación*. The ad ran in *El Mercurio* and *La República* for several weeks in November 1866. The complainant was supposedly a government official. After several days the nuns succeeded in halting the free-for-all, but only after some sixty-seven orphans had been removed. The available records from this period show no appreciable up-tick in placements, though this may be because these transactions were not recorded.

62. Cf. *El Padre Cobos*, 11 diciembre 1875, #29; 4 mayo 1882, #155; 6 mayo 1882, #156; 13 mayo 1882, #159. The newspaper's unfavorable portrayal of the nuns and priests is predictable given its open anticlericalism, but the fact that the paper begrudged religious officials this particular transgression is telling. Occasionally individuals did indeed bring legal action against asylums in an attempt to recover children: Secundina Brito contra Paulina Carrasco, 1899, AJSF, Caja 115; José Segundo Cepeda con Sor Isabel Veronesi, sobre entrega de una hija, *Gaceta*, 1887, #3207, p. 2190.

63. On children's rural labor, see Atropos, "El Inquilino," 607; Bengoa, *Poder y subordinación*, 49; Balmaceda, *Manual del hacendado*.

64. Johnson, "Family and Household Structure," especially 639–45. Johnson finds that on some estates a majority of households contained allegados.

65. María Gutiérrez contra Nicolás Gamboa y otros por robo con violencia, 1893, AJSF, Caja 80. It is unclear whether the Carvallos were inquilinos or smallholders.

66. Bauer, *Chilean Rural Society*, 159–61; 160.

67. Salazar and Pinto, *Historia contemporánea* V, 165.

68. Loveman, *Struggle in the Countryside*, 33.

69. Del Pozo, *Historia del vino*, 135, and "Viña Santa Rita." A single request for a child from a resident of Santa Rita, dated 1927, was found misfiled among admissions records. See the epilogue for more on this case. El Principal requests are recorded in CHLS 1922–30. These placements occurred from March 1927 to December 1929. An additional child was placed in a household on the García Huidobro estate in 1923.

70. There are two available volumes of placement records, one covering the 1850s and 1860s, the other corresponding to the 1920s. Both are incomplete. The latter records the placement of 239 children from 1922 to 1930, at least 46 on haciendas. Most of the placement details are ambiguous, and the number is probably much higher. Additional information on the haciendas is taken from Valenzuela, *Álbum de la zona central*.

71. The letter from Administrator Miguel Dávila was published in the local press: "Los huérfanos," *El Mercurio*, 26 de junio 1855. It is reprinted in Morin, *Historia de la Congregación*, 96–99. Morin noted that the administrator's petition was a success.

72. Miers-Cox owned Hacienda Mansel in Paine. Valledor's hacienda, Lo Valledor, was donated to the Casa upon his death.

73. Loveman, *Struggle in the Countryside*, 35.

74. Doña Pascuala Armijo c. Don Pedro Méndez por entrega de una hija, 1852, AJS, serie 2a, Leg. 1079.

75. Cases of multigenerational servitude, in which children joined or succeeded mothers or aunts in service to the same family, include Los hijos naturales de don José María Barahona contra su viuda e hijos legítimos, sobre alimentos, 1832, AJCU, Leg. 4, 39; AGLA, Vol. 6, solicitudes 1813–69; Juana Ferrá con Gabriela Cisternas sobre entrega de un niño, 1885, AJV, Leg. 1430,

19; José Ramón Vidaurre con Beatriz Vidaurre sobre impugnación de lejitimidad, ESC, julio 1901, Segundo Juzgado del Crimen de Valparaíso; Contra Felisa
Mallea por maltrato de Victoria Cavieres, ESC, 1918, Tercer Juzgado del Crimen de Valparaíso; Victoria Torres con Superiora del Buen Pastor sobre entrega de una hija, 1890, AJT, Leg. 711, 3; Contra Francisco Cuadra y Carlos
Blanchard por rapto, ESC, 1898, Segundo Juzgado del Crimen de Valparaíso.

76. This case is discussed in the introduction. Contra Wenceslao Plaza,
Alejandro Moraga, y Luis Avila por el homicidio de la niña Elena Valencia, ESC,
octubre 1895, Primer Juzgado del Crimen de Santiago.

77. In a typical pattern, the family filed suit after Ramírez removed the girl
from the household and the family demanded compensation for her crianza. In
this instance, the two parties were joined in a larger complex of dependency
and obligation. By the time they filed suit, they were no longer inquilinos,
suggesting that this dispute was part of a broader rupture between the hacendado and his dependents. Ramírez also later placed an illegitimate son with the
overseer of peons on his estate. Doña Juana Josefa Madariaga con Don Pedro
Antonio Ramíres por divorcio perpetuo, 1867/8, AAZ, rollo 1855307, Leg.
813–14. Other prominent fathers whose illegitimate children are reared in
manifestly inferior households include Francisco Salvador Alvarez, discussed
in chapter 2, and the fathers in the following cases: María Bartola Olivos con
Mateo A de los Olivos por alimentos, 1851, AJS, serie 2a, Leg. 1193, 23; Bernales de N. Eloisa con Manuela Bernales y otra sobre declaración de hija
natural, 1881, AJS, Leg. B58, 6; Hilario Pino contra Gumercindo García por
violación y rapto, ESC, 1895, Primer Juzgado del Crimen de Santiago.

78. McCracken, "Exchange of Children," 307, 306.

79. Nicanor González contra Elvira Moreno y otra por lesiones, 1894, AJSF,
Caja 88.

80. The phrase comes from Stephanie McCurry's study of yeoman households in antebellum South Carolina.

81. Fonseca makes a parallel observation about the social status of natal and
foster families in contemporary Brazilian child circulation, "Inequality Near
and Far," 419.

82. Premo also highlights the role of "nonpatriarchs" in rearing children in
colonial Lima. *Children of the Father-King.* Once Rojas produced his daughter's
baptismal certificate, the court ordered Galán to hand the minor over to her
father. Antecedentes sobre entrega de la menor Fortunata Rojas a su padre
Ramón Rojas, ESC, septiembre 1894, Primer Juzgado del Crimen de Santiago.

83. On migration in the eighteenth and nineteenth centuries, see Góngora,
"Vagabundaje y sociedad fronteriza"; Johnson, "Internal Migration"; Romero,
Qué hacer; Salazar, *Labradores, peones, y proletarios*.

84. Pinto [Pérez], *El huérfano*, 36. Apparently, attempts to bind criados
through ideologies of loyalty and gratitude were not always operative. Pérez's
account creates the impression of patrones who ruthlessly worked him for as
long as he would stay.

85. Of course in one key respect, Pérez's life experience is completely atypical: he is able to write about it. It is unclear where and when he became literate. He says only that he was always "thoughtful and dedicated to study and work" (151). For more on this source, see chapter 3.

86. Narciso Flores por doble matrimonio, 1856, AJT, Leg. 738, 16.

87. Pinto [Pérez], *El huérfano*, 37–38. Thereafter, in narrating his litany of jobs, Pérez always notes how much he earned and how, in the many instances in which he was not paid, he would promptly leave the job. On peon wages, see Bauer, "Chilean Rural Labor," 1080.

88. Examples of cases of girls sent from the countryside to Santiago include Contra Prosperina Saavedra por parricidio, 1895, AJS, Leg. 1638, 6; Contra María Ramírez por hurto, ESC, 1895, Primer Juzgado de Crimen de Santiago; Antecedentes sobre la remisión de la menor Adelaida Martínez, ESC, 1894, Primer Juzgado del Crimen de Santiago; Doña Pascuala Armijo c. Don Pedro Méndez por entrega de una hija, 1852, AJS, serie 2a, Leg. 1079; Contra Manuel Salas y Domingo Soza por violación de Filomena Roldán, ESC, febrero 1894, Primer Juzgado del Crimen de Santiago. Unfortunately, I have found no rich diachronic narratives of female life histories such as exist for Pérez and Flores. On adult women's migration, see Johnson, "Internal Migration"; Salazar, *Labradores, peones y proletarios*.

89. Examples of adult women who continued to live in the households in which they were reared include the plaintiff in María Bartola Olivos con Mateo A de los Olivos por alimentos, 1851, AJS, serie 2a, Leg. 1193, 23; Juana Paez in Nicanor González contra Elvira Moreno y otra por lesiones, 1894, AJSF, Caja 88; the plaintiffs Agustina Olmedo y María Cordero con Don Pablo Herrera y Don José Marcoleta sobre servicios personales . . . , 1854, AJSF, Caja 11; and the defendant in Sumario sobre la muerte de un recien nacido en el Bosque contra Flora Peralta por infanticidio, 1899, AJCO, Leg. 1150, 13. Stationary men include a fifty-year-old man resident in the nonnatal household where he was reared (in the Olivos case, above) and a seventeen-year-old male allegado in María Gutiérrez contra Nicolás Gamboa y otros por robo con violencia, 1893, AJSF, Caja 80. Given that judicial materials by definition involve cases of conflict, criados (of either sex) who remained indefinitely with their masters may well be underrepresented in this source.

90. I found no cases of male runaways whose masters went to court to get them back. Cases involving female adolescent criadas who run away from masters include Gino Baudrán con Echeverría sobre entrega de menor, ESC, 1916, Segundo Juzgado Civil de Valparaíso; Contra María Ramírez por hurto, ESC, 1895, Primer Juzgado de Crimen de Santiago; Denuncio de Don Luis Siderey sobre secuestro de una menor, ESC, julio 1918, Tercer Juzgado del Crimen de Valparaíso; Contra Bernardina Carrera por hurto, ESC, 20 abril 1916, n. 7976, Juzgado del Crimen de Santiago; Contra Gorgonio Cortez por rapto, *Gaceta*, 1862, 1032, #810, p. 306; Antecedentes sobre la remisión de la menor Adelaida Martínez, ESC, 1894, Primer Juzgado del Crimen de Santiago.

91. Of course women also experienced domestic tutelage as wives. But the dependence of marriage harbored very different meanings from that of domestic service. See the introduction and Milanich, "From Domestic Servant."

92. Criminal contra Gregorio Pradines por urto de un niño, *Gaceta*, 1844, 123.

93. Denuncio de Don Luis Siderey sobre secuestro de una menor, ESC, julio 1918, Tercer Juzgado del Crimen de Valparaíso; Francisco Díaz con Pedro Romero sobre entrega de un niño, 1884, AJV, Leg. 1408, 30; Petronila Muñoz con Edelmira Prado por entrega de un niño, 1885, AJSF, Caja 128; Contra Gorgonio Cortez por rapto, *Gaceta*, 1862, 1032, #810, p. 306.

94. Pinto [Pérez], *El huérfano*.

95. They might also appropriate their masters' property as a form of compensation. A case of a young apprentice who says he took several items as payment is Contra Gregorio Diaz por hurto, *Gaceta*, 1855, 666, #2584, p. 5877.

96. Cases of runaways who turn up in other households include Contra María Ramírez por hurto, ESC, 1895, Primer Juzgado de Crimen de Santiago, as well as the cases of "kidnapped" criados cited above.

97. Some patrones sought a mantle of legitimacy by disingenuously referring to criados as "pupils" and their authority as "guardianship." Cf. Contra Bernardina Carrera por hurto, ESC, 20 abril 1916, n. 7976, Juzgado del Crimen de Santiago, discussed in Milanich, "Children of Fate," 263–64.

98. Denuncio de Don Luis Siderey sobre secuestro de una menor, ESC, julio 1918, Tercer Juzgado del Crimen de Valparaíso.

99. Poeppig, *Un testigo*, 199.

100. Kuznesof, "Puzzling Contradiction"; Meznar, "Orphans"; Szuchman, *Order, Family and Community*; Premo, *Children of the Father-King*. Peruvian municipal regulations are discussed in Milanich, "Degrees of Bondage."

101. Valenzuela, *Adopción*, 54.

102. "If marriage has formally governed the legal rights and status of some women, other women have lived in the shadow of marriage, regulated by marriage's normative framework even as they have inhabited terrain outside of its formal boundaries." Dubler, "In the Shadow of Marriage," 1645–46. Her analysis in turn draws on Mnookin and Kornhauser's notion of the "shadow of the law," in "Bargaining in the Shadow."

103. This estimation is based on DeShazo's figures, which show child workers earning just over three pesos per day in 1921. Since industrial laborers likely worked five days a week, whereas Pérez may well have worked more, her wage might in fact have been lower. DeShazo, *Urban Workers*, 31.

EPILOGUE

1. Gazmuri, *Chile del centenario*.

2. Therborn, *Between Sex and Power*, offers this characterization of marriage rates and sketches in broad strokes the changes narrated here, 169–72.

3. The letter, dated December 28, 1927, and numbered 2165, was found misfiled among admissions records. It does not, apparently, represent an isolated dealing. Casa records show that two years earlier the Santa Cruz Ossa family had taken María Peña, a twenty-year-old who had been reared in the Casa, to their rural property in San Fernando. CHRE-BHM, 1894–1914.

4. The high-water mark was 1924, when more than a thousand children entered in a single year, Delgado, "Marginación e integración," 50. Thereafter, the numbers began to decrease, less because of dampened demand than because of aggressive new policies encouraging mothers to keep their children.

5. Morin, *Historia de la Congregación*, 234.

6. For example, it appears that some children designated as "adopted," whose average age was eight, were in fact laborers. CHM, 1901–2; 1902; Milanich, "Casa de Huérfanos," 326–27; San Cristóbal J., "Labor que realiza el Servicio Social."

7. Contra Felisa Mallea por maltrato de Victoria Cavieres, ESC, 1918, Tercer Juzgado del Crimen de Valparaíso; Denuncio de Don Luis Siderey sobre secuestro de una menor, ESC, julio 1918, Tercer Juzgado del Crimen de Valparaíso; Gino Baudrán con Echeverria sobre entrega de menor, ESC, 1916, Segundo Juzgado Civil de Valparaíso; María B. Güemes por homicidio de María L. Caballero, 1915, AJS, Leg. 1657, 10; Secuestro de Ema Basso, ESC, 1921, Tercer Juzgado del Crimen de Valparaíso; Contra Manuel Mancilla por maltrato al niño Eduardo Calderon, ESC, julio 1919, Tercer Juzgado del Crimen de Valparaíso; Contra Bernardina Carrera por hurto, ESC, 20 abril 1916, n. 7976, Juzgado del Crimen de Santiago. I am grateful to Soledad Zárate and Ivonne Urriola for sharing this last reference. That all of these cases derive from Valparaíso and Santiago courts reflects the availability of early-twentieth-century records. Unfortunately, the dearth of judicial materials after about 1920 makes it impossible to trace these cases further forward. See the methodological appendix.

8. Of course, not all children left at the foundling home lost their origins. In the years after 1910, just over 14 percent were reclaimed by their families, a significantly higher proportion than in earlier decades. Delgado, "Marginación e integración," 217–18.

9. CHM, 1902, 49; Morin, *Historia de la Congregación*, 234.

10. AJB, sesiones, mayo 1906–abril 1910, Santiago, 0507, 4 de agosto 1908, fj 302–3.

11. AJB, 10 de junio 1924; AJB, 14 de junio 1929. La Casa Nacional del Niño continues to function, albeit on a significantly reduced scale, to this day.

12. SPIRE, 1894–1902.

13. Cited in Rojas Flores, *Niños cristaleros*, 60. The quote is from 1918. A typical account of child labor that ignores domestic servitude is Letelier González, *Protección de la infancia*. On child welfare and child rights in early-twentieth-century Chile, see Rojas Flores, "Los derechos del niño." On the law's blinkered approach to child labor, see Milanich, "Informalidad, extralegalidad y niños."

14. On "essayists of the crisis," see Gazmuri, *Chile del centenario*. This edited volume includes only nonfiction essayists, but as Gazmuri notes, he could well have included *Juana Lucero* as a fictional exemplar of this genre (20).

15. James O. Morris counts seventy theses on "labor and social subjects" (including unionism, labor law, workplace issues, housing, and women and child labor) among graduates between 1898 and 1924. *Elites, Intellectuals and Consensus*, 38. Venerable jurists who wrote on illegitimacy in this period include Luis Claro Solar, Manuel Somarriva Undurraga, Arturo Alessandri Rodríguez, and Eliodoro Yáñez. Moisés Poblete Troncoso, who would become a renowned scholar of labor and political economy, wrote his law thesis on illegitimacy, as did Eugenio Matte Hurtado, a future cofounder of the Socialist Party.

16. Vargas Guerra, *La ilejitimidad en Chile*, 3.

17. Moya con Muñoz, *RDJ* 22, 1925, 575–86.

18. As Luis Claro Solar prefaced a case in 1908, "Filiation suits in which pre-Civil Code law can be applied are few, and in a few years more they will have disappeared completely." Albornoz con Ordinario Eclesiástico de Santiago, *RDJ* 5, #8, julio 1908, 368–71. In a few instances, it was illegitimates' heirs who pursued legal action.

19. Indeed the consensus on this reform was apparently hemispheric: the Fourth Pan-American Child Congress, held in Santiago in 1924, called for all Latin American legislatures to permit paternity suits.

20. Illegitimacy also tended to be identified with defects in the civil marriage law of 1883. The law did not make civil procedure a precondition to the religious rite, and people who contracted Catholic nuptials only were not legally married. Establishing "civil precedence," critics argued, would expand the penumbra of legal marriage to more couples and their children.

21. Highly placed persons: Vega, *Necesidad de reformar la condición jurídica*, 13–14; scoundrel: Fernández Martorell, *Investigación de la paternidad ilegítima*, 23–24.

22. Legitimate children: Ipinza Besoain, *De la natalidad ilegítima*; different categories: Iturrieta Sarmiento, *De los hijos ilegítimos*, 19.

23. Fernández Martorell, *La investigación de la paternidad ilejítima*, 27.

24. Valdés Valdés, "El huérfano," 394; hatred: Diputado Moreno Echavarria, CamDip, 18a extraordinaria, 27 noviembre 1929; goldmine: Errázuriz Tagle and Eyzaguirre Rouse, *Monografía de una familia obrera*, 66.

25. Rencoret A., *Estudio sobre la situación civil*, 18.

26. This was true, once again, in Chile and elsewhere in Latin America. The same hemispheric child welfare congresses that called for paternity investigation also recommended the incorporation of adoption laws by participating countries.

27. In a hemispheric child welfare publication, a Uruguayan jurist went so far as to call for the reinstitution of archaic legal mechanisms of adoption deriving from the Iberian codes. Coral Luzzi, "La arrogación."

28. Rafael Moreno Echevarría, CamDip, 87a ordinaria, 2 enero 1929.

29. The student was Ciro Salazar Monroy. See Salazar Monroy, *Hijo natural*, 15. A slightly earlier opponent of reform (1897) is Badilla Acuña, *Filiación natural.* I have not been able to identify the party affiliation of either writer.

30. Yáñez, *Del reconocimiento de los hijos naturales.* Alessandri Rodríguez's counterargument was published a year later, *Reconocimiento de hijo natural.* The case is also detailed in Parra con Avello, *RDJ*, 23, 1926, 73–99.

31. Lavrín, *Women, Feminism, and Social Change*, chapter 6.

32. Felicitas Klimpel's survey of women's progress from 1910 to 1960, *La mujer chilena*, includes a long discussion of women's juridical status but hardly mentions the issue of filiation reform. Likewise, in a survey of women and the law for a 1920s compilation celebrating Chilean women's educational progress, the noted feminist Elena Caffarena dwelled on the rights and incapacities of married women but made no mention of filiation law; see "Situación jurídica."

33. Mistral quote: Figueroa, Silva, and Vargas, *Tierra, indio, mujer*, 107. The quote dates from 1927. Labarca: Asunción Lavrín cites an essay by Labarca to this effect published in *Acción Femenina*. She also cites an article on illegitimacy appearing in the early 1930s in *Nosotras*, a publication of the Unión Femenina de Chile. *Women, Feminism, and Social Change*, 399.

34. Stoner, *From the House to the Streets*, 63–65, 67–69, 94, 160–65. A reform of filiation law was passed in 1940.

35. Lavrín, *Women, Feminism and Social Change*, 212–13.

36. Palacios, *Raza chilena*, 12.

37. Letelier, "Los pobres," 139; Poblete Troncoso, *Legislación sobre hijos ilejítimos.* The congressional bills were sponsored by Ramon Briones Luco and Santiago Rubio. CamDip, 5a ordinaria, 15 junio 1916; CamDip, 2a ordinaria, 28 mayo 1928.

38. Mancilla Cheney, *De la investigación de la paternidad ilegítima*, 122.

39. Pearson, "El niño roto."

40. López Morales, "Legado de Baldomero Lillo." The story, "Era él solo," originally appeared in the second edition of Lillo's celebrated short story collection, *Sub-Terra.*

41. Hutchison, *Labors Appropriate to Their Sex*; Rojas Flores, *Niños cristaleros.*

42. Elizabeth Quay Hutchison, Karin Rosemblatt, and Heidi Tinsman, among others, have documented the patriarchal commitments of the Chilean left.

43. Hutchison, "Fruto envenenado," discusses this scenario, painted frequently in the labor press. It also appeared in critiques of filiation law: cf. Poblete Troncoso, *Legislación sobre hijos ilejítimos.*

44. Matte H., *Natalidad ilegítima en Chile.* Matte participated in the founding of the party fifteen years later, in 1933.

45. Klubock, *Contested Communities*, and Rosemblatt, *Gendered Compromises*, offer compelling analyses of this process.

46. Rosemblatt, *Gendered Compromises*, especially chapter 2.

47. Lavrín, *Women, Feminism, and Social Change*, 145–46; Therborn, *Between Sex and Power*, 169–71.

48. Lewin, *Surprise Heirs, II*.

49. Ley 5.343 of 1934 established adoption as a juridical institution; subsequently, Ley 7.613 of 1943 modified the structure of the law. Ley 5.750 of 1935 legalized paternity investigation only for the purpose of establishing rights to basic support. The reform also excised the most stigmatized natal category, that of "damaged union." Law 10.271 of 1952 extended paternity investigation to natural filiation.

50. Ramos Pazos, "Análisis crítico."

51. Ley 19.585. In 2005, yet another reform simplified procedures introduced in the previous law in order to make the rights it guaranteed more accessible. In addition, in 1999, adoption law was reformed to eliminate different tiers of adoptive status and further formalize adoption procedures (Ley 19.620).

52. Ramos Pazos, "Análisis crítico."

53. Htun, *Sex and the State* argues that the Catholic Church's role in restoring human rights and helping end the Pinochet dictatorship gave it enduring moral legitimacy and political capital in democratic Chile. This political strength has in turn allowed the Church to successfully press its social agenda.

54. Ibid., 139.

55. Hudson, *Chile*.

56. Leach, "Characterization of Caste and Class Systems," cited in Martínez-Alier, *Marriage, Class and Colour*, 9.

APPENDIX

1. The notion of "urban" here is relative. In the mid-nineteenth century, neither Santiago nor Valparaíso was much of a bustling metropolis. In 1865, Santiago's population was around 115,000; that of Valparaíso, 70,000. Loveman, *Hispanic Capitalism*, 146. Moreover, given the fact that patterns of land tenure and household structure could vary significantly from one rural area to another, San Felipe cannot be taken as representative of "rural society" in general.

2. Stern, *Secret History*, 37–40; Socolow's critique of Stern's book, "Review"; Caulfield, *Defense of Honor*, 12–13; Premo, *Children of the Father-King*, introduction.

3. Delgado, "Marginación e integración."

4. Since some volumes of the Registros de Entradas are housed at the Biblioteca de Historia de la Medicina, while others are located at the Casa Nacional del Niño, in citing this source I specify location (CHRE-BHM or CHRE-CNN).

5. Bauer, "Chilean Rural Labor," 1067; Atropos, "El Inquilino," 736.

BIBLIOGRAPHY

Archival Collections

Archivo del Arzobispado de Santiago, Microfilm Collection, Church of Jesus
    Christ of the Latter-Day Saints
    Archivo del Provisor, Asuntos Matrimoniales

Archivo Nacional, Santiago, Chile*
    Archivo de la Gobernación de Los Andes
    Archivo de la Gobernación de La Unión
    Archivo de la Intendencia de Colchagua
    Archivo Judicial de Concepción
    Archivo Judicial de Constitución
    Archivo Judicial de Copiapó
    Archivo Judicial de Curicó
    Archivo Judicial de La Serena
    Archivo Judicial de Linares
    Archivo Judicial de Parral
    Archivo Judicial de Putaendo
    Archivo Judicial de Quirihue
    Archivo Judicial de Rancagua
    Archivo Judicial de San Carlos
    Archivo Judicial de San Felipe
    Archivo Judicial de San Fernando
    Archivo Judicial de Santiago
    Archivo Judicial de Talca
    Archivo Judicial de Valparaíso
    Archivo del Ministerio de Guerra
    Archivo del Ministerio de Justicia
    Archivo del Ministerio del Interior
    Archivo de la Municipalidad de Santiago
    Archivo de la Municipalidad de Valparaíso
    Archivo Notarial de Curicó
    Archivo Notarial de Quillota
    Archivo Notarial de Rengo
    Archivo Notarial de San Bernardo

    **Including uncatalogued judicial materials from various civil and criminal
      courts*

Ministerio del Interior, *Memorias de la Casa de Expósitos en Santiago*
Sesiones de la Cámara de Diputados
Sesiones de la Cámara de Senadores

Archivo del Siglo XX (Archivo Nacional de la Administración), Santiago, Chile
    Archivo del Ministerio de Higiene, Asistencia, y Previsión Social
    Archivo Notarial de Casablanca
    Archivo Notarial de San Felipe
    Archivo Notarial de Santiago

Biblioteca Museo Nacional de Medicina Enrique Laval, Facultad de Medicina,
    Universidad de Chile, Santiago, Chile
    Actas de la Junta de Beneficencia de Santiago
    Manuscript collection, Biblioteca de Historia de la Medicina
    Registros de Entradas, Casa de Huérfanos (Fondo Beneficencia, serie expósitos)
    Ministerio del Interior, *Memorias de la Casa de Expósitos en Santiago*
    Libros de Entradas, San Juan de Dios and San Francisco de Borja

Casa Nacional del Niño (Casa de Huérfanos), Santiago, Chile
    Libro de Amas, Casa de Huérfanos
    Libro de Correspondencia, Casa de Huérfanos
    Libros de Entradas, Casa de Huérfanos
    Libros de Salidas, Casa de Huérfanos
    Registros de Entradas, Casa de Huérfanos

Congregación de las Hermanas de la Providencia, Santiago, Chile
    Archivo Bernarda Morin

Congregación de las Hijas de San José, Protectoras a la Infancia, Santiago, Chile
    Carpetas: "Documentos de importancia. Fundación y entrega obras";
        "Memorias de obras entregadas"; "Correspondencia[s] diversas e
        importantes, 1890–1906"

Sociedad Protectora de la Infancia, Santiago, Chile
    Libro de Actas
    Registro de Entradas

Published Primary Sources

Abalos, José Vicente. "Memoria sobre filiación i derechos de los hijos habidos
    fuera del matrimonio." *Anales de la Universidad de Chile* (1848): 316–33.
*Actividades femeninas en Chile. (Obra publicada con motivo del
    cincuentenario del decreto que concedió a la mujer chilena el derecho de
    validar sus exámenes secundarios).* Santiago: Imprenta y Litografía La
    Ilustración, 1928.
Alegato de bien probado en el juicio que sigue doña Rejina Guzmán sobre

filiación de un hijo natural de ésta y del finado sr D. Manuel Cifuentes . . .
Santiago: Imprenta de Julio Belin i Ca., 1851.

Alessandri Rodríguez, Arturo. *Reconocimiento de hijo natural y trasmisión de derechos hereditarios.* Santiago: Balcells and Co., 1925.

Allende, Salvador. *La realidad médico-social chilena.* Santiago: Ministerio de Salubridad, Previsión y Asistencia Social, 1939.

Almanaque del Patronato Nacional de la Infancia. Santiago: Balcells and Co., various years.

Alvarez, Secundino. *Resumen de algunos puntos principales de la prueba rendida por ambas partes en el juicio que siguen Don Secundino Alvarez i Don José Francisco Vergara sobre filiación.* Santiago: Imprenta de la Libreria del Mercurio, 1877.

———. *Antecedentes del juicio sobre filiación natural, seguido por Secundino Alvarez en contra de la sucesión de Francisco Salvador Alvarez.* Valparaíso: Imprenta de La Patria, 1876.

Amador Fuenzalida, Enrique. *Galeria contemporánea de hombres notables de Chile, 1850–1901.* Valparaíso: Imprenta del Universo del Guillermo Helfmann, 1901.

Antecedentes, actas, y trabajos del Primer Congreso Nacional de Gotas de Leche, celebrado en Santiago, Sept. 1919. Santiago: Imprenta Universitaria, 1919.

"Apuntes sobre chilenismos y otros vocablos." *Revista Católica* 20 (1911): 649–51.

Aránguiz, Horacio. "Cartas políticas de Don Domingo Santa María a Don José Francisco Vergara (1878–1882)." *Estudios de Historia de las Instituciones Políticas y Sociales* 1 (1966): 313–70.

Astaburuaga Cueto, E. *Memoria de Prueba (Si el reconocimiento de hijo natural hecho por testamento puede ser revocado).* Santiago: Imprenta Cervantes, 1901.

Atropos. "El inquilino en Chile." *Revista del Pacífico* 5 (1861): 92–104; 599–613; 735–43.

Badilla Acuña, Eduardo Aníbal. *Filiación natural, anterior i posterior a la vijencia de nuestro Código Civil.* Santiago: Imprenta San Buenaventura, 1897.

Balmaceda, Manuel José. *Manual del hacendado chileno: Instrucciones para la dirección i gobierno de los fundos que en Chile se llaman haciendas.* Santiago: Imprenta Franklin, 1875.

Barros O., Salustio, and Luis Calvo Mackenna, "La beneficencia y los niños abandonados." *Revista de Beneficencia Pública* 7, no. 1 (1923): 217–24.

Bello, Andrés. *Selected Writings of Andrés Bello.* Edited by Iván Jaksic. Oxford: Oxford University Press, 1997.

———. "Civil Code: Presentation of the Bill to the Congress." In *Selected Writings,* 270–86.

——. "Discurso del Presidente de la República en 1852." In *Antología de discursos y escritos*, edited by José Vila Selma, 157–72. Madrid: Editora Nacional, 1976.

——. *Obras completas.* Vol. IX, *Opúsculos jurídicos.* Santiago: Impreso por Pedro G. Ramírez, 1885.

——. "Responsabilidad de los jueces de primera instancia." In *Obras completas,* Vol. IX, *Opúsculos jurídicos,* 195–200.

——. "Observancia de la lei." In *Obras completas*, Vol. IX, *Opúsculos jurídicos,* 201–9.

Bladh, C. E. *La república de Chile, 1821–1828.* Santiago: Imprenta Universitaria, 1951.

Blest Gana, Alberto. *Martín Rivas.* Buenos Aires: Javier Vergara Editor, 1979.

Calvo Mackenna, Luis. *Memoria de la Casa Nacional del Niño: Breve reseña de su labor desde 1927 a 1933, inclusive.* Santiago: Imprenta Casa Nacional del Niño, 1934.

del Campo, S. "Datos genealógicos de la familia del Ilmo Sr Obispo D. José Hipólito Salas." *Revista Católica* 23 (1912): 507–11.

Casa Nacional del Niño. *Informe acerca de las actividades de la Casa Nacional del Niño y talleres.* Santiago: Imprenta Casa Nacional del Niño, 1936.

Casanova, Mariano. "Pastoral sobre la propaganda de doctrinas irreligiosas y antisociales." In *La "cuestión social" en Chile: Ideas y debates precursores (1804–1902),* edited by Sergio Grez, 401–10. Santiago: Ediciones de la Dirección de Bibliotecas, Archivos y Museos, 1995.

——. *Obras oratorias.* Santiago: Imprenta Cervantes, 1891.

Chacón, Jacinto. *Esposición razonada y estudio comparativo del Código Civil chileno.* Valparaíso: Imprenta del Mercurio, 1868.

Claro Solar, Luis. "Proyecto de Reforma del Código Civil." *Revista de Derecho y Jurisprudencia* 12, no. 1 (1915): 1–8.

——. *Explicaciones de derecho civil chileno y comparado.* Vols. I and II. Santiago: Establecimiento Poligráfico Roma, 1898–1902.

Código Civil. [1855]. In *Colección de códigos de la República de Chile.* Santiago: Roberto Miranda, 1891.

Código Penal. [1874]. In *Colección de códigos de la República de Chile.* Santiago: Roberto Miranda, 1891.

Colección de ordenanzas, reglamentos i decretos supremos referentes a los establecimientos de beneficencia de Santiago: Desde el año de 1833 hasta el de 1867. Santiago: Imprenta del Independiente, 1867.

Concha, Antenor. *La claúsula testamentaria que se consigna el reconocimiento del hijo natural, ¿es revocable?* Santiago: Establecimiento Poligráfico Roma, 1897.

Consejo Superior de Protección a la Infancia: Ley y Reglamento sobre Protección a la Infancia Desválida. Santiago: Imprenta y Encuadernación Chile, 1913.

La Congregación de las Hermanas de la Providencia en Chile. Santiago:
Imprenta de San José, 1924.

Constitución política de la República Chilena. [1831]. *Colección de códigos de
la República de Chile.* Santiago: Roberto Miranda, 1891.

Coral Luzzi, P. Federico. "La arrogación obligatoria y restringida como
institución legal máxima de protección a la infancia abandonada, ilegítima
o natural." *Boletín del Instituto Internacional Americano de Protección a la
Infancia* 9, no. 3 (1936): 425–37.

Correa, María Rosa. *Crónica del Asilo de la Providencia de San José en
Valparaíso y de su sucursal La Casa de la Providencia en Limache.*
Santiago: Imprenta de San José, 1897.

Croizet, E. *Lucha social contra la mortalidad infantil en el período de
lactancia.* Conferencia dada en la Universidad de Chile el 7 de septiembre
de 1912. Santiago: Imprenta, Litografía y Encuadernación Barcelona, 1913.

Dávila Boza, Ricardo. "Mortalidad de los niños en Santiago: Sus causas i sus
remedios." *Revista Chilena de Higiene* 5 (1899): 265–392.

D'Halmar, Augusto. *Juana Lucero: Los vicios de Chile.* Santiago: Imprenta
Turín, 1902.

Dirección General de Estadística. *Anuario Estadístico de la República de
Chile, años 1929–1930.* Santiago: Dirección General de Estadística, 1931.

Egaña, Mariano. *Alegato pronunciado ante la Iltma Corte de Apelaciones de
Valparaíso por el abogado Don Mariano Egaña patrocinante de los
derechos de Da Fidelia Carril en el juicio que sigue contra ella Da Matilde
Lamarca, v. del Carril sobre aclaración de la sentencia que la reconoció
como hija natural de Don Manuel Benito del Carril.* Valparaíso: Imprenta
del Comercio, 1894.

Errázuriz Tagle, Jorge, and Guillermo Eyzaguirre Rouse. *Estudio social:
Monografía de una familia obrera de Santiago.* Santiago: Imprenta
Barcelona, 1903.

Escriche, Joaquín. *Diccionario razonado de legislación y jurisprudencia.*
Madrid: Imprenta Eduardo Cuesta, 1874–76.

Estatutos de la Sociedad "La Igualdad" de Obreras de Valparaíso. Valparaíso:
Imprenta Excelsior, 1892.

Fermandois, José Luis [Jotavé]. *Diablofuerte.* 4th ed. Santiago: Imprenta y
Editorial S. Corazón de Jesús, 1939.

Fernández Martorell, Alfonso. *La investigación de la paternidad ilejítima.*
Santiago: Imprenta La Ilustración, 1912.

Fernández Pradel, Arturo. "La investigación y la prueba de la paternidad
ilegítima." *Revista de Derecho y Jurisprudencia* 14, no. 6 (1917): 127–43.

Figueroa (Talquino), Virjilio. *Diccionario histórico, biográfico, y bibliográfico
de Chile.* Vols. 1–5. Santiago: Balcells and Co., 1929.

Fleury, José Eugenio de. *La ilustre Casa de Larraín.* Santiago: Imprenta
Cervantes, 1917.

Gaete Varas, Benjamín. *Estado civil: Leyes, decretos, circulares i documentos diversos relativos al matrimonio i al rejistro civil.* Santiago: Imprenta Nacional, 1892.

Graham, Maria. *Journal of a Residence in Chile during the Year 1822.* Edited by Jennifer Hayward. Charlottesville: University of Virginia Press, 2003.

Guerra, Emigdio. *Instrucciones para los jueces de subdelegación i del distrito.* Santiago: Imprenta de la República, 1876.

Guía comercial de Valparaíso para 1895. Valparaíso: Imprenta de La Patria, 1895.

Hernández C., Roberto. "Mirando al pasado: La inauguración del 'Camino de Hierro' entre Valparaíso y Viña del Mar en 1855." In *Crónicas viñamarinas,* by Benjamín Vicuña Mackenna. Valparaíso: Talleres Gráficos Salesianos, 1931, 11–33.

Ipinza Besoain, Arnaldo. *De la natalidad ilegítima: Sus causas y modo de remediarlas.* Santiago: Imprenta de San José, 1920.

Iturrieta Sarmiento, Manuel. *De los hijos ilegítimos no reconocidos solemnemente segun el título XIV del Código Civil.* Santiago: Imprenta Albion, 1898.

Lambert, C. J. *Sweet Waters: A Chilean Farm.* Westport, Conn.: Greenwood Press, 1975.

Lastarria, José Victorino. "El manuscrito del diablo" [1849]. In *La "cuestión social" en Chile: Ideas y debates precursores,* edited by Sergio Grez Toso, 93–109. Santiago: Ediciones de la Dirección de Bibliotecas, Archivos y Museos, 1995.

Lei de Organización i Atribuciones de los Tribunales. [1875]. In *Colección de códigos de la República de Chile.* Santiago: Roberto Miranda, 1891.

Lei de Rejistro Civil. [1884]. In *Colección de códigos de la República de Chile.* Santiago: Roberto Miranda, 1891.

Lei sobre el efecto retroactivo de las leyes. [1861]. In *Colección de códigos de la República de Chile.* Santiago: Roberto Miranda, 1891.

Letelier, Valentín. "Los pobres" [1896]. *Anales de la Universidad de Chile* año CXV 105 (1957): 137–44.

Letelier González, Hipólito. *La protección de la infancia.* Santiago: Imprenta S.B., 1918.

Lillo, Baldomero. *Sub-Terra: Cuadros mineros.* Santiago: Imprenta Moderna, 1904.

Mancilla Cheney, Antonio. *De la investigación de la paternidad ilegítima: Especialmente en Chile, Francia, Bélgica, Suiza y Alemania.* Santiago: Empresa Editorial "La Semana," 1928.

Matte H., Eugenio. *Natalidad ilegítima en Chile.* Santiago: Imprenta Claret, 1918.

Memoria de los 25 años del Apostolado Popular del Sagrado Corazon, 1917–1942. Santiago: Imprenta El Imparcial, [1942].

Meyer, Adolfo. *Guía médica de higiene y beneficencia*. Santiago: Imprenta Barcelona, 1902.

Miers-Cox, Nathaniel. *Los Cox de Chile: Narración genealógica y biográfica*. Santiago: Imprenta de El Diario Popular, 1903.

Molinare, Nicanor. *Manual para los oficiales del rejistro civil*. Santiago: Imprenta Victoria de H. Izquierdo, 1889.

[Morin, Bernarda]. *Historia de la Congregación de la Providencia de Chile*. Vol. 1. Santiago: Imprenta de San José, 1899.

Orrego Concha, Abelardo. *Cuestiones sobre reconocimiento de hijo natural*. Valparaíso: Imprenta del Pacifico, 1908.

Orrego Luco, Augusto. "La cuestión social en Chile" [1884]. *Anales de la Universidad de Chile*, nos. 121–22 (1961): 43–55.

Palacios, Nicolás. *Raza chilena*. 4th ed. Santiago: Ediciones Colchagua, 1988.

Pérez Rosales, Vicente. *Recuerdos del pasado, 1814–1860*. Santiago: Imprenta Gutenberg, 1886.

Pinto, P. N. [Pablo Pérez]. *El huérfano: Historia verdadera contada por un expósito de la Casa de Maternidad de Santiago*. Curicó: El Industrial, 1898.

Poblete Troncoso, Moisés. *Lejislación sobre los hijos ilejítimos (cuestión social)*. Santiago: Imprenta Progreso, 1912.

Poeppig, Eduardo. *Un testigo en la alborada de Chile, 1826–1829*. Santiago: Zig-Zag, 1960.

Ravest, José. "Memoria sobre la filiación natural i sus derechos." *Anales de la Universidad de Chile* (1848): 391–419.

Ravest, José Ramón. *Diccionario de jurisprudencia de las Cortes de Justicia de la República de Chile: Estudio jurídico de la Gaceta de los Tribunales, 1878–1887*. Santiago: Imprenta Barcelona, 1893.

Real Academia Española. *Diccionario de la Lengua Castellana*. 10th ed. Madrid: Imprenta Nacional, 1852.

La Regla i constituciones de las Relijiosas de la Congregación de la Casa de María. Santiago: Imprenta del Independiente, 1866.

Rencoret A., Luis F. *Estudio sobre la situación civil de los hijos ilejítimos i naturales*. Santiago: Imprenta Nacional, 1915.

Rodríguez, Arturo Alessandri. *Precedencia del matrimonio civil al relijioso: Estudio de actualidad*. Santiago: Imprenta Universitaria, 1916.

Rodríguez, Zorobabel. *Diccionario de chilenismos*. Santiago: Imprenta del Independiente, 1875.

Román, Manuel Antonio. *La Casa de María: Relato histórico presentado a la Asamblea Católica de 1886*. Santiago: Imprenta de la Union, 1887.

Rudolph, Federico G. *Estudio sobre el estado civil de hijo natural*. Valparaíso: Imprenta Moderna. 1912.

Russel, William Howard. *A Visit to Chile and the Nitrate Fields of Tarapacá*. London: J. S. Virtue, 1890.

Salazar Monroy, Ciro. *Hijo natural: Modo de adquirir este estado civil.*
    Santiago: Imprenta Bellavista, 1909.

San Cristóbal J., Blanca. "Labor que realiza el Servicio Social de la Casa
    Nacional del Niño." *Anuario Médico Social de la Casa Nacional del Niño,
    año 1935.* Santiago: Imprenta Talleres Casa Nacional del Niño, 1936.

Sierra M., Lucas, and Eduardo Moore. *La mortalidad de los niños en Chile.*
    Valparaíso: Imprenta y Litografia Central, 1895.

Smith, Edmond Reuel. *The Araucanians, or, Notes of a Tour among the Indian
    Tribes of Southern Chili.* New York: Harper and Brothers, 1855.

La [Sociedad] Protectora de Valparaíso. *Cuarta memoria anual: 21 mayo
    1883.* Valparaíso: Imprenta del Progreso, 1883.

Thayer Ojeda, Luis. *Orígenes de Chile, elementos étnicos, apellidos, familias.*
    Santiago: Editorial Andrés Bello, 1989.

———. *Familias chilenas.* Santiago: Guillermo Miranda, 1905.

Tornero, Recaredo Santos. *Chile ilustrado: Guía descriptiva del territorio de
    Chile. . . .* Valparaíso: Librerías i Agencias de El Mercurio, 1872.

Valdés Valdés, Ismael. "El huérfano." *Revista de Beneficencia Pública* 9, no. 2
    (September 1925): 387–95.

[Valdivieso, Rafael Valentín]. "Ordenanza sobre libros parroquiales e
    informaciones matrimoniales." *Boletín Eclesiástico* 2, no. 21 (1853–60):
    15–42.

Valenzuela, Luis. *La adopción ante la lei chilena: Estudio hecho a propósito del
    primer caso de adopción que se presenta ante nuestros tribunales.* Santiago:
    Imprenta Gutenberg, 1885.

Valenzuela O., Juvenal. *Álbum de la zona central de Chile, 1923.* Santiago:
    Imprenta Universitaria, 1923.

Vargas Guerra, Eduardo. *La ilejitimidad en Chile i sus consecuencias.*
    Santiago: Imprenta Camilo Henríquez, 1917.

Vega A., Julio Alberto. *Necesidad de reformar la condición jurídica de la
    madre e hijos ilejítimos.* Santiago: Imprenta de Enrique Blanchard-Chessi,
    1900.

Venegas, José. *Deberes de la mujer cristiana.* Santiago: Imprenta Barcelona,
    1891.

Vera, Robustiano. *Manual para los jueces de distrito i de subdelegación.* 2nd
    ed. Santiago: Imprenta de la Librería del Mercurio, 1876.

Vergara Keller, J. M. "Nodrizas mercenaries." In *Antecedentes, Actas, y
    Trabajos del Cuarto Congreso Panamericano del Niño.* (Santiago de Chile,
    Octubre 1924). Tomo Tercero/Sección Higiene. Santiago: Imprenta
    Cervantes, 1926.

Vergara L., Armando. *Población de Chile: Estudio sobre su composición i
    movimiento.* Santiago: Imprenta del Centro Editorial La Prensa, 1900.

Vicuña Mackenna, Benjamín. *Historia de la campaña de Tacna i Arica, 1879–
    1880.* 2nd ed. Santiago: Rafael Jover, 1893.

——. *Historia crítica y social de la ciudad de Santiago: Desde su fundación hasta nuestros dias (1541–1868)*. Vol. II. Valparaíso: Imprenta del Mercurio, 1869.

Vidal, Severo. "Memoria leida ante la Facultad de Leyes . . . [Reflexiones sobre administración de justicia]." *Anales de la Universidad de Chile* 12 (1850): 560–67.

Villarruel, José de los Dolores. "Discurso de recepción del señor Don José de los Dolores Villarruel, sobre las ventajas que reportaría Chile del establecimiento de las Hermanas de la Caridad." *Anales de la Universidad de Chile* 10 (1858): 141–48.

Vowell, Richard Longeville. *Campaigns and Cruises, in Venezuela and New Grenada, and in the Pacific Ocean; from 1817 to 1830*. Vol. 1. London: Longman and Co., 1831.

Yáñez, Eliodoro. *Del reconocimiento de los hijos naturales conforme a la Ley XI de Toro y del derecho de trasmisión hereditaria de las acciones de estados*. Concepcion: Corte Suprema de Justicia, 1924.

Yrarrázabal, Miguel. *Circular a los oficiales del registro civil por el inspector del ramo*. Santiago: Imprenta Nacional, 1888.

Zagal Anabalón, Armando. *Lactancia y nodrizas asalariadas (Ley Roussel)*. Santiago: Imprenta El Progreso, 1918.

Zapata, Martín. *Alegación en derecho ante la Ilustrísima Corte de Apelaciones en favor de los herederos del finado D. Santiago Yngram contra la filiación natural que se atribuye al menor D. Jorje Laureaud*. Santiago: Imprenta de Julio Belin i Ca., 1850.

——. "Discusión jurídica sobre la prueba en materia de filiación natural." *Gaceta de los tribunales*, November 2, 1850, 3000–3045.

Zorrilla Moreira, Manuel. *La Casa Nacional del Niño: Algunos de sus problemas*. Santiago: Talleres Gráficos Casa Nacional del Niño, 1942.

Secondary Sources

Aguirre, Carlos. "Patrones, esclavos y sirvientes domésticos en Lima (1800–1860)." In *Familia y vida privada en la historia de Iberoamérica*, edited by Pilar Gonzalbo Aizpuru y Cecilia Rabell Romero, 401–22. Mexico City: Colegio de México, Universidad Nacional Autónoma de México, 1996.

Alonso, Ana María. *Thread of Blood: Colonialism, Revolution, and Gender on Mexico's Northern Frontier*. Tucson: University of Arizona Press, 1995.

Amado, Jorge. *Gabriela, Clove and Cinnamon*. New York: Avon Books, 1988.

Andreucci Aguilera, Rodrigo. "La Pragmática de Carlos III sobre el matrimonio de los hijos de familiay y su pervivencia en el derecho chileno." *Revista de Estudios Histórico-Jurídicos* 22 (2000): 213–23.

Araya, Alejandra. "Sirvientes contra amos: Las heridas en lo íntimo propio."

In *Historia de la vida privada en Chile*. Vol. 1, *El Chile Tradicional: De la Conquista a 1840*, edited by Rafael Sagredo and Cristián Gazmuri, 161–97. Santiago: Taurus, 2005.

Arrom, Silvia. *Containing the Poor: The Mexico City Poor House, 1774–1871*. Durham, N.C.: Duke University Press, 2000.

——. "Changes in Mexican Family Law in the Nineteenth Century: The Civil Codes of 1870 and 1884." *Journal of Family History* 10, no. 3 (1985): 305–17.

Balmori, Diana, and Robert Oppenheimer. "Family Clusters: Generational Nucleation in Nineteenth-Century Argentina and Chile." *Comparative Studies in Society and History* 21, no. 2 (1979): 231–61.

Balmori, Diana, Stuart Voss, and Miles Wortman. *Notable Family Networks in Latin America*. Chicago: University of Chicago Press, 1984.

Barbier, Jacques. "Elite and Cadres in Bourbon Chile." *Hispanic American Historical Review* 52, no. 3 (1972): 416–35.

Bauer, Arnold. *Chilean Rural Society from the Conquest to 1930*. New York: Cambridge University Press, 1975.

——. "Chilean Rural Labor in the Nineteenth Century." *American Historical Review* 76, no. 4 (1971): 1059–83.

Bengoa, José. *Historia social de la agricultura chilena*. Vol. 1, *El poder y la subordinacion*. Santiago: Ediciones SUR, 1988.

Benton, Lauren. *Law and Colonial Cultures: Legal Regimes in World History, 1400–1900*. New York: Cambridge University Press, 2002.

Besse, Susan K. *Restructuring Patriarchy: The Modernization of Gender Inequality in Brazil, 1914–1940*. Chapel Hill: University of North Carolina Press, 1996.

Bethell, Leslie, ed. *Chile since Independence*. New York: Cambridge University Press, 1993.

Blakemore, Harold. "From the War of the Pacific to 1890." In Bethell, ed., *Chile since Independence*, 33–85.

Bliss, Katherine. *Compromised Positions: Prostitution, Public Health, and Gender Politics in Revolutionary Mexico City*. University Park: Pennsylvania State University Press, 2001.

Blum, Ann. "Conspicuous Benevolence: Liberalism, Public Welfare, and Private Charity in Porfirian Mexico City, 1877–1910." *The Americas* 58, no. 1 (2001): 7–38.

——. "Public Welfare and Child Circulation, Mexico City, 1877 to 1925." *Journal of Family History* 23, no. 3 (1998): 240–71.

Boswell, John. *The Kindness of Strangers: The Abandonment of Children in Western Europe from Late Antiquity to the Renaissance*. New York: Pantheon, 1988.

Brennan, Teresa, and Carol Pateman. "Mere Auxiliaries to the Commonwealth: Women and the Origins of Liberalism." In *Feminism and Politics*, edited by Anne Phillips, 93–115. Oxford: Oxford University Press, 1998.

Bridikhina, Eugenia. "Las criadas y ahijadas: Servicio doméstico de los menores en La Paz." In *Historia de la infancia en América Latina*, edited by Pablo Rodríguez and María Emma Mannarelli, 281–96. Bogotá: Universidad Externado de Colombia, 2007.

Brinton, Crane. *French Revolutionary Legislation on Illegitimacy, 1789–1804*. Cambridge, Mass.: Harvard University Press, 1936.

Brito Peña, Alejandra. "Del rancho al conventillo: Transformaciones en la identidad popular-femenina (Santiago de Chile, 1850–1920)." In *Voces femeninas y construcción de identidad*, edited by Marcia Rivera, 13–59. Buenos Aires: CLACSO, 1995.

Bunster, Enrique. "Los amores de Portales." *Chilenos en California*, 29–35. Santiago: Editorial de Pacífico, 1958.

Cadet, Jean-Robert. *Restavec: From Haitian Slave Child to Middle-Class American*. Austin: University of Texas Press, 1998.

Caffarena Morice, Elena. "Situación jurídica de la mujer chilena." In *Actividades femeninas*, [no author], 75–84. Santiago: La Ilustración, 1928.

Calvo, Thomas. "The Warmth of the Hearth: Seventeenth-Century Guadalajara Families." In *Sexuality and Marriage in Colonial Latin America*, edited by Asunción Lavrín, 287–312.

———. "Familia y registro parroquial: El caso tapatío en el siglo XVIII." *Relaciones: Estudios de Historia y Sociedad* 3, no. 10 (1982): 53–68.

Caplan, Jane, and John Torpey, eds. "Introduction." In *Documenting Individual Identity: The Development of State Practices in the Modern World*. Princeton, N.J.: Princeton University Press, 2001.

Cardoso, Ruth C. L. "Creating Kinship: The Fostering of Children in Favela Families in Brazil." In *Kinship Ideology and Practice in Latin America*, edited by Raymond T. Smith, 196–203. Chapel Hill: University of North Carolina Press, 1984.

Caulfield, Sueann. "The History of Gender in the Historiography of Latin America." *Hispanic American Historical Review* 81, nos. 3–4 (2001): 449–90.

———. *In Defense of Honor: Sexual Morality, Modernity, and Nation in Early-Twentieth-Century Brazil*. Durham, N.C.: Duke University Press, 2000.

Caulfield, Sueann, Sarah C. Chambers, and Lara Putnam. *Honor, Status, and Law in Modern Latin America*. Durham, N.C.: Duke University Press, 2005.

Cavieres F., Eduardo. "Consensualidad, familia e hijos naturales: Aconcagua en la segunda mitad del siglo XVIII." *Cuadernos de Historia* 15 (December 1995): 219–39.

Cavieres F., Eduardo, and René Salinas Meza. *Amor, sexo, y matrimonio en Chile tradicional*. Valparaíso: Universidad Católica de Valparaíso, Serie monografias, 5, 1991.

Centeno, Miguel Angel. "The Disciplinary Society in Latin America." In *The

Other Mirror: Grand Theory through the Lens of Latin America, edited by Miguel Angel Centeno and Fernando López-Alves, 289–308. Princeton, N.J.: Princeton University Press, 2000.

Chambers, Sarah C. "A Right to Support: State Responsibility for Family Welfare in 19th-Century Chile." Paper presented at "Common Vocabularies, Different Perspectives: New Political History on Nineteenth Century Latin America" Symposium, Columbia University, New York City, May 4–5, 2007.

——. "Private Crimes, Public Order: Honor, Gender, and the Law in Early Republican Peru." In Caufield, Chambers, and Putnam, eds., *Honor, Status, and Law in Modern Latin America*, 27–49.

——. *From Subjects to Citizens: Honor, Gender, and Politics in Arequipa, Peru 1780–1854*. University Park: Pennsylvania State University Press, 1999.

Charney, Paul. "Negotiating Roots: Indian Migrants in the Lima Valley during the Colonial Period." *Colonial Latin American Historical Review* 5, no. 1 (1996): 1–20.

Coates, Timothy J. *Convicts and Orphans: Forced and State-Sponsored Colonizers in the Portuguese Empire, 1550–1755*. Stanford, Calif.: Stanford University Press, 2001.

Collier, Simon, and William Sater. *A History of Chile, 1808–1994*. Cambridge: Cambridge University Press, 1996.

Cope, Douglas. *The Limits of Racial Domination: Plebeian Society in Colonial Mexico City, 1660–1720*. Madison: University of Wisconsin Press, 1994.

Cramaussel, Chantal. "Ilegítimos y abandonados en la frontera norte: Parral y San Bartolomé en el siglo XVII." *Colonial Latin American Historical Review* 4, no. 4 (1995): 405–39.

Cunningham, Hugh. Review of Steven Mintz, *Huck's Raft: A History of American Childhood*. H-Childhood, H-Net Reviews. February 2006. Online at http://www.h-net.org (visited November 21, 2008).

Davis, Natalie Zemon. *The Return of Martin Guerre*. Cambridge, Mass.: Harvard University Press, 1983.

Deere, Carmen Diana, and Magdalena León. "Liberalism and Married Women's Property Rights in Nineteenth-Century Latin America." *Hispanic American Historical Review* 85, no. 4 (2005): 627–78.

Delgado Valderrama, Manuel. "La infancia abandonada en Chile, 1770–1930." *Revista de Historia Social y de las Mentalidades* 5 (2001): 101–26.

——. "Marginación e integración social en Chile: Los expósitos, 1750–1930." Master's thesis, Universidad Católica de Valparaíso, Instituto de Historia, 1986.

Delgado Valderrama, Manuel, and René Salinas Meza. "Los hijos del vicio y del pecado: La mortalidad de los niños abandonados, 1750–1930." *Proposiciones* 19 (1990): 44–54.

DeShazo, Peter. *Urban Workers and Labor Unions in Chile, 1902–1927*. Madison: University of Wisconsin Press, 1983.

Dias, Maria Odila Silva. *Power and Everyday Life: Working Women in Nineteenth-Century Brazil.* New Brunswick, N.J.: Rutgers University Press, 1995.

Díaz, Arlene. *Female Citizens, Patriarchs, and the Law in Venezuela, 1786–1904.* Lincoln: University of Nebraska Press, 2004.

——. "Women, Order, and Progress in Guzmán Blanco's Venezuela, 1870–1888." In Aguirre, Joseph, and Salvatore, eds., *Crime and Punishment in Latin America*, 56–82.

Donoso, Ricardo. *Desarrollo político y social de Chile desde la Constitución de 1833.* Santiago: Imprenta Universitaria, 1942.

Dore, Elizabeth. "One Step Forward, Two Steps Back: Gender and the State in the Long Nineteenth Century." In Dore and Molyneux, eds., *Hidden Histories of Gender and the State in Latin America*, 3–32.

——. "Property, Households, and Public Regulation of Domestic Life: Diriomo, Nicaragua, 1840–1900." In Dore and Molyneux, eds., *Hidden Histories of Gender and the State in Latin America*, 147–71.

——. "The Holy Family: Imagined Households in Latin American History." In *Gender Politics in Latin America: Debates in Theory and Practice*, edited by Elizabeth Dore, 101–17. New York: Monthly Review Press, 1997.

Dore, Elizabeth, and Maxine Molyneux, eds. *Hidden Histories of Gender and the State in Latin America.* Durham, N.C.: Duke University Press, 2000.

Dougnac Rodríguez, Antonio. *Esquema del derecho de familia indiano.* Santiago: Ediciones del Instituto del Derecho Juan de Solorzano y Pereyra, 2003.

Dubler, Ariela. "In the Shadow of Marriage: Single Women and the Legal Construction of the Family and the State." *Yale Law Journal* 112 (2003): 1641–715.

Dueñas Vargas, Guiomar. *Los hijos del pecado: Ilegitimidad y vida familiar en la Santafé de Bogotá colonial.* Bogotá: Editorial Universidad Nacional, 1997.

Felstiner, Mary Lowenthal. "Family Metaphors: The Language of an Independence Revolution." *Comparative Studies in Society and History* 25, no. 1 (1983): 154–80.

Figueroa, Lorena, Keiko Silva, and Patricia Vargas. *Tierra, indio, mujer: Pensamiento social de Gabriela Mistral.* Santiago: Ediciones LOM, 2000.

Findlay, Eileen Suárez. *Imposing Decency: The Politics of Sexuality and Race in Puerto Rico, 1870–1920.* Durham, N.C.: Duke University Press, 1999.

Fonseca, Claudia. "Inequality Near and Far: Adoption as Seen from the Brazilian Favelas." *Law and Society Review* 36, no. 2 (2002): 397–432.

——. *Caminos de adopción.* Buenos Aires: Eudeba, 1998.

——. "Pais e filhos na família popular (Início do século XX)." In *Amor e família no Brasil*, edited by Maria Angela d'Incao, 95–128. São Paulo: Editora Contexto, 1989.

Fonseca, Claudia, and Irene Rizzini. *As meninas no universo do trabalho*

doméstico no Brasil: Aspectos históricos culturais e tendências atuais.
Brasilia: Organização Internacional de Trabalho, 2002.

Foucault, Michele. *Power/Knowledge: Selected Interviews and Other Writings, 1972, 1977.* New York: Pantheon, 1980.

Fraser, Nancy. "Rethinking the Public Sphere: A Contribution to the Critique of Actually Existing Democracy." In *Habermas and the Public Sphere,* edited by Craig Calhoun, 109–42. Cambridge, Mass.: MIT Press.

Fuchs, Rachel. *Abandoned Children: Foundlings and Child Welfare in Nineteenth-Century France.* Albany: State University of New York Press, 1984.

Gager, Kristin. *Blood Ties and Fictive Ties: Adoption and Family Life in Early Modern France.* Princeton, N.J.: Princeton University Press, 1996.

Gálvez Pérez, Thelma, and Rosa Bravo Barja. "Siete décadas de registro del trabajo femenino, 1854–1920." *Revista de Estadística y Economía* 5 (1992): 1–52.

García Alaniz, Anna Gicelle. *Ingênuos e libertos: Estratégias de sobrevivência familiar em épocas de transição, 1871–1895.* Campinas: UNICAMP, 1997.

Garrido A., Eugenia. "Los orígenes de Viña del Mar y su proceso de industrialización, un caso específico: Lever, Murphy y Cía." *Revista Archivum* 6 (2004): 74–86.

Gazmuri, Cristián. *El Chile del centenario: Los ensayistas de la crisis.* Santiago: Pontifica Universidad Católica de Chile, 2001.

——. *El "48" chileno: Igualitarios, reformistas, radicales, masones y bomberos.* Santiago: Editorial Universitaria, 1992.

Glave, Luis. "Mujer indígena, trabajo doméstico y cambio social en el virreinato peruano del siglo XVII: La ciudad de La Paz y el sur andino en 1684." *Bulletin de l'Institut français d'études andines* 16, nos. 3–4 (1987): 39–69.

Goicovic, Igor. "Mecanismos de solidaridad y retribución en la familia popular del Chile tradicional." *Revista de Historia Social y de las Mentalidades* 3 (1999): 61–88.

——. "Familia y estrategias de reproducción social en Chile tradicional. Mincha, 1854." *Valles: Revista de Estudios Regionales* (Museo de la Ligua, Chile) 4, no. 4 (1998): 13–35.

Góngora, Mario. "Vagabundaje y sociedad fronteriza en Chile (siglos XVII a XIX)." *Cuadernos del Centro de Estudios Socioeconómicos* 2 (1966): 1–41.

González, Ondina E., and Bianca Premo, eds. *Raising an Empire: Children in Early Modern Iberia and Colonial Latin America.* Albuquerque: University of New Mexico Press, 2007.

Graham, Sandra Lauderdale. *House and Street: The Domestic World of Servants and Masters in Nineteenth-Century Rio de Janeiro.* Austin: University of Texas Press, 1992.

Grez Toso, Sergio. *La "cuestión social" en Chile: Ideas y debates precursores (1804–1902)*. Santiago: Ediciones de la Dirección de Bibliotecas, Archivos y Museos, 1995.

Grossberg, Michael. "Who Gets the Child? Custody, Guardianship, and the Rise of a Judicial Patriarchy in Nineteenth-Century America." *Feminist Studies* 9, no. 2 (1983): 235–60.

Gutiérrez, Ramón A. *When Jesus Came, the Corn Mothers Went Away: Marriage, Sexuality, and Power in New Mexico, 1500–1846*. Stanford, Calif.: Stanford University Press, 1991.

Guy, Donna. "Parents before the Tribunals: The Legal Construction of Patriarchy in Argentina." In Dore and Molyneux, eds., *Hidden Histories of Gender and the State in Latin America*, 172–93.

———. *Sex and Danger in Buenos Aires: Prostitution, Family, and Nation in Argentina*. Lincoln: University of Nebraska Press, 1991.

———. "Lower-Class Families, Women and the Law in Nineteenth-Century Argentina." *Journal of Family History* 10, no. 3 (1985): 305–17.

———. "Women, Peonage and Industrialization: Argentina, 1810–1914." *Latin American Research Review* 16, no. 3 (1981): 65–89.

Guzmán Brito, Alejandro. *La codificación civil en Iberoamérica: Siglos XIX y XX*. Santiago: Editorial Jurídica de Chile, 2000.

Guzmán Brito, Alejandro, et al. *El "Proyecto no completo de un código civil para Chile escrito por el señor D. Maríano Egaña": Primer proyecto de código civil de Chile*. Santiago: Editorial Jurídica de Chile, 1978.

Hale, Charles A. "Political Ideas and Ideologies in Latin America, 1870–1930." In *Ideas and Ideologies in Twentieth-Century Latin America*, edited by Leslie Bethell, 133–206. Cambridge: Cambridge University Press, 1996.

Hartmann, Heidi. "The Family as the Locus of Gender, Class and Political Struggle: The Example of Housework." *Signs* 6, no. 3 (1981): 366–94.

Hay, Douglas, E. P. Thompson, Peter Linebaugh, John G. Rule, and Cal Winslow. *Albion's Fatal Tree: Crime and Society in Eighteenth-Century England*. New York: Pantheon Books, 1975.

Hecht, Tobias, ed. *Minor Omissions: Children in Latin American History and Society*. Madison: University of Wisconsin Press, 2002.

Heywood, Colin. *Childhood in Nineteenth-Century France: Work, Health and Education among the Classes Populaires*. New York: Cambridge University Press, 1988.

Hoffer, Peter C., and N. E. H. Hull. *Murdering Mothers: Infanticide in England and New England, 1558–1803*. New York: New York University Press, 1984.

Htun, Mala. *Sex and the State: Abortion, Divorce and the Family under Latin American Dictatorships and Democracies*. Cambridge: Cambridge University Press, 2003.

Hudson, Rex A., ed. *Chile: A Country Study*. Washington: GPO for the Library of Congress, 1994. Online at http://countrystudies.us/chile/3.htm (visited July 17, 2008).

Hull, Isabel V. *Sexuality, State, and Civil Society in Germany, 1700–1815.* Ithaca, N.Y.: Cornell University Press, 1996.

Hunefeldt, Christine. *Liberalism in the Bedroom: Quarreling Spouses in Nineteenth-Century Lima.* University Park: Pennsylvania State University Press, 2000.

Hutchison, Elizabeth Quay. "From 'La Mujer Esclava' to 'La Mujer Limón': Anarchism and the Politics of Sexuality in Early-Twentieth-Century Chile. *Hispanic American Historical Review* 81, nos. 3–4 (2001): 519–54.

——. *Labors Appropriate to their Sex: Gender, Labor, and Politics in Urban Chile, 1900–1930.* Durham, N.C.: Duke University Press, 2001.

——. "La historia detrás de las cifras: La evolución del censo chileno y la representación del trabajo femenino, 1895–1930." *Historia* (Chile) 33 (2000): 417–34.

——. "'El fruto envenenado del arbol capitalista': Women Workers and the Prostitution of Labor in Urban Chile, 1896–1925." *Journal of Women's History* 9 (1998): 131–51.

Jablonka, Ivan. *Ni père ni mère: Histoire des enfants de l'Assistance publique (1874–1939).* Paris: Seuil, 2006.

Jaksic, Iván. "La República del orden: Simon Bolívar, Andrés Bello, y las transformaciones del pensamiento político de la Independencia." *Historia* 36 (2003): 191–218.

——. *Andrés Bello: Scholarship and Nation-Building in Nineteenth-Century Latin America.* New York: Cambridge University Press, 2001.

——. Introduction. *Selected Writings of Andrés Bello.* Oxford: Oxford University Press, 1997.

Johnson, Ann Hagerman. "The Impact of Market Agriculture on Family and Household Structure in Nineteenth-Century Chile." *Hispanic American Historical Review* 58, no. 4 (1978): 625–48.

——. "Internal Migration in Chile to 1920: Its Relationship to the Labor Market, Agricultural Growth, and Urbanization." Ph.D. dissertation, University of California, Davis, Department of History, 1978.

Johnson, Lyman L., and Sonya Lipsett-Rivera, eds. *The Faces of Honor: Sex, Shame, and Violence in Colonial Latin America.* Albuquerque: University of New Mexico Press, 1998.

Joseph, Gilbert M. "Preface." In Salvatore, Aguirre, and Joseph, eds., *Crime and Punishment in Latin America,* ix–xxi.

Joseph, Gilbert M., and Daniel Nugent, eds. *Everyday Forms of State Formation: Revolution and the Negotiation of Rule in Modern Mexico.* Durham, N.C.: Duke University Press, 1994.

Kertzer, David. *Sacrificed for Honor: Italian Infant Abandonment and the Politics of Reproductive Control.* Boston: Beacon Press, 1993.

Klimpel, Felicitas. *La mujer en Chile (El aporte femenino al Progreso de Chile, 1910–1960)*. Santiago: Editorial Andrés Bello, 1962.

Klubock, Thomas M. *Contested Communities: Class, Gender, and Politics in Chile's El Teniente Copper Mine, 1904–1951*. Durham, N.C.: Duke University Press, 1998.

Koven, Seth, and Sonya Michel. *Mothers of a New World: Maternalist Politics and the Origins of Welfare States*. New York: Routledge, 1993.

Kuznesof, Elizabeth Anne. "The Home, the Street, Global Society: Latin American Families and Childhood in the Twenty-First Century." *Journal of Social History* 38, no. 4 (2005): 859–72.

———. "The Puzzling Contradictions of Child Labor, Unemployment, and Education in Brazil." *Journal of Family History* 23, no. 3 (1998): 225–39.

———. "Sexual Politics, Race, and Bastard-Bearing in Nineteenth-Century Brazil: A Question of Culture or Power?" *Journal of Family History* 16, no. 3 (1991): 241–61.

———. "A History of Domestic Service in Spanish America, 1492–1980." In *Muchachas No More: Household Workers in Latin America and the Caribbean,* edited by Elsa M. Chaney and Mary Garcia Castro, 17–36. Philadelphia: Temple University Press, 1989.

———. "The Role of the Female-Headed Household in Brazilian Modernization: São Paulo, 1765 to 1836." *Journal of Social History* 13, no. 4 (1980): 589–613.

Kuznesof, Elizabeth Anne, and Robert Oppenheimer. "The Family and Society in Nineteenth-Century Latin America: An Historiographical Introduction." *Journal of Family History* 10, no. 3 (1985): 215–35.

Larraín, Carlos J. *Historia de Viña del Mar*. Santiago: Imprenta Nascimento, 1946.

Lavrín, Asunción. *Women, Feminism, and Social Change in Argentina, Chile, and Uruguay, 1890–1940*. Lincoln: University of Nebraska Press, 1995.

———, ed. *Sexuality and Marriage in Colonial Latin America*. Lincoln: University of Nebraska Press. 1989.

Leinaweaver, Jessaca. *The Circulation of Children: Kinship, Adoption, and Morality in Andean Peru*. Durham, N.C.: Duke University Press, 2008.

———. "On Moving Children: The Social Implications of Andean Child Circulation." *American Ethnologist* 34, no. 1 (2007): 163–80.

Lewin, Linda. *Surprise Heirs, I: Illegitimacy, Patrimonial Rights, and Legal Nationalism in Luso-Brazilian Inheritance, 1750–1821*. Stanford, Calif.: Stanford University Press, 2003.

———. *Surprise Heirs, II: Illegitimacy, Inheritance Rights, and Public Power in the Formation of Imperial Brazil, 1822–1889*. Stanford, Calif.: Stanford University Press, 2003.

———. "Natural and Spurious Children in Brazilian Inheritance Law from Colony to Empire: A Methodological Essay." *The Americas* 48, no. 3 (1992): 351–96.

Lipsett-Rivera, Sonya. "Introduction: Children in the History of Latin America." *Journal of Family History* 23, no. 3 (1998): 221–24.

Lira Montt, Luis. "El estatuto de limpieza de sangre en Indias." *Boletín de la Academia Chilena de la Historia* 108–109 (1998–99): 85–112.

Lira Urquieta, Pedro. *El Código Civil chileno y su época*. Santiago: Editorial Jurídica de Chile, 1956.

López Morales, Berta. "El legado de Baldomero Lillo." Online at http://www .cervantesvirtual.com/bib—autor/lillo/obra.shtml (visited January 16, 2009).

Loveman, Brian. *Chile: The Legacy of Hispanic Capitalism*. New York: Oxford University Press, 1988.

——. *Struggle in the Countryside: Politics and Rural Labor in Chile, 1919–1973*. Bloomington: Indiana University Press, 1976.

Mallon, Florencia. "Decoding the Parchments of the Latin American Nation-State: Peru, Mexico, and Chile in Comparative Perspective." In *Studies in the Formation of the Nation-State in Latin America*, edited by James Dunkerley, 13–53. London: Institute of Latin American Studies, 2002.

Mamalakis, Markos. *Historical Statistics of Chile*. Vol. 2, *Demography and Labor Force*. Westport, Conn.: Greenwood Press, 1980.

Mannarelli, María Emma. *Pecados públicos: La ilegitimidad en Lima, siglo XVII*. Lima: Ediciones Flora Tristán, 1993.

Mannarelli, María Emma, and Pablo Rodríguez, eds. *Historia de la infancia en América Latina*. Bogotá: Universidad Externado de Colombia, 2007.

Marcílio, Maria Luiza. *História social da criança abandonada*. São Paulo: Editora HUCITEC, 1998.

Martínez-Alier [Stolke], Verena. *Marriage, Class and Colour in Nineteenth-Century Cuba: A Study of Racial Attitudes and Sexual Values in a Slave Society*. Ann Arbor: University of Michigan Press, 1974.

Martínez Baeza, Sergio. "Cinco documentos para la historia de Viña del Mar." *Revista Archivum* 3, no. 4 (2002): 165–83.

Martínez-Vergne, Teresita. *Shaping the Discourse on Space: Charity and its Wards in Nineteenth-Century San Juan, Puerto Rico*. Austin: University of Texas Press, 1999.

McCaa, Robert. *Marriage and Fertility in Chile: Demographic Turning Points in the Petorca Valley, 1840–1976*. Boulder, Colo.: Westview Press, 1983.

——. "Chilean Social and Demographic History: Sources, Issues, and Methods." *Latin American Research Review* 13, no. 2 (1978): 104–26.

McCracken, Grant. "The Exchange of Children in Tudor England: An Anthropological Phenomenon in Historical Context." *Journal of Family History* 8 (1983): 303–13.

McCurry, Stephanie. *Masters of Small Worlds: Yeoman Households, Gender Relations, and the Political Culture of the Antebellum South Carolina Low Country*. New York: Oxford University Press, 1995.

Meade, Teresa A. *"Civilizing" Rio: Reform and Resistance in a Brazilian City, 1889–1930.* University Park: Pennsylvania State University Press, 1997.

Meznar, Joan. 1994. "Orphans and the Transition to Free Labor in Northeast Brazil: The Case of Campina Grande, 1850–1888." *Journal of Social History* 27, no. 3 (1994): 499–515.

Milanich, Nara. "Degrees of Bondage: Children's Tutelary Servitude in Latin America." In *Children and Slavery*, edited by Joseph Miller, Suzanne Miers, and Gwyn Campbell. Athens: Ohio University Press, forthcoming 2010.

——. "El perfil local del patriarcado legal transnacional: El Código Civil chileno en una perspectiva comparativa." In *Ampliando miradas: Chile y su historia en un tiempo global*, edited by Fernando Purcell and Alfredo Riquelme. Santiago: Pontificia Universidad Católica, 2009.

——. "Service and Circulation: Women, Children, and Domestic Labor in Nineteenth-Century Chile." Unpublished paper, 2008.

——. "Informalidad y extralegalidad de los niños en América Latina: Del período colonial hasta el presente." In Mannarelli and Rodríguez, eds., *Historia de la infancia en América Latina*, 591–613.

——. "Whither Family History? A Road Map from Latin America." *American Historical Review* 112, no. 2 (2007): 439–58.

——. "Women, Gender and Family, 1800–2000." In *A Companion to Latin American History*, edited by Thomas H. Holloway, 461–79. New York: Blackwell, 2007.

——. "Merceditas and Secundino: Sons, Daughters and Illegitimacy in Nineteenth-Century Chile." Paper delivered at the Latin American Studies Association, San Juan, Puerto Rico, March 2006.

——. "From Domestic Servant to Working-Class Housewife: Poor Women, Family, and Labor in Chile." *Estudios Interdisciplinarios de América Latina* 16, no. 1 (2005): 11–39.

——. "The Casa de Huérfanos and Child Circulation in Late-Nineteenth-Century Chile." *Journal of Social History* 38, no. 2 (2004): 311–40.

——. "Historical Perspectives on Illegitimacy and Illegitimates in Latin America." In Hecht, ed., *Minor Omissions: Children in Latin American History and Society*, 72–101.

——. "The Children of Fate: Families, Class and the State in Chile, 1857–1930." Ph.D. dissertation, Yale University, Department of History, 2002.

Milton, Cynthia. "Wandering Waifs and Abandoned Babes: The Limits and Uses of Juvenile Welfare in Eighteenth-Century Audiencia of Quito." *Colonial Latin Historical Review* 13, no. 1 (2004): 103–28.

Mintz, Steven. *Huck's Raft: A History of American Childhood.* Cambridge. Mass.: Belknap Press of Harvard University Press, 2004.

Mirow, Matthew. *Latin American Law: A History of Private Law and Institutions in Spanish America.* Austin: University of Texas Press, 2004.

——. "Borrowing Private Law in Latin America: Andrés Bello's Use of the Code Napoleón in Drafting the Chilean Civil Code." *Louisiana Law Review* 61, no. 2 (2001): 291–329.

Mnookin, Robert, and Lewis Kornhauser. "Bargaining in the Shadow of the Law: The Case of Divorce." *Yale Law Journal* 88 (1979): 950–97.

Molyneux, Maxine. "Twentieth-Century State Formations in Latin America." In Dore and Molyneux, eds., *Hidden Histories of Gender and the State in Latin America*, 33–81.

Montecinos, Sonia. *Madres y huachos: Alegorias del mestizaje chileno.* Santiago: Editorial Cuarto Propio, 1991.

Morris, James O. *Elites, Intellectuals, and Consensus: A Study of the Social Question and the Industrial Relations System in Chile.* Ithaca, N.Y.: Cornell University School of Industrial Labor Relations, 1966.

Nazzari, Muriel. "An Urgent Need to Conceal." In Johnson and Lipsett-Rivera, eds., *The Faces of Honor: Sex, Shame, and Violence in Colonial Latin America*, 103–26.

——. "Concubinage in Colonial Brazil: The Inequalities of Race, Class, and Gender." *Journal of Family History* 21, no. 2 (1996): 107–24.

Nedelsky, Jennifer. "Reconceiving Autonomy: Sources, Thoughts, and Possibilities." *Yale Journal of Law and Feminism* 1, no. 1 (1989): 7–16.

Neff, Charlotte. "Pauper Apprenticeship in Early Nineteenth Century Ontario." *Journal of Family History* 21, no. 2 (1996): 144–71.

Offen, Karen. "Defining Feminism: A Comparative Historical Approach." *Signs* 14, no. 1 (1988): 119–57.

Okin, Susan Moller. "Gender, the Public and the Private." In Phillips, ed., *Feminism and Politics*, 116–41.

O'Phelan Godoy, Scarlett, and Margarita Zegarra Flórez, eds. *Mujeres, familia y sociedad en la historia de América Latina, siglos XVIII–XXI.* Lima: Institut français d'études andines, 2006.

Palma Alvarado, Daniel. "*De apetitos y de cañas*: El consumo de alimentos y bebidas en Santiago a fines del siglo XIX." *Historia* 37, no. 2 (2004): 391–417.

Pateman, Carol. *The Sexual Contract.* Stanford, Calif.: Stanford University Press, 1988.

Patterson, Orlando. *Slavery and Social Death: A Comparative Study.* Cambridge, Mass.: Harvard University Press, 1982.

Pearson, Lon. "El niño roto en la ficción chilena." In *El niño en las literaturas hispánicas*, edited by J. Cruz Mendizabal, 137–62. Hispanic Literatures Fourth Annual Conference. Indiana, Penn.: Indiana University of Pennsylvania, 1978.

Phillips, Anne, ed. *Feminism and Politics.* Oxford: Oxford University Press, 1998.

Potthast, Barbara, and Sandra Carrera, eds. *Entre la familia, la sociedad y el estado; Niños y jóvenes en América Latina (siglos XIX–XX).* Madrid: Iberoamericana, 2005.

Pozo, José del. *Historia del vino chileno: Desde 1850 hasta hoy.* Santiago: Editorial Universitaria, 2004.

——. "Viña Santa Rita and Wine Production in Chile since the Mid-Nineteenth Century." *Journal of Wine Research* 6, no. 2 (1995): 133–42.

Premo, Bianca. *Children of the Father-King: Youth, Minority and Authority in Colonial Lima.* Chapel Hill: University of North Carolina Press, 2005.

Priore, Mary del, ed. *História das crianças no Brasil.* São Paolo: Editoria Contexto. 1999.

Putnam, Lara. *The Company They Kept: Migrants and the Politics of Gender in Caribbean Costa Rica, 1870–1960.* Chapel Hill: University of North Carolina Press, 2002.

Ramos, Fábio Pestana. "A história trágico-marítima das crianças nas embarcações portuguesas do século XVI." In Priore, ed., *História das crianças no Brasil*, 19–54.

Ramos Pazos, René. "Análisis crítico de la Ley N° 19.585." *Revista de Derecho* 10 (December 1999): 125–34.

Restrepo Zea, Estela. "El concertaje laboral de los niños abandonados en Bogotá, 1642–1885." In *Historia de la infancia en América Latina*, edited by Pablo Rodríguez and María Emma Mannarelli. Bogotá: Universidad Externado de Colombia, 2007.

Reyes G., Caetano. "Expósitos e hidalgos: La polarización social de la Nueva España." *Boletín del Archivo General de la Nación* (Mexico) 16, 3a ser., vol. 5, no. 2 (April–June 1981): 3–5.

Rizzini, Irene. "Pequenos trabalhadores do Brasil." In Priore, ed., *História das crianças no Brasil*, 376–406.

Rodríguez, Pablo. "Iluminando sombras: Ilegitimidad, abandono infantil y adopción en la historia colombiana." In O'Phelan Godoy and Zegarra Flórez, eds., *Mujeres, familia y sociedad en la historia de América Latina, siglos XVIII–XXI*, 57–76.

Rodríguez S., Eugenia. "Civilizing Domestic Life in the Central Valley of Costa Rica, 1750–1850." In Dore and Molyneux, eds., *Hidden Histories of Gender and the State in Latin America*, 85–107.

Rojas Flores, Jorge. "Los derechos del niño en Chile: Una aproximación histórica, 1910–1930." *Historia* 40, no. 1 (2007): 129–64.

——. *Los niños cristaleros: Trabajo infantil en la industria: Chile, 1880–1950.* Santiago: DIBAM, 1996.

Romero, Luis Alberto. *¿Qué hacer con los pobres? Elite y sectores populares en Santiago de Chile, 1840–1895.* Buenos Aires: Editorial Sudamericana, 1997.

Rosemblatt, Karin Alejandra. *Gendered Compromises: Political Cultures and the State in Chile, 1920–1950.* Chapel Hill: University of North Carolina Press, 2000.

Sabato, Hilda, and Luis Alberto Romero. *Los trabajadores de Buenos Aires:*

La experiencia del mercado, 1859–1880. Buenos Aires: Editorial
Sudamericana, 1992.

Salazar, Gabriel. *Ser niño "huacho" en la historia de Chile.* Santiago: Ediciones
LOM, 2006.

——. "Ser niño huacho en la historia de Chile (siglo XIX)." *Proposiciones* 19
(1990): 55–83.

——. *Labradores, peones y proletarios.* Santiago: Ediciones Sur, 1985.

Salazar, Gabriel, and Julio Pinto. *Historia contemporánea de Chile V: Niñez y
juventud.* Santiago: Ediciones LOM, 2002.

——. *Historia contemporánea de Chile II: Actores, identidad y movimiento.*
Santiago: Ediciones LOM, 1999.

Salinas Meza, René. "Lo público y lo no confesado: Vida familiar en Chile
tradicional, 1700–1880." *Revista de Historia Social y de la Mentalidades* 3
(1999): 31–60.

——. "Orphans and Family Disintegration in Chile: The Mortality of
Abandoned Children, 1750–1930." *Journal of Family History* 16, no. 3
(1991): 315–29.

——. "Familia y hogar en Chile central a mediados del siglo XIX: Los Andes,
1835–1865." In *História e População: Estudos sobre a América Latina,*
edited by Sérgio Odiolon Nadalin, Maria Luiza Marcílio, and Altiva Pillati
Balhana, 194–201. São Paulo: Fundação SEADE, 1990.

Salinas Meza, René, and Nicolás Corvalán. "Transgresores sumisos,
pecadores felices: Vida afectiva y vigencia del modelo matrimonial en
Chile tradicional." *Cuadernos de Historia* 16 (1996): 9–39.

Salvatore, Ricardo D., Carlos Aguirre, and Gilbert M. Joseph, eds. *Crime and
Punishment in Latin America: Law and Society since Late Colonial Times.*
Durham, N.C.: Duke University Press, 2001.

Sater, William. *Chile and the War of the Pacific.* Lincoln: University of
Nebraska Press, 1986.

Schell, Patience A. "Nationalizing Children through Schools and Hygiene:
Porfirian and Revolutionary Mexico City." *The Americas* 60, no. 4 (2004):
559–87.

Scott, James. *Seeing Like a State: How Certain Schemes to Improve the Human
Condition Have Failed.* New Haven, Conn.: Yale University Press, 1998.

Seed, Patricia. *To Love, Honor, and Obey in Colonial Mexico.* Stanford, Calif.:
Stanford University Press, 1988.

Shelton, Laura. "Like a Servant or Like a Son? Child Circulation in Northern
Mexico." In González and Premo, eds., *Raising an Empire,* 219–37.

Sherwood, Joan. *Poverty in Eighteenth-Century Spain: The Women and
Children of the Inclusa.* Toronto: University of Toronto Press, 1988.

Socolow, Susan. Review of *The Secret History of Gender: Women, Men, and
Power in Latin Colonial Mexico* by Steve Stern. *The Americas* 53, no. 1
(1996): 163–65.

Somarriva Undurraga, Manuel. *Evolución del Código Civil chileno.* Bogotá: Temis, 1983.

Stabili, Maria Rosaria. *Il sentimento aristocratico: Élites cilene allo specchio, 1860–1960.* Lecce: Congedo, 1996.

Stern, Steve. *The Secret History of Gender: Women, Men, and Power in Late Colonial Mexico.* Chapel Hill: University of North Carolina Press, 1995.

Stoler, Ann Laura. *Carnal Knowledge and Imperial Power: Race and the Intimate in Colonial Rule.* Berkeley: University of California Press, 2002.

——. "Tense and Tender Ties: The Politics of Comparison in North American History and (Post) Colonial Studies." *Journal of American History* 88, no. 3 (2001): 829–65.

Stoner, K. Lynn. *From the House to the Streets: The Cuban Woman's Movement for Legal Reform, 1898–1940.* Durham, N.C.: Duke University Press, 1991.

Súsnik, Branislava. *Los indios del Paraguay.* Madrid: Mapfre, 1995.

Szuchman, Mark D. *Order, Family, and Community in Buenos Aires, 1810–1860.* Stanford, Calif.: Stanford University Press, 1988.

Therborn, Göran. *Between Sex and Power: Family in the World, 1900–2000.* London: Routledge, 2004.

Tinsman, Heidi. *Partners in Conflict: The Politics of Gender, Sexuality and Labor in the Chilean Agrarian Reform, 1950–1973.* Durham, N.C.: Duke University Press, 2002.

Twinam, Ann. "The Church, the State, and the Abandoned: Expósitos in Late-Eighteenth-Century Havana." In González and Premo, eds., *Raising an Empire,* 163–86.

——. *Public Lives, Private Secrets: Gender, Honor, Sexuality, and Illegitimacy in Colonial Spanish America.* Stanford, Calif.: Stanford University Press, 1999.

Vassberg, David E. 1998. "Orphans and Adoption in Early Modern Castilian Villages." *History of the Family: An International Quarterly* 3, no. 4 (1998): 441–58.

Vaughan, Mary Kay. *Cultural Politics in Revolution: Teachers, Peasants, and Schools in Mexico: 1930–1940.* Tucson: University of Arizona Press, 1997.

Venâncio, Renato Pinto. *Famílias abandonadas: Assistência à criança de camadas populares no Rio de Janeiro e em Salvador, séculos XVIII e XIX.* Rio de Janeiro: Papirus, 1999.

——. "Os aprendizes da guerra." In Priore, ed., *História das crianças no Brasil,* 192–209.

Vergara Quiroz, Sergio. *Cartas de mujeres en Chile, 1630–1885.* Santiago: Editorial Andrés Bello, 1987.

Vial, Gonzalo. "Aplicación en Chile de la Pragmática sobre matrimonios de los hijos de familia." *Revista Chilena de Historia del Derecho* 6 (1970): 335–62.

Vicuña, Manuel. *La belle époque chilena.* Santiago: Sudamericana, 2001.

Wadsworth, James E., and Tamera L. Marko. "Children of the Pátria: Representations of Childhood and Welfare State Ideology around the 1922 Rio de Janeiro International Centennial Exposition." *The Americas* 58, no. 1 (2001): 65–90.

Waldman Mitnick, Gilda. "Chile: Indígenas y mestizos negados." *Política y Cultura* 21 (2004): 97–110.

Walmsley, Emily. "Raised by Another Mother: Informal Fostering and Kinship Ambiguiuties in Northwest Ecuador." *Journal of Latin American and Caribbean Anthropology* 13, no. 1 (2008): 1–28.

Windler, Erica. "City of Children: Boys, Girls, Family and State in Imperial Rio de Janeiro, Brazil." Ph.D. dissertation, University of Miami, Department of History, 2003.

Yeager, Gertrude. "The Club de la Unión and Kinship: Social Aspects of Political Obstructionism in the Chilean Senate, 1920–1924." *The Americas* 35, no. 4 (1979): 539–72.

Zárate, María Soledad. "Proteger a las madres: Origen de un debate público, 1870–1920." *Nomadias* 1 (1999): 163–82.

Zeitlin, Maurice, and Richard Earl Ratcliff. *Landlords and Capitalists: The Dominant Class of Chile.* Princeton, N.J.: Princeton University Press, 1988.

Zelizer, Viviana. *Pricing the Priceless Child: The Changing Social Value of Children.* New York: Basic Books, 1985.

INDEX

Page numbers in italics represent illustrations.

genealogy, lineage (*cont.*)
  tion of, 4, 10, *11*, 107; enduring sig-
    nificance of, 152–54; family honor
    and, 146, 148–49; incorporations
    into, 100; *limpieza de sangre* and,
    107, 154, 272n6; plebeian indiffer-
    ence to, 114–15; plebeian valoriza-
    tion of, 111; in post-Code paternity
    suits, 75; public scandal and, 53, 59,
    149; social congruity and, 79; social
    fortune changes of, 89. *See also* elite
    families
generational hierarchy: *alimentos* suits
    and, 112; ascending, descending
    losses in, 125–26; child circulation
    and, 165, 206–7, 230; children as
    revealing, 26; *criados* in, 190–91,
    296n25; domestic service wages
    and, 193, 297n33; elite vs. plebeian
    reproduction and, 4; illegitimates
    viewed as threat to, 232; *inquilinos*
    and, 14, 116; kinship, family as re-
    vealing, 6, 12; kinship's social bene-
    fits and, 130; of kinship vs. charity,
    81–82; law and, 7, 23, 28, 42, 56,
    253n51; multigenerational servi-
    tude and, 205–6; tutelary servitude
    and, 196, 214; vernacular kinship as
    transcending, 157–59
Graham, Maria, 185, 188
Graham, Sandra Lauderdale, 124
guardianship, 61, 123, 177, 212, 291n68

hacendados: Casa's relationship with,
    203, 205, 301n71; child circulation
    and, 82–84, 166, 206, 268n34; de-
    pendencies involving, 9–11, 201–2;
    in filiation cases, 47, 71, 76, 93,
    256n18; land appropriation by, 14;
    Miers-Cox, 109; peon use by, 117;
    prominent alleged fathers among,
    255n14, 302n77; Sociedad Nacional
    de Agricultura and, 108

haciendas: Casa children circulated to,
    218–19, 269n50, 301n70; child cir-
    culation on, 26, 82–84, 166–67,
    178, 181, 187, 203; dependencies in-
    volving, 201–2; gender and, 15,
    288n28; *inquilinos* and, 116, 274;
    methodologically elusive social, la-
    bor relations on, 244; in Pablo
    Pérez's narrative, 208–9; peon
    wages on, 298n35; in portraits, *11*,
    202; tutelary servitude and, 268n31
Hale, Charles A., 25
Hermanas de la Providencia, 103–4,
    172, 203, 243, 280n26; Bernarda
    Morin and, 199–201, 219–20,
    295n11, 300n61, 301n71. *See also*
    Casa de Huérfanos
hijos ajenos, 33, 214, 227
hijos de familia, 12, 19, 178, 214,
    250n11
hijos naturales: Code's distinction be-
    tween *hijo ilegítimo* and, 291n63; in
    Code vs. pre-Code taxonomy of na-
    tal statuses, 45, 60–61, 261–
    262n62; illegitimacy, honor and,
    145; inheritance rights of, 61; recog-
    nition of, in courts, 95; rights of as
    varied, 262n63; social congruity
    and, 74, 77; social status of parents
    and, 97, 270n64; in will
hijos simplemente ilegítimos, 60–61,
    265n9
honor: as argument for Latin Ameri-
    can child abandonment, 114;
    changes, continuities in colonial
    ideas about, 148–51; civil registry's
    revelation of illegitimacy and, 145–
    47; colonial public/private dichot-
    omy and, 283–284n60; illegitimacy
    and, 277n58; kinlessness and, 124;
    limpieza de sangre and, 107, 154,
    272n6; as male entitlement and,
    150. *See also* genealogy, lineage

filiation cases in U.S., 264n80; interpretive vs. codified law standards in, 74, 265n8; paternity recognition and fees of, 95, 270n56; paternity recognition and social class biases of, 95; pre-Code paternity rulings by, 45–49, 51–52, 258n28, 258n31, 258n33; social congruity applied by, 74–79, 265n9, 265–266n10, 266n14, 266–267n18; vernacular practice appropriation by, 178

Junta de Beneficencia, 138, 280n25

kinlessness: as ascending and descending, 124–26; baptism records and, 121–22; civil registry and, 147; in criminal cases, 119–20, 124, 275n44, 275n45, 277n60; direct causes of, 106; foundlings left with notes and, 139; *hijos de la iglesia* and, 114, 273n25; honor and, 124; *huachismo* as, 16–17; in Latin American societies, 113–15; law, bureaucracy as selectively imposing, 153; legal orphanhood and, 138; through *libreta de familia*, 144, 282–283n47; as marriage impediment, 121–24, 276n50; natal alienation as, 272n5; as necessitating charity, 112–13; among newspaper boys, 121, 219, 276n47, 276n48; among peons, 116–17; as self-perpetuating, 124; societal factors in, 114; state as generating, 7, 66; state formation's effect on, 151–54; as stigmatized underclass, 105; strategic advantages of, 115, 274n30; surname changes and, 118–19, 275n41; twentieth-century persistence of, 217, 219; valorization of origins vs. stigmatization of, 111, 273n15. *See also* identity; orphans

kin practices, vernacular: categories

of, as fluid, 173–75, 290n54; *crianza, compadrazgo* as, 157; as devalued, 169; as extralegal, 158, 160, 172–76; kinship's narrowed legal definition as encouraging, 160–61, 179–80; kinship vs., 27; law's disjuncture with, 23; plebeian family, household, community building through, 159, 182; state institutions as indirectly fomenting, 215; state power as in counterpoint with, 27, 30; state-sanctioned kinship practices as coexisting with, 170–71, 290n52; state's appropriation of, 178; twentieth-century reform and, 227, 233; types of, 18–19

kinship: as administrative, legal category, 130, 133, 279n9; adoption recognition by plebeians vs. state and, 172–73; *ajeno, extraño* statuses and, 6; *alimentos* and material negotiations of, 111–12; *alimentos* and practices of, 131, 273n20; through baptism, 140; boundaries of, as fluid, 236; charity vs. obligations of, 81–85, 112–13; child circulation and survival of, 118; civic identity and, 134; Code's transformation of, 42, 44; elite categories of, 181, 290n59; elite power through, 10; *estado civil* as tying civil identity to, 154; family exclusivity vs. universality in, 137; family law and boundaries of, 22–23; in filiation case records, 72–73; identity and allegations of false, 135–36, 279n17; individual, familial identity and, 132; individual and collective identity through, 126; among *inquilinos* vs. *gañanes*, 116; kin dispossession and, 124–25; kinlessness as stigmatized vs. valorization of, 111, 273n15; legal, bureaucratic discrimination

cial status ambiguities and, 80–83.
See also Alvarez paternity suit; social congruity principle

paternity suits, pre-Code: analysis of,
265n16; community influences on,
49, 51–52, 58–59, 258n33; D'Huique
example of, 41–42, 45–46, 65–66,
254n3; elite fathers as subjects of, 75,
265n11; gender, class and, 45–46,
255n13, 265n15; illegitimate victories
in, 46–49; informal justice in, 49; judicial sources for, 240; legal paternalism toward women, children in, 51–
52, 257–258n26, 258n29, 258n31;
lower vs. higher courts and, 64–65,
263n77; social dependency in,
267n20; ubiquity of, 42

patria potestad, 12, 175, 178, 182, 212,
229, 259n37

patriarchal households. *See* households, patriarchal

patriarchy: civil law's dogmatic eleva-
tion of, 99; colonial, liberal states as,
44; feminists, filiation law and, 229,
307n32; in imagined norms vs. reality, 18, 106; Latin American, republican citizenship as rooted in,
134; liberalism and, 25–26; paternal
identity erasure and, 142; in pre-
Code filiation cases, 52–53

patrones. See servitude, (children's) tutelary domestic

Patterson, Orlando, 105, 125–26,
272n5

peons: child circulation, rootlessness
of, 207–8; *criados'* common adult
destiny as, 36, 184, 201–2, 205–10,
214; definition of, 9; gender and,
250n15; increase in, 14, 120; *inquilino* dependencies with, 11, 201–
2, 302n77; *inquilinos* compared
with, 116–17; kinship ties among,
in elite critiques, 181; orphanages'

roles in generating, 230; Pablo
Pérez's literacy as uncharacteristic
of, 303n85; turn-of-nineteenth-
century as peak in, 120; waged autonomy among, 209, 298n35,
303n87

Pérez, Pablo: after book publication,
127; children-and-nation rhetoric
of, 180; literacy of, 303n85. *See also
Orphan: True Story Recounted by a
Foundling of the Casa de Maternidad de Santiago, The* (Pablo
Pérez)

Pérez Rosales, Vicente, 264n1

Peru, 35, 103, 128, 160, 185, 213, 224,
291n62

plebeian children: campaigns on behalf
of, 21–22, 216, 221–22; dependencies as ambiguous and, 13, 28, 33; in
elite commentary, 18; fate vs. agency
of, 236–37; as harbingers of disorder
and, 20–21, 232; as *hijos de la patria*,
22, 38, 180; massive numbers as deprived of parental responsibility and,
179; massive numbers in circulation
and, 177; in mid-nineteenth century
vs. early twentieth century, 232–33;
The Orphan (Pablo Pérez) and, 103–
4; as protagonists in literature, 20,
104, 251n31, 271n3, 273n24

plebeian families: adoption as common in, 176–77; children circulated
in households of, 163–64; *criados* in
households of, 191–92; "familial
anomie" critiques of, 18–21; genealogical indifference of, 114–15; genealogical valorization by, 111;
infant mortality among, 164; *inquilino*, 116; kinlessness cycles
among, 117; patriarchal households
of, in early twentieth century, 232–
33; patterns of, 14–21. *See also* kin
practices, vernacular

NARA B. MILANICH

IS AN ASSISTANT PROFESSOR OF HISTORY

AT BARNARD COLLEGE, COLUMBIA UNIVERSITY.

Library of Congress Cataloging-in-Publication Data

Milanich, Nara B., 1972–
Children of fate : childhood, class, and the state in chile,
1850–1930 / Nara B. Milanich.
p. cm.
Includes bibliographical references and index.
ISBN 978-0-8223-4557-2 (cloth : alk. paper)
ISBN 978-0-8223-4574-9 (pbk. : alk. paper)
1. Children—Chile—Social conditions—History.
2. Family—Chile—History.
3. Family policy—Chile—History.
4. Illegitimacy—Chile—History.
5. Social classes—Chile—History.
6. Kinship—Chile—History. I. Title.
HQ792.C47M55 2009
305.23086'9450983—dc22
2009013111